Dr. Clarice R. Ford ▪ Yolanda H. Beamon

University of Illinois—Springfield

Necessary Steps

Road map for First Generation College Students Success

Kendall Hunt
publishing company

Cover image © Shutterstock, Inc.

Kendall Hunt
publishing company

www.kendallhunt.com
Send all inquiries to:
4050 Westmark Drive
Dubuque, IA 52004-1840

Copyright © 2014 by Dr. Clarice R. Ford and Yolanda H. Beamon

ISBN 978-1-4652-4096-5

Printed in the United States of America

Contents

Foreword

By Darlena Jones, PhD

As a first-generation college student, I was faced with the same challenges you're facing. How do I apply for student loans? What are residence halls like? Should I get involved in Greek life? Will I flunk out after the first semester? How do I handle my family responsibilities in addition to college? Most students have a college-educated parent to help them navigate college life, but first-generation students don't.

Because I was a first-generation college student who was successful in college when others weren't, I have always felt an obligation to help students be successful. In my work at EBI MAP-Works, I have access to data from students during the transition into college. Taking that data, I have conducted research on behaviors that make first-generation college students successful and I have presented those results to college educators in the hopes they better understand and improve the student experience.

I was one of the lucky ones because my family was very supportive of my college career and easily forgave me when school work took precedent over family time. However my research shows most first-generation college students struggle with balancing family obligations with school work and find the pressure of family overwhelming.

While my family was supportive of college, they were not supportive of my being involved in student activities and organizations. They did not understand how time spent in cocurricular activities would enhance my education; they saw it as a waste of time and money. Looking back, I regret not getting involved in student activities. From my research, involvement and engagement in student activities helps first-generation college students find a peer group who are interested in similar activities; a strong peer group in college helps students survive challenging times.

Because I was a first-generation college student and had no one to ask, I didn't understand how to finance college. I didn't know there were many scholarships, grants, and work study opportunities to help with tuition and expenses; I depended on student loans and work. My research shows first-generation college students experience higher levels of financial stress than others.

Probably the most difficult feelings I experienced as a first-generation college student was the fear of flunking out. That nagging feeling stayed with me throughout my college career. My research shows first-generation college students are inherently less confident in their academic abilities than other students even when they achieve high grades.

When I was in college, no one focused on helping first-generation college students succeed. However, you have Dr. Clarice Ford and her valuable book as your guide.

In 2010, I met Dr. Clarice Ford through a shared passion for first-generation college student success. Both of us were first-generation college students and knew firsthand the uncertainties facing students like us. She and I collaborated on many scholarly presentations; we shared my research into behaviors that make first-generation students successful and her practitioner experience working directly with these students. The success she has had in helping first-generation college students be successful is inspiring.

Her work in student success is what led to this book. Necessary Steps: Roadmap to First-generation College Student Success is an easy-to-read guide for anyone wanting to be successful in college. Dr. Ford explains, in a superb way, her own personal life experiences about how she was successful as a first-generation college student. The book reflects Dr. Ford's passion for helping college students be successful.

Necessary Steps: Road map to First-Generation College Student Success identifies the challenges you might face like how to live with roommates; the effect homesickness has on your ability to handle stress; and where to find help on campus if needed. This book also helps you identify your next steps after college by helping you to create a full life plan. It also serves as a useful guide to your family; so they can better understand your experience.

You, as a first-generation student, might think you don't need special attention, but you do. As someone who has been in your shoes, I advise you to pay special attention to the advice in this book and apply it to your daily life. Dr. Ford's book provides insight into the challenges you might face and shows you how to avoid those challenges. The important work within these pages provides a roadmap to your college success.

Congratulations! You are about to embark on an amazing college career. Most importantly, you are paving the way for future generations to be successful college graduates.

Darlena Jones, PhD
Director of Education and Program Development
EBI MAP-Works
Springfield, MO

Acknowledgments

I would like to thank all my students former, present, and future for allowing me the opportunity to sow a seed in your life and be able to see you grow into *greatness*. Thanks to Becky Martino for bringing books home from work and showing me that the color of one's skin does not dictate how to love one another. Mr. Messitt, thank you for being my role model on the importance of teaching and supporting students, I will never forget you. To my father, who was denied the right to be educated in America because of the color of his skin, and my mother, who became a registered nurse despite the odds. Last but not least, thanks to my family, friends, and Traffic, for your unconditional love, and to every student who reads this book—WIT (Whatever It Takes) Graduate!!

I would like to thank Raymond Bady for telling me a simple phrase as a young girl: "look up, because sky is the limit." I have lived and functioned with that phrase in mind from the beginning of my college, career, and now life. I would like to thank my parents Ricky and Yolanda Beamon, who are my heroes. They show me every day what love looks like. The fact that they decided not to further their education fueled the motivation to make my family's name one that would be positively read about in books. Hence this project. My brothers— Eugene (Syrena), Renardell-Bahli (Andrea), and Ricky Jr. (Tawanda)— thank you so much for supporting me and expecting greatness from me. I spend plenty of time making sure that I live a life that you all would be proud of, as your baby sister. To my nephews and nieces— DaMonte, Eugene Jr., Eric, Yazmin, Ayva, Ricky III, Olajuwon, Zaria, and Tyler Kobe and Jada London— whenever you wonder where Auntie Missy is, I want you to know that I always wanted to watch you grow up, but I was out, leaving my footprint on the world. I would like to thank, DeJuan Dennis, Leah Dennis, and LeShay Dennis, when you entered into my life, I felt obligated to set the example of greatness for you to follow. Though Juan was taken from us early, I still work tirelessly to prove to you three that the depth of your struggle determines the height of your success. Hard work and the ambiguous desire to be amazing exemplify my drive and motivation. I would like to offer a sincere thank-you to Ms. Charlotte Scott for always expecting great things from me and pushing me beyond my broken heart. I thank you so much for that. I would like to offer a deep and sincere thank-you to Dr. Clarice R. Ford, the words thank you cannot begin to express my appreciation to you as my mentor and friend. Your belief in my ability to be great took a while to understand; while I'm still on this life journey, you have set an unattainable standard for greatness that I could only scratch at. Thank you for laughing at me only after I told you I was fine, when I fell in the middle of the street after signing the contract to write this book. I will continue to be your Elisha and you will forever be my Elijah. I would like to offer a special thank-you to Charles L. Olivier, for being on my team, even when I didn't have a "team." You're a good friend! Thank you for being you. I would like to thank the guy who has my heart; I look forward to the day that we meet. I anticipate our conversations and time together to be intellectual, intriguing yet simple and romantic. To all of my students, past, present, and future, thank you for growing me up! My expectations for you should never exceed your expectations for yourself. Mine are pretty high, as you all know! Always remember, you can make excuses or you can make changes but you can't do both.

Contributors:
Dr. Sarah Colby Weaver
Dr. Van Vierrgge
Dr. Patricia Cunningham
Jennifer Sanders
Monique Williams
Daniel Garcia
Nehemiah Bishop
Justin Keenan
Dr. Michael Scurlock
Edward Bempong
Andreas Laras
Jane Roqueplot

About the Authors

Clarice Ford holds a doctoral degree in Educational Leadership from Fielding University and a Master's Degree in Multicultural/Diversity Education from Antioch University. Ford has researched, taught, and/or consulted in areas of Greek life, diversity, leadership, student success, first-generation students and families, race and ethnic relations, retention, relationships, cultural adaptation, African American males, international students, LGBTQ communication, juvenile/adult corrections, and spirituality. She has facilitated workshops on working with college students in religious and secular organizations nationwide, student and academic affairs and diversity. Ford has made numerous presentations and authored articles on college success for first-generation and African American males. She is the author of the book "Pass the P's Please" and host of a weekly radio show on WLJX radio heard by many on issues of relationships, spirituality, education, and overcoming obstacles. Ford is currently the Executive Director of Diversity Center and Associate Vice Chancellor of Student Services at the University of Illinois Springfield.

Yolanda Beamon holds a Master's Degree in Public Administration from the University of Illinois Springfield. Beamon has spent time researching, teaching, and consulting in areas of diversity, leadership, student success, first first-generation students and families, retention, LGBTQA communication, and spirituality. She has a strong passion for researching and teaching student leadership, iY Generation, and first-generation college students. Student leadership, retention, and student success are the crux of her passion in the field of higher education. Currently, she is the Director of New Student Orientation and Parent Relations at the University of Illinois Springfield.

Who Are First-Generation Students?

1

PURPOSE

Understanding that you are a first-generation college student is empowering as you begin to learn the systems of your institution of higher education. Thus, the first step in student empowerment is embracing personal pride and learning the necessary steps needed in order to be successful. You will begin to take ownership for your reasons to attend college and gain the tools needed in order to be successful.

ACTIVATE YOUR THOUGHTS

When you hear the phrase "first-generation college student," the first words that come to your mind are . . .

Why are you in college and what do you expect from it?

First-Generation College Student is defined as a student whose parents have not graduated from a four-year college or university.

WHY DO FIRST-GENERATION COLLEGE STUDENTS ATTEND COLLEGE?

Students attend college for many reasons. Your reason for attending may or may not differ from the many peers that will attend college with you. Take a moment and reflect on your reason for attending college. An important part of that reflection as a first-generation college student typically involves the "job-related benefits of going to college." According to the Cooperative Institutional Research Program, " incoming freshmen cited 'to be able to get a better job' as a very important reason for attending college reached an all-time high of 87.9 percent in 2012, an increase from 85.9 percent in 2011 and considerably higher than the low of 67.8 percent in 1976." In the minds of today's college students, getting a better job continues to be the most prevalent reason to go to college. Many incoming students also said the ability "to make more money" was a very important reason to attend college; this percentage rose from 71.7 in 2011 to 74.6 in 2012, another all-time high" (Pryor et al. 2012).

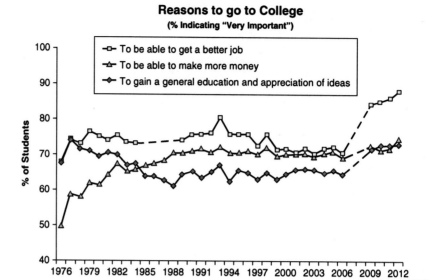

Common reasons to attend college include money, finding a philosophy of life, becoming a more cultured person, or satisfying their parents' wishes. As a first-generation student, examining your reasons for enrolling in higher education can help you determine what you can "realistically" hope to achieve as a student. However, as a first-generation college student, your ability to navigate the process of higher education may prove to be a great feat without the necessary reference resources.

> "Do the best until you know better, when you know better do better."
> —Maya Angelou

The idea of being a first-generation college student is not a new concept. However, the demographic of people who attend college has drastically changed. "People attending American colleges and universities were mostly white and male," but without fail were children of parents who had attended college (Davis 2010). The privilege of attending college was exactly that; a privilege. The ideology of "privilege" did not benefit the American College System. In fact several factors weakened the American College System as compared to the evolution of the undergraduate education and the pursuit of training the intellect and building character (Bok 2006). The Yale model of 1828 "held that the principal aim of college instruction was not to supply all of the important information that students might some day use but to instill mental discipline" (Bok 2006).

The undergraduate institution of the twenty-first century has very little resemblance to the evolution of American colleges and undergraduate education of post Civil War institutions. The linkage to religious entities and finishing schools deemed the transition of what the American college once looked like (Bok 2006). Exclusion of people whose parents did not attend college was more harmful to the American College System than any of the above named ideas. Exclusion was "harmful to the people who were excluded, but also harmful to the people included" (Davis 2010).

This leads to the continued plight of the first-generation college student being more visible than ever before. First-generation students not having a point of reference for skills, attitudes, and habits needed, in order to be successful in college, further plagues the idea of success.

> First Generation college students is uttered more often these days by college presidents and other high-level administrators in communication to general public, the category still remains oddly emergent"First Generation college students although educational leaders know them to be extremely important to the continued health of the education system, remain somewhat ill defined and, more important, underserved in the sense that a well articulated practice to help them earn college degrees more easily and efficiently has not been presented." (Davis 2010)

Surviving college involves an element of understanding the necessary skills needed to navigate life. Several studies have been done that inaccurately depict the first-generation college student as a student with every possible odd against them. When in actuality there are specific components of development and programming that can be put in place to assist matriculation through higher education.

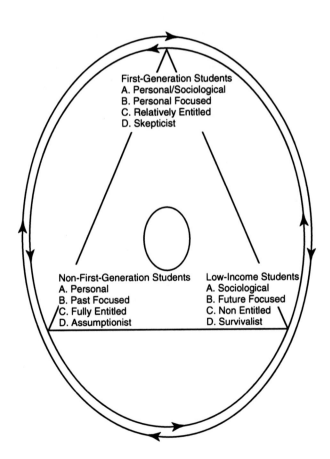

First-Generation Students
A. Personal/Sociological
B. Personal Focused
C. Relatively Entitled
D. Skepticist

Non-First-Generation Students
A. Personal
B. Past Focused
C. Fully Entitled
D. Assumptionist

Low-Income Students
A. Sociological
B. Future Focused
C. Non Entitled
D. Survivalist

Consequently, first-generation college students have needs, which require a wide range of support programs (Jamelske 2009). From the perspective of the first-generation college student, retention and graduation are personally imperative and for the success of the student's entire family.

Being the first often implies extreme pressure with the lack of understanding from family members who do not fully understand the college process. Remaining in an institution as a student is often equated with the fact that a degree pays. In 2003, the median annual salary in the United States was $30,800 for a worker with only a high school diploma. This was lower than the median earnings of $49,900 for those with a bachelor's degree (The College Board 2005).

INTERNATIONAL FIRST-GENERATION COLLEGE STUDENTS

Today United States university officials are recruiting international students to diversify campuses and assist in the financial crunch many are facing. For example, Chinese undergraduates are driving the growth in foreign students attending U.S. institutions, according to NAFSA: Association of International Educators. Last year Chinese undergraduate enrollment grew by 31%. China is the leading sender of students to the United States, and no end to this movement in sight.

Many of our international students are the first in their family to attend college. They are more diverse in financing sources, majors, hometowns, and academic motivation. As single-children from newly affluent middle-class families, they also lack the cultural capital as first-generation students. They have been coddled by parents and grandparents like most first-generation students. This has allowed them to be more liberal and independent-minded but most of all more practical and less politically ideological. Most educators believe this would help international students be successful on U.S. campuses, but often, they don't.

First-generation international students can struggle to make decisions about daily life and the ability to navigate the collegiate environment as domestic first-generation students. Being reluctant to integrate and seek outside help continues to be a common denominator. Newfound freedom from parents, insomnia, depression, and suicide may mark a dark side to campus life and plague the success of matriculation for the First-generation international college student. What can a First-generation international student do to secure a productive academic and social experience at college? Let's discuss!

1. Create a relationship with the Office of International Student Services. They are there to help you with all your needs from immigration to social services. The office provides workshops on American culture, tax preparation, career opportunities, and social activities. Many colleges provide a briefing before arrival to explain the challenges, including language through electronic media and newsletters just to name a few.

2. To address academic expectations speak with advisors on "how to learn"—how to deal with assignments and communicate with peers and professors. Understanding plagiarism is a must! It's important to understand after you get a good TOEFL score, you still have a long way to go in order to secure

a successful academic experience. In order to improve your communication skills, consider living with a U.S. roommate. Ask the resident assistant to help you discuss noise, religious beliefs, and other behaviors including culinary practices with roommates. Living Learning communities for First-generation students, like the Necessary Steps Mentoring Program at the University of Illinois Springfield, can provide a community to live, learn, and grow.

3. Cultural differences, real and perceived can hinder you from U.S. campus life in ways that can prevent you from being successful. Many international students tend to receive information about where to eat, live, and the best courses. Unfortunately, the information may not always be accurate. Just because your friends are getting good grades on paper does not mean they are doing well mentally, spiritually, and physically.

4. Counseling centers on U.S. campuses are for all students. Many countries do not have school counselors so this maybe a new concept. College counselors/professionals are licensed to assist you. The information you share will be kept in strict confidence. In your culture, sharing one's problems with strangers is a matter of face. This is not a question of language but of culture among first-generation students. It's much easier to ask family and friends for advice but they may not always have the answer needed to assist you in college. Don't use drugs or alcohol to "self-medicate," improve your mood, or make you less inhibited in social gatherings. Drinking and using drugs will make your problems worse. It's important to find healthy solutions to alleviate your stress.

5. When you attend a college, you agree to abide by the institution's rules and regulations. There are rules from drinking to plagiarism. Residence life also has rules that you must abide including your classroom. If you violate campus policies you may be referred to the Dean of Students Judicial Affairs Board to hear your case. Many students mistakenly forget they can be subject to city, state, and federal laws when violations occur on campus. You can wind up sharing a city or county jail cell with other lawbreakers. Many students have experienced this, and they find it to be one of the most humiliating and regrettable experiences of their lives. International students' consulate can be notified concerning any law-breaking activities.

6. Identity theft/scams/fraud are being targeted toward international students. This means someone has taken some of your personal informations such as your social security number and used it to create one or more identities that can be used to gain access to your financial accounts. Do not carry PIN numbers or passwords in a wallet with the cards you activate. Never reply to emails that ask for personal information. Be sure to carefully check your bank statements and credit card statements for accuracy in transaction amounts.

Being a first-generation international student can be daunting. Remember to attend every class, be organized, manage your time and resources well, be successful in and out of class, take good notes, know how to read a college level textbook, reduce test anxiety, and utilize student services. Seek a first-generation student program on campus to assist you with a mentor and community to grow and succeed.

Ralph G. Nichols can be quoted saying, "The most basic of all human needs is the need to understand and be understood. The best way to understand people is to listen to them." (Nichols) It is also stated, "First Generation college students are unfamiliar with the culture of college and, to one degree or another unfamiliar with what it means to be a college student." (Davis 2010)

Next you will have the opportunity to benefit from the experiences of those who have lived through the college experience as a first-generation college student. Use the personal anecdotes of the generation as motivation to succeed.

VOICES FROM A GENERATION

Dr. Patricia Cunningham, African American female, The Ohio State University

In the Beginning there was Early Childhood Education and a Notion

I am a first-generation college student. How could I forget? When I was born, my family was homeless, yet, I had an older sibling in college. It was a conundrum. It is isolating and maddening when you have a sibling who is a generation older than you. That means even if she could be helpful, the rules and guidelines had changed for college. She was a Title IX recipient, I was the kid brought up on welfare and food lines. She was exposed to the Black Power movement and was in Detroit during the riots. I was born in the boom of technology with access to none of it and my k-12 education was ethnocentric and Eurocentric. My mother, Mama Pat, gave me two options; Uncle Sam or college. She did not know how to get to or do either, but her plan did help shape my thinking early in life. I was born a philomath, a lover of learning.

I knew that I did not want to stay in the Section 8 housing, I was living in and I did not want to be like the folks who lived around me. Education was my method and my love to get out of my neighborhood. College was a way for me to help myself, help my family, and help others. I knew it even before I could prove it.

Early Childhood Education makes a difference. I was enrolled in Head Start (federally funded program for low income folks to have early childhood education) when I was three and learned to read that same year. Having that early education exposure and preparation meant that as a student of color, I would not be tracked to a lower grade. Being in advanced classes early on made sure I was learning long division in third grade and thinking complexly about the world I lived in.

Teachers who care make an Impact

I had several teachers along the way who allowed me to be a full person and challenge the process. In high school there was Mr. Manoloff. He taught my Advanced Preparatory (AP) government course. He wanted his class to read novels outside the normal class content. I, however, did not want to read a "Tom Clancy" book; I wanted to read a nonfiction text that actually meant something. Mr. Manoloff acquiesced to my request, and I read Black Power books for my supplemental reading. He was apprehensive, in a sense, thinking I had adopted these radical ideas but we discussed it that I was no radical at that point.

He believed in me and we are still close to this day. He was not just a mentor but a father figure and I fondly refer to him as "dad."

Pre Collegiate Support Outside the Classroom

Upward Bound, which is a federally funded program under TRIO, was that important last leg that allowed me a direct path to college. Because of being so poor, Upward Bound paid for my ACT and SAT and they also paid for my college applications. I know that my mother had no idea how I even made it to college. She just knows I graduated from Ohio State three times. Upward Bound had college students for counselors in the summer and during most of the summers I was there, I was allowed to take college courses at Wittenberg University that I transferred to my institution.

This university course preparation was clutch because I could not afford to take the AP tests at my own high school. I took a great number of those courses but the tests were over 100 dollars each and I could not afford the cost. However, taking the harder courses was good for college preparation. I also assembled my first "dream team." Having friends around me who were driven about college and were not distracted by teenage angst and statistics. I had to have a support system of peers because I really could not get that from my family at that time. We were too volatile.

However, when it came to family, Odessa taught me how to be a good person and stay humble. She was always serving the community, and even at 90 years old, she was the example of a person civically engaged because she went canvassing for Obama presidency. Age was a number we were not bound to and her life always made me feel that I could do anything and I was only limited by my mind. Support can come from intentional and unintentional places.

"Aha" Moments and How to be Resilient in College

I went to college to be an astrophysicist. After spending a year working in a lab when I was a junior, I realized that I liked astronomy but I did not want to live it. I wanted to make a difference in the everyday lives of people and social justice advocacy with scholarship called to me. I knew that the history of social change on large scale was related to education and higher education for the past century and I needed to figure out how to do that. This lead to me earning a master's degree in higher education/student affairs and knowing I could not stop there. I also know I wanted a doctorate because I believe the PhD gives you the license to create knowledge.

To be the first doctor in my family actually is not a big a deal to them as it is to the world. To be part of the 1% has not made negotiating the remnants of poverty any easier. To be first comes with an unspoken burden that folks do not realize when they come from that middle class family. Having done things by myself when other peers have had so many helping hands made even more isolating.

I continued the dream team approach in undergraduate. I found friends, and I made for a lifetime. I have been in 22 weddings and have traveled to spend time with the people who helped to shape me into the person I am today. We had our share of tears and laughter. From that particular cohort though, I was the poorest kid and the only first-generation person. Graduate school allowed me to help other first generation students and minority students to equip them with all the things I formerly lacked. I was paying it forward, back, sideways, and made new pathways.

Daniel Garcia, Hispanic/Latino Male, First Year Graduate Student, Marquette University

College seemed like something for only well-to-do kids. As I got older and started going to school, I only seemed to be going through the motions, not having any choice in the matter. It was not until eighth grade when local and private high schools visited to "recruit" students did the word "college" enter into my vocabulary. These representatives kept saying their school was "college preparatory" and I became convinced I would do well at these places.

I attended a private, catholic, "college preparatory" high school, primarily on financial aid, as an honor student. As an athlete, I floated by academically with a B average in almost every class. The only classes I thrived in were History and Government. My History and Government teachers were the first people to really tell me about college and how it would benefit my future. My junior year, with the support of my teachers and family, I committed to studying and for the first time I attained an A average. I knew I needed to work harder if I was going to get into college and receive scholarships.

My parents were extremely supportive when I told them I wanted to go to college. The most influential person during this experience was my older sister, who had already gone off to college. Having not attending college themselves, my parents had a hard time understanding the process of applying to college, especially when filling out the FAFSA. After applying to seven schools, I was admitted into five, and conditionally or waitlisted by the other two. However, paying for these schools was a big issue and I did not receive as much financial aid that I needed to attend.

Instead, I chose a school that had my academic program, and offered me the best financial assistance package. My parents and older sister were supportive, from spending their last on college essentials, to making sure I had every book. Due to my college of choice being located 3 hours from home, my parents had a hard time letting go of me because my family was so close.

Throughout my college experience I was constantly torn between my family and my academics. If I were not in contact with my parents every day, or at least every 30 hours, they would call me concerned about my well-being. It was hard to really "get away" from my parents.

My mother and father looked to my sister and I as counselors for their personal and financial issues because they saw us as more educated and more knowing. When my father lost his job, I went home and helped him navigate the unemployment office. Similarly, when he began applying for work, I was helping him tweak his resume and fill out online applications.

I balanced by education, extracurricular activities, and part time jobs, at first, chaotically. After attending a lot of programs by my university, I began to develop good study habits and what everyone called "time management" which I just changed to "priority management." I would balance everything in my life by prioritizing everything. Whatever was more important that day or the next day or in a week, I would focus on that priority. I quickly learned to plan ahead, accomplishing tougher tasks first.

My personal philosophy centers on family. I work to live, not live to work. At the end of the day, I look forward to spending time with my fiancé, my dog, my family, and my friends. I strive to achieve a proper work-life balance with more emphasis on life.

I am striving to achieve a career in student affairs where I can impact the lives of current and future students. Having been formed and molded by many staff in my college experience, as a first-generation college student, these people were my mentors and advisors who helped me become the person I am today. Someday, I want students to talk about me the same way I talk about my mentors. At the end of the day, the cyclical nature of this mentoring created my passion to work with college students. I am currently a graduate student studying College Student Personnel Administration at Marquette University.

Managing my first-generation life plan, having a subconscious need to constantly "prove" myself, will be a process of reformation. I feel I have to reassess my success and determine what tools, skills, and support I utilized to get where I am. As a first-generation college student, I know there are others in similar positions and want to give back.

Monique Williams, African American Female, Academic Professional, University of Illinois Springfield

Throughout my childhood I was always told by my parents that "cost does not matter" when looking for colleges and universities. So, you can guess my surprise when I actually started applying to schools and it suddenly became all about affordability. In a sense I was hurt to find out that money mattered more than anything. I felt tricked into believing that I could go to any school I wanted. I will admit, it was a struggle to come down to reality of taking cost into consideration. However, when I did take it into consideration, I decided, that I would not let finances overshadow my goal of getting a degree.

I chose Lincoln College in Illinois as my school of choice. It was a private two year college about three hours away from home so it was perfect. I took cost into consideration and I thought it would fit into my budget however my dad did not. I think he was upset about this decision for many reasons: financial obligations, it was mainly an all-white school and I was the last child to leave home. I think the last child held a lot of weight especially since I'm a girl. He tried his hardest to get me to stay home or attend college in Arkansas with my brother. In fact, I can remember him calling the college my brother attended. He tried to get a discount on tuition since two of his kids "would" be attending the same school. I had to explain to him that it did not work that way. Tuition was a set rate no matter how many kids attended the same school.

It wasn't until the college process began that I started to realize that I had to educate my parents on the process. Up until that point, I thought they knew everything and had all the answers to all questions I would ever have. This was a hard realization and it did change my view of them. In fact, I was in awe of them for guiding me in the right direction. Though, I also realized my position changed as well. They looked to me, to guide them in the college process as well. They had to rely on me to interpret information for them especially when it came to dealing with financial aid, housing, and scholarships.

When the time came to take me to college, the first stop before moving into my residence hall was the Financial Aid Office. I went inside with my parents to complete some last minute paperwork. They explained to me that I would need to take out a loan for $5,000 to cover the year. I understood this, as a necessity to get a degree however, my dad did not think so. We got into an argument and he said that "We can get back into the car and you can go to community college or you can stay here and be in debt for the rest of your life." Up until that point, my parents made all the decisions for me, I knew that I would never finish at a community college and that I would end up working at the local Wal-Mart. So, I looked at him and told him that I wanted to stay. I felt accomplished in making this decision but terrified as well. At that time, I didn't even know how I was going to afford books or even get a job. I can say that everything worked itself out, but it took a lot of determination and help from others. The process of affording the cost often confused me. So it was no shock when I received a call from the financial aid office saying that I stilled owed money that was due by a certain date. I called home to talk to my dad about it. He wanted me to get scholarships but the period for applying for them was over. He also suggested going to the financial aid office every day to see if they could give me any extra money. I was not too keen on this idea. I thought of it as begging, something I would not do. Instead, I joined the cross-country team because they offered a scholarship; I also worked two jobs on-campus; so I could make payments. Every week when I got my paycheck, I would take $25 for myself and put the rest of the money toward my student account.

Though this held me for my first semester, I knew I would owe the same amount of money for the following year. I must admit that in high school I never cared about academics; however, I realized that academics was the number one way to get college paid for. I worked my butt off and excelled in my academics. When I look back on this period, I realized that I would go from one project to the next with five hours of sleep a night. It was a vicious circle of cross-country practice in the morning, classes during the day, and work in the evening. What set me apart and allowed me to excel was the people I placed myself with. I worked in the tutoring lab as well as worked in the library. Since there was little time during the day to study, the librarian would let me into the library at 5:00 a.m. to study before practice and let me stay until 3:00 a.m. in the morning. I know it's unusual for students to love the library that much, but I knew I needed to get my work done before I could allow myself to have fun.

I also had the opportunity to surround myself with a good group of friends and a good church family. We made our own community. Sometimes we would argue like a family, have dinner and lunch together, and partied together. No matter what, we were accountable for each other. The Pastor who took us to church on Sundays even knew our class schedules and when we had an upcoming test. She would invite us to have dinner with her so we could have some time off campus. Most importantly she would pray with us in the good times and bad. This was our community, this was my community, and this allowed me the opportunity to graduate with my Associate's Degree.

Jennifer Sanders, White female, Graduate Student, Lincoln Seminary

I started college in 1995 and stopped in 2000 because I was undecided about the degree, I wanted to pursue. The opportunity was presented to me in 2008 to finish my degree in the ministry. I have two sons and was able to do school work during the day while they were at school. I attended school one night a week. I found the nontraditional route to be a good fit for me. I think the most important decision I made was returning to school to get my bachelor's degree. During my life journey, I found my way back to a church, renewed my belief in God, got baptized, and started serving in my church. I have accomplished being the first in my family to get a bachelor's degree. I feel a lot of pride and very accomplished for doing something my parents had not done. My parents, husband, and children celebrated with me. Showing my children that graduating from college can be achieved, allows me to believe they will go on as well to further their education to get a college degree. I am thankful for the many professors I had to teach me as well as my mentor. The role my mentor played in my decision to complete college had everything to do with his leadership style in the ministry environment. The leadership qualities he exhibited help me to serve many roles as well. He gave me a sense of ownership to my education and allowed me to learn and grow. He was always there to lead and to help guide me. He was still there as a mentor when I went off to be a lay pastor at church for seniors. He has been there along the way through the many ideas and passions. I had been going to school and trying to figure out if my role was to be a pastor or a teacher. Accomplishing one goal has lead to other goals and I am currently in the seminary finishing up a master's in Christian Education. After receiving my bachelor's degree, my mentor told me I could pursue becoming a substitute teacher. I have been a substitute teacher for three years within the school district. After I complete my Christian education master's degree, I will pursue a master's degree in special education. Each new step I have taken has opened up new avenues to learn and grow. If I had not accomplished the first goal of getting a bachelor's degree I am not sure I would have had the confidence to continue and be where I am today.

Nehemiah Bishop, African American Male, Undergraduate Student, University of Illinois Chicago

My journey to college would be considered typical for some but unusual for most. I was born and raised in Chicago but also spent a significant amount of my life in the south suburbs of Chicago. Growing up under a single mother with six children warranted a daily uphill challenge. During the earlier years of my life, we were evicted more times than I can count on my fingers. We had experienced what it was like to live in shelters, hotels, family members' homes, and even on our van. These moments in my life may have been the toughest experiences I ever have to go through, but they wouldn't be the reason I quit on life. Two majors factors that played a significant role in pushing me through these challenging times was my other brother William Hatten and my church First Pentecost Assemblies International Church. William always taught me to harness the pain and struggles we've endured and use them to propel myself into a successful future. He has been their every step of the way for me. From the moment of birth to the day I walked across the high school graduation stage. Church was a second home for me; it was the safe haven I needed in order to keep faith that I would overcome these tough circumstances. It was a phrase I constantly heard their, "Tough times don't last, but tough people do." Without these two positive reinforcements in my life, I would be completely altered into an unknown path. Upon reaching high school, college was always the end goal but being part of a family with low income made me skeptical that I would reach an institution of higher learning. My high school counselor Elizabeth Fushi-Peterson made sure my doubts wouldn't become part of my reality. She guided me through the college application process, scholarships applications, and even obstacles that weren't school related. Being accepted into the University of Illinois at Chicago (UIC) also with scholarships and grants to fund my education was definitely one of the happiest moments of my life. Those moments solidified the idea that yours dreams can become reality.

Entering campus, I knew there would be a transition process but I didn't know how much it would alter my life. I knew UIC was one of the most diverse institutions in the nation and that I wouldn't just be surrounded by African and Latino Americans like my previous neighborhoods. The transition at first was difficult. Conversing with individuals of different cultures, ethnicities, and backgrounds can create barriers if you aren't willing to respect and understand the other person background. I always was the type of individual who is eager to learn about others' backgrounds. So I began to search for things we have in common. The topic that my current friends and me continued to talk about was sports, specifically basketball. They shared the same passion and love I had for it and once we had something in common, it open the conversations to more and more topics to the point that I could call these individuals my friend. We understood that there were many differences that were hard to understand at first but we also figured out that we had more in common with each other than we realized. We all enjoyed the same quality of food, movies, art, books, and music. We found ourselves becoming closer than anyone could ever predict. I'm proud to say that my closest friends in college are: Bangladeshian, Vietnamese, Puerto Rican, Pilipino, Nigerian, Bulgarian, and African American.

My philosophy on life is to always be respectful. Treat others the way you want to be treated is a saying I apply to my life everyday. It may be a cliché phrase that is used constantly, but I feel respect is the number one characteristic a human being can have. Whether your opinions perfects align or completely disagree with an individual, as long as there is respect for one another an agreement and understanding can always be reached.

The value and purpose of education in my opinion is right behind God, family, and then education. Education in my opinion is what defines you as a human being. Education isn't just what you learn in a classroom, but also the atmosphere outside of the classroom. The experiences we go through in life educate us just as much as the knowledge we acquire in a textbook. Through education, you cross paths with new information that will help define you as a person, whether it's history, math, science, or the environment you grew up in. All this newly acquired intel will guide individuals towards your life passions. It will help mode your values and beliefs. I don't look at education as something you just learn at an institution, but also the life lesson that educates us daily.

My career explorations are to acquire my bachelor's degree in accounting with a minor in finance. I plan to acquire my masters in order to fulfill the 150 hours that is required to take the Certified Public Accountant Exam (CPA). Once I acquire my CPA exam, I want to partake in Corporate Accounting. The end goal is to eventually open my on CPA firm and lend advice to small businesses. Outside of my career goals however, I plan to fulfill my life passions of helping others. I am currently a member of the 100 Black Men of Chicago. Helping and uplifting the community is main goal of this organization, which is why I am such a heavy participant.

There are many facets that make up my cultural capital. My Church is cultural capital to me. During slavery, the only outlet for African American slaves had been church. It was an uplifting vice that kept my ancestors pushing forward. Even though slavery isn't a problem for African Americans today, church for me is still a vice I use to get me past the challenges I face. These advocates I have in my life are my cultural capital. You can't by family, friends, or loyalty, which makes having these individuals that much more valuable. They have been in my corner and are currently still there. Without William Hatten, Melinda Chapple, Michael Thomas, Cathy Thomas, Joseph Fields, Demetrius Chapple, Antonio Chapple, Daniel Corona, Elizabeth Fushi-Peterson, Mariba Smith-Woods, and Bishop Ernest Owens, there wouldn't be the Nehemiah Bishop you see today. I'm honored to have these individuals in my life, which leads to my cultural obligation of giving back to my community. If these great people weren't there to guide me, I may have been a lost soul. I must try and help those children who need me to be the same advocate that I needed growing up.

My advice to incoming first generation students entering into higher education would be to enter without fear. Understand that there are unlimited possibilities and opportunities in this world, and they just have to be willing to try. Don't be afraid to ask for help. One of the biggest regrets that I have about my experiences when I came on to a college campus was that I would ask for help. During my freshman year, I tried to tackle every challenge I had alone instead of going to the individuals whose jobs were to help me. Once I began to utilize the African American Academic Network at my university, my life as a collegiate student became so much easier. I would highly advise finding individuals on campus that would love nothing more than to see you succeed.

Justin Keenan, White male, Second Year Graduate Student, University of Illinois Chicago

Being a first-generation college student is not always the easiest thing. Applying for school is was difficult and confusing at times. When you and your parents lack experience in navigating college it becomes a lot more difficult. Furthermore, it is hard to talk to your family about the difficulties of school when they have never had the experience. However, I feel that mentoring programs such as the University of Illinois Springfield Necessary Steps Mentoring Program really do help with the transition from high school to college. Simply having a mentor who can assist to your classroom and give contact information for a certain academic program can be very beneficial. I was not aware of anyone from my hometown attending the University of Illinois Springfield and the Necessary Steps Mentoring Program, helped introduce me to students who had similar experiences. We are good friends to this day! It took a lot of work, but I was able to graduate in four years with honors. I contribute a lot of my success to the UIS Necessary Steps Mentoring Program.

Going into high school I was told that you had to take as many honors and AP classes as possible to get accepted into the college of your choice. My high school (Bremen H.S, Midlothian, IL) did offer a large variety of honors classes. However, AP classes were very limited compared to other schools in the Chicagoland area. The college attendance rate is not that great at my high school, and many of my friends and classmates never planned on going to college. However, I feel that overall Bremen helped prepare me for college. It may not have afforded me the opportunities that students at others schools had, but I felt that every one of my teachers worked hard to make sure that each and every student succeeded.

My parents divorced when I was very young, and I had limited contact with my father. My father actually passed away the summer between my sophomore and junior year. However, I have always had a strong network of family members (grandparents, aunts, uncles) who supported me, and helped me reach my goals. My mother has always pushed my brother and myself to do great things with our lives, and we want nothing more than to make her proud.

During the summer between my sophomore and junior year in college, I studied in Harbin, China for 5 weeks. I had already taken one year of Mandarin Chinese, and I wanted to study in China to improve my language skills. Although I worked hard to lobby other students to go with me, I ended up going alone. The trip was amazing, and I learned a lot about Chinese culture and customs. Furthermore, my Mandarin skills improved dramatically. I cannot wait to go back in the future.

Without an education today there really is no future. Jobs that once only required a high school diploma now require a four-year degree. Although I have a bachelor's degree, in the field that I want to work, a master's degree is generally required. That is why I am in the Urban Planning and Policy Masters Program at the UIC. I am currently specializing in economic development, and I really want to work with struggling communities to see what they can do to improve their local economies.

Over the course of my time at UIS, I interned at a variety of government agencies to see what career path I wanted to take. My freshman and sophomore year I worked in the Illinois General Assembly as a Page. My sophomore year I also worked with the Illinois Historic Preservation Agency at the Old State Capitol. The summer after my junior year, I interned with my hometown local municipal government (Midlothian, IL). My senior year, I interned with the Springfield-Sangamon County Regional Planning Commission (SSCRP). My time with the SSCRP and the Midlothian Municipal Government helped show me that I would really like to work with local governments in either the planning or the administration departments. This is the major reason why I am in the Master of Urban Planning Policy pogram at UIC. I am currently the administrative Intern with the Village of Glen Ellyn, IL. My current internship has really confirmed my interest in local government, and I hope to find a job after grad school with a local government in the Chicago land area.

I have always really liked the quote "remember the past or be damned to repeat it" because I feel that it is really fitting for life. I have made a lot of mistakes over the 22 years that I have been on this earth, and I know that I will make plenty more in the future. However, it is very important to make sure that you learn from each mistake to see what you can do to change the outcome in the future. I also work hard to make sure that I treat everyone with kindness and consideration. I am not better than everyone else, and I try to stay level headed at all times. I am a First Generation Success!

Clarice Ford

Whatever It Takes

When I arrived at college, I was afraid to ask for help, to say no to the party people and yes to the study circles. I failed every class including tennis! The hole I had dug for myself was difficult to climb out of and I quit school. Every door of advancement in the job sector was closed in my face because I did not have a college degree. As I returned to college later on in life, a professor placed a small yellow stickem in my hand with the letters WIT written in black ink. She said "Whatever it takes for you to graduate … long nights, early rises with the sun, you must graduate in order to win this race." Those three letters were motivation to win the race not just once but four times (associate, bachelor, masters, doctorate).

From *A Guide to Surviving and Thriving in College* by Berry College. Edited by Katherine Powell. Reprinted by permission of Kendall Hunt Publishing Company.

Critical Thinking

1. What are some general goals and objectives of higher education according to the chapter?
2. How good is a college education?
3. How strong do you identify as a first-generation student?
4. What did you learn from reading the voices of a generation?

Works Cited

1. Bok, Derek. 2006. *Our Underachieving Colleges: A Candid Look at How Much Students Learn and Why They Should be Learning More.* Princeton, NJ: Princeton University Press.
2. Davis, Jeff. 2010. *The First Generation Student Experience.* Sterling, VA: Stylus.

3. Jamelske, Eric. 2009. "Measuring the impact of a university first-year experience program on student GPA and retention." *Higher Education* 57(3):373–391.

4. Pryor, J. H., M. K. Eagan, Blake L. Palucki, S. Hurtado, J. Berdan, and M. H. Case. 2012. "The American Freshman: National Norms Fall 2012." *Higher Education Research Institute home of the Cooperative Institutional Research Program.* Accessed September 17, 2013. www.heri.ucla.edu.

5. The College Board. *Education Pays.* Washington, DC: The College Board, 2005.

6. Tinto, Vincent. "Learning Better Together: The Impact of Learning Communities on Student Success." *Promoting Student Success in College* (Higher Education Monograph Series).

Transition From High School to College

2

WHO IS A FIRST-GENERATION STUDENT?

Definition: A student whose parents have not graduated from a four-year college or university.

PURPOSE

First-generation students are attending colleges and universities across the globe. They are representing the fastest growing population in higher education enrollments in the United States of America.

The purpose of this chapter is to assist you as define who you are as a first-generation student.

ACTIVATE YOUR THOUGHTS

When I am called a "first-generation student" what are my first thoughts and why?

TRANSITION FROM HIGH SCHOOL TO COLLEGE

A major shift that has occurred in colleges and universities is the increase of first-generation college students. In the past, being a first generation was a liability because we tend to come from working class families from various cultural and ethnic backgrounds, receive less support from our families, lack of understanding from our families, and pressure to succeed. Today a new intellectual thought has risen and is being heard and seen all over the world. Due to the many first-generation graduates and famous individuals such as William Clinton (fourty-second President of the United States), Sonia Sotomayor (United States Supreme Court Justice), Oprah Winfrey (CEO, Journalist, Actress), and John Legend (singer), matriculation is achievable for first-generation students.

PRECOLLEGIATE CHARACTERISTICS

Research on first-generation students is usually categorized by the following categories as suggested by Pascarella (2006). They are the precollegiate characteristics, transition, and college experience. The relationship between the characteristics and experiences are represented in Figure 1.1.

First Category   Second Category   Third Category

Precollege Characteristics	Transition	College Experience
Expectations	High School to College	Persistence
College Choices	Sustainability	Educational Attainment
HS Graduation— Mid-term	Freshman—Sophomore	Graduation

Today, I realize how my expectations of college were never articulated to me in middle school for the academic, emotional, and social preparation needed to be successful in college and society. I remember the excitement of receiving my first acceptance letter to college. I had decent SAT scores and good academic performance in high school but I only knew about college by what I saw on television. Television showed more fun than the discipline needed to be successful in the classroom. I didn't realize it was going to be hard since I went away to summer camp and was able to make friends quite easily. The more information on what I needed for college waited for me in the mailbox, the more I began to ask the question "Am I good enough to be a college student?" despite my parents bragging to everyone that their little girl was leaving the neighborhood to attend college.

I thought I should just stay home and attend the community college to help my family financially and be with my friends who were not able to leave because they are going to think I am "better" than them. College choices began to play with my head and heart. I was also accepted to a university in another state and FEAR removed the thought of attending that institution from the list. It is important to note the key construct for first-generation students to understand college is cultural capital. Bourdieu described this, with respect to differences in educational success by individual's socioeconomic status. Parents sharing cultural capital (information and beliefs) to their children are needed to succeed in college (Bourdieu 1973). This information in higher education is the value the students gain from their parents that supports and assists them as they navigate the college experience and seek a higher social status and greater social mobility (Stanton-Salazar and Dornbusch 1995).

The parents of first-generation students understand the importance of getting a college education but lack the tools to assist through the process. They do not have details from their lived experiences in the area of higher education. London and many others have studied the social and educational interactions of the first-generation students and have concluded that the lack of cultural capital leaves us vulnerable to low achievement and failure to attain a degree (London 1989).

We are likely as first-generation students to enter college with less academic preparation and to have limited access to information about the college experience, either first-hand or from relatives (Thayer 2000). I remember all the variables involved in preparing to be accepted to college:

- Researching Institutions (Public, Private, Historically Black Colleges, Hispanic-Serving Institutions, and Native American Non-Tribal Institutions)
- Financial Aid (Grants, loans, scholarships, work study, and parental contribution)
- General Education expectations (Foreign Language, Science, English, Math, and read several of The Great Books)
- College Terminology (Grade Point Average, Residence Halls, internships, and matriculation)
- Campus Resources (TRIO Programs, Career Center, Writing Center, Math Lab, Center for Academic Success, Diversity Center, and Student Life)

Many colleges and universities understand the importance of cultural capital. Today parents are going through the admission process, partaking in the orientation process, sharing coffee with faculty and administrators, taking classes online for parents and developing help-seeking skills to assist their students in the process. According to Purswell, Yazedjian, and Toews, first-generation students usually know their parents care about their accomplishments but insufficient parental engagement combined with insufficient **cultural capital** can be a barrier to success (Purswell, Yazedijan, and Toews 2008).

You might feel "different" because you might not know the processes and procedures at your college or aware of the resources available to you today. Most importantly, gain confidence, remember to persevere and with hard work graduation will always be in sight. We hope this textbook will be your roadmap for success as a First-Generation Student.

KEY TRANSITIONAL TASKS

College students especially those who are first in the family to attend college must effectively complete key transitional tasks (such as adapting to the campus culture, establishing one's identity, time management, and balancing freedom and responsibility) (Ward, Siegel, and Davenport 2012).

We as first-generation college students often feel such a sense of pride about being the first in our families but also for our cultural heritage. All students including first-generation students walk through the process of **anticipatory socialization** before arriving to the campus (Shields 2002). When you arrive to campus, reality begins to slowly take over your emotions and thoughts. This process of reconciliation and change is critical because students who do not adequately complete it are more likely to perceive a mismatch with their college choice, to be dissatisfied with their experience, and to fail to achieve academic and social integration (Tinto 1993). As first-generation students, you must reconcile what you expect from yourself as a student and also what your family expects of you. This is critical for your success to examine how to fulfill your family obligations (such as working at the family business on the week-ends, working to help to contribute to the family finances, helping with a sick parent/grandparent, and maintain your grade point average for scholarship renewal). You might have been able to attend high school, live at home, work, and maintain decent grades, but college is different.

Let's examine the transition from High School to College.

First Generation

Transition From High School to College

Category	High School	College	Adult Graduate
Books	Free	Buy/Rentals	Buy
Housing	Live at home free	Live with others cost + deposit	Credit check, deposit, and monthly rent
Attendance	Excuse from home	Attendance defined on syllabus	Attendance defined by employer
Academic Integrity	Meet with the principal	Meet with professor, committee, could earn F, student disciplinary actions by the Dean of Students and/or expulsion from the college.	Ethics Officer/Supervisor at place of employment. Job could be terminated.
Food	Free/reduced/or cash	Meal plans required. Must buy if you reside on campus	Responsible for your food purchases.
Study Halls/Tables	Part of class schedule.	You decide to attend if not mandated by the professor.	
Library	Part of the school time activity. Free	You decide whether to utilize the library physically or online. Paid through student fees.	Must purchase library card.

Meet with Teacher	Usually means you are in trouble or failing the class.	You are required to take the initiative to make an appointment to meet with the professor, advisors, and/or administrators.	
Technology	Free at school	Paid by fees. Technology is used for classes, communication, billing, and assignments.	Usually have to purchase internet service outside of work.
Extracurricular activities	Free—Show School ID	Fees—Show School ID	Must pay when required.
Classes	Classes—Free Prepared for you by the Guidance Counselor.	Paid by your tuition cost. Must meet with advisors to discuss classes, to drop and/or add classes, withdrawals	

KNOW YOURSELF-GENERATION iY

Change happens extremely fast; in the blink of an eye, technology can change, life can change, people can change. Understanding and recognizing the changes you will experience, as a first-generation college student is important. The shift from one phase to another takes intentional effort to recognize.

Imagine for one second that you fell asleep one night in 1985 and did not wake up until 2013. All this time your parents have been living life and growing and expanding with the changes that are occurring. Continue to think about being a first-generation college student to parents who have experienced the Tylenol scare of 1982, "Halloween hotlines, advisories and statutes, national coverage about dangers to children, divorce, child abuse, abortion, violent crime, alcohol consumption, illegal drugs as well as safety concerns about everything from venetian blinds to peanut butter" (Elmore 2010). As time continued to tick away, traumatic and life changing events happened within schools and adolescent children that forced parents to protect and sometimes over protect their children.

Being a child of a parent from Generation X or a Boomer indicated that you're the future for your family. Have you started questioning why we are discussing the issues that parents have faced since the 80's? If not, now is the time for you to begin to understand why parents of first-generation college students are the way that they are. If you were born between the years of 1982-present, we are the generation of the "era of the wanted child." Beginning to understand why our parents are so involved or not involved at all is the foundation of understanding the importance of getting an education as a first-generation.

Success in college requires that you manage both time and money. You will need time to study and money to pay for your education. The first step in managing time and money is to think about the goals that you wish to accomplish in your life. Having goals that are important to you provides a reason and motivation for managing time and money. This chapter provides some useful techniques for managing time and money so that you can accomplish the goals you have set for yourself.

What Are My Lifetime Goals?

Setting goals helps you to establish what is important and provides direction for your life. Goals help you to focus your energy on what you want to accomplish. Goals are a promise to yourself to improve your life. Setting goals can help you turn your dreams into reality. Steven Scott, in his book *A Millionaire's Notebook,* lays out five steps in this process:

1. Dream or visualize.
2. Convert the dream into goals.
3. Convert your goals into tasks.
4. Convert your task into steps.
5. Take your first step, and then the next.[1]

As you begin to think about your personal goals in life, make your goals specific and concrete. Rather than saying, "I want to be rich," make your goal something that you can break into specific steps. You might want to start learning about money management or begin a savings plan. Rather than setting a goal for happiness, think about what brings you happiness. If you want to live a long and healthy life, think about the health habits that will help you to accomplish your goal. You will need to break your goals down into specific tasks to be able to accomplish them.

HAGAR © 2010 Distributed by King Features Syndicate, World Rights Reserved.

Here are some criteria for successful goal setting:

1. **Is it achievable?** Do you have the skills, abilities, and resources to accomplish this goal? If not, are you willing to spend the time to develop the skills, abilities, and resources needed to achieve this goal?
2. **Is it realistic?** Do you believe you can achieve it? Are you positive and optimistic about this goal?

From *College and Career Success* by Marsha Fralick. Copyright © 2011 by Kendall Hunt Publishing Company. Reprinted by permission.

3. **Is it specific and measurable?** Can it be counted or observed? The most common goal mentioned by students is happiness in life. What is happiness, and how will you know when you have achieved it? Is happiness a career you enjoy, owning your own home, or a travel destination?

4. **Do you want to do it?** Is this a goal you are choosing because it gives you personal satisfaction, rather than meeting a requirement or an expectation of someone else?

5. **Are you motivated to achieve it?** What are your rewards for achieving it?

6. **Does the goal match your values?** Is it important to you?

7. **What steps do you need to take to begin?** Are you willing to take action to start working on it?

8. **When will you finish this goal?** Set a date to accomplish your goal.

REFLECTION ●

Write a paragraph about your lifetime goals. Use any of these questions to guide your thinking:

- What is your career goal? If you do not know what your career goal is, describe your preferred work environment. Would your ideal career require a college degree?

- What are your family goals? Are you interested in marriage and family? What would be your important family values?

- What are your social goals (friends, community, and recreation)?

- When you are older and look back on your life, what are the three most important life goals that you want to have accomplished?

A Goal or a Fantasy?

One of the best questions ever asked in my class was, "What is the difference between a goal and a fantasy?" As you look at your list of lifetime goals, are some of these items goals or fantasies? Think about this question as you read the following scenario:

When Linda was a college student, she was walking through the parking lot, noticed a beautiful red sports car, and decided that it would become a lifetime goal for her to own a similar car one day. However, with college expenses and her part-time job, it was not possible to buy the car. She would have to be content with the used car that her dad had given her so that she could drive to college. Years passed by, and Linda now has a good job, a home, and a family. She is reading a magazine and sees a picture of a similar red sports car. She cuts out this picture and tapes it to the refrigerator. After it has been on the refrigerator for several months, her children ask her why the picture is on the refrigerator. Linda replies, "I just like to dream about owning this car."

One day, as Linda is driving past a car dealership, she sees the red sports car on display and stops in for a test drive. To her surprise, she decides that she does not like driving the car. It doesn't fit her lifestyle, either. She enjoys outdoor activities that would require a larger car. Buying a second car would be costly and reduce the amount of money that the family could spend on vacations. She decides that vacations are more important than owning the sports car. Linda goes home and removes the picture of the red sports car from the refrigerator.

There are many differences between a goal and a fantasy. A fantasy is a dream that may or may not become a reality. A goal is something that we actually plan to achieve. Sometimes we begin with a fantasy and later it becomes a goal. A fantasy can become a goal if steps are taken to achieve it. In the preceding example, the sports car is a fantasy until Linda actually takes the car for a test drive. After driving the car, she decides that she really does not want it. The fantasy is sometimes better than the reality. Goals and fantasies change over a lifetime. We set goals, try them out, and change them as we grow and mature and find out what is most important in life. Knowing what we think is important, and what we value most, helps us make good decisions about lifetime goals.

What is the difference between a goal and a fantasy? A goal is something that requires action. Ask yourself if you are willing to take action on the goals you have set for yourself. Begin to take action by thinking about the steps needed to accomplish the goal. Then take the first step and continue. Change your goals if they are no longer important to you.

REFLECTION ⬤

Write a paragraph about how you will accomplish one of your important lifetime goals. Start your paragraph by stating an important goal from the previous journal entry. What is the first step in accomplishing this goal? Next, list some additional steps needed to accomplish it. How can you motivate yourself to begin taking these steps?

For example:

One of my important lifetime goals is _____. The first step in accomplishing this goal is . . . Some additional steps are . . . I can motivate myself to accomplish this goal by . . .

The ABCs of Time Management

Using the **ABCs of time management** is a way of thinking about priorities. Priorities are what you think is important. An **A priority** is a task that relates to your lifetime goal. For example, if my goal is to earn a college degree, studying becomes an A priority. This activity would become one of the most important tasks that I could accomplish today. If my goal is to be healthy, an A priority would be to exercise and plan a healthy diet. If my goal is to have a good family life, an A priority would be to spend time with family members. Knowing about your lifetime goals and spending time on those items that are most important to you will help you to accomplish the goals that you have set for yourself. If you do not spend time on your goals, you may want to look at them again and decide which ones are fantasies that you do not really value or want to accomplish.

A **B priority** is an activity that you have to do, but that is not directly related to your lifetime goal. Examples of B priorities might be getting out of bed, taking a shower, buying groceries, paying bills, or getting gas for the car. These activities are less important, but still are necessary for survival. If I do not put gas in the car, I cannot even get to school or work. If I do not pay the bills, I will soon have financial difficulties. While we often cannot postpone these activities in order to accomplish lifetime goals, we can learn efficient time management techniques to accomplish these tasks quickly.

A **C priority** is something that I can postpone until tomorrow with no harmful effect. For example, I could wait until tomorrow or another day to wash my car, do the laundry, buy groceries, or organize my desk. As these items are postponed, however, they can move up the list to a B priority. If I cannot see out of my car window or have no clean clothes to wear, it is time to move these tasks up on my list of priorities.

Have you ever been a victim of "**C fever**"? This is an illness in which we do the C activities first and do not get around to doing the A activities that are connected to lifetime goals. Tasks required to accomplish lifetime goals are often ones that are more difficult, challenge our abilities, and take some time to accomplish. These tasks are often more difficult than the B or C activities. The C activities can fill our time and exhaust the energy we need to accomplish the A activities. An example of C fever is the student who cleans the desk or organizes the CD collection instead of studying. C fever is doing the endless tasks that keep us from accomplishing goals that are really important to us. Why do we fall victim to C fever? C activities are often easy to do and give us a sense of accomplishment. We can see immediate progress without too much effort. I can wash my car and get a sense of accomplishment and satisfaction in my shiny clean car. The task is easy and does not challenge my intellectual capabilities.

ACTIVITY

Setting Priorities

To see how the ABCs of time management work, read the profile of Justin, a typical college student, below.

Justin is a 19-year-old college student who plans to major in physical therapy. He is athletic and values his good health. He cares about people and likes helping others. He has a part-time job working as an assistant in the gym, where he monitors proper use of the weightlifting machines. Justin is also a member of the soccer team and practices with the team every afternoon.

Here is a list of activities that Justin would like to do today. Label each task as follows:

A if it relates to Justin's lifetime goals
B if it is something necessary to do
C if it is something that could be done tomorrow or later

_____ Get up, shower, get dressed   _____ Study for biology test that is tomorrow

_____ Eat breakfast   _____ Meet friends for pizza at lunch

_____ Go to work   _____ Call girlfriend

_____ Go to class   _____ Eat dinner

_____ Visit with friends between classes   _____ Unpack gear from weekend camping trip

_____ Buy a new battery for his watch   _____ Watch football game on TV

_____ Go shopping for new gym shoes   _____ Play video games

_____ Attend soccer practice   _____ Do math homework

_____ Do weightlifting exercises

While Justin is the only one who can decide how to spend his time, he can take some steps toward accomplishing his lifetime goal of being healthy by eating properly, exercising, and going to soccer practice. He can become a physical therapist by studying for the biology test and doing his math homework. He can gain valuable experience related to physical therapy by working in the gym. He cares about people and likes to maintain good relationships with others. Any tasks related to these goals are high-priority A activities.

What other activities are necessary B activities? He certainly needs to get up, shower, and get dressed. What are the C activities that could be postponed until tomorrow or later? Again, Justin needs to decide. Maybe he could postpone shopping for a new watch battery and gym shoes until the weekend. He would have to decide how much time to spend visiting with friends, watching TV, or playing video games. Since he likes these activities, he could use them as rewards for studying for the biology test and doing his math homework.

How to Estimate Study and Work Time

Students are often surprised at the amount of time necessary for study to be successful in college. A general rule is that you need to study two hours for every hour spent in a college class. A typical weekly schedule of a full-time student would look like this:

Typical College Schedule

> 15 hours of attending class
> +30 hours of reading, studying, and preparation
> 45 hours total

A full-time job involves working 40 hours a week. A full-time college student spends 45 hours or more attending classes and studying. Some students will need more than 45 hours a week if they are taking lab classes, need help with study and learning skills, or are taking a heavy course load.

Some students try to work full-time and go to school full-time. While some are successful, this schedule is extremely difficult.

The Nearly Impossible Schedule

> 15 hours attending class
> 30 hours studying
> +40 hours working
> 85 hours total

This schedule is the equivalent of having two full-time jobs! Working full-time makes it very difficult to find the time necessary to study for classes. Lack of study causes students to do poorly on exams and to doubt their abilities. Such a schedule causes stress and fatigue that make studying difficult. Increased stress can also lead to problems with personal relationships and emotional problems. These are all things that lead to dropping out of college.

Many students today work and go to college. Working during college can provide some valuable experience that will help you to find a job when you finish college. Working can teach you to manage your time efficiently and give you a feeling of independence and control over your own future. Many people need to work to pay for their education. A general guideline is to work no more than 20 hours a week if you plan to attend college full-time. Here is a workable schedule.

Part-Time Work Schedule

> 12 hours attending class
> 24 hours studying
> +20 hours working
> 56 hours total

A commitment of 56 hours a week is like having a full-time job and a part-time job. While this schedule takes extra energy and commitment, many students are successful with it. Notice that the course load is reduced to 12 hours. This schedule involves taking one less class per semester. The class missed can be made up in summer school, or the time needed to graduate can be extended. Many students take five years to earn the bachelor's degree because they work part-time. It is better to take longer to graduate than to drop out of college or to give up because of frustration. If you must work full-time, consider reducing your course load to one or two courses. You will gradually reach your goal of a college degree.

Part-Time Student Schedule

```
   6 hours attending class
  12 hours studying
+40 hours working
  58 hours total
```

Add up the number of hours you are attending classes, double this figure for study time, and add to it your work time, as in the above examples. How many hours of commitment do you have? Can you be successful with your current level of commitment to school, work, and study?

To begin managing your schedule, use the weekly calendar located at the end of this chapter to write in your scheduled activities such as work, class times, and athletics.

Schedule Your Success

If you have not used a schedule in the past, consider trying a schedule for a couple of weeks to see if it is helpful in completing tasks and working toward your lifetime goals. There are several advantages to using a schedule:

- It gets you started on your work.
- It helps you avoid procrastination.
- It relieves pressure because you have things under control.
- It frees the mind of details.
- It helps you find time to study.
- It eliminates the panic caused by doing things at the last minute.
- It helps you find time for recreation and exercise.

Once you have made a master schedule that includes classes, work, and other activities, you will see that you have some blanks that provide opportunities for using your time productively. Here are some ideas for making the most of your schedule:

1. Fill in your study times. Use the time immediately before class for previewing and the time immediately after class for reviewing. Remember that you need to study two hours or more for each hour spent in a college class.

2. Break large projects such as a term paper or test into small tasks and begin early. Double your time estimates for completion of the project. Larger projects often take longer than you think. If you finish early, use the extra time for something fun.

3. Use the daylight hours when you are most alert for studying. It may take you longer to study if you wait until late in the day when you're tired.

4. Think about your day and see if you can determine when you are most alert and awake. Prime time differs with individuals, but it is generally earlier in the day. Use the prime time when you are most alert to accomplish your most challenging tasks. For example, do your math homework during prime time. Wash your clothes during nonprime time, when you are likely to be less alert.

5. Set priorities. Make sure you include activities related to your lifetime goals.

6. Allow time for sleep and meals. It is easier to study if you are well rested and have good eating habits.

7. Schedule your time in manageable blocks of an hour or two. Having every moment scheduled leads to frustration when plans change.

8. Leave some time unscheduled to use as a shock absorber. You will need unscheduled time to relax and to deal with unexpected events.

9. Leave time for recreation, exercise, and fun.

Return to the schedule at the end of this chapter. After you have written in classes, work times, and other scheduled activities, use the scheduling ideas listed earlier to write in your study times and other activities related to your lifetime goals. Leave some unscheduled time to provide flexibility in the schedule.

If You Dislike Schedules

Some personality types like more freedom and do not like the structure that a schedule provides. There are alternatives for those who do not like to use a schedule. Here are some additional ideas.

1. A simple and fast way to organize your time is to use a to-do list. Take an index card or small piece of paper and simply write a list of what you need to do during the day. You can prioritize the list by putting an A or star by the most important items. Cross items off the list as you accomplish them. A list helps you focus on what is important and serves as a reminder not to forget certain tasks.

2. Another idea is to use monthly or yearly calendars to write down important events, tasks, and deadlines. Use these calendars to note the first day of school, when important assignments are due, vacations, and final exams. Place the calendars in a place where they are easily seen.

3. Alan Lakein, who wrote a book titled *How to Get Control of Your Time and Your Life*, suggests a simple question to keep you on track.[2] Lakein's question is, "What is the best use of my time right now?" This question works well if you keep in mind your goals and priorities.

4. Use reminders and sticky notes to keep on track and to remind yourself of what needs to be done each day. Place the notes in a place where you will see them, such as your computer, the bathroom mirror, or the dashboard of your car.

5. Some families use their refrigerators as time management devices. Use the refrigerator to post your calendars, reminders, goals, tasks, and to-do lists. You will see these reminders every time you open the refrigerator.

6. Invent your own unique ideas for managing time. Anything will work if it helps to accomplish your goals.

Manage Your Time with a Web Application

There are thousands of new web applications available to organize your life. You can use a web application on your phone, laptop, computer, or other mobile device to:

- Create a to-do list or schedule.
- Send reminders when assignments are due.
- Organize your calendar and plan your tasks.
- Organize your study time and plan assignments.
- Avoid procrastination.
- Create a virtual assistant to keep you organized.

QUIZ

Time Management, Part I

Test what you have learned by selecting the correct answers to the following questions.

1. The most important difference between a goal and a fantasy is
   a. imagination.
   b. procrastination.
   c. action.

2. An A priority is
   a. related to your lifetime goals.
   b. something important.
   c. something you have to do.

3. A general rule for college success is that you must spend ___ hours studying for every hour spent in a college class.
   a. one
   b. four
   c. two

4. For a workable study schedule,
   a. fill in all the blank time slots.
   b. leave some unscheduled time to deal with the unexpected.
   c. plan to study late at night.

5. To complete a large project such as a term paper,
    a. break the project into small tasks and begin early.
    b. schedule large blocks of time the day before the paper is due.
    c. leave time for exercise, recreation, and fun before beginning on the project.

How did you do on the quiz? Check your answers: 1. c, 2. a, 3. c, 4. b, 5. a

Time Management Tricks

Life is full of demands for work, study, family, friends, and recreation. Time management tricks can help you get started on the important tasks and make the most of your time. Try the following techniques when you are feeling frustrated and overwhelmed.

Divide and Conquer

When large tasks seem overwhelming, think of the small tasks needed to complete the project and start on the first step. For example, suppose you have to write a term paper. You have to take out a paper and pencil, log onto your computer, brainstorm some ideas, go to the library to find information, think about your main ideas, and write the first sentence. Each of these steps is manageable. It's looking at the entire project that can be intimidating.

I once set out hiking on a mountain trail. When I got to the top of the mountain and looked down, I enjoyed a spectacular view and was amazed at how high I had climbed. If I had thought about how high the mountain was, I might not have attempted the hike. I climbed the mountain by taking it one step at a time. That's the secret to completing any large project: break it into small, manageable parts, then take the first step and keep going.

Learning a small part at a time is also easy and helps with motivation for learning. While in college, carry around some material that you need to study. Take advantage of five or ten minutes of time to study a small part of your material. In this way you make good use of your time and enhance memory by using distributed practice. Don't wait until you have large blocks of uninterrupted study time to begin your studies. You may not have the luxury of large blocks of time, or you may want to spend that time in other ways.

Do the First Small Step

The most difficult step in completing any project is the first step. If you have a challenging project to do, think of a small first step and complete that small step. Make the first step something that you can accomplish easily and in a short amount of time. Give yourself permission to stop after the first step. However, you may find that you are motivated to continue with the project. If you have a term paper to write, think about some small step you can take to get started. Log onto your computer and look at the blank screen. Start writing some ideas. Type the topic into a computer search engine and see what information is available.

Go to the library and see what is available on your topic. If you can find some interesting ideas, you can motivate yourself to begin the project. Once you have started the project, it is easier to continue.

The 80/20 Rule

Alan Lakein is noted for many useful time management techniques. One that I have used over the years is the 80/20 rule. Lakein says, "If all items are arranged in order of value, 80 percent of the value would come from only 20 percent of the items, while the remaining 20 percent of the value would come from 80 percent of the items."[3] For example, if you have a list of ten items to do, two of the items on the list are more important than the others. If you were to do only the two most important items, you would have accomplished 80 percent of the value. If you are short on time, see if you can choose the 20 percent of the tasks that are the most valuable. Lakein noted that the 80/20 rule applies to many situations in life:

- 80 percent of file usage is in 20 percent of the files.
- 80 percent of dinners repeat 20 percent of the recipes.
- 80 percent of the washing is done on the 20 percent of the clothes worn most frequently.
- 80 percent of the dirt is on the 20 percent of the floor used most often.

Think about how the 80/20 rule applies in your life. It is another way of thinking about priorities and figuring out which of the tasks are C priorities. This prioritizing is especially important if you are short on time. The 80/20 rule helps you to focus on what is most important.

Aim for Excellence, Not Perfection

Are you satisfied with your work only if it is done perfectly? Do you put off a project because you cannot do it perfectly? Aiming for perfection in all tasks causes anxiety and procrastination. There are times when perfection is not necessary. Dave Ellis calls this time management technique "It Ain't No Piano."[4] If a construction worker bends a nail in the framing of a house, it does not matter. The construction worker simply puts in another nail. After all, "it ain't no piano." It is another matter if you are building a fine cabinet or finishing a piano. Perfection is more important in these circumstances. We need to ask: Is the task important enough to invest the time needed for perfection? A final term paper needs to be as perfect as we can make it. A rough draft is like the frame of a house that does not need to be perfect.

In aiming for excellence rather than perfection, challenge yourself to use perspective to see the big picture. How important is the project and how perfect does it need to be? Could your time be better invested accomplishing other tasks? This technique requires flexibility and the ability to change with different situations. Do not give up if you cannot complete a project perfectly. Do the best that you can in the time available. In some situations, if life is too hectic, you may need to settle for completing the project and getting it in on time rather than doing it perfectly. With this idea in mind, you may be able to relax and still achieve excellence.

Make Learning Fun by Finding a Reward

Time management is not about restriction, self-control, and deprivation. If it is done correctly, time can be managed to get more out of life and to have fun while doing it. Remember that behavior is likely to increase if followed by a reward. Think about activities that you find rewarding. In our time management example with Justin who wants to be a physical therapist, he could use many tasks as rewards for completing his studies. He could meet friends for pizza, call his girlfriend, play video games, or watch TV. The key idea is to do the studying first and then reward the behavior. Maybe Justin will not be able to do all of the activities we have mentioned as possible rewards, but he could choose what he enjoys most.

Studying first and then rewarding yourself leads to peace of mind and the ability to focus on tasks at hand. While Justin is out having pizza with his friends, he does not have to worry about work that he has not done. While Justin is studying, he does not have to feel that he is being deprived of having pizza with friends. In this way, he can focus on studying while he is studying and focus on having a good time while relaxing with his friends. It is not a good idea to think about having pizza with friends while studying or to think about studying while having pizza with friends. When you work, focus on your work and get it done. When you play, enjoy playing without having to think about work.

Take a Break

If you are overwhelmed with the task at hand, sometimes it is best to just take a break. If you're stuck on a computer program or a math problem, take a break and do something else. As a general rule, take a break of 10 minutes for each hour of study. During the break, do something totally different. It is a good idea to get up and move around. Get up and pet your cat or dog, observe your goldfish, or shoot a few baskets. If time is really at a premium, use your break time to accomplish other important tasks. Put your clothes in the dryer, empty the dishwasher, or pay a bill.

Study in the Library

If you are having difficulty with studying, try studying at school in the library. Libraries are designed for studying, and other people are studying there as well. It is hard to do something else in the library without annoying the librarian or other students. If you can complete your studying at school, you can go home and relax. This may be especially important if family, friends, or roommates at home easily distract you.

Learn to Say No Sometimes

Learn to say no to tasks that you do not have time to do. Follow your statement with the reasons for saying no: you are going to college and need time to study. Most people will understand this answer and respect it. You may need to say no to yourself as well. Maybe you cannot go out on Wednesday night if you have a class early on Thursday morning. Maybe the best use of your time right now is to turn off the TV or get off the Internet and study for tomorrow's test. You are investing your time in your future.

Dealing with Time Bandits

Time bandits are the many things that keep us from spending time on the things we think are important. Another word for a time bandit is a time waster. In college, it is tempting to do many things other than studying. We are all victims of different kinds of bandits.

ACTIVITY

Put a checkmark next to the items that waste your time. Add your own personal time wasters at the end of the list.

_____ TV	_____ Phone	_____ Sleeping in
_____ Other electronic devices	_____ Household chores	_____ Shopping
_____ Daydreaming	_____ Roommates	_____ Being easily distracted
_____ Social networking	_____ Video games	_____ Studying at a bad time
_____ Saying yes when you mean no	_____ Partying	_____ Reading magazines
_____ Friends	_____ Children	_____ Studying in a distracting place
_____ Internet	_____ iPod	
_____ Social time	_____ Waiting time	_____ Movies
_____ Family	_____ Girlfriend, boyfriend, spouse	_____ Commuting time (travel)

List some of your personal time bandits here.

_____

_____

Here are some ideas for keeping time bandits under control:

- **Schedule time for other people.** Friends and family are important, so we do not want to get rid of them! Discuss your goal of a college education with your friends and family. People who care about you will respect your goals. You may need to use a Do Not Disturb sign at times. If you are a parent, remember that you are a role model for your children. If they see you studying, they are more likely to value their own education. Plan to spend quality time with your children and the people who are important to you. Make sure they understand that you care about them.

- **Remember the rewards.** Many of the time bandits listed above make good rewards for completing your work. Put the time bandits to work for you by studying first and then enjoying a reward. Enjoy the TV, Internet, iPod, video games, or phone conversations after you have finished your studies. Aim for a balance of work, study, and leisure time.

- **Use your prime time wisely.** Prime time is when you are most awake and alert. Use this time for studying. Use non-prime time for the time bandits. When you are tired, do household chores and shopping. If you have little time for household chores, you might find faster ways to do them. If you don't have time for shopping, you will notice that you spend less and have a better chance of following your budget.

- **Remind yourself about your priorities.** When time bandits attack, remind yourself of why you are in college. Think about your personal goals for the future. Remember that college is not forever. By doing well in college, you will finish in the shortest time possible.

- **Use a schedule.** Using a schedule or a to-do list is helpful in keeping you on track. Make sure you have some slack time in your schedule to handle unexpected phone calls and deal with the unplanned events that happen in life. If you cannot stick to your schedule, just get back on track as soon as you can.

REFLECTION ●

Write a paragraph about how you will manage your time to accomplish your goal of a college education. Use any of these questions to guide your thinking:

- What are your priorities?
- How will you balance school, work, and family/friends?
- What are some time management tools you plan to use?
- How can you deal with time bandits?

Dealing with Procrastination

Procrastination means putting off things until later. We all use delaying tactics at times. Procrastination that is habitual, however, can be self-destructive. Understanding some possible reasons for procrastination can help you use time more effectively and be more successful in accomplishing goals.

Why Do We Procrastinate?

There are many psychological reasons for procrastinating. Just becoming aware of these may help you deal with procrastination. If you have serious difficulty managing your time for psychological reasons, visit the counseling center at your college or university. Do you recognize any of these reasons for procrastination in yourself or others?

- **Fear of failure.** Sometimes we procrastinate because we are afraid of failing. We see our performance as related to how much ability we have and how worthwhile we are as human beings. We may procrastinate in our college studies because of doubts about our ability to do the work. Success, however, comes from trying and learning from mistakes. There is a popular saying: falling down is not failure, but failing to get up or not even trying is failure.

- **Fear of success.** Most students are surprised to find out that one of the reasons for procrastination is fear of success. Success in college means moving on with your life, getting a job, leaving a familiar situation, accepting increased responsibility, and sometimes leaving friends behind. None of these tasks is easy. An example of fear of success is not taking the last step required to be successful. Students sometimes do not take the last class needed to graduate. Some good students do not show up for the final exam or do not turn in a major project. If you ever find yourself procrastinating on an important last step, ask yourself if you are afraid of success and what lies ahead in your future.

- **Perfectionism.** Some people who procrastinate do not realize that they are perfectionists. Perfectionists expect more from themselves than is realistic and more than others expect of themselves. There is often no other choice than to procrastinate because perfectionism is usually unattainable. Perfectionism generates anxiety that further hinders performance. Perfectionists need to understand that perfection is seldom possible. They need to set time limits on projects and do their best within those time limits.

- **Need for excitement.** Some students can only be motivated by waiting until the last minute to begin a project. These students are excited and motivated by playing a game of "Beat the Clock." They like living on the edge and the adrenaline rush of responding to a crisis. Playing this game provides motivation, but it does not leave enough time to achieve the best results. Inevitably, things happen at the last minute to make the game even more exciting and dangerous: the printer breaks, the computer crashes, the student gets ill, the car breaks down, or the dog eats the homework. These students need to start projects earlier to improve their chances of success. It is best to seek excitement elsewhere, in sports or other competitive activities.

- **Excellence without effort.** In this scenario, students believe that they are truly outstanding and can achieve success without effort. These students think that they can go to college without attending classes or reading the text. They believe that they can pass the test without studying. They often do not succeed in college the first semester, which puts them at risk of dropping out of school. They often return to college later and improve their performance by putting in the effort required.

- **Loss of control.** Some students fear loss of control over their lives and procrastinate to gain control. An example is students who attend college because others (such as parents) want them to attend. Procrastination becomes a way of gaining control over the situation by saying, "You can't make me do this." They attend college but accomplish nothing. Parents can support and encourage education, but students need to choose their own goals in life and attend college because it is an important personal goal.

Tips for Dealing with Procrastination

When you find yourself procrastinating on a certain task, think about the consequences. Will the procrastination lead to failing an exam or getting a low grade? Think about the rewards of doing the task. If you do well, you can take pride in yourself and celebrate your success. How will you feel when the task is completed? Will you be able to enjoy your leisure time without guilt about not doing your work? How does the task help you to achieve your lifetime goals?

Maybe the procrastination is a warning sign that you need to reconsider lifetime goals and change them to better suit your needs.

Procrastination Scenario

George is a college student who is on academic probation for having low grades. He is required to make a plan for improving his grades in order to remain in college. George tells the counselor that he is making poor grades because of his procrastination. He is an accounting major and puts off doing homework because he dislikes it and does not find it interesting. The counselor asks George why he had chosen accounting as a major. He replies that accounting is a major that is in demand and has a good salary. The counselor suggests that George consider a major that he would enjoy more. After some consideration, George changes his major to psychology. He becomes more interested in college studies and is able to raise his grades to stay in college.

Most of the time, you will reap benefits by avoiding procrastination and completing the task at hand. Jane Burka and Lenora Yuen suggest the following steps to deal with procrastination:

1. Select a goal.
2. Visualize your progress.
3. Be careful not to sabotage yourself.
4. Stick to a time limit.
5. Don't wait until you feel like it.
6. Follow through. Watch out for excuses and focus on one step at a time.
7. Reward yourself after you have made some progress.
8. Be flexible about your goal.
9. Remember that it does not have to be perfect.[5]

QUIZ

Time Management, Part II

Test what you have learned by selecting the correct answers to the following questions.

1. To get started on a challenging project,
   a. think of a small first step and complete it.
   b. wait until you have plenty of time to begin.
   c. wait until you are well rested and relaxed.

2. If you are completing a to-do list of 10 items, the 80/20 rule states that
   a. 80% of the value comes from completing most of the items on the list.
   b. 80% of the value comes from completing two of the most important items.
   c. 80% of the value comes from completing half of the items on the list.

3. It is suggested that students aim for
   a. perfection.
   b. excellence.
   c. passing.

4. Sometimes students procrastinate because of
   a. fear of failure.
   b. fear of success.
   c. all of the above.

5. Playing the game "Beat the Clock" when doing a term paper results in
   a. increased motivation and success.
   b. greater excitement and quality work.
   c. increased motivation and risk.

How did you do on the quiz? Check your answers: 1. a, 2. b, 3. b, 4. c, 5. c

REFLECTION ●

Write a paragraph about how you will avoid procrastination. Consider these ideas when thinking about procrastination: fear of failure, fear of success, perfectionism, need for excitement, excellence without effort, and loss of control. How will you complete your assignments on time?

My Lifetime Goals: Brainstorming Activity

Name _____   Date _____

1. Think about the goals that you would like to accomplish in your life. At the end of your life, you do not want to say, "I wish I would have _____." Set a timer for five minutes and write whatever comes to mind about what you would like to do and accomplish over your lifetime. Include goals in these areas: career, personal relationships, travel, and financial security or any area that is important to you. Write down all your ideas. The goal is to generate as many ideas as possible in five minutes. You can reflect on which ones are most important later. You may want to do this as part of a group activity in your class.

Look over the ideas you wrote above and highlight or underline the goals that are most important to you.

2. Ask yourself what you would like to accomplish in the next five years. Think about where you want to be in college, what you want to do in your career, and what you want to do in your personal life. Set a timer and write whatever comes to mind in five minutes. The goal is to write down as many ideas as possible.

Again, look over the ideas you wrote and highlight or underline the ideas that are most important to you.

3. What goals would you like to accomplish in the next year? What are some steps that you can begin now to accomplish your lifetime goals? Consider work, study, leisure, and social goals. Set your timer for five minutes and write down your goals for the next year.

Review what you wrote and highlight or underline the ideas that are most important to you. When writing your goals, include fun activities as well as taking care of others.

Looking at the items that you have highlighted or underlined, make a list of your lifetime goals using the form that follows. Make sure your goals are specific enough so that you can break them into steps you can achieve.

My Lifetime Goals

Name _____   Date _____

Using the ideas that you brainstormed in the previous exercise, make a list of your lifetime goals. Make sure your goals are specific and concrete. Begin with goals that you would like to accomplish over a lifetime. In the second section, think about the goals you can accomplish over the next one to three years.

Long-Term Goals (lifetime goals)

Short-Term Goals (one to three years)

What are some steps you can take now to accomplish intermediate and long-term goals?

Successful Goal Setting

Name _____   Date _____

Look at your list of lifetime goals. Which one is most important? Write the goal here:

Answer these questions about the goal you have listed above.

1. What skills, abilities, and resources do you have to achieve this goal? What skills, abilities, and resources will you need to develop to achieve this goal?

2. Do you believe you can achieve it? Write a brief positive statement about achieving this goal.

3. State your goal in specific terms that can be observed or counted. Rewrite your goal if necessary.

4. Write a brief statement about how this goal will give you personal satisfaction.

5. How will you motivate yourself to achieve this goal?

6. What are your personal values that match this goal?

7. List some steps that you will take to accomplish this goal.

8. When will you finish this goal?

9. What roadblocks will make this goal difficult to achieve?

10. How will you deal with these roadblocks?

Weekly College Schedule

Name _____   Date _____

Copy the following schedule to use in future weeks or design your own schedule. Fill in this schedule and try to follow it for at least one week. First, fill in scheduled commitments (classes, work, activities). Next, fill in the time you need for studying. Put in some tasks related to your lifetime goals. Leave some blank time as a shock absorber to handle unexpected activities.

Time	Monday	Tuesday	Wednesday	Thursday	Friday	Saturday	Sunday
7 A.M.							
8							
9							
10							
11							
Noon							
1 P.M.							
2							
3							
4							
5							
6							
7							
8							
9							
10							
11							

Weekly To-Do Chart

Name _____   Date _____

Using a to-do list is an easy way to remind yourself of important priorities each day. This chart is divided into three areas representing types of tasks that college students need to balance: academic, personal, and social.

Weekly To-Do List

	Monday	Tuesday	Wednesday	Thursday	Friday
Academic					
Personal					
Social					

Study Schedule Analysis

Name _____   Date _____

Before completing this analysis, use the schedule form to create a master schedule. A master schedule blocks out class and work times as well as any regularly scheduled activities. Looking at the remaining time, write in your planned study times. It is recommended that you have two hours of study time for each hour in class. For example, a three-unit class would require six hours of study time. A student with 12 units would require 24 hours of study time. You may need more or fewer hours, depending on your study skills, reading skills, and difficulty of courses.

1. How many units are you enrolled in?

2. How many hours of planned study time do you have?

3. How many hours do you work each week?

4. How many hours do you spend in relaxation/social activities?

5. Do you have time planned for exercise?

6. Do you get enough sleep?

7 . What are some of your time bandits (things that take up your time and make it difficult to accomplish your goals)?

Write a few discovery statements about how you use your time.

8. Are you spending enough time to earn the grades you want to achieve? Do you need to spend more time studying to become successful?

9. Does your work schedule allow you enough time to study?

10. How can you deal with your time bandits?

11. How can you use your time more effectively to achieve your goals?

Name _____   Date _____

This circle represents 24 hours. Each piece is six hours. Draw a slice of pie to represent how much time you spend on each of these activities in a typical day: sleeping, attending classes, studying, work, family, friends, and other activities.

Thinking about your values is the first step in setting goals. How you spend your time determines whether you will accomplish these goals. Are you using your time to accomplish your goals? Make some intention statements for the future on how you want to spend your time.

I intend to:

KEEPING TRACK: HOW TO CALCULATE YOUR GPA

Your GPA (grade point average) is based on the following point system:

A	4.0	C	2.0
A−	3.7	C−	1.7
B+	3.3	D+	1.3
B	3.0	D	1.0
B−	2.7	F	0
C+	2.3		

The sample grade report below illustrates how to calculate a GPA.

Course No.	Title	Credits	Grade	Credit × Grade	Grade Points
BCC 100	Freshman Seminar	1	A	1.0 × 4.0	4.0
ENG 101	Composition	3	C+	3.0 × 2.3	6.9
MAT 105	Nature of Math	3	B−	3.0 × 2.7	8.1
PSY 101	Introduction to Psychology	3	C	3.0 × 2.0	6.0
MUS 215	Appreciation of Music	3	A	3.0 × 4.0	12.0
Total number of credits attempted		=	13	Total grade points earned =	37.0
Total grade points earned divided by total number of credits attempted: 37 ÷ 13 = 2.85 GPA					

Use this table to help estimate your first semester GPA.

Course No.	Title	Credits	Grade	Credit × Grade	Grade Points
BCC 100	Freshman Seminar	1		1.0 ×	
Total number of credits attempted =				Total grade points earned =	
Total grade points earned divided by total number of credits attempted = anticipated GPA					

From *A Guide to Surviving and Thriving in College* by Berry College. Edited by Katherine Powell. Reprinted by permission of Kendall Hunt Publishing Company.

THE MOST POWERFUL RESEARCH-BASED PRINCIPLES OF COLLEGE SUCCESS

Research on human learning and student development indicates four powerful principles of college success:

1. Active involvement
2. Use of campus resources
3. Interpersonal interaction and collaboration
4. Personal reflection and self-awareness (Astin, 1993; Kuh et al., 2005; Light, 2001; Pascarella & Terenzini, 1991; 2005; Tinto, 1993).

These principles are introduced and examined carefully in this opening chapter for two reasons:

1. You can put them into practice to establish good habits for early success in college.
2. They represent the foundational bases for the success strategies recommended throughout this book.

The four principles of success can be remembered by visualizing them as the four bases of a baseball diamond—as depicted in Figure 2.1.

TOUCHING THE FIRST BASE OF COLLEGE SUCCESS: ACTIVE INVOLVEMENT

Research indicates that active involvement may be the most powerful principle of human learning and college success (Astin, 1993; Kuh et al., 2005). The bottom line is this: To maximize your success in college, you cannot be a passive spectator; you need to be an active player.

FIGURE 2.1

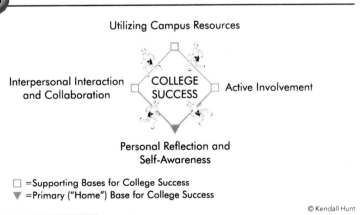

Utilizing Campus Resources

Interpersonal Interaction and Collaboration — COLLEGE SUCCESS — Active Involvement

Personal Reflection and Self-Awareness

☐ =Supporting Bases for College Success
▼ =Primary ("Home") Base for College Success

© Kendall Hunt

The Diamond of College Success

Student
Perspective

"You don't have to be smart to work hard."

—24-year-old first-year student who has returned to college

"It is not so much what the individual thinks or feels but what the individual does, how he or she behaves, that defines and identifies involvement."

—Alexander Astin, professor emeritus at University of California, Los Angeles, identified as the "most frequently cited author" in higher education and the person "most admired for creative insightful thinking"

Student
Perspective

"My biggest recommendation: GO TO CLASS. I learned this the hard way my first semester. You'll be surprised what you pick up just by being there. I wish someone would have informed me of this before I started school."

—Advice to new students from a college sophomore (Walsh, 2005)

The principle of active involvement includes the following key components:

- The amount of personal time devoted to learning in college.
- The degree of personal effort or energy (mental and physical) put into the learning process.

Think of something you do with intensity, passion, and commitment. If you were to approach academic work in the same way, you would be faithfully implementing the principle of active involvement.

One way to ensure that you're actively involved in the learning process and putting forth high levels of energy or effort is to take action on what you're learning. You can engage in any of the following actions to ensure that you are investing a high level of effort and energy:

- **Writing.** Write in response to what you're trying to learn. Example: Write notes when reading rather than passively underlining sentences.
- **Speaking.** Say aloud what you're trying to learn. Example: Explain course concepts to a study-group partner rather than studying them silently.
- **Organizing.** Connect or integrate the ideas you're trying to learn. Example: Create an outline, diagram, or concept map to visually connect ideas, as illustrated in Figure 2.1.

The following section explains how you can apply both key components of active involvement—spending time and expending energy—to the major learning challenges that you will encounter in college.

Time Spent in Class

The total amount of time you spend on learning is associated with how much you learn and how successfully you learn. This association leads to a straightforward recommendation: Attend all class sessions in all your courses. It may be tempting to skip or cut classes because college professors are less likely to monitor your attendance or take roll than your high school teachers. However, don't let this new freedom fool you into thinking that missing classes has no impact on your college grades. Over the past 75 years, many research studies in many types of courses have shown a direct relationship between class attendance and course grades—as one goes up or down, so does the other (Anderson & Gates, 2002; Credé, Roch, & Kieszczynka, 2010; Grandpre, 2000; Kowalewski, Holstein, & Schneider, 1989; Launius, 1997; Shimoff & Catania, 2001). **Figure 2.2** represents the results of a study conducted at the City Colleges of Chicago, which shows the relationship between students' class attendance during the first five weeks of the term and their final course grades.

© Lisa F. Young, 2013. Under license from Shutterstock, Inc.

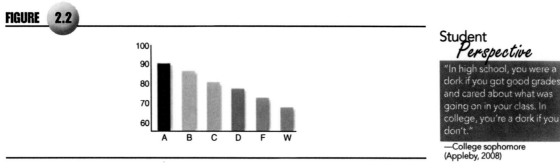

Relationship between Class Attendance Rate and Course Final Grades

Time Spent on Coursework outside the Classroom

In college, you will spend fewer hours per week sitting in class than you did in high school; however, you will be expected to spend more of your own time on academic work outside of class. Studies clearly show that when college students spend more time on academic work outside of class, it results in better learning and higher grades (National Survey of Student Engagement, 2009). For example, one study of more than 25,000 college students found that the percentage of students receiving mostly "A" grades was almost three times higher for students who spent 40 or more hours per week on academic work than it was for students who spent between 20 and 40 hours. Among students who spent 20 or fewer hours per week on academic work, the percentage receiving grades of mostly "C" or below was almost twice as high as it was for students who spent 40 or more hours on academic work (Pace, 1990; 1995).

Unfortunately, less than 40 percent of beginning college students report having studied for six or more hours per week during their final year in high school (Pryor, De Angelo, Palucki-Blake, Hurtado, & Tran, 2012), and only one-third expect to spend more than 20 hours per week preparing for class in college (National Survey of Student Engagement, 2009). Also, less than 10 percent say they will study for at least two hours out of class for every hour spent in class, which is what most college faculty believe is necessary to do well in college (Kuh, 2005). This has to change if new college students are to earn good grades. Just as successful athletes need to put in time and often work hard to improve their physical performance, successful students need to do the same to improve their academic performance.

If you need further motivation to achieve good grades, keep in mind that higher grades earned in college are related to higher prospects for career success after college. Research on college graduates indicates that the higher their grades were in college, the higher: (1) their annual salary, (2) the status (prestige) of their first job, (3) their career mobility (ability to change jobs or move into different positions). This relationship between college grades and career advantages exists for students at all types of colleges and universities, regardless of the reputation or prestige of the institution that the students are attending (Pascarella & Terenzini, 1991; 2005). In other words, how well you do academically in college matters more to your career success than where you went to college.

"All genuine learning is active, not passive. It is a process in which the student is the main agent, not the teacher."

—Mortimer Adler, American professor of philosophy and educational theorist

REFLECTION ●———

During your senior year of high school, how many hours per week did you spend on schoolwork outside of class?

Active Listening and Note Taking

You'll find that college professors rely heavily on the lecture method—they profess their knowledge by speaking for long stretches of time, and the students' job is to listen and take notes on the knowledge they dispense. This method of instruction places great demands on your ability to listen carefully and take notes that are both accurate and complete.

Remember _____

Research shows that, in all subject areas, most test questions on college exams come from the professor's lectures, and that students who take better class notes get better course grades (Brown, 1988; Cuseo, Fecas, & Thompson, 2007; Kiewra, 2000).

The best way to apply the principle of active involvement during a class lecture is to engage in the physical action of writing notes. Writing down what your instructor is saying in class "forces" you to pay closer attention to what is being said and reinforces your retention of what was said. By taking notes, you not only hear the information (auditory memory), you also see it on paper (visual memory) and feel it in the muscles of your hand as you write it (motor memory).

Remember _____

Your role in the college classroom is not to be a passive spectator or an absorbent sponge that sits back and simply soaks up information through osmosis. Instead, your role is more like that of an aggressive detective or investigative reporter who's on a search-and-record mission. You need to actively search for information by picking your instructor's brain, picking out your instructor's key points, and recording your "pickings" in your notebook.

See **Do It Now! 2.1** for top strategies on classroom listening and note taking that you can put into action right now.

Active Class Participation

You can become actively involved in the college classroom by arriving at class prepared (e.g., having done the assigned reading), by asking relevant questions, and by contributing thoughtful comments during class discussions. When you communicate orally, you elevate your level of active involvement in the learning process because speaking requires you to exert both mental energy (thinking about what you are going to say) and physical energy (moving your lips to say it). Thus, class participation will increase your ability to stay alert and attentive in class. It also sends a clear message to the instructor that you are a motivated student who takes the course seriously and wants to learn.

DO IT NOW

Listening and Note Taking

One task that you'll be expected to perform at the start of your first term in college is taking notes in class. Studies show that professors' lecture notes are the number one source of test questions (and test answers) on college exams. Get off to a fast start by using the following strategies to improve the quality of your note taking:

© Joanne Harris and Daniel Bubnich, 2013. Under license from Shutterstock, Inc.

1. **Get to every class.** Whether or not your instructors take roll, you're responsible for all material covered in class. Remember that a full load of college courses (15 units) only requires that you be in class about 13 hours per week. If you consider your class work to be a full-time job, any job that requires you to show up for about 13 hours a week is a pretty sweet deal. It's a deal that supplies you with much more educational freedom than you had in high school. To miss a class session in college when you're required to spend so little time in class per week is an abuse of this educational freedom. It's also an abuse of the money you, your family, or taxpaying American citizens pay to support your college education.

2. **Get to every class on time.** During the first few minutes of a class session, instructors often share valuable information, such as reminders, reviews, and previews.

3. **Get organized.** Bring the right equipment to class. Get a separate notebook for each class, write your name on it, date each class session, and store all class handouts in it.

4. **Get in the right position.**
   - The ideal place to sit is in the front and center of the room, where you're in the best position to hear and see what's going on.
   - The ideal posture is upright and leaning forward, because your body influences your mind. If your body is in an alert and ready position, your mind is likely to follow.
   - The ideal social position is to be near people who will not distract you or detract from the quality of your note taking.

Remember

These attention-focusing strategies are particularly important during the first year of college, when class sizes tend to be larger. In a large class, students tend to feel more anonymous, which can reduce their sense of personal responsibility and their drive to stay focused and actively involved. Thus, in large class settings, it's especially important to use effective strategies that eliminate distractions and attention drift.

5. **Get in the right frame of mind.** Get psyched up; come to class with attitude—an attitude that you're going to pick your instructor's brain, pick up answers to test questions, and build up your course grade.

6. **Get it down (in writing).** Actively look, listen, and record important points at all times in class. Pay special attention to whatever information instructors put in writing, whether it is on the board, on a slide, or in a handout.

7. **Don't let go of your pen.** When in doubt, write it out; it's better to have it and not need it than to need it and not have it.

8. **Finish strong.** During the last few minutes of class, instructors often share valuable information, such as reminders, reviews, and previews.

9. **Stick around.** When class ends, don't immediately bolt; instead, hang out for a few moments and quickly review your notes (by yourself or with a classmate). If you find any

gaps, check them out with your instructor before the instructor leaves the classroom. This quick end-of-class review will help your brain retain the information it just received.

Remember

Most college professors do not write all important information on the board for you; instead, they expect you to listen carefully to what they're saying and write it down for yourself.

Finish class with a rush of attention, not a rush out the door!

Since class participation accounts for a portion of your final grade in many courses, your attentiveness and involvement in class can have a direct, positive effect on your final grade.

REFLECTION ●━━━━━━━━━━━━━

When you enter a classroom, where do you usually sit?

Why do you sit there? Is it a conscious choice or more like an automatic habit?

Do you think that your usual seat places you in the best possible position for listening and learning in the classroom?

Active Reading

Writing not only promotes active listening in class but also can promote active reading out of class. Taking notes on information that you're reading (or on information you've highlighted while reading) keeps you actively involved in the reading process because it requires more mental and physical energy than merely reading the material or passively highlighting sentences. (See **Do It Now! 1.2** for top tips on reading college textbooks that you can put into practice immediately.)

DO IT NOW!

Top Strategies: Improving Textbook Reading Comprehension and Retention

If you haven't already acquired textbooks for your courses, get them immediately and get ahead on your reading assignments. Information from reading assignments ranks right behind lecture notes as a source of test questions on college exams. Your professors are likely to deliver class lectures with the expectation that you have done the assigned reading and can build on that knowledge when they're lecturing. If you haven't done the reading, you'll have more difficulty following and taking notes on what your instructor is saying in class. Thus, by not doing the reading you pay a double penalty: You miss information that will appear directly on course exams, and you miss information delivered by your instructor in class because you don't have the background knowledge to make sense of it. College professors also expect you to relate or connect what they talk about in class to the reading they have assigned. Thus, it's important to start developing

Student *Perspective*

"I recommend that you read the first chapters right away because college professors get started promptly with assigning certain readings. Classes in college move very fast because, unlike high school, you do not attend class five times a week but two or three times a week."

—Advice to new college students from a first-year student

good reading habits now. You can do so by using the following strategies to improve your reading comprehension and retention.

1. **Read with the right equipment.**

   - Bring tools to record and store information. Always bring a writing tool (pen or pencil) to record important information and a storage space (notebook or laptop) in which you can save and retrieve information acquired from your reading for later use on tests and assignments.

   - Have a dictionary nearby to quickly find the meaning of unfamiliar words that may interfere with your ability to comprehend what you're reading. Looking up definitions of unfamiliar words does more than help you understand what you're reading: it's also an effective way to build your vocabulary. A strong vocabulary will improve your reading comprehension in all college courses, as well as your performance on standardized tests, such as those required for admission to graduate and professional schools.

   - Check the back of your textbook for a list of key terms included in the book. Each academic subject or discipline has its own vocabulary, and knowing the meaning of these terms is often the key to understanding the concepts covered in the text. Don't ignore the glossary; it's more than an ancillary or afterthought to the textbook. Use it regularly to increase your comprehension of course concepts. Consider making a photocopy of the glossary of terms at the back of your textbook so that you can have a copy of it in front of you while you're reading, rather than having to repeatedly stop, hold your place, and go to the back of the text to find the glossary.

2. **Get in the right position.** Sit upright and have light coming from behind you, over the side of your body opposite your writing hand. This will reduce the distracting and fatiguing effects of glare and shadows.

3. **Get a sneak preview.** Approach the chapter by first reading its boldface headings and any chapter outline, summary, or end-of-chapter questions that may be provided. This will supply you with a mental map of the chapter's important ideas before you start your reading trip and provide an overview that will help you keep track of the chapter's major ideas (the "big picture"), reducing the risk that you'll get lost among the smaller details you encounter along the way.

4. **Use boldface headings and subheadings.** Headings are cues for important information. Turn them into questions, and then read to find their answers. This will launch you on an answer-finding mission that will

keep you mentally active while reading and enable you to read with a purpose. Turning headings into questions is also a good way to prepare for tests because you're practicing exactly what you'll be expected to do on tests—answer questions.

5. **Pay attention to the first and last sentences.** Absorb opening and closing sentences in sections beneath the chapter's major headings and subheadings. These sentences often contain an important introduction and conclusion to the material covered in that section of the text.

6. **Finish each of your reading sessions with a short review.** Recall what you have highlighted or noted as important information (rather than trying to cover a few more pages). It's best to use the last few minutes of reading time to "lock in" the most important information you've just read because most forgetting takes place immediately after you stop processing (taking in) information and start doing something else.

Remember _____

Your goal while reading should be to discover or uncover the most important information, and the final step in the reading process is to review (and lock in) the most important information you discovered.

Remember _____

Involvement with campus services is not just valuable, it's also "free"—the cost of these services has already been covered by your college tuition. By investing time and energy in campus resources, you not only increase your prospects for personal success but also maximize the return on your financial investment in college—you get a bigger bang for your buck.

TOUCHING THE SECOND BASE OF COLLEGE SUCCESS: USE OF CAMPUS RESOURCES

Your campus environment contains multiple resources designed to support your quest for educational and personal success. Studies show that students who take advantage of campus resources report higher levels of satisfaction with college and get more out of the college experience (Pascarella & Terenzini, 1991, 2005).

Using your campus resources is an important, research-backed principle of college success, and it is a natural extension of the principle of active involvement. Successful students are active learners not only inside the classroom, but outside of class as well. Active involvement outside of class includes making use of campus resources. An essential first step in making effective use of campus resources is to become aware of what they are and what they're designed to do.

The following sections describe what key campus services are offered on most college campuses and why they should be utilized.

Learning Center (a.k.a. Academic Support or Academic Success Center)

This is your campus resource for strengthening your academic performance. The individual and group tutoring provided by this campus service can help you master difficult course concepts and assignments, and the people working here are professionally trained to help you learn how to learn. While your professors may have expert knowledge of the subject matter they teach, learning resource specialists are experts on the process of learning. These specialists can equip you with effective learning strategies and show you how you can adjust or modify your learning strategies to meet the unique demands of different courses and teaching styles you encounter in college.

Studies show that college students who become actively involved with academic support services outside the classroom are more likely to attain higher grades and complete their college degree, particularly if they begin their involvement with these support services during the first year of college (Cuseo, 2003). Also, students who seek and receive assistance from the Learning Center show significant improvement in academic self-efficacy— that is, they develop a stronger sense of personal control over their academic performance and higher expectations for academic success (Smith, Walter, & Hoey, 1992).

Despite the powerful advantages of using academic support services, these services are typically underused by college students, especially by those students who need them the most (Cuseo, 2003; Knapp & Karabenick, 1988; Walter & Smith, 1990). Some students believe that seeking academic help is admitting they are not smart, self-sufficient, or unable to succeed on their own. Do not buy into this belief system. Using academic support services doesn't mean you're helpless or clueless; instead, it indicates that you're a motivated and resourceful student who is striving to achieve academic excellence.

Writing Center

Many college campuses offer specialized support for students who would like to improve their writing skills. Typically referred to as the Writing Center, this is the place where you can receive assistance at any stage of the writing process, whether it be collecting and organizing your ideas, composing your first draft, or proofreading your final draft. Since writing is an academic skill that you will use in many of your courses, if you improve your writing, you're likely to improve your overall academic performance. Thus, we strongly encourage you to capitalize on this campus resource.

"Do not be a PCP (Parking Lot→ Classroom→ Parking Lot) student. The time you spend on campus will be a sound investment in your academic and professional success."

—Drew Appleby, professor of psychology

"The impact of college is not simply the result of what a college does for or to a student. Rather, the impact is a result of the extent to which an individual student exploits the people, programs, facilities, opportunities, and experiences that the college makes available."

—Ernest Pascarella and Patrick Terenzini, *How College Affects Students*

Student *Perspective*

"Where I learn the material best is tutoring because they go over it and if you have questions, you can ask, you can stop, they have time for you. They make time."

—First-year college student

"At colleges where I've taught, it's always been found that the grade point average of students who use the Learning Center is higher than the college average and honors students are more likely to use the center than other students."

—Joe Cuseo, professor of psychology and lead author of this text

Disability Services (a.k.a. Office for Students with Special Needs)

If you have a physical or learning disability that is interfering with your performance in college, or think you may have such a disability, Disability Services is the campus resource to consult for assistance and support. Programs and services typically provided by this office include:

- Assessment for learning disabilities;
- Verification of eligibility for disability support services;
- Authorization of academic accommodations for students with disabilities; and
- Specialized counseling, advising, and tutoring.

College Library

"The next best thing to knowing something is knowing where to find it."

—Dr. Samuel Johnson, English literary figure and original author of the *Dictionary of the English Language* (1747)

The library is your campus resource for finding information and completing research assignments (e.g., term papers and group projects). Librarians are professional educators who provide instruction outside the classroom. You can learn from them just as you can learn from faculty inside the classroom. Furthermore, the library is a place where you can acquire skills for locating, retrieving, and evaluating information that you may apply to any course you are taking or will ever take.

Your college library is your campus resource for developing research skills that let you access, retrieve, and evaluate information, which are skills for achieving both educational and occupational success.

Academic Advising Center

Whether or not you have an assigned academic advisor, the Academic Advising Center is a campus resource for help with course selection, educational planning, and choosing or changing a major. Studies show that college students who have developed clear educational and career goals are more likely to persist in college until they complete their college degree (Willingham, 1985; Wyckoff, 1999). Research indicates that beginning college students need help clarifying their educational goals, selecting an academic major, and exploring careers (Cuseo, 2005; Frost, 1991). As a first-year college student, being undecided or uncertain about your educational and career goals is nothing to be embarrassed about. However, you should start thinking about your future now. Connect early and often with an academic advisor to help you clarify your educational goals and find a field of study that best complements your interests, talents, and values.

Office of Student Life

The Office of Student Life is your campus resource for student development opportunities outside the classroom, including student clubs and organizations, recreational programs, leadership activities, and volunteer experiences. Research consistently shows that experiential learning that takes place outside the classroom is as important to your personal development and future success as learning from course work (Kuh, 1995; Kuh, Douglas, Lund, & Ramin-Gyurnek, 1994; Pascarella & Terenzini, 2005). (This is why they are referred to as "co-curricular experiences" rather than "extracurricular activities.") More specifically, studies show students who become actively involved in campus life are more likely to:

- Enjoy their college experience;
- Graduate from college; and
- Develop leadership skills that enhance career performance beyond college (Astin, 1993).

Devoting some out-of-class time to these co-curricular experiences should not interfere with your academic performance. Keep in mind that in college you'll be spending much less time in the classroom than you did in high school. As mentioned previously, a full load of college courses (15 units) only requires that you be in class about 13 hours per week. This should leave you with enough time to become involved in learning experiences on campus. Evidence indicates that college students who become involved in co-curricular, volunteer, and part-time work experiences that total *no more than 15 hours per week* earn higher grades than students who do not get involved in any out-of-class activities (Pascarella, 2001; Pascarella & Terenzini, 2005).

Although it is important to get involved in co-curricular experiences on your campus, limit your involvement to no more than two or three major campus organizations at any one time. Restricting the number of your out-of-class activities should enable you to keep up with your studies; it will be more impressive to future schools or employers because a long list of involvement in numerous activities may suggest you're padding your resume with things you did superficially (or never really did at all).

> "Just a [long] list of club memberships is meaningless; it's a fake front. Remember that quality, not quantity, is what counts."
> —Lauren Pope, director of the National Bureau for College Placement

Financial Aid Office

This campus resource is designed to help you finance your college education. If you have questions concerning how to obtain assistance in paying for college, the staff of this office is there to guide you through the application process. The paperwork needed to apply for and secure financial aid can sometimes be confusing or overwhelming. Don't let this intimidate you enough to prevent you from seeking financial aid; assistance is available to you from the knowledgeable staff in the Financial Aid Office. You can also seek help from this office to find:

- Part-time employment on campus through a work-study program;
- Low-interest student loans;
- Grants; and
- Scholarships.

If you have any doubt about whether you are using the most effective plan for financing your college education, make an appointment to see a professional in your Financial Aid Office.

Remember ——————

Co-curricular experiences are also resume-building experiences, and campus professionals with whom you interact regularly while participating in co-curricular activities (e.g., the director of student activities or dean of students) are valuable resources for personal references and letters of recommendation to future schools or employers.

Counseling Center

Counseling services can provide you with a valuable source of support in college, not only for helping you cope with the stress associated with the transition to college, but also by helping you gain self-awareness and reach your full potential. Personal counseling can promote your self-awareness and self-development in social and emotional areas of your life that are important for mental health, wellness, and personal growth.

Health Center

Making the transition from high school to college often involves adjustments and decisions affecting your health and wellness. Good health habits help you cope with stress and reach peak levels of performance. The Health Center on your campus is the resource for information on how to manage your physical health and maintain wellness. It is also the place to go for help with illnesses, sexually transmitted infections or diseases, and eating or nutritional disorders.

Career Development Center (a.k.a. Career Center)

Research on college students indicates that they are more likely to stay in school and graduate when they have some sense of how their present academic experience relates to their future career goals (Levitz & Noel, 1989; Tinto, 1993; Wyckoff, 1999). Studies also show that most new students are uncertain about what career they would like to pursue (Gordon & Steele, 2003). So, if you are uncertain about your future career, welcome to the club that includes a very large number of other first-year students. This uncertainty is normal because you haven't had the opportunity for hands-on work experience in the real world of careers.

The Career Development Center is the place to go for help in finding a meaningful answer to the important question of how to connect your current college experience with your future career goals. This campus resource typically provides such services as personal career counseling, workshops on career exploration and development, and career fairs where you are able to meet professionals working in different fields. Although it may seem like the beginning of your career is light-years away because you're just beginning college, the process of exploring, planning, and preparing for career success starts in the first year of college.

> "The college years are an important growing period in which new social and intellectual experiences are sought as a means of coming to grips with the issue of adult careers. Students enter college with the hope that they will be able to formulate for themselves a meaningful answer to that important question."
>
> —Vincent Tinto, nationally known scholar on student success

TOUCHING THE THIRD BASE OF COLLEGE SUCCESS: INTERPERSONAL INTERACTION AND COLLABORATION

Learning is strengthened when it takes place in a social context that involves interpersonal interaction. As some scholars put it, human knowledge is "socially constructed" or built up through interpersonal interaction and dialogue. According to these scholars, your conversations with others become internalized as ideas in your mind and influence your way of thinking (Bruffee, 1993; Johnson, Johnson, & Smith, 1998). Thus, by having frequent, intelligent conversations with others, you broaden your knowledge and deepen your thinking.

REFLECTION ●————————————

Look back at the major campus resources that have been mentioned in this section. Which two or three of them do you think you should use *immediately*?

Why have you identified these resources as your top priorities right now?

Ask your course instructor for recommendations about what campus resources you should consult during your first term on campus. Compare their recommendations with your selections.

Four particular forms of interpersonal interaction have been found to be strongly associated with student learning and motivation in college:

1. Student-faculty interaction
2. Student-advisor interaction
3. Student-mentor interaction
4. Student-student (peer) interaction

Interacting with Faculty Members

Studies repeatedly show that college success is strongly influenced by the quality and quantity of student-faculty interaction *outside the classroom*. Such contact is associated with the following positive outcomes for college students:

- Improved academic performance;
- Increased critical thinking skills;
- Greater satisfaction with the college experience;
- Increased likelihood of completing a college degree; and
- Stronger desire to seek education beyond college (Astin, 1993; Pascarella & Terenzini, 1991; 2005).

These positive outcomes are so strong and widespread that we encourage you to immediately begin seeking interaction with college faculty outside of class time. Here are some of the easiest ways to do so.

1. **Seek contact with your instructors immediately after class.** If you are interested in talking about something that was discussed in class, approach your instructor as soon as the class session ends. Interaction with instructors immediately after class can help them get to know you as an individual, which should increase your confidence and willingness to seek subsequent contact in other settings.

2. **Seek interaction with your course instructors during their office hours.** One of the most important pieces of information on a course syllabus is your instructor's office hours. Make note of them and make an earnest attempt to capitalize on them. College professors specifically reserve out-of-class time for office hours during which they are expected to be available to students. Try to make at least one visit to the office of each of your instructors, preferably early in the term, when quality time is easier to find, rather than at midterm, when major exams and assignments begin to pile up. Even if your early contact with instructors is only for a few minutes, it can be a valuable icebreaker that helps your instructors get to know you as a person and helps you feel more comfortable interacting with them in the future.

3. **Connect with your instructors through e-mail.** Electronic communication is another effective way to interact with an instructor, particularly if that professor's office hours conflict with your class schedule, work responsibilities,

Student
Perspective

"I wish that I would have taken advantage of professors' open-door policies when I had questions, because actually understanding what I was doing, instead of guessing, would have saved me a lot of stress and re-doing what I did wrong the first time."

—College sophomore (Walsh, 2005)

or family commitments. If you are a commuter student who does not live on campus, or if you are an adult student juggling family and work commitments along with your academic schedule, e-mail communication may be an especially effective and efficient mode of student-faculty interaction. In one national survey, almost half of college students reported that e-mail has allowed them to communicate their ideas with professors on subjects that they would not have discussed in person (Pew Internet & American Life Project, 2002). If you're shy or hesitant about "invading" your professor's office space, e-mail can provide a less threatening way to interact and may give you the self-confidence to eventually seek face-to-face contact with an instructor.

However, you should never e-mail faculty with the following questions after missing class:

- Did I miss anything in class today?
- Could you send me your teaching notes or PowerPoint from the class I missed?

Also, when you are with faculty in the classroom, use the following guidelines with respect to use of personal technology.

Guidelines for Civil and Responsible Use of Personal Technology in the College Classroom	
• Turn your cell phone completely off, or leave it out of the classroom. In the rare case of an emergency when you think you need to leave it on, inform your instructor. • Don't check your cell phone during the class period by turning it off and on.	• Don't text message during class. • Don't surf the Web during class. • Don't touch your cell phone during any exam because this may be viewed by the instructor as a form of cheating.

Interaction with Academic Advisors

An academic advisor may serve as a very effective referral agent who can direct you to, and connect you with, campus support services that can promote your success. An advisor can also help you understand college procedures and navigate the bureaucratic maze of college policies and politics.

Your academic advisor should be someone whom you feel comfortable speaking with, someone who knows your name, and someone who's familiar with your personal interests and abilities. Give your advisor the opportunity to get to know you personally, and seek your advisor's input on courses, majors, and personal issues that may be affecting your academic performance.

REFLECTION ●━━━━━━━━━━━━━━━

Do you have a personally assigned advisor?

If yes, do you know who this person is and where he or she can be found?

If no, do you know where to go if you have questions about your class schedule or academic plans?

If you have been assigned an advisor and cannot develop a good relationship with this person, ask the director of advising or academic dean if you could be assigned to someone else. Ask other students about their advising experience and whether they know an advisor they can recommend to you.

If your college does not assign you a personal advisor, but offers advising services in an Advising Center on a drop-by or drop-in basis, you may see a different advisor each time you visit the center. If you are not satisfied with this system of multiple advisors, find one advisor with whom you feel most comfortable and make that person your personal advisor by scheduling your appointments in advance. This will enable you to consistently connect with the same advisor and help you develop a close, ongoing relationship with that person.

Remember _____

An academic advisor is not someone you see just once per term when you need to get a signature for class scheduling and course registration. Advisors can be much more than course schedulers: they can be mentors. Unlike your course instructors, who will change from term to term, your academic advisor may be the one professional on campus with whom you have regular contact and a stable, ongoing relationship throughout your college experience.

Interaction with a Mentor

A mentor may be described as an experienced guide who takes personal interest in you and the progress you're making toward your goals. (For example, in the movie *Star Wars*, Yoda served as a mentor for Luke Skywalker.) Research in higher education demonstrates that a mentor can make first-year students feel significant and enable them to stay on track until they complete their college degree (Campbell & Campbell, 1997; Knox, 2004). A mentor can assist you in troubleshooting difficult or complicated issues that you may not be able to resolve on your own and is someone with whom you can share good news, such as your success stories and personal accomplishments. Look for someone on campus with whom you can develop this type of trusting relationship. Many people on campus have the potential to be outstanding mentors, including the following:

- Your academic advisor
- Your instructor in a first-year seminar or experience course
- Faculty in your intended major
- Juniors, seniors, or graduate students in your intended field of study
- Working professionals in careers that interest you
- Academic support professionals (e.g., professional tutors in the Learning Center)
- Career counselors
- Personal counselors
- Learning assistance professionals (e.g., from the Learning Center)
- Student development professionals (e.g., the director of student life or residential life)
- Campus minister or chaplain
- Financial aid counselors

Interaction with Peers (Student-Student Interaction)

Studies repeatedly point to the power of the peer group as a source of social and academic support during the college years (Pascarella, 2005). One study of more than 25,000 college students revealed that when peers interact with one another while learning they achieve higher levels of academic performance and are more likely to persist to degree completion (Astin, 1993). In another study that involved in-depth interviews with more than 1,600 college students, it was discovered that almost all students who struggled academically had one particular study habit in common: They always studied alone (Light, 2001).

Peer interaction is especially important during the first term of college. At this stage of the college experience, new students have a strong need for belonging and social acceptance because many of them have just left the lifelong security of family and hometown friends. As a new student, it may be useful to view the early stage of your college experience through the lens of psychologist Abraham Maslow's hierarchy of human needs (see **Figure 2.3**). According to Maslow's hierarchy of needs, humans cannot reach their full potential and achieve peak performance until their more basic emotional and social needs have been met (e.g., their needs for personal safety, social acceptance, and self-esteem). Making early connections with your peers helps you meet these basic human needs, provides you with a base of social support to ease your integration into the college community, and prepares you to move up to higher levels of the need hierarchy (e.g., achieving educational excellence and fulfilling your potential).

© Andresr, 2013. Under license from Shutterstock, Inc.

Getting involved with campus organizations or activities is one way to connect you with other students. Also, try to interact with students who have spent more time at college than you. Sophomores, juniors, and seniors can be valuable social resources for a new student. You're likely to find that they are willing to share their experiences with you because you have shown an interest in hearing what they have to say. You may be the first person who has ever asked them what their experiences have been like on your campus. You can learn from their experiences by asking them which courses and instructors they would recommend or what advisors they found to be most well informed and personable.

REFLECTION

Think about the students in your classes this term. (1) Are there any students who might be good members to connect with and form learning teams? (2) Do you have any classmates who are currently in more than one class with you and who might be good peer partners to team up with and work together on the courses you have in common?

Collaboration with Peers

Simply defined, collaboration is the process of two or more people working interdependently toward a common goal, rather than working independently or competitively. Collaboration involves true teamwork, in which teammates support each other's success and take equal responsibility for helping the team move

Remember ———————

Your peers can be more than competitors or a source of negative peer pressure: they can also be collaborators, a source of positive social influence, and a resource for college success. Be on the lookout for classmates who are motivated to learn and willing to learn with you, and keep an eye out for advanced students who are willing to assist you. Start building your social support network by surrounding yourself with success-seeking and success-achieving students. They can be a stimulating source of positive peer power that can drive you to higher levels of academic performance and heighten your drive to complete college.

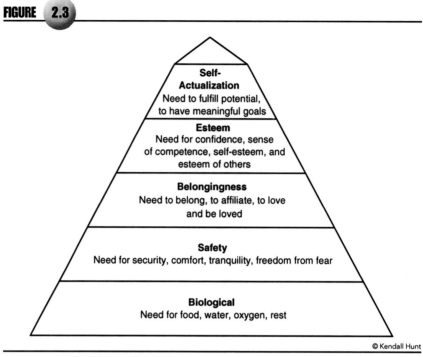

FIGURE 2.3

Abraham Maslow's Hierarchy of Needs

"TEAM = **T**ogether **E**veryone **A**chieves **M**ore"
—Author unknown

toward its shared goal. Research shows that when students collaborate in teams, from kindergarten through college, their academic performance and interpersonal skills improve significantly (Cross, Barkley, & Major, 2005; Cuseo, 1996; Gilles & Adrian, 2003; Johnson et al., 1998).

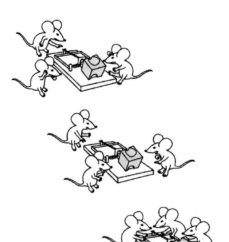

Research shows that when peers work collaboratively to reach a common goal, they learn more effectively and achieve "higher levels" of thinking.

To maximize the power of collaboration, use the following guidelines to make wise choices about teammates who will contribute positively to the quality and productivity of your learning team:

1. Observe your classmates with an eye toward identifying potentially good teammates. Look for fellow students who are motivated and who will likely contribute to your team's success, rather than those whom you suspect may just be hitchhikers looking for a free ride.

2. Don't team up exclusively with peers who are similar to you in terms of their personal characteristics, backgrounds, and experiences. Instead, include teammates who differ from you in age; gender; ethnic, racial, cultural, or geographical background; learning style; and personality characteristics. Such variety brings different life experiences, styles of thinking, and learning strategies to your team, which enrich not only its diversity but its quality as well. If your team consists only of friends or classmates whose interests and lifestyles are similar to your own, this familiarity can interfere with your team's focus and performance because your common experiences can get you off track and on to topics that have nothing to do with the learning task (e.g., what you did last weekend or what you are planning to do next weekend).

Keep in mind that learning teams are not simply study groups formed the night before an exam. Effective learning teams collaborate more regularly and work on more varied academic tasks than late-night study groups. Following are various types of learning teams that you may join or form to improve your performance on key academic tasks in college.

> "Surround yourself with only people who are going to lift you higher."
> —Oprah Winfrey, actress and talk-show host

Remember ————
Seek diversity; capitalize on the advantages of collaborating with peers with varied backgrounds and lifestyles. Simply stated, studies show that we learn more from people who are different from us than we do from people who are similar to us (Pascarella, 2001; Thompson & Cuseo, 2012).

Note-Taking Teams

Immediately after a class session ends, take a couple of minutes to team up with other students to compare and share notes. Since listening and note taking are demanding tasks, it's likely that a student may pick up an important point that the others overlooked and vice versa. Also, by teaming up immediately after class to review your notes together, your team has the opportunity to consult with the instructor about any missing or confusing information before your instructor leaves the room.

Expert's Experience

During my first term in college, I was having difficulty taking complete notes in my biology course because the instructor spoke rapidly and with an unfamiliar accent. I noticed another student (Alex) sitting in the front row who was trying to take notes as best he could, but he was experiencing the same difficulty. Following one particularly fast and complex lecture, we looked at each other and noticed that we were both shaking our heads in frustration and began talking about it. We decided to team up immediately after every class and compare our notes to identify points we missed or found confusing. First, we helped each other by comparing and sharing our notes in case one of us got something that the other missed. If there were points that we both missed or couldn't figure out, we went to the front of class together to consult with the instructor before he left the classroom. At the end of the course, Alex and I finished with the highest grades in the course.

Joe Cuseo

Reading Teams

After completing your reading assignments, team up with classmates to compare your highlighting and margin notes. Compare notes on what you identified as the most important points in the reading that should be studied for upcoming exams.

Writing Teams

Students can provide each other with feedback that they can use to revise and improve the quality of their own writing. Studies show that when peers assess each other's writing, the quality of their writing and their attitudes toward writing improve (Topping, 1998). You can form peer writing teams to help at any or all of the following stages in the writing process:

1. **Topic selection and refinement.** To help each other come up with a list of possible topics and subtopics to write about;
2. **Pre-writing.** To clarify your writing purpose and audience;
3. **First draft.** To improve your general writing style and tone; and
4. **Final draft.** To proofread and correct mechanical errors before submitting your written work.

Library Research Teams

Many first-year students are unfamiliar with the process of conducting academic research at a college or university library. Some students experience "library anxiety" and will try to avoid even setting foot in the library, particularly if it's large and intimidating (Malvasi, Rudowsky, & Valencia, 2009). Forming library research teams is an effective way for you to develop a social support group that can make trips to the library less intimidating and transform library research from a solitary experience into a collaborative venture that's done as a team.

Team-Instructor Conferences

Visiting instructors in their office with other classmates is an effective way to get additional assistance in preparing for exams and completing assignments for the following reasons:

- You're likely to feel more comfortable about venturing onto your instructors' "turf" in the company of peers, rather than entering this unfamiliar territory on your own. As the old expression goes, "There's safety in numbers."
- When you make an office visit as a team, the information shared by the instructor is heard by more than one person, so your teammates may pick up some useful information that you may have missed, misinterpreted, or forgotten to write down (and vice versa).
- You save your instructors time by allowing them to help multiple students at the same time, which reduces the likelihood that they'll have to engage in "repeat performances" for individual students making separate visits at different times.
- You send a message to instructors that you're serious about the course and are a motivated student because you've taken the time—ahead of time—to connect with your peers and prepare for the office visit.

Remember

It's perfectly acceptable and ethical to team up with others to search for and share resources. This isn't cheating or plagiarizing—as long as your final product is completed individually and what you turn in to the instructor represents your own work.

"Two heads are better than one, not because either is infallible, but because they are unlikely to go wrong in the same direction."

—C.S. Lewis, English novelist and essayist

Study Teams

Research clearly demonstrates that college students learn as much from peers as they do from instructors and textbooks (Astin, 1993; Pascarella, 2005). When seniors at Harvard University were interviewed, nearly every one of them who had participated in study groups considered the experience to be crucial to their academic progress and success (Light, 1990, 1992; 2001).

Additional research on study groups indicates that they are effective only if each member has done required course work in advance of the team meeting—for example, if each group member has done the required readings and other course assignments (Light, 2001). Thus, to fully capitalize and maximize the power of study teams, each team member should study individually *before* studying with the group. Each member should come prepared with specific information or answers to share with teammates and specific questions or points of confusion about which they hope to receive help from the team. This ensures that all team members are individually accountable and equally responsible for doing their own learning and contributing to the learning of their teammates.

Test Results-Review and Assignment-Review Teams

After receiving the results of course examinations and assignments, you can collaborate with peers to review your results as a team. When you compare your answers to the answers of other students, you're better able to identify the sources of your mistakes; by seeing the answers of teammates who received maximum credit on certain questions, you get a clearer picture of where you went wrong and what you should do to get it right next time.

Teaming up after tests and assignments early in the term is especially effective because it enables you to get a better idea of what the instructor expects from students throughout the remainder of the course. You can use this information as early feedback to diagnose your mistakes, improve your next performance, and raise your course grade while there's still plenty of time left in the term to do so.

Learning Communities

Your college may offer you the opportunity to participate in a learning community program, in which the same group of students registers for the same block of courses during the same term. If this opportunity is available to you, try to take advantage of it because research suggests that students who participate in learning community programs are more likely to:

- Become actively involved in classroom learning,
- Form their own learning groups outside of class,
- Report greater intellectual gains, and
- Continue their college education (Tinto, 1997; 2000).

If learning community programs are not offered on your campus, consider creating smaller, more informal learning communities on your own by finding other first-year students who are likely to be taking the same courses as you (e.g., the same general education or pre-major courses). Team up with these students during registration to see if you can enroll in the same two or three courses together. This will allow you to reap the benefits of a learning community, even though your college may not offer a formal learning-community program.

Studies repeatedly show that students who become socially integrated or connected with other members of the college community are more likely to complete their first year of college and continue on to complete their college degree (Tinto, 1993; Pascarella & Terenzini, 2005). (For effective ways to make these interpersonal connections, see **Do It Now! 2.3.**)

DO IT NOW!

Making Connections with Members of Your College Community

Consider these top 10 tips for making important interpersonal connections in college. Start making these connections now so that you can begin constructing a base of social support that will strengthen your performance during your first term and, perhaps, throughout your college experience.

1. Connect with a peer or student development professional whom you may have met during orientation.

2. Connect with peers who live near you or who commute to school from the same community in which you live. If your schedules are similar, consider carpooling together.

3. Join a college club, student organization, campus committee, intramural team, or volunteer service group whose members may share the same personal or career interests as you. If you can't find a club or organization you were hoping to join, consider starting it on your own. For example, if you're an English major, consider starting a writing club or a book club.

4. Connect with a peer leader who has been trained to assist new students (e.g., peer tutor, peer mentor, or peer counselor) or with a peer who has more college experience than you (e.g., sophomore, junior, or senior).

5. Connect with classmates and team up with them to take notes, complete reading assignments, and study for exams. (Look especially to team up with a peer who may be in more than one class with you.)

6. Connect with faculty members, particularly in a field that you're considering as a major, by visiting them during office hours, conversing briefly with them after class, or communicating with them via e-mail.

7. Connect with an academic support professional in your college's Learning Center for personalized academic assistance or tutoring related to any course in which you'd like to improve your performance.

8. Connect with an academic advisor to discuss and develop your educational plans.

9. Connect with a college librarian to get early assistance and a head start on any research project that you've been assigned.

10. Connect with a personal counselor or campus minister to discuss any college adjustment or personal life issues that you may be experiencing.

REFLECTION ●──────────────────────────────

Four categories of people have the potential to serve as mentors for you in college:

1. Experienced peers

2. Faculty (instructors)

3. Administrators (e.g., office and program directors)

4. Staff (e.g., student support professionals and administrative assistants)

Think about your first interactions with faculty, staff, and administrators on campus. Do you recall anyone who impressed you as being approachable, personable, and helpful? If you did, make a note of the person's name in case you'd like to seek out that person again. (If you haven't met such a person yet, when you do, be sure you remember who it is, because that person may be someone who can serve as a mentor for you.)

TOUCHING THE FOURTH (HOME) BASE OF COLLEGE SUCCESS: PERSONAL REFLECTION AND SELF-AWARENESS

The final step in the learning process, whether it be learning in the classroom or learning from experience, is to step back from the process, thoughtfully review it, and connect it to what you already know. Reflection may be defined as the flip side of active involvement; both processes are necessary for learning to be complete. Learning requires not only effortful action but also thoughtful reflection. Active involvement gets and holds your focus of *attention*, which enables information to reach your brain, and personal reflection promotes *consolidation*, which locks that information into your brain's long-term memory (Bligh, 2000; Roediger, Dudai, & Fitzpatrick, 2007).

Brain research reveals that different brain wave patterns are associated with the mental states of involvement and reflection (Bradshaw, 1995). In **Figure 2.4**, the pattern on the left shows the brain waves of someone who is actively involved in the learning task and attending to it. The pattern on the right shows the brain waves of someone who is thinking deeply about information that has been attended to and taken in, which will help consolidate or lock that information into the person's long-term memory. Thus, effective learning combines active mental involvement (characterized by high-amplitude "beta" brain waves) with thoughtful reflection (characterized by high-frequency "alpha" brain waves— similar to someone in a meditative state).

REFLECTION ●———

Think about the students in your classes this term. Are there any students whom you might want to join with to form learning teams?

Do you have any classmates who are in more than one class with you and who might be good peer partners for the courses you have in common?

"We learn to do neither by thinking nor by doing; we learn to do by thinking about what we are doing."

—George Stoddard, professor emeritus, University of Iowa

Personal reflection also involves introspection—turning inward and inspecting yourself to gain deeper *self-awareness* of what you've done, what you're doing, or what you intend to do. Two forms of self-awareness are particularly important for success in college:

1. Self-assessment
2. Self-monitoring

Self-Assessment

Simply defined, self-assessment is the process of reflecting on and evaluating characteristics of your "self," such as your personality traits, learning habits, personal strengths, and personal weaknesses that need improvement. Self-assessment is the critical first step in the process of self-improvement, personal planning, and effective decision making. The following are important target areas for self-assessment because they reflect personal characteristics that play a pivotal role in promoting success in college and beyond:

- **Personal interests.** What you like to do or enjoy doing.
- **Personal values.** What is important to you and what you care about doing.
- **Personal abilities or aptitudes.** What you do well or have the potential to do well.
- **Learning habits.** How you go about learning and the usual approaches, methods, or techniques you use to learn.
- **Learning styles.** How you prefer to learn—the way you like to:
  - Receive information—the learning format you prefer (e.g., learning by reading, listening, or experiencing);
  - Perceive information—what sensory modality you prefer to use (e.g., vision, sound, or touch);

FIGURE 2.4 ———

High-Amplitude Brain Waves Associated with a Mental State of *Active Involvement*.

High-Frequency Brain Waves Associated with a Mental State of *Reflective Thinking*.

© Kendall Hunt

- Process information—how you prefer to deal with or think about information you've taken in (e.g., whether you like to think about it on your own or discuss it with others).

- **Personality traits.** Your temperament, emotional characteristics, and social tendencies (e.g., whether you lean toward being outgoing or reserved);

- **Academic self-concept.** What kind of student you think you are and how you perceive yourself as a learner (e.g., your level of self-confidence and whether you believe academic success is within your control or depends on factors beyond your control).

REFLECTION

How would you rate your academic self-confidence at this point in your college experience? (Circle one.)

very confident   somewhat confident

somewhat unconfident   very unconfident

Why did you make this choice?

Self-Monitoring

Research indicates that one characteristic of successful learners is that they monitor or watch themselves and maintain self-awareness of:

- Whether they're using effective learning strategies (e.g., they are aware of their level of attention or concentration in class);

- Whether they're comprehending what they are attempting to learn (e.g., if they're understanding it at a deep level or merely memorizing it at a surface level); and

- How to regulate or adjust their learning strategies to meet the demands of different academic tasks and subjects (e.g., they read technical material in a science textbook more slowly and stop to test their understanding more often than when they're reading a novel; Pintrich, 1995; Pintrich & Schunk, 2002; Weinstein, 1994; Weinstein & Meyer, 1991).

Remember _____

Successful students are self-aware learners who know their learning strategies, styles, strengths, and shortcomings.

"Successful students know a lot about themselves."

—Claire Weinstein and Debra Meyer, professors of educational psychology at the University of Texas

Student *Perspective*

"I wasn't sure what this class was about. Now I understand this class and I really like it. I learned a lot about myself."

"In the start of the semester I thought this class would be a waste of time and busy work. But I realized it is an important way of learning who and what you are . . . I underestimated this class."

—Comments made by first-year students when evaluating their first-year experience course

You can begin to establish good self-monitoring habits by creating a routine of periodically pausing to reflect on the strategies you're using to learn and "do" college. For instance, you can ask yourself the following questions:

- Am I listening attentively to what my instructor is saying in class?

- Do I comprehend what I am reading outside of class?

Remember ────────────

Successful students and successful people are mindful—they watch what they're doing and remain aware of whether they're doing it effectively and to the best of their ability.

- Am I effectively using campus resources that are designed to support my success?
- Am I interacting with campus professionals who can contribute to my current success and future development?
- Am I interacting and collaborating with peers who can contribute to my learning and increase my level of involvement in the college experience?
- Am I effectively implementing the success strategies identified in this book?

REFLECTION ● ──────────────────────

How would you rate your academic self-confidence at this point in your college experience? (Circle one.)

very confident	somewhat confident
somewhat unconfident	very unconfident

Why?

A Checklist of Success-Promoting Principles and Practices

1. **Active Involvement**
   Inside the classroom, I:
   - ☑ Get to class. Treat it like a job; if you cut, your pay (grade) will be cut.
   - ☑ Get involved in class. Come prepared, listen actively, take notes, and participate.

   Outside the classroom, I:
   - ☑ **Read actively.** Take notes while you read to increase attention and retention.
   - ☑ **Double up.** Spend twice as much time on academic work outside the classroom than you spend in class—if you're a full-time student, that makes it a 40-hour academic workweek (with occasional "overtime").

2. **Use of Campus Resources**
   I capitalize on academic and student support services, such as the following:
   - ☑ Learning Center
   - ☑ Writing Center
   - ☑ Disability Services
   - ☑ College library
   - ☑ Academic Advising Center
   - ☑ Office of Student Life
   - ☑ Financial Aid Office
   - ☑ Counseling Center
   - ☑ Health Center

☑ Career Development Center
☑ Experiential Learning Resources

3. **Interpersonal Interaction and Collaboration**

I interact with the following people:

☑ **Peers.** I join student clubs and participate in campus organizations.

☑ **Faculty members.** I connect with professors and other faculty members immediately after class, in their offices, or via e-mail.

☑ **Academic advisors.** I see an advisor for more than just course registration. I've found an advisor with whom I can relate and develop an ongoing relationship.

☑ **Mentors.** I try to find experienced people on campus who can serve as trusted guides and role models.

I collaborate by doing the following:

☑ **Forming learning teams.** I join not only last-minute study groups but also teams that collaborate more regularly to work on such tasks as taking lecture notes, completing reading and writing assignments, conducting library research, and reviewing results of exams or course assignments.

☑ **Participating in learning communities.** I enroll in two or more classes with the same students during the same term.

4. **Personal Reflection and Self-Awareness**

I engage in:

☑ **Self-Assessment.** I reflect on and evaluate my personal traits, habits, strengths, and weaknesses.

☑ **Self-Monitoring.** I maintain self-awareness of how I'm learning in college and whether I'm using effective strategies that will enable me to do college well.

REFLECTION ●────────────────────────

Before exiting this chapter, look back at the Checklist of Success-Promoting Principles and Practices and see how these ideas compare with those you recorded at the start of this chapter, when we asked you how you thought college would be different from high school and what it would take to be successful in college.

What ideas from your list and our checklist tend to match?

Were there any ideas on your list that were not on ours, or vice versa?

Blueprint for First Generation College Success Exercises

Birds of a Different Feather: High School versus College

Read the following list of differences between high school and college and rate each difference on a scale from 1 to 4 in terms of how aware you were of this difference when you began college (1 = totally unaware; 2 = not fully aware; 3 = somewhat aware, 4 = totally aware)

Class schedules are typically made for high school students.

College students make their own class schedules, either on their own or in consultation with an academic advisor.

Awareness Rating _____

High school classes are scheduled back-to-back at the same time every day with short breaks in between.

Larger time gaps can occur between college classes, and they are scheduled at various times throughout the day (and night).

Awareness Rating _____

Class attendance in high school is mandatory and checked daily.

Class attendance in college is not mandatory; in many classes, attendance is not even taken.

Awareness Rating _____

> "In college, if you don't go to class, that's you. Your professor doesn't care really if you pass or fail."
> —First-year student (Engle, Bermeo, & O'Brien, 2006).

High school teachers often write all important information they cover in class on the board.

College professors frequently expect students to write down important information contained in their lectures without explicitly writing it on the board or including it on PowerPoint slides.

Awareness Rating _____

High school teachers often re-teach material in class that students were assigned to read.

College professors often do not teach the same material covered in assigned reading and information from the assigned reading still appears on exams.

Awareness Rating _____

High school teachers often take class time to remind students of assignments and their due dates.

College professors list their assignments and due dates on the course syllabus and expect students to keep track of them on their own.

Awareness Rating _____

> "College teachers don't tell you what you're supposed to do. They just expect you to do it. High school teachers tell you about five times what you're supposed to do."
> —College sophomore (Appleby, 2008)

Homework assignments (e.g., math problems) in high school are typically turned in to the teacher, who checks and grades the students' work.

Assigned work in college often is not turned in to be checked or graded; students are expected to have the self-discipline to do the work on their own.

Awareness Rating _____

High school students spend most of their learning time in class; they spend much less time studying outside of class than they spend in class.

College students typically spend no more than 15 hours per week in class and are expected to spend at least two hours studying out of class for every hour they spend in class.

Awareness Rating _____

Tests in high school often take place frequently and cover limited amounts of material. College exams are given less frequently (e.g., midterm and final) and tend to cover large amounts of material.

Awareness Rating _____

Make-up tests and extra-credit opportunities are often available to students in high school.

In college, if an exam or assignment is missed, rarely do students have a chance to make it up or to recapture lost points through extra-credit work.

Awareness Rating _____

A grade of "D" in high school is still passing.

In college, a grade point average below "C" puts a student on academic probation, and if it doesn't improve to C or higher, the student may be academically dismissed.

Awareness Rating _____

In high school, students go to offices of campuses only if they have to or are required to (e.g., if they forgot to do something or did something wrong).

In college, students go to campus offices to enhance their success by taking advantage of the services and support they provide.

Awareness Rating _____

> "In high school, they're like, 'Okay, well, I'll give you another day to do it.' In college, you have to do it that day . . . and the teachers are like, 'If you don't do it, that's your problem.'"
>
> —First-year student (Engle, Bermeo, & O'Brien, 2006)

(Adapted from the following source: Altshuler Learning Enhancement Center, Southern Methodist University: www. smu.edu/alec/transition.asp)

Constructing a Master List of Campus Resources

Construct a master list of all support services that are available to you on your campus. Your final product should be a list that includes the following:

- The names of different support services your campus offers
- The types of support each service provides

- A short statement indicating whether you think you would benefit from each particular type of support
- The name of a person whom you could contact for support from each service

Use each of the following sources to gain more in-depth knowledge about the support services available on your campus:

- Information published in your college catalog and student handbook
- Information posted on your college's Web site
- Information gathered by speaking with professionals in different offices or centers on your campus

Use the form on the following page to help you construct your master lists of campus resources.

Notes

- You can team up with other classmates to work collaboratively on this assignment. For instance, different team members could identify different campus resources to research and each member could bring information about one resource to share with other members of the team. Working together with a peer on any research task can reduce your anxiety, increase your energy, and generate synergy, which results in a final product that is superior to what could have been produced by one person working alone (independently).
- After you complete this assignment, save your master list of support services for future use. You might not have an immediate need for some of these services during your first term in college, but all of them are likely to be useful to you at some point in your college experience.

Support Services

Learning Center

How will I benefit?   Whom should I contact?

_____

Writing Center

How will I benefit?   Whom should I contact?

_____

Disability Services

How will I benefit?   Whom should I contact?

_____

College Library

How will I benefit?   Whom should I contact?

_____

Academic Advising Center

How will I benefit?   Whom should I contact?

_____

Office of Student Life

How will I benefit?   Whom should I contact?

_____

Financial Aid Office

How will I benefit?   Whom should I contact?

_____

Counseling Center

How will I benefit?   Whom should I contact?

_____

Health Center

How will I benefit?   Whom should I contact?

Career Development Center

How will I benefit?   Whom should I contact?

Experiential Learning Resources

How will I benefit?   Whom should I contact?

Other Types of Support Available on Campus

How will I benefit?   Whom should I contact?

Alone and Disconnected: Feeling Like Calling It Quits

Josephine is a first-year student in her second week of college. She doesn't feel like she's fitting in with other students on her campus. She also feels guilty about the time she's taking time away from her family and her old high school friends who are not attending college, and she fears that her ties with them will be weakened or broken if she continues spending so much time at school and on schoolwork. Josephine is feeling so torn between college and her family and former friends that she's beginning to have second thoughts about whether she should have gone to college.

Reflection and Discussion Questions

1. What would you say to Josephine that might persuade her to stay in college?

2. What could Josephine's college have done more during her first two weeks on campus to make her (and other students) feel more connected with college and less disconnected from family?

3. What could Josephine do for herself right now to minimize the conflict she's experiencing between her commitment to college and her commitment to family and high school friends?

STAGES IN THE LEARNING AND MEMORY PROCESS

Learning deeply, and remembering what you've learned, is a process that involves three key stages:

1. **Sensory input (perception).** Taking information into your brain;
2. **Memory formation (storage).** Saving that information in your brain; and
3. **Memory recall (retrieval).** Bringing information back to mind when you need it.

These three stages in the learning-memory process are summarized visually in **Figure 2.5**.

You can consider these stages of the learning and memory process to be similar to the way information is processed by a computer: (1) information is typed onto the screen (input), (2) the information is saved in a file (storage), and (3) the saved information is recalled and used when it's needed (retrieval). This three-stage process can be used to create a systematic set of strategies for effectively using the two major routes through which you acquire information and knowledge in college: taking notes as you listen to lectures, and reading textbooks.

EFFECTIVE LECTURE-LISTENING AND NOTE-TAKING STRATEGIES

The importance of effective listening skills in the college classroom is highlighted by a study of more than 400 first-year students who were given a listening test at the start of their first term in college. At the end of their first year in college, 49 percent of those students who scored low on the listening test were on academic probation, compared to only 4.4 percent of students who scored high on the listening test. On the other hand, 68.5 percent of students who scored high on the listening test were eligible for the honors program at the end of their first year—compared to only 4.17 percent of those students who had low listening test scores (Conaway, 1982).

FIGURE 2.5

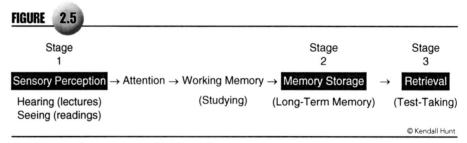

Key Stages in the Learning and Memory Process

REFLECTION ⬤

Do you think writing notes in class helps or hinders your ability to pay attention and learn from your instructors' lectures?

Why?

Studies show that information delivered during lectures is the number one source of test questions (and answers) on college exams (Brown, 1988; Kuhn, 1988). When lecture information that hasn't been recorded in the student's notes appears on a test, it has only a 5 percent chance of being recalled (Kiewra et al., 2000). Students who write notes during lectures achieve higher course grades than students who just listen to lectures (Kiewra, 1985, 2005), and students with a more complete set of notes are more likely to demonstrate higher levels of overall academic achievement (Johnstone & Su, 1994; Kiewra & DuBois, 1998; Kiewra & Fletcher, 1984).

Contrary to popular belief that writing while listening interferes with the ability to listen, students report that taking notes actually increases their attention and concentration in class (Hartley, 1998; Hartley & Marshall, 1974). Studies also show that when students write down information that's presented to them, rather than just sitting and listening to it, they're more likely to remember the most important aspects of that information when tested later (Bligh, 2000; Kiewra et al., 1991). One study discovered that students with grade point averages (GPAs) of 2.53 or higher recorded more information in their notes and retained a larger percentage of the most important information than did students with GPAs of less than 2.53 (Einstein, Morris, & Smith, 1985). These findings are not surprising when you consider that *hearing* information, *writing* it, and then *seeing* it after you've written it produces three different memory traces (tracks) in the brain, which combine to multiply your chances of remembering it. Furthermore, students with a good set of notes have a written record of that information, which can be reread and studied later.

These research findings suggest that you should view each lecture as a test-review session during which your instructor is giving out test answers and you're given the opportunity to write all those answers in your notes. Come to class with the attitude that your instructors are dispensing answers to test questions as they speak, and your job is to pick out and pick up these answers.

Remember _____

If important points your professor makes in class make it into your notes, they can become points learned; these learned points will turn into earned points on your exams (and higher grades in the course).

The next sections give strategies for getting the most out of lectures at three stages in the learning process: *before*, *during*, and *after* lectures.

Pre-Lecture Strategies: What to Do before Lectures

1. **Check your syllabus to see where you are in the course and determine how the upcoming class fits into the total course picture.** Checking your syllabus before individual class sessions strengthens learning because you will see how each part (individual class session) relates to the whole (the entire course). This strategy also capitalizes on the brain's natural tendency to seek larger patterns and see the "big picture." Rather than seeing things in separate parts, the brain is naturally inclined to connect parts into a meaningful whole (Caine & Caine, 1991). In other words, the brain looks for meaningful patterns and connections rather than isolated bits and pieces of information (Jensen, 2000). In **Figure 2.6**, notice how your brain naturally ties together and fills in the missing information to perceive a meaningful whole pattern.

2. **Get to class early so that you can look over your notes from the previous class session and from any reading assignment that relates to the day's lecture topic.** Research indicates that when students preview information related to an upcoming lecture topic, it improves their ability to take more accurate and complete lecture notes (Kiewra, 2005; Ladas, 1980). Thus, a good strategy to help you learn from lectures is to review your notes from the previous class session and read textbook information related to an upcoming lecture topic—*before* hearing the lecture. This strategy will help you better understand and take more detailed notes on the lecture. Reviewing previously learned information also activates your previous knowledge, enabling you to build a mental bridge from one class session to the next, connecting new information to what you already know—a key to deep learning (Bruner, 1990; Piaget, 1978; Vygotsky, 1978). Acquiring knowledge isn't a matter of simply pouring information into the brain as if it were an empty jar. It's a matter of attaching or connecting new ideas to ideas that are already stored in the brain. When you learn deeply, a physical connection is

FIGURE 2.6

You perceive a white triangle in the middle of this figure. However, if you use three fingers to cover up the three corners of the white triangle that fall outside the other (background) triangle, the white triangle suddenly disappears. What your brain does is take these corners as starting points and fill in the rest of the information on its own to create a complete or whole pattern that has meaning to you. (Also, notice how you perceive the background triangle as a complete triangle, even though parts of its left and right sides are missing.)

© Kendall Hunt

Triangle Illusion

FIGURE 2.7

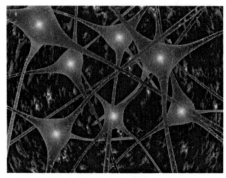

When something is learned, it's stored in the brain as a link in an interconnected network of brain cells. Thus, deep learning involves making connections between what you're trying to learn and what you already know.

© Jurgen Ziewe, 2013. Under license from Shutterstock, Inc.

Network of Brain Cells

actually made between nerve cells in your brain (Alkon, 1992), as illustrated in **Figure 2.7**.

3. **Adopt a seating location that maximizes your focus of attention and minimizes sources of distraction.** Many years of research show that students who sit in the front and center of class tend to earn higher exam scores and course grades (Tagliacollo, Volpato, & Pereira, 2010; Benedict & Hoag, 2004; Rennels & Chaudhair, 1988). These results are found even when students are assigned seats by their instructor, so it's not just a matter of more motivated and studious students tending to sit in the front of the room: instead, the better academic performance achieved by students sitting in the front and center of the room likely results from a learning advantage provided by this seating location. Front-and-center seating benefits students' academic performance by improving their vision of material written on the board or screen and their ability to hear the instructor's lectures. In addition, this seating position allows for better eye contact with the instructor, which can increase students' level of attention, reduce their feeling of anonymity, and heighten their sense of involvement in the classroom. Sitting in the front of class can also reduce your level of anxiety about speaking up in class because, when you speak, you will not have numerous classmates sitting in front of you turning around to look at you while you speak.

The bottom line: When you enter a classroom, get in the habit of heading for a seat in the front and center of class. In large classes, it's even more important to get "up close and personal" with your instructors, not only to improve your attention, note taking and participation in class, but also to improve your instructors' ability to remember who you are and how well you performed in class—which will work to your advantage when it comes time to ask your instructors for letters of recommendation.

4. **Sit by people who will enable (not disable) your ability to learn.** Intentionally sit near classmates who will not distract you or interfere with the quality of your note taking. Attention comes in degrees or amounts; you can

Student *Perspective*

"I tend to sit at the very front of my classrooms. It helps me focus and take notes better. It also eliminates distractions."

—First-year college student

Student *Perspective*

"[In high school] the teacher knows your name. But in college they don't know your name; they might see your face, but it means nothing to them unless you make yourself known."

—First-year college student

Student
Perspective

"I like to sit up front so I am not distracted by others and I don't have to look around people's heads to see the chalkboard."

—First-year college student

give all of your attention or part of it to whatever task you're performing. Trying to grasp complex information in class is a task that demands your undivided attention.

Remember _____

When you enter a class, you have a choice about where you're going to sit. Choose wisely by selecting a location that will maximize your attentiveness to the instructor and the effectiveness of your note taking.

The evolution of student attention from the back to the front of class.

5. **Adopt a seating posture that screams attention.** Sitting upright and leaning forward increases your attention because these bodily signals will reach your brain and increase mental alertness. If your body is in an alert and ready position, your mind tends to pick up these physical cues and follow your body's lead by also becoming alert and ready (to learn). Just as baseball players assume a ready position in the field before a pitch is delivered to put their bodies in position to catch batted balls, learners who assume a ready position in the classroom put themselves in a better position to catch ideas batted around in the classroom. Studies show that when humans are mentally alert and ready to learn, greater amounts of the brain chemical C-kinase are released at the connection points between brain cells, which increases the likelihood that a learning connection will form between them (Howard, 2000).

There's another advantage to being attentive in class: You send a clear message to your instructor that you're a conscientious and courteous student. This can influence your instructor's perception and evaluation of your academic performance, which can earn you the benefit of the doubt at the end of the term if you're on the border between a lower and higher course grade.

Listening and Note-Taking Strategies: What to Do during Lectures

1. **Take your own notes in class.** Don't rely on someone else to take notes for you. Taking your own notes in your own words focuses your attention and ensures that you're taking notes that make sense to you. Research shows that students who record and review their own notes earn higher scores on

memory tests for that information than do students who review the notes of others (Fisher, Harris, & Harris, 1973; Kiewra, 2005). These findings point to the importance of taking and studying your own notes because they will be most meaningful to you. You can collaborate with classmates to compare notes for completeness and accuracy or to pick up points you may have missed. However, don't routinely rely on someone else to take notes for you.

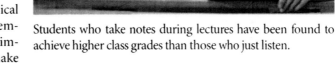

Students who take notes during lectures have been found to achieve higher class grades than those who just listen.

2. **Focus full attention on the most important information.** Attention is the critical first step to successful learning and memory. Since the human attention span is limited, it's impossible to attend to and make note of (or take notes on) everything. Thus, you need to use your attention *selectively* to focus on, detect, and select information that matters most. Here are some strategies for attending to and recording the most important information delivered by professors in the college classroom:

   - Pay attention to information your instructors put *in print*—on the board, on a slide, or in a handout. If your instructor takes the time and energy to write it out or type it out, that's usually a good clue that the information is important and you're likely to see it again—on an exam.

   - Pay attention to information presented during the first and last few minutes of class. Instructors are more likely to provide valuable reminders, reviews, and previews at these two points in time.

   - Use your instructor's *verbal and nonverbal cues* to detect important information. Don't just tune in when the instructor is writing something down and tune out at other times. It's been found that students record almost 90 percent of information written on the board, but less than 50 percent of important ideas that professors state but don't write on the board (Johnstone & Su, 1994; Locke, 1977; Titsworth & Kiewra, 2004). Don't fall into the reflex-like routine of just writing something in your notes when you see your instructor writing on the board. Listen actively to receive and record important ideas in your notes that you *hear* your instructor saying. In **Do It Now! 2.4,** you'll find strategies for detecting clues to important information that professors deliver during lectures.

3. **Take organized notes**. Keep taking notes in the same paragraph if the instructor is continuing on the same point or idea. When the instructor shifts to a new idea, skip a few lines and shift to a new paragraph. Be alert to phrases that your instructor may use to signal a shift to a new or different idea (e.g., "Let's turn to . . ." or "In addition to . . ."). Use these phrases as cues for taking notes in paragraph form. By recording different ideas in different paragraphs, you improve the organizational quality of your notes, which will improve your comprehension and retention of them. Also, be sure to leave extra space between paragraphs (ideas) to give yourself room to add

DO IT NOW!

Detecting When Instructors Are Delivering Important Information during Class Lectures

1. **Verbal cues**
   - Phrases signal important information (e.g., "The point here is . . ." or "What's most significant about this is . . .").
   - Information is repeated or rephrased in a different way (e.g., "In other words . . .").
   - Stated information is followed with a question to check understanding (e.g., "Is that clear?" "Do you follow that?" "Does that make sense?" or "Are you with me?").

2. **Vocal (tone of voice) cues**
   - Information is delivered in a louder tone or at a higher pitch than usual, which may indicate excitement or emphasis.
   - Information is delivered at a slower rate or with more pauses than usual, which

may be your instructor's way of giving you more time to write down these important ideas.

3. **Nonverbal cues**
   - Information is delivered by the instructor with more than the usual
     a. facial expressiveness (e.g., raised or furrowed eyebrows);
     b. body movement (e.g., more gesturing and animation); or
     c. eye contact (e.g., looking more directly and intently at the faces of students to see whether they are following or understanding what's being said).
   - The instructor moves closer to the students (e.g., moving away from the podium or blackboard).
   - The instructor's body is oriented directly toward the class (i.e., both shoulders directly or squarely face the class).

information later that you may have initially missed, or to translate the professor's words into your own words that are more meaningful to you.

Another popular strategy for taking organized notes, called the Cornell Note-Taking System, is summarized in **Do It Now! 2.5.**

4. **Keep taking notes even if you don't immediately understand what your instructor is saying.** If you are uncertain or confused about what your instructor is saying, don't stop taking notes, because your notes will at least leave you with a record of the information to review later—when you have more time to think about and grasp their meaning. If you still don't understand it after taking time to review it, check it out in your textbook, with your instructor, or with a classmate.

Remember _____

Your primary goal during lectures is to get important information into your brain long enough to note it mentally and then physically in your notes. Making sense of that information often has to come later, when you have time to reflect on the notes you took in class.

DO IT NOW

The Cornell Note-Taking System

1. On the page on which you're taking notes, draw a horizontal line about 2 inches from the bottom edge of the paper.

2. If there's no vertical line on the left side of the page, draw one line about 2½ inches from the left edge of the paper (as shown in the scaled-down illustration here).

3. When your instructor is lecturing, use the large space to the right of the vertical line (area A) to record your notes.

4. After a lecture, use the space at the bottom of the page (area B) to summarize the main points you recorded on that page.

5. Use the column of space on the left side of the page (area C) to write questions that are answered in the notes on the right.

6. Quiz yourself by looking at the questions listed in the left margin while covering the answers to them that are found in your class notes on the right.

Note: You can use this note-taking and note-review method on your own, or you could team up with two or more students and do it collaboratively.

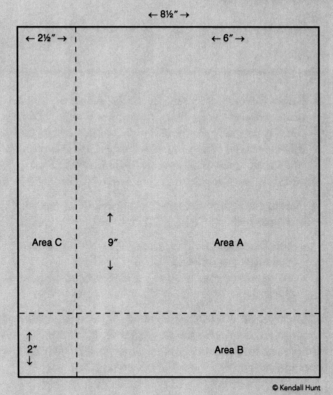

Post-Lecture Strategies: What to Do after Lectures

1. **As soon as class ends, quickly check your notes for missing information or incomplete thoughts.** Since the information is likely to be fresh in your mind immediately after class, a quick check of your notes at this time will allow you to take advantage of your short-term memory. By reviewing and reflecting on it, you can help move the information into long-term memory before forgetting takes place. This quick review can be done alone or, better yet, with a motivated classmate. If you both have gaps in your notes, check them out with your instructor before he or she leaves the classroom. Even though it may be weeks before you will be tested on the material, the quicker you address missed points and clear up sources of confusion, the better, because you'll be able to use your knowledge to help you understand and learn upcoming material. Catching confusion early in the game also enables you to avoid the mad last-minute rush of students seeking help from the instructor just before test time. You want to reserve the critical time just before exams for studying a set of notes that you know are complete and accurate, rather than rushing around trying to find missing information and getting cheap fast-food help on concepts that were presented weeks ago.

REFLECTION ●—————————————————————————

What do you tend to do immediately after a class session ends?

Why?

2. **Before the next class session meets, reflect on and review your notes to make sense of them.** Your professors will often lecture on information that you may have little prior knowledge about, so it is unrealistic to expect that you will understand everything that's being said the first time you hear it. Instead, you'll need to set aside time for making notes or taking notes on your own notes (i.e., rewriting them in your own words so that they make sense to you).

During this reflect-and-rewrite process, we recommend that you take notes on your notes by:

- Translating technical information into your own words to make it more meaningful to you; and
- Reorganizing your notes to get ideas related to the same point in the same place.

Studies show that when students organize lecture information into meaningful categories, they demonstrate greater recall for that information on a delayed memory test than do students who simply review their notes without organizing them into categories (Howe, 1970; Kiewra, 2005).

Remember _____

Look at note taking as a two-stage process: Stage 1 involves actively taking notes in class, and Stage 2 takes place later, when you have time to reflect on your notes and process them more deeply.

Expert's Experience   My first year in college was mainly spent trying to manipulate my schedule to find some free time. I took all of my classes in a row without a break to save some time at the end of the day for relaxation and hanging out with friends before I went to work. Seldom did I look over my notes and read the material that I was assigned on the day I took the lecture notes and received the assignment. Thus, on the day before the test I was in a panic trying to cram the lecture notes into my head for the upcoming test. Needless to say, I did not perform well on many of these tests. Finally, I had a professor who told me that if I spent time each day after a couple of my classes catching up on reading and rewriting my notes, I would retain the material longer, improve my grades, and decrease my stress at test time. I employed this system, and it worked wonderfully.

— *Aaron Thompson*

READING STRATEGICALLY TO COMPREHEND AND RETAIN TEXTBOOK INFORMATION

Second only to lecture notes as a source of test questions on college exams is information found in assigned readings (Brown, 1988). You're likely to find exam questions containing information that your professors didn't talk about specifically in class (or even mention in class), but that was contained in your assigned reading. College professors often expect you to relate or connect what they lecture about in class with material that you've been assigned to read. Furthermore, they often deliver class lectures with the assumption that you have done the assigned reading, so if you haven't done it, you're likely to have more difficulty following what your instructor is talking about in class.

Remember _____

Do the assigned reading and do it according to the schedule your instructor has established. It will help you better understand class lectures, improve the quality of your participation in class, and raise your overall course grade.

REFLECTION ●———————————————————————

Rate yourself in terms of how frequently you use these note-taking strategies according to the following scale:

4 = always, 3 = sometimes, 2 = rarely, 1 = never

1. I take notes aggressively in class.	4	3	2	1
2. I sit near the front of the room during class.	4	3	2	1
3. I sit upright and lean forward while in class.	4	3	2	1
4. I take notes on what my instructors say, not just what they write on the board.	4	3	2	1

5. I pay special attention to information presented at the start and end of class.	4	3	2	1
6. I take notes in paragraph form.	4	3	2	1
7. I review my notes immediately after class to check that they are complete and accurate.	4	3	2	1

When completing your reading assignments, use effective reading strategies that are based on sound principles of human learning and memory, such as those listed here.

What follows is a series of research-based strategies for effective reading at three key stages in the learning process: before, during, and after reading.

Pre-Reading Strategies: What to Do before Reading

1. **Before jumping into your assigned reading, look at how it fits into the overall organizational structure of the book and course.** You can do this efficiently by taking a quick look at the book's table of contents to see where the chapter you're about to read is placed in the overall sequence of chapters, especially its relation to chapters that immediately precede and follow it. Using this strategy will give you a sense of how the particular part you're focusing on connects with the bigger picture. Research shows that if learners gain access to advanced knowledge of how information they're about to learn is organized—if they see how its parts relate to the whole—*before* they attempt to start learning the specific parts, they're better able to comprehend and retain the material (Ausubel, Novak, & Hanesian, 1978; Mayer, 2003). Thus, the first step toward improving reading comprehension and retention of a book chapter is to see how it relates to the whole book before you begin to examine the chapter part by part.

REFLECTION

When you open a textbook to read a chapter, how do you start the reading process? That is, what's the first thing you do?

2. **Preview the chapter you're about to read by reading its boldface headings and any chapter outline, objectives, summary, or end-of-chapter questions that may be included.** Before jumping right into the content, get in the habit of previewing what's in a chapter to gain an overall sense of its organization. If you dive into the specific details first, you lose sight of how the smaller details relate to the larger picture. The brain's natural tendency is to perceive and comprehend whole patterns rather than isolated bits of information. Start by seeing how the parts of the chapter are integrated into the whole. This will enable you to better connect the separate pieces of information you encounter while you read, similar to seeing the whole picture of a completed jigsaw puzzle before you start assembling is pieces.

3. **Take a moment to think about what you already know that relates to the material in the chapter you're about to read.** By thinking about knowledge you possess about the topic you're about to read, you activate the areas of your brain where that knowledge is stored, thereby preparing it to make meaningful connections with the material you're about to read.

Strategies to Use while Reading

1. **Read selectively to locate the most important information.** Rather than jumping into reading and randomly highlighting, effective reading begins with a plan or goal for identifying what should be noted and remembered. Here are three strategies to use while reading to help you determine what information should be noted and retained.

    Use boldface or dark-print headings and subheadings as cues for identifying important information. These headings organize the chapter's major points; thus, you can use them as "traffic signs" to direct you to the most important information in the chapter. Better yet, turn the headings into questions and then read to find answers to these questions. This question-and-answer strategy will ensure that you read actively and with a purpose. (You can set up this strategy when you preview the chapter by placing a question mark after each heading contained in the chapter.) Creating and answering questions while you read also keeps you motivated; the questions help stimulate your curiosity and finding answers to them serves to reward or reinforce your reading (Walter, Knudsbig, & Smith, 2003). Lastly, answering questions about what you're reading is an effective way to prepare for tests because you're practicing exactly what you'll be expected to do on exams—answering questions. You can quickly write the heading questions on separate index cards and use them as flash cards to review for exams. Use the question on the flash card as a way to flash back and trigger your recall of information from the text that answers the question.

    Pay special attention to words that are *italicized*, <u>underlined</u>, or appear in boldface print. These are usually signs for building-block terms that must be understood and built on before you can proceed to understand higher-level concepts covered later in the reading. Don't simply highlight these words because their special appearance suggests they are important. Read these terms carefully and be sure you understand their meaning before you continue reading.

    Pay special attention to the first and last sentences in each paragraph. These sentences contain an important introduction and conclusion to the ideas covered in the paragraph. It's a good idea to reread the first and last sentences of each paragraph before you move on to the next paragraph, particularly when reading sequential or cumulative material (e.g., science or math) that requires full comprehension of what was previously covered to understand what will be covered next.

    Reread your chapter notes and highlights after you've listened to your instructor lecture on the material contained in the chapter. You can use your lecture notes as a guide to help you focus on what information in the chapter your instructor feels is most important. If you adopt this strategy, your reading before lectures will help you understand the lecture and take better class notes, and your reading after lectures will help you locate and learn information in the textbook that your instructor is emphasizing in class—which is likely to be the information your instructor thinks is most important and is most likely to show up on your exams. Thus, it's a good idea to have your class notes nearby when you're completing your reading assignments to help you identify what you should pay special attention to while reading.

Remember

Your goal when reading is not merely to cover the assigned pages, but to uncover the most important information and ideas contained on those pages.

"I would advise you to read with a pen in your hand, and enter in a little book of short hints of what you find that is curious, or that might be useful; for this will be the best method of imprinting such particulars in your memory, where they will be ready."

—Benjamin Franklin, 18th-century inventor, newspaper writer, and signer of the *Declaration of Independence*

"I had the worst study habits and the lowest grades. Then I found out what I was doing wrong. I had been highlighting with a black magic marker."

—Jeff Altman, American comedian

2. **Take written notes on what you're reading.** Just as you should take notes in class, you should take notes in response to the author's words in the text. Writing requires more active thinking than highlighting because you're creating your own words rather than passively highlighting words written by somebody else. Don't get into the habit of using your textbook as a coloring book in which the artistic process of highlighting what you're reading with spectacular kaleidoscopic colors distracts you from the more important process of learning actively and thinking deeply.

If you can express what someone else has written in words that make sense to you, this means that you're relating it to what you already know—a sign of deep learning (Demmert & Towner, 2003). A good time to pause and summarize what you've read in your own words is when you encounter a boldface heading, because this indicates you've just completed reading about a major concept and are about to begin a new one.

Highlighting textbooks in spectacular colors is a very popular reading strategy among college students, but it's a less effective strategy for producing deep learning than taking written notes on what you read.

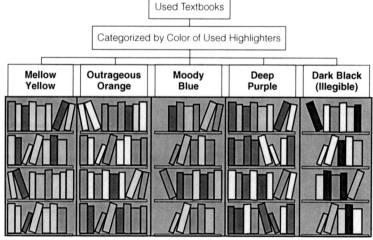

© Kendall Hunt

Remember _____

Effective reading isn't a passive process of covering pages: it's an active process in which you uncover meaning in the pages you read.

_____

3. **Use the visual aids included in your textbook.** Don't fall into the trap of thinking that visual aids can or should be skipped because they're merely secondary supplements to the written words in the body of the text. Visual aids, such as charts, graphs, diagrams, and concept maps, are powerful learning and memory tools for a couple of reasons: (1) they enable you to "see" the information in addition to reading (hearing) it, and (2) they organize and connect separate pieces of information into an integrated whole.

REFLECTION ●—————————————————————

When reading a textbook, do you usually have the following tools on hand?

Highlighter:	yes	no
Pen or pencil:	yes	no
Notebook:	yes	no
Class notes:	yes	no
Dictionary:	yes	no
Glossary:	yes	no

Furthermore, visual aids allow you to experience a form of information input other than repeatedly processing written words. This occasional change of sensory input brings variety to the reading process, which can recapture your attention and recharge your motivation.

Post-Reading Strategies: What to Do after Reading

1. **End a reading session with a short review of the information you've noted or highlighted.** Most forgetting that takes place after you receive and process information occurs immediately after you stop focusing on the information and turn your attention to another task (Baddeley, 1999; Underwood, 1983). (See **Figure 2.8.**) Taking a few minutes at the end of your reading time to review the most important information works to lock that information into your memory before you turn your attention to something else and forget it.

The graph in **Figure 2.8** represents the results of a classic experiment on how well information is recalled at various times after it was originally learned. As you can see on the far left of the graph, most forgetting occurs soon after information has been taken in (e.g., after 20 minutes, the participants in the study forgot more than 60 percent of it). The results of this classic study, which have been confirmed multiple times (Schacter, 2001), point to the importance of reviewing information you've acquired through reading immediately after you've

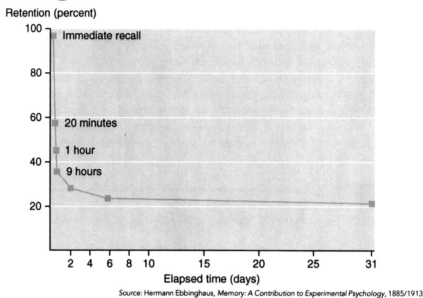

Source: Hermann Ebbinghaus, Memory: A Contribution to Experimental Psychology, 1885/1913

The Forgetting Curve

read it. When you do so, your memory for that information will improve dramatically because you're intercepting the forgetting curve at its steepest point of memory loss—immediately after information has been read.

2. **For difficult-to-understand concepts, seek out other information sources.** If you find you can't understand a concept explained in your text, even after rereading and repeatedly reflecting on it, try the following strategies:

   Look at how another textbook explains it. Not all textbooks are created equally: some do a better job of explaining certain concepts than others. Check to see whether your library has other texts in the same subject as your course, or check your campus bookstore for textbooks in the same subject area as the course you're taking. A different text may be able to explain a hard-to-understand concept much better than the textbook you purchased for the course.

   Seek help from your instructor. If you read carefully and made every effort to understand a particular concept but still can't grasp it, most instructors should be willing to assist you. If your instructor is unavailable or unwilling, seek help from the professionals and peer tutors in the Learning Center or Academic Support Center on campus.

STUDY STRATEGIES FOR LEARNING DEEPLY AND REMEMBERING LONGER

The final step in the learning process is to save the information in your brain and bring it back to mind at the time you need it—e.g., test time. Described here is a

SQ3R: A Method for Improving Reading Comprehension and Retention

A popular reading strategy for organizing and remembering information is the SQ3R method. SQ3R is an acronym for five steps you can take to increase textbook reading comprehension and retention, particularly when reading highly technical or complex material. The following sequences of steps comprise this method:

1. Survey
2. Question
3. Read
4. Recite
5. Review

S = Survey: Get a preview and overview of what you're about to read.

1. Read the title to activate your thoughts about the subject and prepare your mind to receive information related to it.
2. Read the introduction, chapter objectives, and chapter summary to become familiar with the author's purpose, goals, and most important points.
3. Note the boldface headings and subheadings to get a sense of the chapter's organization before you begin to read. This creates a mental structure or framework for making sense of the information you're about to read.
4. Take note of any graphics, such as charts, maps, and diagrams; they provide valuable visual support and reinforcement for the material you're reading.
5. Pay special attention to reading aids (e.g., italics and boldface font) that you can use to identify, understand, and remember key concepts.

Q = Question: Stay active and curious.
As you read, use the boldface headings to formulate questions you think will be answered in that particular section. When your mind is actively searching for answers to questions, it becomes more engaged in the learning process. As you read, add any questions that you have about the reading.

R = Read: Find the answer to the questions you've created.
Read one section at a time, with your questions in mind, and search for answers to these questions. Also, keep an eye out for new questions that need to be asked.

R = Recite: Rehearse your answers.
After you complete reading each section, recall the questions you asked and see whether you can answer them from memory. If not, look at the questions again and practice your answers to them until you can recall them without looking. Don't move on to the next section until you're able to answer all questions in the section you've just completed.

R = Review: Look back and get a second view of the whole picture.
Once you've finished the chapter, review all the questions you've created for different parts or sections. See whether you can still answer them without looking. If not, go back and refresh your memory.

series of effective study strategies for acquiring knowledge, keeping that knowledge in your brain (memory storage), and accessing that information when you need it (memory retrieval).

The Importance of Undivided Attention

The human attention span has limited capacity; we have only so much of it available to us at any point in time, and we can give all or part of it to whatever task we're working on. If study time is spent engaging in other activities besides studying (e.g., listening to music, watching TV, or text-messaging friends), the attention available for studying is subtracted and divided among the other activities. In other words, studying doesn't receive your undivided attention.

Studies show that when people multitask they don't pay equal attention to all tasks at the same time. Instead, they divide their attention by shifting it back and forth between tasks (Howard, 2000) and their performance on the task that demands the most concentration or deepest thinking is what suffers the most (Crawford & Strapp, 1994). Furthermore, research shows that multitasking can increase boredom for the task that requires the most intense concentration. One study found that with even a low level of stimulation from another source of sensory input, such as a TV turned on a low volume in the next room, students were more likely to describe the mental task they were concentrating on as "boring" (Damrad-Frye & Laird, 1989).

REFLECTION ●————————————————

Rate yourself in terms of how frequently you use these reading strategies according to the following scale:

4 = always, 3 = sometimes, 2 = rarely, 1 = never

1. I read the chapter outlines and summaries before I start reading the chapter content.	4	3	2	1
2. I preview a chapter's boldface headings and subheadings before I begin to read the chapter.	4	3	2	1
3. I adjust my reading speed to the type of subject I am reading.	4	3	2	1
4. I look up the meaning of unfamiliar words and unknown terms that I come across before I continue reading.	4	3	2	1
5. I take written notes on information I read.	4	3	2	1
6. I use the visual aids included in my textbooks.	4	3	2	1
7. I finish my reading sessions with a review of important information that I noted or highlighted.	4	3	2	1

When performing complex mental tasks that cannot be done automatically or mindlessly, other tasks and sources of external stimulation interfere with the quiet internal reflection needed for permanent connections to form between brain cells—which is what must happen if deep, long-lasting learning is to take place (Jensen, 2000).

Making Meaningful Associations

Connecting what you're trying to learn to something you already know is a powerful memory-improvement strategy because knowledge is stored in the form of a connected network of brain cells (Coward, 1990; Chaney, 2007).

Studies show that doing challenging academic work while multitasking divides up attention and drives down comprehension and retention.

The brain's natural tendency to seek meaningful, connected patterns applies to words as well as images. This is illustrated in the following passage that once appeared anonymously on the Internet. See whether you can read it and grasp its meaning.

> Aoccdrnig to rscheearch at Cmabridge Uinverstisy, it deos't mattaer in what order the ltteers in a word are, the only iprmoetnt thing is that the frist and lsat ltteer be at the rghit pclae. The rset can be a total mses and you can still raed it wouthit a porbelm. This is bcusae the human mind deos not raed ervey lteter by istlef, but the word as a wlohe. Amzanig huh?

Notice how easily you found the meaning of the misspelled words by naturally transforming them into correctly spelled words—which you knew because the correctly spelled words were already stored in your brain. Thus, whenever you learn meaningfully, you do so by connecting what you're trying to understand to what you already know.

Learning by making meaningful connections is referred to as *deep learning* (Biggs & Tang, 2007; Entwistle & Ramsden, 1983). It involves moving beyond shallow memorization to deeper levels of understanding. This is a major a shift from the old view that learning occurs by passively absorbing information like a sponge—for example, by receiving it from the teacher or text and studying it in the same prepackaged form as you received it. Instead, you want to adopt an approach to learning that involves actively transforming the information you receive into a form that's meaningful to you (Feldman & Paulsen, 1994; Mayer, 2002). This transforms short-term, surface-level learning (memorization of information) into deep and meaningful long-term learning (acquisition of knowledge).

So, instead of immediately trying to learn something by repeatedly pounding it into your brain like a hammer, your first strategy should be to try hooking or hanging it onto something that's already stored in your brain—something you already know and is meaningful to you. It may take a little while and a little work to find the right hook, but once you've found it, you'll learn the information

"The extent to which we remember a new experience has more to do with how it relates to existing memories than with how many times or how recently we have experienced it."
—Morton Hunt, *The Universe Within: A New Science Explores the Human Mind*

faster and retain it longer. For instance, here's a meaningful way to learn and remember how to correctly spell one of the most frequently misspelled words in the English language: *separate* (not *seperate*). If you remember that *par* means "to divide," as in the words *part*s or *partition*, it makes sense that *separate* should be spelled *separate* because its meaning is "to divide into parts."

Each of the academic subjects that comprise the college curriculum has a specialized vocabulary that can sound like a foreign language to someone who has no experience with the subject area. Before you start to brutally beat these terms into your brain through sheer repetition, try to find some meaning in them. One way you can make a term more meaningful to you is by looking up its word root in the dictionary or by identifying its prefix or suffix, which may give away the term's meaning. For instance, suppose you're taking a biology course and studying the autonomic nervous system—the part of the nervous system that operates without your conscious awareness or voluntary control (e.g., your heart beating and lungs breathing). The meaning of the phrase is given away by the prefix *auto*, which means self-controlling, as in the word *automatic* (e.g., automatic transmission).

If looking up the term's root, prefix, or suffix doesn't give away its meaning, see if you can make it meaningful to you in some other way. For instance, suppose you looked up the root of the term *artery* and nothing about the origins of this term suggested its meaning or purpose. You could create your own meaning for this term by taking its first letter (a), and have it stand for "away"—to help you remember that arteries carry blood away from the heart. Thus, you've taken a biological term and made it personally meaningful (and memorable).

REFLECTION ●─────────────────────

Think of a key term or concept you're learning in a course this term that you could form a meaningful association to remember?

What is the information you're attempting to learn?

What is the meaningful association you could use to help you remember it?

Remember _____

If what you're learning is meaningful to you, you'll learn it more deeply and you'll remember it longer.

Compare and Contrast

When you're studying something new, get in the habit of asking yourself the following questions:

1. Is this idea similar or comparable to something that I've already learned? (Compare)

2. How does this idea differ from what I already know? (Contrast)

Research indicates that this simple strategy is one of the most powerful ways to promote learning of academic information (Marzano, Pickering, & Pollock, 2001). Asking yourself the question "How is this similar to and different from concepts that I already know?" makes learning more personally meaningful because you are relating what you're trying to learn to what you already know.

Integration and Organization

Integrate or connect ideas from your class notes and assigned readings that relate to the same major point by organizing them into the same category. For example, get these related ideas in the same place by recording then on the same index card under the same category heading. Index cards are a good tool for such purposes; you can use each card as a miniature file cabinet for different categories of information. The category heading on each card functions like the hub of a wheel, around which individual pieces of related information are attached like spokes. Integrating information related to the same topic in the same place and studying it at the same time divides the total material you're learning into identifiable and manageable parts. In contrast, when ideas pertaining to the same point or concept are spread all over the place, they're more likely to take that form in your mind—leaving them mentally disconnected and leaving you confused (as well as feeling stressed and overwhelmed).

Remember

Just as important as organizing course materials is organizing course concepts. Ask yourself the following questions: How can this specific concept be categorized or classified? How does this particular idea relate to or "fit into" something bigger?

Divide and Conquer

Effective learning depends not only on *how* you learn (your method), but on *when* you learn (your timing). Although cramming just before exams is better than not studying, it's far less effective than studying that's spread out across time. Rather than cramming all your studying into one long session, use the method of *distributed practice*: spread or distribute your study time over several shorter sessions. Research consistently shows that short, periodic practice sessions are more effective than a single marathon session.

Spreading out your studying into shorter sessions improves your memory by reducing loss of attention due to fatigue.

Distributing study time over several shorter sessions improves your learning and memory by:

- Reducing loss of attention due to fatigue or boredom; and

- Reducing mental interference by giving your brain some downtime to cool down and lock in information it has received before it's interrupted by the need to deal with additional information (Malmberg & Murnane, 2002; Murnane & Shiffrin, 1991).

If the brain's downtime is interfered with by the arrival of additional information, it gets overloaded and its capacity for handling information becomes impaired. This is what cramming does—it overloads the brain with lots of information in a limited period of time. In contrast, distributed study does just the opposite—it uses shorter sessions with downtime between sessions, thereby giving the brain the time and opportunity to retain the information that it has received and processed (studied).

Another major advantage of distributed study is that it's less stressful and more motivating than cramming. Shorter sessions provide you with an incentive to start studying because you know that you're not going to be doing it for a long stretch of time or lose any sleep over it. It's easier to maintain your interest and motivation for any task that's done for a shorter rather than a longer period. Furthermore, distributing studying makes exam preparation easier because you know that if you run into difficulty understanding anything, you'll still have plenty of time to get help with it before you're tested and graded on it.

The "Part-to-Whole" Study Method

The part-to-whole method of studying is a natural extension of the distributed practice just discussed. With the part-to-whole method, you break up the material you need to learn into smaller parts and study those parts in separate sessions in advance of the exam; then you use your last study session just before the exam to review (restudy) all the parts you previously studied in separate sessions. Thus, your last session is not a cram session or even a study session: it's a review session.

Research shows that students of all ability levels learn material in college courses more effectively when it's studied in small units and when progression to the next unit takes place only after the previous unit has been mastered or understood (Pascarella & Terenzini, 1991, 2005). This strategy has two advantages: (1) it reinforces your memory for what you previously learned and (2) it builds on what you already know to help you learn new material. These advantages are particularly important in cumulative subjects that require memory for problem-solving procedures or steps, such as math and science. When you repeatedly practice these procedures, they become more automatic and you're able to retrieve them quicker (e.g., on a timed test). This enables you to use them efficiently without having to expend a lot of mental effort and energy (Samuels & Flor, 1997), freeing your working memory for more important tasks—such as critical thinking and creative problem solving (Schneider & Chein, 2003).

REFLECTION ●——————————————

Are you more likely to study in advance of exams or cram just before exams?

Why?

———————————————————————————————

Don't buy into the myth that studying in advance is a waste of time because you'll forget it all by test time. As discussed in Chapter 4, this is a myth that procrastinators often use to rationalize their habit of putting off studying until the very last moment, which forces them to cram frantically the night before exams.

Do not underestimate the power of breaking material to be learned into smaller parts and studying those parts some time before a major exam. Even if you cannot recall what you previously studied, when you start reviewing it you'll find that you will relearn it much faster than when you studied it the first time. This proves that studying in advance is not a waste of time, because it takes less time to relearn the material, indicating that information studied in the earlier sessions was still retained in your brain (Kintsch, 1994).

Build Variety into the Study Process

You can increase your concentration and motivation by using the following strategies to infuse variety and a change of pace into your study routine.

Periodically vary the type of academic work you do while studying. Changing the nature of your work activities or the type of mental tasks you're performing while studying increases your level of alertness and concentration by reducing *habituation*—attention loss that occurs after repeated engagement in the same type of mental task (McGuiness & Pribram, 1980). To combat attention loss due to habituation, occasionally vary the type of study task you're performing. For instance, shift periodically among tasks that involve reading, writing, studying, and problem-solving skills (e.g., math or science problems).

Study different subjects in different places. Studying in different locations provides different environmental contexts for learning, which reduces the amount of interference that normally builds up when all information is studied in the same place (Rankin et al., 2009). In addition to spreading out your studying at different times, it's also a good idea to spread it out in different places. The great public speakers in ancient Greece and Rome used this method of changing places to remember long speeches by walking through different rooms while rehearsing their speech, learning each major part of their speech in a different room (Higbee, 1998).

Changing the nature of the learning task and place provides a change of pace that infuses variety into the learning process, which, in turn, stimulates your attention, concentration, and motivation. Although it's useful to have a set time and place to study for getting you into a regular work routine, this doesn't mean that learning occurs best by habitually performing all types of academic tasks in the same place. Instead, research suggests that you should periodically change the learning tasks you perform and the environment in which you perform them to maximize attention and minimize interference (Druckman & Bjork, 1991).

Remember _____

Changes of pace and place while studying can stimulate your attention to what you're studying as well as your interest in and motivation for studying.

Mix long study sessions with short study breaks that involve physical activity (e.g., a short jog or brisk walk). Study breaks that include physical activity not only refresh the mind by giving it a rest from studying, but also stimulate the mind by increasing blood flow to your brain, which will help you retain what you've already studied and regain concentration for what you'll study next.

FIGURE 2.9

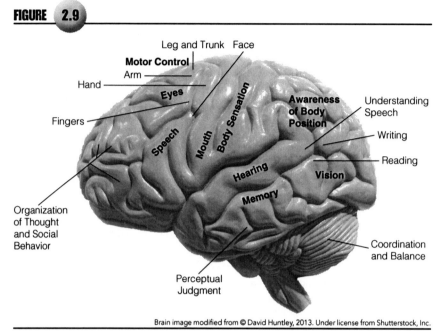

Brain image modified from © David Huntley, 2013. Under license from Shutterstock, Inc.

A Map of the Functions Performed by the Outer Surface of the Human Brain

Learn with all of your senses. When studying, try to use as many sensory channels as possible. Research shows that information perceived through multiple sensory modalities is remembered better because it creates multiple interconnections in long-term memory areas of the brain (Bjork, 1994; Shams & Seitz, 2011; Zull, 2002). When a memory is formed in the brain, different sensory aspects of it are stored in different areas. For example, when your brain receives visual, auditory (hearing), and motor (movement) input while learning, each of these forms of sensory input is stored as memory trace in a different part of the brain. **Figure 2.9** shows a map of the outer surface of the human brain; you can see how different parts of the brain are specialized to receive input from different sensory modalities. When you use all of these sensory modalities while learning, multiple memory traces of what you're studying are recorded in different parts of your brain, which leads to deeper learning and stronger memory for what you have learned (Education Commission of the States, 1996).

REFLECTION ●

Would you say that you're more of a visual learner or verbal learner?

How do you think most people would answer this question?

FIGURE 2.10

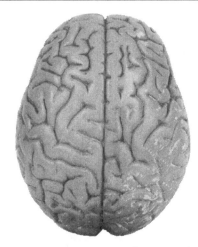

The human brain consists of the left hemisphere, which processes words, and the right hemisphere, which processes images.

© JupiterImages Corporation.

Learn visually. The human brain consists of two hemispheres (half spheres): the left and the right (see **Figure 2.10**). Each hemisphere of the brain specializes in a different type of learning. In most people, the left hemisphere specializes in verbal learning, dealing primarily with words. In contrast, the right hemisphere specializes in visual-spatial learning, dealing primarily with perceiving images and objects that occupy physical space. If you use both hemispheres while studying, you lay down two different memory traces in your brain: one in the left hemisphere where words are stored, and one in the right hemisphere where images are stored. This process of laying down a double memory trace (verbal and visual) is referred to as *dual coding* (Paivio, 1990). When this happens, memory for what you're learning is substantially strengthened, primarily because two memory traces are better than one.

To capitalize on the advantage of dual coding, be sure to use any visual aids that are available to you, including those provided in your textbook and by your instructor in class. You can also create your own visual aids by drawing pictures, symbols, and concept maps, such as flowcharts, Venn diagrams, spider webs, wheels with spokes, or branching tree diagrams. (For example, see **Figure 2.11** for a tree diagram that could be used to help you remember the parts and functions of the human nervous system.)

Remember _____

Drawing and other forms of visual illustration are not just artistic exercises: they can also be powerful learning tools—you can draw to learn! Drawing keeps you actively involved in the process of learning, and by representing what you're learning in visual form, you're able to dual-code the information you're studying, which doubles the number of memory traces recorded in your brain. As the old saying goes, "A picture is worth a thousand words."

FIGURE 2.11

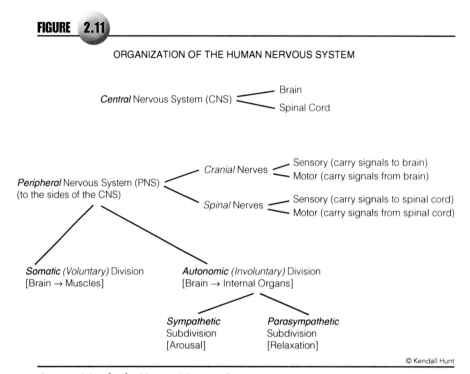

ORGANIZATION OF THE HUMAN NERVOUS SYSTEM

Central Nervous System (CNS) — Brain / Spinal Cord

Peripheral Nervous System (PNS)
(to the sides of the CNS)

Cranial Nerves — Sensory (carry signals to brain) / Motor (carry signals from brain)

Spinal Nerves — Sensory (carry signals to spinal cord) / Motor (carry signals from spinal cord)

Somatic (Voluntary) Division
[Brain → Muscles]

Autonomic (Involuntary) Division
[Brain → Internal Organs]

Sympathetic
Subdivision
[Arousal]

Parasympathetic
Subdivision
[Relaxation]

© Kendall Hunt

Concept Map for the Human Nervous System

REFLECTION ●

Think of a course you're taking this term in which you're learning related pieces of information that could be joined together to form a concept map. In the space that follows, make a rough sketch of this map that includes the information you need to remember.

Learn by moving or using motor learning (a.k.a. muscle memory). In addition to hearing and seeing, movement is a sensory channel. When you move, your brain receives kinesthetic stimulation—the sensations generated by your muscles. Research shows that memory traces for movement are commonly stored in an area of your brain that plays a major role for all types of learning (Middleton & Strick, 1994). Thus, associating movement with what you're learning can improve your ability to retain it because you add a muscle memory trace in the motor control area of your brain. (See Figure 2.9.)

Expert's Experience I was talking about memory in class one day and mentioned that when I temporarily forget how to spell a word, its correct spelling comes back to me once I start to write it. One of my students raised her hand and said the same thing happens to her when she forgets a phone number—it comes back to her when she starts dialing it. Both of these experiences illustrate how motor memory brings information back to mind that was temporarily forgotten, pointing to the power of movement for promoting learning and memory.

Joe Cuseo

You can use movement to help you learn and retain academic information by using your body to act out what you're studying or to symbolize it with your hands (Kagan & Kagan, 1998). For example, if you're trying to remember five points about something (e.g., five consequences of the Civil War), when you're studying these points, count them on your fingers as you try to recall each of them. Also, remember that talking involves muscle movement of your lips and tongue. Thus, by speaking aloud when you're studying, either to a friend or to yourself, you can improve your memory of what you're studying by adding kinesthetic stimulation to the auditory or sound stimulation your brain receives from hearing what you're saying.

Remember _____

Try to make the learning process a total body experience—hear it, see it, say it, and move it.

Student *Perspective*

"When I have to remember something, it's better for me to do something with my hands so I could physically see it happening."

—First-year college student

Learn with emotion. Information reaches the brain through your senses and is stored in the brain as a memory trace; the same is true of emotions. Numerous connections occur between brain cells in the emotional and memory centers (Zull, 1998). For instance, when you're experiencing emotional excitement about what you're learning, adrenaline is released and is carried through the bloodstream to the brain. Once adrenaline reaches the brain, it increases blood flow and glucose production, which stimulates learning and strengthens memory (LeDoux, 1998; Rosenfield, 1988). In fact, emotionally intense experiences can release such a substantial amount of adrenaline into the bloodstream that memories for them can be immediately stored in long-term memory and last an entire lifetime. For instance, most people remember exactly what they were doing at the time they experienced such emotionally intense events as the September 11 terrorist attack on the United States, their first kiss, or their favorite team winning a world championship.

What does this emotion-memory link have to do with helping you remember academic information while studying? Research indicates that emotional intensity, excitement, and enthusiasm strengthen memory of academic information just as they do for memory for life events and personal experiences. If you get psyched up about what you're learning, you have a much better chance of learning and remembering it. When you're passionate or intense about what you're learning and convince yourself that what you're learning is really important to know, you're more likely to remember it (Howard, 2000; Minninger, 1984). So, keep in mind the importance or significance of what you're learning. For instance, if you're learning about photosynthesis, remind yourself that you're not just learning about a chemical reaction, you're learning about the driving force that underlies all plant life on the planet! If you aren't aware of the importance or significance of a particular concept you're studying, ask your instructor or a student majoring in the field. Enthusiasm can be contagious; you may catch it and become more passionate about learning the concept.

Remember _____

You learn most effectively when you actively involve all your senses (including bodily movement) and when you learn with passion and enthusiasm. In other words, learning grows deeper and lasts longer when you put your whole self into it—your heart, your mind, and your body.

"We are born for cooperation, as are the feet, the hands, the eyelids, and the upper and lower jaws."

—Marcus Aurelius, Roman emperor

Learn by collaborating with others. Research indicates that college students who work regularly in small groups of four to six become more actively involved in the learning process and learn more (Light, 2001). To maximize the power of study groups, each member should study individually *before* studying in a group and should come prepared with specific information or answers to share with teammates, as well as questions or points of confusion that the team can attempt to help answer or clarify. (For specific team-learning strategies, see Chapter 1.)

Expert's Experience

When I was in my senior year of college, I had to take a theory course by independent study because the course would not be offered again until after I planned to graduate. Another senior found himself in the same situation. The instructor allowed both of us to take this course together and agreed to meet with us every two weeks. My classmate and I studied independently for the first two weeks.

I prepared for the biweekly meetings by reading thoroughly, yet I had little understanding of what I had read. After our first meeting, I left with a strong desire to drop the course but decided to stick with it. Over the next two weeks, I spent many sleepless nights trying to prepare for our next meeting and was feeling pretty low about not being the brightest student in my class of two. During the next meeting with the instructor, I noticed that the other student was also having difficulty, and so did the instructor. After that meeting, the instructor gave us study questions and asked us to read separately and then get together to discuss the questions. During the next two weeks, my classmate and I met several times to discuss what we were learning (or attempting to learn). By communicating with each other about the issues we were studying, we both ended up gaining greater understanding. Our instructor was delighted to see that he was able to suggest a collaborative learning strategy that worked for both of us.

Aaron Thompson

Self-Monitor Your Learning

Student *Perspective*

"I would suggest students get to know [each] other and get together in groups to study or at least review class material. I find it is easier to ask your friends or classmates with whom you are comfortable asking 'dumb' questions."

—Advice to first-year students from a college sophomore (Walsh, 2005)

Successful learners just don't put in study time; they reflect and check on themselves to see if they're putting in quality time and really understanding what they're attempting to learn. They monitor their comprehension as they go along by asking themselves questions such as "Am I following this?" "Do I really understand it?" and "Do I know it for sure?"

How do you know if you really know it? Probably the best answer to this question is "I find *meaning* in it—that is, I can relate to it personally or put it in terms that make sense to me" (Ramsden, 2003).

Following are some strategies for checking whether you truly understand what you're trying to learn. They help you answer the question "How do I know if I really know it?" These strategies can be used as indicators or checkpoints for determining whether you're just memorizing or learning at a deeper level.

Can you paraphrase (restate or translate) what you're learning into your own words? When you can paraphrase what you're learning, you're able to complete the following sentence: "In other words . . ." If you can complete that sentence in your own words, this is a good indication that you've moved beyond memorization to comprehension because you've transformed what you're learning into words that are meaningful to you. You know you know it if you're not stating it the same way your instructor or textbook stated it, but restating it in words that are your own.

Can you explain what you're learning to someone who is unfamiliar with it? Simply put, if you can't explain it to someone else, you probably don't really understand it yourself. If you can explain to a friend what you've learned, this is a good sign that you've moved beyond memorization to comprehension because you're able to translate it into language that's understandable to anyone. Studies show that students gain deeper levels of understanding for what they're learning when they're asked to explain it to someone else (Chi et al., 1994). Sometimes, we only become aware of how well we know or don't know something until we have to explain it to someone who's never heard it before (just ask any teacher). If you cannot find someone else to explain it to, then explain it aloud as if you were talking to an imaginary friend.

Can you think of an example of what you've learned? If you can come up with an instance or illustration of what you're learning that's your own—not one given by your instructor or textbook—this is a good sign that you truly understand it. It shows you're able to take a general, abstract concept and apply it to a specific real-life experience (Bligh, 2000). Furthermore, a personal example is a powerful memory tool. Studies show that when people retrieve a concept from memory, they first recall an example of it. The example then serves a memory-retrieval cue to trigger their memory of other details about the concept, such as its definition and relationship to other concepts (Norman, 1982; Okimoto & Norman, 2010; Park, 1984).

Can you represent or describe what you've learned in terms of an analogy or metaphor that compares it to something with similar meaning, or which works in a similar way? Analogies and metaphors are basically ways of learning something new by understanding it in terms of its similarity to something you already understand. For instance, the computer can be used as a metaphor for the human brain to get a better understanding of learning and memory as a three-stage process in which information is (1) inputted—perceived or received (through lectures and readings), (2) stored or saved—by studying, and (3) retrieved—recalled from storage at test time. If you can use an analogy or metaphor to represent what you're learning, you're grasping it at a deep level because you're building a mental bridge that connects it to what you already know (Cameron, 2003).

Can you apply what you're learning to solve a new problem that you haven't previously seen? The ability to use knowledge by applying it in a different situation is a good indicator of deep learning (Erickson & Strommer, 2005). Learning specialists refer to this mental process as *decontextualization*—taking what you learned in one context (situation) and applying it to another (Bransford, Brown, & Cocking, 1999). For instance, you know that you've learned a mathematical concept deeply when you can use that concept to solve math problems that are different from the ones used by your instructor

"When you know a thing, to recognize that you know it; and when you do not, to know that you do not know; that is knowledge."
—Confucius, influential Chinese thinker and educator

Student
Perspective

"Most things used to be external to me—of out a lecture or textbook. It makes learning a lot more interesting and memorable when you can bring your experiences into it. It makes you want to learn."
—Returning adult student

"You do not really understand something unless you can explain it to your grandmother."
—Albert Einstein, considered the "father of modern physics" and named "Person of the (20th) Century" by *Time Magazine*

Student
Perspective

"I learn best through teaching. When I learn something and teach it to someone else, I find that it really sticks with me a lot better."
—College sophomore

or your textbook. This is why your math instructors rarely include on exams the exact problems that they solved in class or were solved in your textbook. They're not trying to trick you at test time: they're trying to see whether you've learned the concept or principle deeply.

REFLECTION ⬤

Rate yourself in terms of how frequently you use these study strategies according to the following scale:

                    4 = always, 3 = sometimes, 2 = rarely, 1 = never

1. I block out all distracting sources of outside stimulation when I study.	4	3	2	1
2. I try to find meaning in technical terms by looking at their prefixes or suffixes or by looking up their word roots in the dictionary.	4	3	2	1
3. I compare and contrast what I'm currently studying with what I've already learned.	4	3	2	1
4. I organize the information I'm studying into categories or classes.	4	3	2	1
5. I integrate or pull together information from my class notes and readings that relates to the same concept or general category.	4	3	2	1
6. I distribute or spread out my study time over several short sessions in advance of the exam, and I use my last study session before the test to review the information I previously studied.	4	3	2	1
7. I participate in study groups with my classmates.	4	3	2	1

Information delivered during lectures is most likely to form questions and answers on college tests. Students who do not record information presented during lectures in their notes have a slim chance of recalling the information at test time. Thus, effective note taking is critical to successful academic performance in college.

Information from reading assignments is the next most common source of test questions on college exams. Professors often don't discuss information contained in assigned reading during class lectures. Thus, doing the assigned reading, and doing it in a way that's most effective for promoting comprehension and retention, plays an important role in your academic success.

The most effective strategies for promoting effective classroom listening, textbook reading, and studying are those that reflect three of the college success principles discussed in Chapter 1: (1) active involvement, (2) collaboration, and (3) self-awareness.

Active involvement is critical for learning from lectures (e.g., actively taking notes while listening to lectures) and learning from reading (e.g., actively taking notes while reading). While active involvement is necessary for learning because it engages your attention and enables information to enter the brain, personal reflection is also necessary for deep learning because it keeps that information in the brain by locking it into long-term memory. Reflection also encourages deep learning by promoting self-awareness. By periodically pausing to reflect on whether you're truly understanding what you're studying, you become a more self-aware learner and a more successful student.

Learning is also deepened when it's a multisensory experience—when you engage as many senses as possible in the learning process, particularly the sense of vision. Lastly, learning is strengthened when it's done collaboratively. You can collaborate with peers to take better notes in class, to identify what's most important in your assigned reading, and to study lecture and reading notes in preparation for course exams.

Summary and Conclusion

Research reviewed in this chapter points to the conclusion that successful students are:

1. **Involved.** They invest time and effort in the college experience;
2. **Resourceful.** They capitalize on their surrounding resources;
3. **Interactive**. They interact and collaborate with others; and
2. **Reflective.** They are self-aware learners who assess and monitor their own performance.

Successful students are students who could honestly check almost every box in the following self-assessment checklist of success-promoting principles and practices.

Learning More through the World Wide Web

Internet-Based Resources for Further Information on Liberal Arts Education

For additional information related to promoting your success in college, we recommend the following Web sites:

www.cgcc.cc.or.us/StudentServices/TipsCollegeSuccess.cfm

www.dartmouth.edu/~acskills/success/

www.studygs.net

Strategic Learning and Study Strategies:

www.Dartmouth.edu/~acskills/success/index.html

www.muskingum.edu/~cal/database/general/

Learning Math and Overcoming Math Anxiety:

www.mathacademy.com/pr/minitext/anxiety

www.onlinemathlearning.com/math-mnemonics.html

Works Cited

Bourdieu, P. "Cultural Reproduction and Social Reproduction." In *Knowledge, education and social change*, edited by R. Brown, 71–112. London: Tavistock, 1973.

Elmore, Tim. *IY Generation: Our Last Chance to Save Their Future.* Atlanta, Georgia: Poet Gardener Publishing, 2010.

London, H. B. "Breaking away: A study of first generation college students and their families." *American Journal of Education* 97(1989):144–170.

Pascarella, E. T. *How college affects students: A third decade of research.* San Francisco, CA: Jossey-Bass, 2006.

Purswell, K E, A. Yazedijan, and M. L. Toews. "Students' intentions and social support as predictors of self-reported academic behaviors: A Comparison of first generation and continuing generation college students." *Journal of College Student Retention* 10 (2008):191–206.

Shields, N. "Anticipatory socialization, adjustment to university life, and perceived stress." *Social Psychology of Education* 5 (2002):365–392.

Stanton-Salazar, R. D., and S. M. Dornbusch. "Social capital and the reproduction of inequality: Information networks among Mexican origin high school students." *Sociology of Education* 68 (1995):116–135.

Thayer, P. B. "Retaining first generation and low income students." *Opportunity Outlook.* May 2000. www.pellinstitute.org/downloads/trio_clearinghouse-Thayer_mayer00.pdf (accessed September 2013).

Tinto, V. *Leaving College:Rethinking the causes and cures of student attrition.* 2nd Edition. Chicago, IL: University of Chicago Press, 1993.

Strategic Learning and Studying Exercises

Self-Assessment of Note-Taking and Reading Habits

Look back at the ratings you gave yourself for effective note-taking (p. 118), reading (p. 124), and studying (p. 135) strategies. Add up your total score for these three sets of learning strategies (the maximum score for each set is 28):

Note Taking = _____
Reading = _____
Studying = _____
Total Learning Strategy Score = _____

Self-Assessment Questions

1. In which learning strategy area did you score lowest?
2. Do you think that the strategy area in which you scored lowest has anything to do with your lowest course grade at this point in the term?
3. Of the seven strategies listed within the area in which you scored lowest, which ones could you immediately put into practice to improve your lowest course grade this term?
4. What is the likelihood that you will put the preceding strategies into practice this term?

Consulting with a Learning Center or Academic Development Specialist

Make an appointment to visit your Learning Center or Academic Support Center on campus to discuss the results of your note-taking, reading, and studying self-assessment in Exercise 5.1 (or any other learning self-assessment you may have taken). Ask for recommendations about how you can improve your learning habits in your lowest-score area. After your visit, answer the following questions.

Learning Resource Center Reflection

1. Who did you meet with in the Learning Center? _____
2. Was your appointment useful (e.g., did you gain any insights or acquire any new learning or test-taking strategies)?
3. What steps were recommended to you for improving your academic performance?
4. How likely is it that you will take the steps mentioned in the previous question: (a) definitely, (b) probably, (c) possibly, or (d) unlikely? Why?
5. Do you plan to visit the Learning Center again? If yes, why? If no, why not?

Too Fast, Too Frustrating: A Note-Taking Nightmare

Susan Scribe is a first-year student who is majoring in journalism, and she's enrolled in an introductory course that is required for her major (Introduction to Mass Media). Her instructor for this course lectures at a rapid rate and uses vocabulary words that go right over her head. Since she cannot get all her instructor's words down on paper and cannot understand half the words she does manage to write down, she becomes frustrated and stops taking notes. She wants to do well in this course because it's the first course in her major, but she's afraid she will fail it because her class notes are so pitiful.

Reflection and Discussion Questions

1. Can you relate to this case personally, or do you know any students who are in the same boat as Susan?

2. What would you recommend that Susan do at this point?

3. Why did you make the preceding recommendation?

The Value and Purpose of Education for First-Generation Students

3

PURPOSE

The purpose of this chapter is to educate first-generation students about financial literacy and educational and personal financial capital. This chapter will introduce financial principles of fiscal responsibility as global citizens.

ACTIVATE YOUR THOUGHTS

When considering paying for college, why is it important for you to understand the principles of fiscal responsibility?

THE VALUE AND PURPOSE OF EDUCATION FOR FIRST-GENERATION STUDENTS

First-generation college students face a variety of unique challenges that too often make it difficult to complete their studies and receive their degrees. Higher education experts believe factors from unmet expectations to finances that first-generation students often must confront in college can be devastating. A major barrier for many first-generation college students is a lack of financial capital, which is exacerbated when grants, scholarships, and loans are increasingly scarce. It is important to note during the past forty-plus years, federal financial aid has undergone a dramatic policy shift (King 1996). The goal of expanding access to higher education is now jeopardized by a change in how support is being awarded (Hartle 1997), now that higher education is seen as a consumer product rather than a social good (Parsons 2000). The shift for college students has been the lack of grants and scholarships to obtaining more loans. Although loans have served as a viable source of financing for middle- and high-income students, because first-generation students usually come from families with poor credit and extensive debt, the current federal aid policy has reduced the financial options available. (Melvin and Stick 2001).

It is important to note these challenges have implications for loan default prevention, because students who leave college without a degree are at greater risk in the future of defaulting on their education loans. This can hinder your future employment by having a low credit score, unable to get housing (apartment, house, etc.), or purchase a vehicle. Today a credit report is part of the employment decision by the employer.

First-generation students have higher levels of expectation regarding financial and related services. This includes the amount of aid available, the timing of financial aid awards, and the helpfulness of financial aid counselors. Unfortunately, the level of expectation is not equal in relation to student support, tutoring, and accessibility to computer labs. These services are critical to the success of first-generation students and will be discussed in more detail in Chapter 4.

Financial challenges in the last six years globally and domestically have created a strain for everyone. State budgets have led to higher institutional fees and reduced financial access for low- and middle-income students. Today, a greater dependence on student loans means greater debt. This should not be a reason for you as a first-generation student to allow these factors to have a negative impact on access to higher education and persistence.

To cover costs, many first-generation students turn to off-campus employment and are more likely to be employed full-time while attending college. Remember a full load of classes and an off-campus job means less time spent on campus and fewer opportunities to feel connected to your school and friends. Research has shown higher retention rates among students who work on campus, because the students have more opportunities to build supportive relationships with members of the campus community (Carey 2005). This disconnection to the college campus, first-generation students are more likely to drop out of a four-year institution by their second year, and tend to have fewer credit hours after three years of college work (Pascarella and Terenzini 2005). Tseng (2004) found that students from backgrounds that emphasize family interdependence might be expected to fulfill obligations to the family without regard to college responsibilities, causing some first-generation students to question their priorities and eventually leave school.

All college students are required to understand the principles of fiscal responsibility as global citizens. Financial literacy has become a new language to first-generation students in higher education and can be intimidating to those who are unfamiliar to such language. The next pages will introduce economic principles to assist in your growth personally and professionally.

PAYING FOR COLLEGE

One of the challenges incoming college freshmen and their families face is how to pay for a college education. Ideally, families would start saving for the prospective student's secondary education at an early age, but that is often not the case. The cost of a secondary education is more than tuition costs, as it can also include room and board charges, campus service fees, books, and discretionary spending, etc. The mix of these charges and how they are billed varies by institution.

Many college preparation websites discuss that planning for college should begin as a freshman in high school. Taking AP and honors courses to prepare for college level work is important along with a challenging course load that meets college admission requirements. Few, however, discuss the financial planning and preparation that should also begin at that time. There is a common misconception for first-generation families that college costs are a "pay as you go" process. This is not the case.

College financial aide counselors are the best source of information regarding specific financial aide packages offered by that specific institution. Most college financial aid offices have checklists and other financial assistance information. The information explains the differences between loans, scholarships, work-study, and grants.

Families and students unfamiliar with college financing are often the targets for scams from private sources charging for help with securing scholarships and other college financing products. There are free financial aid workshops in most areas for you and your parents to get valuable information. Use the information from these workshops and from financial aid counselors to research and apply for scholarships, loans, and grants. These financial aid student guides explain the differences in financial assistance programs, benefits awarded for veterans and other groups, and the differences in loan types for student and parents. See figure Page 1 of 2 FAFSA worksheet (Federal Student Aid at a glance)

An article by Mudambi (2013) provides a list of words related to college financing that you will encounter as you matriculate.

Award Letter—This is an official document that is sent out by the university to each accepted student. The award letter usually provides the cost of attendance and any financial aid (both need and merit based aid) offered to students.

Cost of Attendance—This is the total amount the college estimates that a student needs to spend to attend the institution for one year. This figure may vary depending on state residency status, whether a student commutes from home or resides on campus, and/or a student's major. The cost of attendance usually includes tuition, fees, books and supplies, transportation, room and board, and personal expenses.

Debt Load—A debt load is a figure creditor's look at when you apply for a loan. The debt load is the total amount of debt one has accumulated. It is a dollar figure that represents your total financial situation when referring to your income in comparison to your debts.

Differential Packaging—Some colleges will provide more aid to students who have qualities that the institution particularly seeks. These qualities may include (but are not limited to) membership to an underrepresented community, academic strength, and/or demonstrated achievement in a sport.

Expected Family Contribution—The amount an institution determines a family can afford to pay according to the results of financial-aid formulas. Elements considered include family and student income and assets.

FAFSA—A federal form that legal, U.S. residents fill out that allows the government to estimate a student's need. Colleges can use this calculation to determine financial aid award packages.

FIGURE 3.1

Do You Need Money for College?

Federal Student Aid at a Glance 2013-14

WHAT is federal student aid?

Federal student aid comes from the federal government—specifically, the U.S. Department of Education. It's money that helps a student pay for higher education expenses (i.e., college, career school, or graduate school expenses).

Federal student aid covers such expenses as tuition and fees, room and board, books and supplies, and transportation. Aid also can help pay for a computer and for dependent care.

There are three main categories of federal student aid: grants, work-study, and loans. Check with your school to find out which programs your school participates in. Information about the federal student aid programs is on page 2 of this document.

WHO gets federal student aid?

Our most basic eligibility requirements are that you must

- demonstrate financial need (for most programs—to learn more, visit **StudentAid .gov/how-calculated**),
- be a U.S. citizen or an eligible noncitizen,
- have a valid Social Security number
- register (if you haven't already) with Selective Service, if you're a male between the ages of 18 and 25,
- maintain satisfactory academic progress in college or career school, and
- show you're qualified to obtain a college or career school education by
  - having a high school diploma or General Educational Development (GED) certificate or
  - completing a high school education in a homeschool setting approved under state law.

Find more details about eligibility criteria at **StudentAid.gov/eligibility.**

HOW do you apply for federal student aid?

1. Complete the *Free Application for Federal Student Aid* (FAFSA℠) at **www.fafsa.gov.**

If you need a paper FAFSA, you can get one from

- our website at **www.fafsa.gov**, where you can download a PDF, or
- our ED Pubs distribution center at **www .edpubs.gov** or toll-free at 1-877-433-7827.

For the 2013–14 award year, you can apply beginning Jan. 1, 2013, you have until June 30, 2014, to submit your FAFSA. But you need to apply as soon as you can! School and states often use FAFSA information to award nonfederal aid. Their deadlines are usually early in the year. You can find state deadlines at **www. fafsa.gov** or on the paper FAFSA. Check with the schools you're interested in for their deadlines.

2. **Review your *Student Aid Report* (SAR).** After you apply, you'll receive a *Student Aid Report*, or SAR. Your SAR contains the information reported on your FAFSA and usually includes your Expected Family Contribution (EFC). The EFC is an index number used to determine your eligibility for federal student aid. Review your SAR information and make any corrections or changes, if necessary. The school(s) you list on your FAFSA will get your SAR data electronically.

3. **Contact the school(s) you might attend.** Make sure the financial aid office at each school you're interested in has all the information needed to determine your eligibility. If you're eligible, each school's financial aid office will send you an award letter showing the amount and types of aid (from all sources) the school will offer you. You can compare award letters from the schools to which you applied and see what aid you can receive from each school.

HAVE QUESTIONS?

Contact or visit the following:

- StudentAid.gov
- a college financial aid office
- studentaid@ed.gov
- 1-800-4-FED-AID (1-800-433-3243) toll-free
- 1-800-730-8913 (toll-free TTY for the hearing impaired)

| Federal |
| **Student** |
| Aid |
| An OFFICE of the U.S. DEPARTMENT of EDUCATION PROUD SPONSOR of the AMERICAN MIND™ |

An Office of the U.S. Department of Education Proud Sponsor of the American Mind™

Federal Student Aid—Financial assistance that comes from the U.S. Department of Education. Federal student aid covers such expenses as tuition and fees, room and board, books and supplies, and transportation. Aid can also help pay for a computer and for dependent care. The three main categories of federal student aid are grants, work-study, and loans. For details about the federal student aid programs, including who qualifies, maximum amounts and loan interest rates, visit www.studentaid.ed.gov/funding.

Financial Aid—Financial assistance in the form of scholarships, grants, loans, and work-study. This aid can be either federal, state or both.

Financial Budget—A financial budget is a means to manage money. A monthly budget of income and expenses gives a snapshot of where the money is coming from and where it's going.

Gift Aid—Financial aid that does not have to be paid back. Scholarships and grants are two types of gift aids.

Grants—Financial aid that does not have to be paid back. Government agencies and universities may offer grants.

Loans—Financial aid that, if accepted, will have to be repaid. Interest is also paid in addition to the amount borrowed.

Master Promissory Note (MPN)—The MPN is a legal document; borrowers must sign before receiving a Direct Loan. By signing, the borrower promises to repay the loan, with interest, in specified installments. The MPN also includes any information about the grace period, deferment or cancellation provisions, and the borrower's rights and responsibilities with respect to the loan.

Merit-Based Aid—Financial aid that is offered based on a student's achievements.

Need—The difference between the cost of attendance and the expected family contribution. Universities are not obligated to meet a student's need. (A university may offer less money than a family is determined to need.)

Need-Based Financial Aid—Financial assistance offered based on students' financial need.

Scholarships—Financial aid that does not need to be repaid. Scholarships may be offered by the government, the college, and outside institutions.

Self-Help Aid—Financial aid that is offered in exchange for student employment.

Students must submit the FAFSA (Free Application for Federal Student Aid) form to be eligible for state and federal financial aid. It is important to submit this form as soon as possible after January 1, of your senior year of high school. And remember, you must reapply for financial aid as soon as possible after January 1, each year that you are in college by filling out a renewal FAFSA. One element of the *FAFSA* is the *EFC* (Expected Family Contribution). The Expected Family Contribution is a measure of your family's financial strength and is calculated according to a formula established by law. Your family's taxed and untaxed income, assets, and benefits (such as unemployment or Social

Security) are all considered in the formula. Also considered are your family size and the number of family members who will attend college during the year.

The information you report on your FAFSA or your *FAFSA4caster* is used to calculate your EFC. Schools use the EFC to determine your federal student aid eligibility and financial aid award.

As mentioned earlier, in addition to the cost of tuition, there could be the cost of room and meals, books, program fees, and incidental expenses.

Room and Board—Depending on the institution you select, there may be a room and board (meal plan) charge on your student bill. Many institutions now require freshmen to live on campus and purchase a meal plan in their first year. Meal plans are available to all students and come in many forms; from declining balance plans, to block meal plans, to a combination of "X" number of meals per week plus campus retail dollars.

Always review the housing (residence life) and food service websites at the institution, to see what is required, what options are offered, and how they are charged. They could be part of your financial aid package.

Textbooks—Some institutions include book rentals as a part of tuition and some do not. Textbooks at most institutions are a separate charge and can be obtained by purchasing a new or used book, renting the book, or renting a digital copy of the book. Some bookstores are operated by the institution and others through a private on-campus provider. Textbook and course pack materials for students in heavy science-based programs could run as much as $1,000 per semester. Most campus book stores offer buy-back services at the end of the semester for books purchased through them. Again, review the bookstore website at the institutions you are interested in attending to see what is required, what options are offered, and how they are charged. They could be part of the financial aid package.

Some institutions or student organizations within the institution charge fees to participate in intramural athletic activities, fraternity/sorority memberships, or student life programs. List the groups or social activities you are interested in pursuing and check their websites for fees they may charge.

There could also be a charge for health insurance if you are not covered under your family's plan. Ask your financial aid advisor if this is included in your financial aid package. Also think about incidental expenses and personal financial needs. Think about how much money you will need for snacks, a movie off-campus, personal hygiene items, eating off-campus, transportation costs, etc. Avoid piling up high credit card debt by planning for these expenses in advance and budgeting for them. Many institutions provide a campus cash, debit card, or bonus bucks program, so that families and students can add money for on-campus incidental spending needs.

One way to pay for some incidental expenses and/or cover room and board charges is to have student employment on-campus (self-help aid). Most institutions have student labor and federal work-study eligible positions. Student labor positions are usually set up for less than twenty hours per week at a minimum wage rate of pay to perform a variety of administrative support functions such as manning help desks, filing, making copies, and some data entry tasks, etc. Federal Work-Study eligible positions perform similar tasks, for a similar number of hours per week, and at a similar rate of pay. The salary, however, is partially subsidized by the U.S. Department of Education. Eligibility for Federal Work Study is based on financial need as determined from the submission of the FAFSA. Internships and off-campus positions are also options but are usually not recommended for freshmen students. Check with the Career Development Center at the institution you are interested in attending for more information on employment opportunities.

Residential Assistant (RA) positions often offer a room and at least a partial meal plan for second semester freshman and above. Each institution has its specific policies and procedures for becoming an RA. Check with the institution you are interested in attending for more information.

Often, student's parents do not share their knowledge of financing, or include their children in financial decision-making as part of the college search process. College financial aid offices can address this through family financial aid counseling. The creation of a family/student cash flow statement that includes student loans and a budget that accounts for debt load, even though they are spread out over four academic years or more, are important tools for a student's financial success. (Berry College Kendall Hunt Publication, Your College Journey Cash Flow Statement)

Most students and/or their parents borrow money so that the student can attend college. It is important that college financial aid offices provide counseling to students and their families so that they recognize the depth of this commitment. This counseling should go beyond basic entrance counseling that is required by federal regulation. Financial aid counselors should meet with students and parents in person during orientation every fall, at which time the student signs the Master Promissory Note (MPN), which lays out the details of their borrowing (Bahls 2011).

If there is a balance due after you have exhausted federal, state and local scholarship, grant and work-study options, consideration must be given to signing a MPN for a student and/or parent federal loan. There are several loan types available for students and the parents of a dependent undergraduate student. The financial aid office at the institution you are interested in attending can provide information on the qualifications and the type of loan that is best for you.

Why take out a federal student loan instead of charging expenses to a credit card or getting a loan from a local bank? Federal student loans offer low fixed interest rates; income based repayment plans; loan forgiveness; and deferment (postpone of repayment) options, including deferment of loan payment when a student returns to school. Generally, repayment of a federal loan does not begin until after the student leaves school. A student receiving a federal loan does not need a credit history or cosigner. Private loans from banks often do not offer such benefits.

The U.S. Department of Education offers low-***interest*** loans to eligible students to help cover the cost of college or career school. What's the difference between Direct Subsidized Loans and Direct Unsubsidized Loans? In short, Direct Subsidized Loans have slightly better terms to help out students with ***financial need.***

Here's a quick overview of Direct Subsidized Loans:

- Direct Subsidized Loans are available to undergraduate students with financial need.
- Your school determines the amount you can borrow, and the amount may not exceed your financial need.
- The U.S. Department of Education pays the interest on a Direct Subsidized Loan while you're in school at least half-time, for the first six months after you leave school (referred to as a *grace period**), and during a period of *deferment* (a postponement of loan payments).

*Note: If you choose not to pay the interest that accrues during your grace period, the interest will be added to your *principal* balance.

Here's a quick overview of Direct Unsubsidized Loans:

- Direct Unsubsidized Loans are available to undergraduate and graduate students; there is no requirement to demonstrate financial need.
- Your school determines the amount you can borrow based on your cost of attendance and other financial aid you receive.
- You are responsible for paying the interest on a Direct Unsubsidized Loan during all periods.
- If you choose not to pay the interest while you are in school and during grace periods and deferment or *forbearance* periods, your interest will accrue (accumulate) and be capitalized (that is, your interest will be added to the principal amount of your loan).
- U.S. Department of Education worksheet (Page 2 of 2)

Interest rates can vary on the type of loan secured, the source of the loan, the length of the loan and the amount of the loan. The riskier the loan, the more interest charged. It can be confusing at times when confronted with all of the financial jargon associated with taking out a loan, particularly when all you really want to know is exactly how much it is going to cost you on a monthly basis.

Having said that, there is much to be gained from having a basic understanding about interest rates, the different types of interest rates that are available, and how interest rates are calculated BEFORE you enter into any loan arrangement. The more you know about interest rate formulas the better you'll be positioned to make a more informed judgment when it comes to taking out a loan and, in doing so, ensure that you keep as much of your money in your pocket as possible.

What Is "Interest"?

In its simplest form, 'interest" is the cost of borrowing money, and it is normally expressed in terms of a percentage of the overall loan. Not only will you have to pay back the original amount of money borrowed (the principal), but you'll also have to pay back the cost of borrowing that money (the interest, plus any setting up fees etc.) How much interest you have to pay on any given loan is subject to a number of different criteria, depending on whom you borrow the money from and the terms of the loan.

FIGURE 3.2

Federal Student Aid Programs 2013–14

Program	Type of Aid	Program Details	Annual Amount
Federal Pell Grant	Grant: does not have to be repaid	Available almost exclusively to undergraduates	2012–13: up to $5,550 (2013–14 amount not determined as of this document's publication date) Total amount may not exceed the equivalent of six years of Pell Grant funding
Federal Supplemental Educational Opportunity Grant (FSEOG)	Grant: does not have to be repaid	For undergraduates with exceptional financial need; Federal Pell Grant recipients take priority; funds depend on availability at school	$100–$4,000
Teacher Education Assistance for College and Higher Education (TEACH) Grant	Grant: does not have to be repaid unless student fails to carry out service obligation, in which case student must repay TEACH Grant as Direct Unsubsidized Loan with interest accrued (accumulated) from date grant was disbursed (paid out to student)	For undergraduate, postbaccalaureate, and graduate students who are or will be taking course work necessary to become elementary or secondary teachers; recipient must sign Agreement to Serve saying he or she will teach full-time in designated teacher shortage area for four complete years (within eight years of completing academic program) at elementary or secondary school serving children from low-income families	Up to $4,000 a year; total amount may not exceed $16,000 Graduate student: Total amount may not exceed $8,000
Iraq and Afghanistan Service Grant	Grant: does not have to be repaid	For students who are not Pell-eligible due only to having less financial need than is required to receive Pell funds; whose parent or guardian died as a result of military service in Iraq or Afghanistan after the events of 9/11; and who, at the time of the parent's or guardian's death, were less than 24 years old or were enrolled at least part-time at an institution of higher education	Maximum is same as Pell Grant maximum; payment adjusted for less-than-full-time study Total amount may not exceed the equivalent of six years of Iraq and Afghanistan Service Grant funding

(continued)

Federal Work-Study	Money earned while attending school; does not have to be repaid	For undergraduate and graduate students; jobs can be on campus or off campus; students are paid at least federal minimum wage	No annual minimum or maximum amounts
Federal Perkins Loan	Loan: must be repaid with interest	For undergraduate and graduate students; must be repaid to school that made the loan; 5% rate	Undergraduate students: up to $5,500; graduate and professional students: up to $8,000 Total amount may not exceed $27,500 for undergraduates and $60,000 for graduate students (including amounts borrowed as an undergraduate)
Direct Subsidized Loan	Loan: must be repaid with interest	For undergraduate students; U.S. Department of Education pays interest while borrower is in school and during grace and deferment periods (if you receive a Direct Subsidized Loan that is first disbursed between July 1, 2012, and July 1, 2014, you will be responsible for paying any interest that accrues during your grace period); student must be at least half-time and have financial need; 6.8% rate	$3,500–$5,500, depending on grade level For total lifetime limit, see **StudentAid.gov/sub-unsub**
Direct Unsubsidized Loan	Loan: must be repaid with interest	For undergraduate and graduate students; borrower is responsible for all interest; student must be at least half-time; financial need is not required; 6.8% rate	$5,500–$20,500 (less any subsidized amounts received for same period), depending on grade level and dependency status For total lifetime limit, see **StudentAid.gov/sub-unsub**
Direct PLUS Loan	Loan: must be repaid with interest	For parents of dependent undergraduate students and for graduate or professional students; student must be enrolled at least half-time; financial need is not required Borrower is responsible for all interest; 7.9% rate	Maximum amount is cost of attendance minus any other financial aid student receives; no minimum amount

Note: The information in this document was compiled in summer 2012. For updates or additional Information, visit **StudentAid.gov.**

Fixed Rate Interest

Fixed rate interest is simply as the name suggests: a "fixed" percentage of the loan must be paid back during the life of the loan. For example (using dollars as our currency), a $1,000 loan with a fixed rate of interest of 5% per annum, means that if the loan amount were to be paid off in 12 months, the total amount the borrower would pay back would be $1,050. Fixed rate interest loans make it very easy to calculate the exact amount of money the borrower will have to pay back each month, as the amount never changes. Simply put, the borrower can add up the amount to be borrowed, the interest amount, and any set up fees and other charges, and then divide that amount by the number of payments to be made (the life of the loan) and he/she will be left with the monthly payments that need to be made.

Variable Rate Interest

Variable rate interest loans allow the lender to set the interest rate to whatever market conditions demand at any given time during the life of the loan. The attraction of variable interest rate loans is that you can benefit from any future drop in market interest rates, as you monthly repayments will be reduced to reflect the market changes. However, the opposite also holds true, that if the market decides it's time for interest rates to rise, so too will your repayments. Mortgage loans, for example, are mostly set up with a variable interest rate, as it is virtually impossible to predict market conditions years ahead. In many cases you can opt for a fixed rate for a few years, and then the loan transfers on to a variable rate, but these deals vary from lender to lender. Make sure you fully understand the consequences of a variable interest rate loan if you are considering taking one out. If interest rates rise dramatically, you could find yourself in financial difficulties.

APR

APR, or "Annual Percentage Rate" is the percentage of interest payable on the loan based on a yearly term. In many countries, financial lenders must disclose the APR so that consumers have the chance to measure all lenders against a common metric. For example, many credit card companies declare their interest rates in terms of a monthly interest rate, say 2%. The actual APR in this instance is 24% (12 months $\times$ 2% = 24%), which doesn't sound so attractive. APR gives borrowers the chance to determine what the actual overall cost of the loan will be, but keep in mind that there may be additional "set up" or "administration" fees that are not included in the APR calculation. Particularly for smaller loans over shorter time periods, these extra fees can make a big impact.

Students should avoid taking out loans for living and unnecessary incidental expenses as it adds to their debt load and can influence future borrowing after graduation. Your debt load can be calculated by taking your gross take home pay and dividing it by your debts. Lenders won't tell you exactly what a good debt load is permissible for any of their loan products but usually anything ranging from 0%–40% should be considered average.

There is a difference between good debt and bad debt (Roberts 2008). Not all debts are considered bad. Some debts can actually improve your credit score and your worthiness as a borrower.

Good Debt—A debt that appreciates in value as time passes is a good debt. In fact, a mortgage loan is considered as a very good debt. As you know, the price of a home property usually increases over time which means the amount of loan you used to purchase your property is so much less than what it would cost after 10 years or more. This is why many people who have the resources choose to buy home properties as an investment.

A student loan can also be called a good debt. Why? Because you're using the money you loan to earn a degree. When you graduate from college, you'll obviously be earning so much more than the amount you used to obtain your student loan.

Bad Debt—Acquiring debts because you need the money for purchasing consumable things can be considered bad debt. For example, obtaining too many credit cards is not a very healthy habit. Using your credit card to spend on things that do not appreciate in value, is a big mistake especially if your credit card has a high interest rate. There have been so many people all over the world who got stuck in debt because they were unable to control their spending using their credit cards. Because credit cards are so easy to use, it is also too easy to splurge and use it in unnecessary expenses.

Another example of bad debt is a vacation loan. Some people tend to spend more than what they can afford on vacation trips because they were able to get a vacation loan. Although, it's a good idea to take a break from time to time, it would be better if you can set aside savings from your own money that you'll be spending for a vacation.

Bad Debt Management—Take a close look at your current financial status. You may have incurred both good and bad debts. If so, then you should prioritize paying off your bad debts first since they do not increase in value. However, this does not mean that you can take on as much debt as you like as long as it's a good debt. It is very important to consider things ten times before acquiring any type of debt. Even if you think it's a good investment, it is not practical to take on new debts, if you know that you don't have the means to pay for it.

Ultimately, whether it's a good debt or a bad debt, you are accountable for it. The best thing you can do as a borrower is to be constantly aware of how much you owe and what you can pay. Be responsible enough to pay back what you owe on time.

College students are target marketed by banks and credit card companies to apply for their credit and debit cards. So what is the difference between a credit card and a debit card (Caldwell 2013)? Debit cards and credit cards are accepted at the same places. Debit cards all carry the symbol of one of the major types of credit cards on them, and can be used anywhere that credit cards are accepted. They both offer convenience. The fundamental difference between a debit card and a credit card account is where the cards pull the money. A debit card takes it from your banking account and a credit card charges it to your line of credit.

Debit cards offer the convenience of a credit but work in a different way. Debit cards draw money directly from your checking account when you make the purchase. They do this by placing a hold on the amount of the purchase. Then the merchant sends in the transaction to their bank and it is transferred to the merchants account. It can take a few days for this to happen, and the hold may drop off before the transaction goes through. For this reason it is important to keep a running balance of your checking account to make sure you do not accidentally overdraw your account. It is possible to do that with a debit card.

A credit card is a card that allows you to borrow money in small amounts at local merchants. You use the card to make your basic transactions. The credit card company then charges you interest on your purchases, though there is generally a grace period of approximately thirty days before interest is charged if you do not carry your balance over from month to month.

In the past many people felt that you needed a credit card to complete certain transactions such as rent a car or to purchase items online. They also felt that it was safer and easier to travel with a credit card rather than carrying cash or trying to use your checkbook. However debit cards offer the same convenience without making you borrow the money to complete the transactions.

The knowledge of financial terms and questions to ask will now assist you in planning, consulting with financial aid couselors and paying attention to deadlines.

VETERANS EDUCATION AND TRAINING BENEFITS

Many first-generation students have served their country and returning to college campuses across the United States to attend college. We are so grateful for their bravely and selfless dedication in serving in the Armed Forces.

Reintegrating into society can be very difficult, and knowing where to begin on campus can also be challenging. Today campuses and universities have the Office of Veteran Services to assist in every resource available to you at the federal, state, and local level.

The following information from the Federal Benefits for Veterans, Dependents and Survivors, 2012 Edition, U.S. Department of Veterans Affairs, provides education and training opportunities along with financial assistance. The goal is to empower and assist you with gaining access to the benefits you deserve and have earned.

Post–9/11 GI Bill

Eligibility: The Post-9/11 GI Bill is an education benefit program for Servicemembers and Veterans who served on active duty after Sept. 10, 2001. Benefits are payable for training pursued on or after Aug. 1, 2009. No payments can be made under this program for training pursued before that date.

To be eligible, the Servicemember or Veteran must serve at least 90 aggregate days on active duty after Sept. 10, 2001, and remain on active duty or be honorably discharged. Active duty includes active service performed by National Guard members under title 32 U.S.C. for the purposes of organizing, administering, recruiting, instructing, or training the National Guard; or under section 502(f) for the purpose of responding to a national emergency.

Veterans may also be eligible if they were honorably discharged from active duty for a service-connected disability after serving 30 continuous days after Sept. 10, 2001. Generally, Servicemembers or Veterans may receive up to 36 months of entitlement under the Post-9/11 GI Bill.

Eligibility for benefits expires 15 years from the last period of active duty of at least 90 consecutive days. If released for a service-connected disability after at least 30 days of continuous service, eligibility ends 15 years from when the member is released for the service-connected disability.

If, on Aug.1, 2009, the Servicemember or Veteran is eligible for the Montgomery GI Bill; the Montgomery GI Bill – Selected Reserve; or the Reserve Educational Assistance Program, and qualifies for the Post-9/11 GI Bill, an irrevocable election must be made to receive benefits under the Post-9/11 GI Bill.

In most instances, once the election to receive benefits under the Post-9/11 GI Bill is made, the individual will no longer be eligible to receive benefits under the relinquished program.

Based on the length of active duty service, eligible participants are entitled to receive a percentage of the following:

1. Cost of in-state tuition and fees at public institutions and for the 2011-2012 academic year, up to $17,500 towards tuition and fee costs at private and foreign institutions (paid directly to the school);

2. Monthly housing allowance equal to the basic allowance for housing payable to a military E-5 with dependents, in the same zip code as the primary school (paid directly to the Servicemember, Veteran, or eligible dependents);

3. Yearly books and supplies stipend of up to $1,000 per year (paid directly to the Servicemember, Veteran, or eligible dependents); and

4. A one-time payment of $500 paid to certain individuals relocating from highly rural areas.

* The housing allowance is not payable to individuals pursuing training at half time or leas.

Approved training under the Post-9/11 GI Bill includes graduate and undergraduate degrees, vocational/technical training, on-the-job training, flight training, correspondence training, licensing and national testing programs, and tutorial assistance.

Individuals serving an aggregate period of active duty after Sept. 10, 2001 can receive the following percentages based on length of service:

Active Duty Service	Maximum Benefit
At least 36 months	100%
At least 30 continuous days and discharged due to service-connected disability	100%

At least 30 months < 36 months (1)	90%
At least 24 months < 30 months (1)	80% (3)
At least 18 months < 24 months (2)	70%
At least 12 months < 18 months (2)	60%
At least 6 months < 12 months (2)	50%
At least 90 days < 6 months (2)	40%

(1) Includes service on active duty in entry level and skill training. (2) Excludes service on active duty in entry level and skill training. (3) If the individual would only qualify at the 70% level when service on active duty in entry level and skill training is excluded, then VA can only pay at the 70% level.

Transfer of Entitlement (TOE): DOD may offer members of the Armed Forces on or after Aug. 1, 2009, the opportunity to transfer benefits to a spouse or dependent children. DOD and the military services must approve all requests for this benefit. Members of the Armed Forces approved for the TOE may only transfer any unused portion of their Post-9/11 GI Bill benefits while a member of the Armed Forces, subject to their period of eligibility.

The Yellow Ribbon G.I. Education Enhancement Program was enacted to potentially assist eligible individuals with payment of their tuition and fees in instances where costs exceed the in-state tuition charges at a public institution or the national maximum payable at private and foreign institutions. To be eligible, the student must be: a Veteran receiving benefits at the 100% benefit rate payable, a transfer-of-entitlement-eligible dependent child, or a transfer-of-entitlement eligible spouse of a Veteran.

The school of attendance must have accepted VA's invitation to participate in the program, state how much student tuition will be waived (up to 50%) and how many participants will be accepted into the program during the current academic year. VA will match the school's percentage (up to 50%) to reduce or eliminate out-of-pocket costs for eligible participants.

Marine Gunnery Sergeant John David Fry Scholarship: This scholarship entities children of those who die in the line of duty on or after Sept. 11, 2001, to use Post-9/11 GI Bill benefits.

Eligible children:

- are entitled to 36 months of benefits at the 100% level
- have 15 years to use the benefit beginning on their 18th birthday.
- may use the benefit until their 33rd birthday
- are not eligible for the Yellow Ribbon Program

Restoring GI Bill Fairness Act of 2011

The Restoring GI Bill Fairness Act of 2011 amended the Post-9/11 GI Bill. The provisions of the bill are applicable to training pursued under the Post-9/11 GI Bill that began on or after Aug. 1, 2011.

The legislation authorizes VA to pay more than the national maximum set for private schools (currently $17,500 or the appropriately reduced amount based on eligibility percentage) in tuition and fees under the Post-9/11 GI Bill for certain students attending private colleges and universities in seven states - Arizona, Michigan, New Hampshire, New York, Pennsylvania, South Carolina and Texas.

To qualify for the increased payment (also referred to as the "grand-fathered" tuition and fee amount), students must have been enrolled in the same college or university since Jan. 4, 2011, and have been enrolled in a program for which the combined amount of tuition and fees for full-time attendance during the 2010-2011 academic year exceeded $17,500.

VOW to Hire Heroes Act of 2011

Included in this new law is the Veterans Retraining Assistance Program (VRAP) for unemployed Veterans, VA and the Department of Labor (DoL) are working together to roll put this new program on July 1, 2012. The program will provide retraining for Veterans hardest hit by current economic conditions.

VRAP offers 12 months of training assistance to unemployed Veterans. To qualify, a Veteran must:

- Be at least 35, but no more than 60 years old
- Be unemployed (as determined by DoL)
- Have an other than dishonorable discharge
- Not be eligible for any other VA education benefit program (e.g., the Post-9/11 GI Bill, Montgomery GI Bill, Vocational Rehabilitation and Employment assistance)
- Not be in receipt of VA compensation due to unemployability
- Not be enrolled in a federal or state job-training program

The program is limited to 45,000 participants during fiscal year 2012, and to 54,000 participants from Oct. 1, 2012, through March 31, 2014. Participants may receive up to 12 months of assistance at the full-time payment rate under the Montgomery GI Bill–Active Duty program (currently $1,473 per month). Applications will be submitted through DoL and benefits paid by VA. DoL will provide employment assistance to every Veteran who participates upon completion of their program.

Participants must be enrolled in a VA-approved program of education offered by a community college or technical school. The program must lead to an associate degree, non-college degree, or a certification, and train the Veteran for a high-demand occupation.

More details will be available at www.gibill.va.gov and on VA's Face-book, which are updated regularly.

Educational and Vocational Counseling Services: Refer to Chapter 10, "Transition Assistance," for detailed information on available services.

Montgomery GI Bill

Eligibility: VA educational benefits may be used while the Service-member is on active duty or after the Servicemember's separation from active duty with a fully honorable military discharge. Discharges "under honorable conditions" and "general" discharges do not establish eligibility.

Eligibility generally expires 10 years after the Servicemember's discharge. However, there are exceptions for disability, re-entering active duty, and upgraded discharges.

All participants must have a high school diploma, equivalency certificate, or have completed 12 hours toward a college degree before applying for benefits.

Previously, Servicemembers had to meet the high school requirement before they completed their initial active duty obligation. Those who did not may now meet the requirement and reapply for benefits. If eligible, they must use their benefits within 10 years from the date of last discharge from active duty.

Additionally, every Veteran must establish eligibility under one of four categories.

Category 1: Service after June 30, 1985.

For Veterans who entered active duty for the first time after June 30, 1985, did not decline MGIB in writing, and had their military pay reduced by $100 a month for 12 months. Servicemembers can apply after completing two continuous years of service. Veterans must have completed three continuous years of active duty, or two continuous years of active duty if they first signed up for less than three years or have an obligation to serve four years in the Selected Reserve (the 2×4 program) and enter the Selected Reserve within one year of discharge.

Servicemembers or Veterans who received a commission as a result of graduation from a service academy or completion of an ROTC scholarship are not eligible under Category 1 unless they received their commission:

1. After becoming eligible for MGIB benefits (including completing the minimum service requirements for the initial period of active duty); or

2. After Sept. 30, 1996, and received less than $3,400 during any one year under ROTC scholarship.

Servicemembers or Veterans who declined MGIB because they received repayment from the military for education loans are also ineligible under Category 1. If they did not decline MGIB and received loan repayments, the months served to repay the loans will be deducted from their entitlement.

Early Separation from Military Service: Servicemembers who did not complete the required period of military service may be eligible under.

Category 1: If discharged for one of the following:

1. Convenience of the government—with 30 continuous months of service for an obligation of three or more years, or 20 continuous months of service for an obligation of less than three years

2. Service-connected disability

3. Hardship

4. A medical condition diagnosed prior to joining the military

5. A condition that interfered with performance of duty and did not result from misconduct

6. A reduction in force (in most cases)

7. Sole Survivorship (if discharged after 9/11/01)

Category 2: Vietnam Era GI Bill Conversion

For Veterans who had remaining entitlement under the Vietnam Era GI Bill on Dec. 31, 1989, and served on active duty for any number of days during the period Oct. 19, 1984, to June 30, 1985, for at least three continuous years beginning on July 1, 1985; or at least two continuous years of active duty beginning on July 1, 1985, followed by four years in the Selected Reserve beginning within one year of release from active duty.

Veterans not on active duty on Oct. 19, 1984, may be eligible under Category 2 if they served three continuous years on active duty beginning on or after July 1, 1985, or two continuous years of active duty at any time followed by four continuous years in the Selected Reserve beginning within one year of release from active duty.

Veterans are barred from eligibility under Category 2 if they received a commission after Dec. 31, 1976, as a result of graduation from a service academy or completion of an ROTC scholarship.

However, such a commission is not disqualifying if they received the commission after becoming eligible for MGIB benefits, or received the commission after Sept. 30, 1996, and received less than $3,400 during any one year under ROTC scholarship.

Category 3: Involuntary Separation/Special Separation

For Veterans who meet one of the following requirements:

1. Elected MGIB before being involuntarily separated; or

2. were voluntarily separated under the Voluntary Separation Incentive or the Special Separation Benefit program, elected MGIB benefits before being separated, and had military pay reduced by $1,200 before discharge.

Category 4: Veterans Educational Assistance Program

For Veterans who participated in the Veterans Educational Assistance Program (VEAP) and:

1. Served on active duty on Oct. 9, 1996.

2. Participated in VEAP and contributed money to an account.

3. Elected MGIB by Oct. 9, 1997, and paid $1,200.

Veterans who participated in VEAP on or before Oct. 9, 1996, may also be eligible even if they did not deposit money in a VEAP account if they served on active duty from Oct. 9, 1996, through April 1, 2000, elected MGIB by Oct. 31, 2001, and contributed $2,700 to MGIB.

Certain National Guard servicemembers may also qualify under Category 4 if they:

1. Served for the first time on full-time active duty in the National Guard between June 30, 1985, and Nov. 29, 1989, and had no previous active duty service.

2. Elected MGIB during the nine-month window ending on July 9, 1997; and

3. Paid $1,200.

Payments: Effective Oct. 1, 2011, the rate for full-time training in college, technical or vocational school is $1,473 a month for those who served three years or more or two years plus four years in the Selected Reserve. For those who served less than three years, the monthly rate is $1,196.

Benefits are reduced for part-time training. Payments for other types of training follow different rules. VA will pay an additional amount, called a "kicker" or "college fund," if directed by DOD. Visit www.gibill.va.gov for more information. The maximum number of months Veterans can receive payments is 36 months at the full-time rate or the part-time equivalent.

The following groups qualify for the maximum: Veterans who served the required length of active duty, Veterans with an obligation of three years or more who were separated early for the convenience of the government and served 30 continuous months, and Veterans with an obligation of less than three years who were separated early for the convenience of the government and served 20 continuous months.

Types of Training Available:

1. Courses at colleges and universities leading to associate, bachelor or graduate degrees, including accredited independent study offered through distance education.

2. Courses leading to a certificate or diploma from business, technical or vocational schools.

3. Apprenticeship or on-the-job training for those not on active duty, including self-employment training begun on or after June 16, 2004, for ownership or operation of a franchise.

4. Correspondence courses, under certain conditions.

5. Flight training, if the Veteran holds a private pilot's license upon beginning the training and meets the medical requirements.

6. State-approved teacher certification programs.

7. Preparatory courses necessary for admission to a college or graduate school.

8. License and certification tests approved for Veterans.

9. Entrepreneurship training courses to create or expand small businesses.

10. Tuition assistance using MGIB as "Top-Up" (active duty servicemembers).

Accelerated payments for certain high-cost programs are authorized.

Work-Study Program: Participants who train at the three-quarter or full-time rate may be eligible for a work-study program in which they work for VA and receive hourly wages. Students under the work-study program must be supervised by a VA employee, and all duties performed must relate to VA. The types of work allowed include:

Working in Veterans-related position at schools or other training facilities.

Providing hospital or domiciliary care at a state home.

Working at national or state Veterans' cemeteries.

Various jobs within any VA facility.

Providing assistance in obtaining a benefit under title 38 U.S.C. at a state Veterans agency.

Assisting in the administration of chapters 1606 or 1607 of title 10 U.S.C. at a Department of Defense, Coast Guard, or National Guard facility.

Working in a Center for Excellence for Veterans Student Success.

Educational and Vocational Counseling Services: Refer to Chapter 10, "Transition Assistance", for detailed information on available services.

Veterans' Educational Assistance Program

Eligibility: Active duty personnel could participate in the Veterans' Educational Assistance Program (VEAP) if they entered active duty for the first time after Dec. 31, 1976, and before July 1, 1985, and made a contribution prior to April 1, 1987.

The maximum contribution is $2,700. Active duty participants may make a lump-sum contribution to their VEAP account. For more information, visit www.gibill.va.gov.

Servicemembers who participated in VEAP are eligible to receive benefits while on active duty if:

1. At least three months of contributions are available, except for high school or elementary, in which only one month is needed.

2. And they enlisted for the first time after Sept 7, 1980, and completed 24 months of their first period of active duty.

Servicemembers must receive a discharge under conditions other than dishonorable for the qualifying period of service. Servicemembers who enlisted for the first time after Sept. 7, 1980, or entered active duty as an officer or enlistee after Oct. 16, 1981, must have completed 24 continuous months of active duty, unless they meet a qualifying exception.

Eligibility generally expires 10 years from release from active duty, but can be extended under special circumstances.

Payments: DoD will match contributions at the rate of $2 for every $1 put into the fund and may make additional contributions, or "kickers," as necessary. For training in college, vocational or technical schools, the payment amount depends on the type and hours of training pursued. The maximum amount is $300 a month for full-time training.

Training, Work-Study, Counseling: VEAP participants may receive the same training, work-study benefits and counseling as provided under the MGIB with the exception of preparatory courses.

Expert's Experience

I was once advising a first-year student (Laura) who intended to major in business. While helping her plan the courses she needed to complete her degree, I pointed out to her that she still needed to take a course in philosophy. Here's how our conversation went after I made this point.

Laura (in a somewhat irritated tone): Why do I have to take philosophy? I'm a business major.

Dr. Cuseo: Because philosophy is an important component of a liberal arts education.

Laura (in a very agitated tone): I'm not liberal and I don't want to be a liberal. I'm conservative and so are my parents; we all voted for Ronald Reagan in the last election!

Joe Cuseo

THE MEANING AND PURPOSE OF A LIBERAL ARTS EDUCATION

If you're uncertain about what the term *liberal arts* means, you're not alone. Most first-year students don't have the foggiest idea what a liberal arts education represents (Hersh, 1997; American Association of Colleges & Universities [AAC&U], 2007). If they were to guess, like Laura, many of them might mistakenly say that it's something impractical or related to liberal politics.

Laura probably would have picked option 1 as her answer to the multiple-choice question posed at the start of this chapter. She would have been wrong; the correct choice is option 5. Literally translated, the term *liberal arts* derives from the Latin words *liberales*, meaning "to liberate or free," and *artes*, meaning "skills." Thus, "skills for freedom" is the most accurate meaning of liberal arts.

The roots of the term *liberal arts* date back to the origin of modern civilization—to the ancient Greeks and Romans, who argued that political power in a democracy rests with the people because they choose (elect) their own leaders. In a democracy, people are liberated from uncritical dependence on a dictator or autocrat. In order to preserve their political freedom, citizens in a democracy must be well-educated critical thinkers so that they can make wise choices about whom they elect as their leaders and lawmakers (Bishop, 1986; Bok, 2006).

The political ideals of the ancient Greeks and Romans were shared by the founding fathers of the United States, who also emphasized the importance of an educated citizenry for preserving America's new democracy. As Thomas Jefferson, third president of the United States, wrote in 1801, "I know of no safe depository of the ultimate powers of a society but the people themselves; and if we think them not enlightened enough to exercise control with a wholesome discretion [responsible decision-making], the remedy is not to take power from them, but to inform their discretion by education" (Ford, 1903, p. 278).

Thus, the liberal arts are rooted in the belief that education is the essential ingredient for preserving democratic freedom. When citizens are educated in the liberal arts, they gain the breadth of knowledge and depth of thinking to vote wisely, preserve democracy, and avoid autocracy (dictatorship).

The importance of a knowledgeable, critically thinking citizenry for making wise political choices is still relevant today. Contemporary political campaigns are using more manipulative media advertisements. These ads rely on short sound bites, one-sided arguments, and powerful visual images that are intentionally designed to appeal to emotions and discourage critical thinking (Goleman, 1992; Boren, 2008).

Over time, the term *liberal arts* has acquired the more general meaning of liberating or freeing people to be self-directed individuals who make personal choices and decisions that are determined by their own well-reasoned ideas and values, rather than blind conformity to the ideas and values of others (Gamson, 1984; Katz, 2008). Self-directed critical thinkers are empowered to resist manipulation by politicians and other societal influences, including:

- Authority figures (e.g., they question excessive use or abuse of authority by parents, teachers, or law enforcers);

"Knowledge will forever govern ignorance; and a people who mean to be their own governors must arm themselves with the power which knowledge gives."

—James Madison, fourth president of the United States, cosigner of the American Constitution, and first author of the Bill of Rights

Remember _____

The original purpose of higher education in America was not just to prepare students for a future profession, but to prepare them for citizenship in a democratic nation.

"It is such good fortune for people in power that people do not think."

—Adolf Hitler, German dictator

"If a nation expects to be ignorant and free, it expects what never was and never will be."

—Thomas Jefferson, principal author of the United States Declaration of Independence and third president of the United States

- Peers (e.g., they resist peer pressure that's unreasonable or unethical); and
- Media (e.g., they detect and reject forms of advertisement designed to manipulate their self-image and dictate their material needs).

In short, a liberal arts education encourages you to be your own person and to ask, "Why?" It's the component of your college education that supplies you with the mental tools needed to be an independent thinker with an inquiring mind who questions authority and resists conformity.

Expert's Experience

I must admit that I graduated from college without ever truly understanding the purpose and value of liberal education. After I became a college professor, two colleagues of mine approached me to help them create a first-year experience course. I agreed and proceeded to teach the course, which included a unit on the meaning and value of a liberal arts education. It was only after preparing to teach this unit that I began to realize that a college education is first and foremost a process of developing enduring (lifelong) learning skills and "habits of mind" that can empower all college graduates to succeed in any career they may pursue. If I hadn't taught a first-year experience course, I don't think I ever would have truly understood the process that was essential to the purpose of a college education and to my role as a college professor.

— Joe Cuseo

THE LIBERAL ARTS CURRICULUM

The first liberal arts curriculum (collection of courses) was designed to equip students with (1) a broad base of knowledge that would ensure they would be well informed in various subjects and (2) a range of mental skills that would enable them to think deeply and critically. Based on this educational philosophy of the ancient Greeks and Romans, the first liberal arts curriculum was developed during the Middle Ages and consisted of the following subjects: logic, language, rhetoric (the art of argumentation and persuasion), music, mathematics, and astronomy (Ratcliff, 1997; AAC&U, 2002, 2007).

The original purpose of the liberal arts curriculum has withstood the test of time. Today's colleges and universities continue to offer a liberal arts curriculum designed to provide students with a broad base of knowledge in multiple subject areas and equip them with critical thinking skills. The liberal arts curriculum today is often referred to as *general education*—representing general knowledge and skills that are applicable to a wide variety of situations. General education is what all college students learn, no matter what their major or specialized field of study may be (AAC&U, 2002).

On some campuses, the liberal arts are also referred to as (1) the *core curriculum*, with "core" standing for what is central and essential for all students to know and do because it contributes to successful performance in any field, or (2) *breadth requirements*, meaning that they are broad in scope, spanning a wide range of subject areas.

Remember _____

Whatever term is used to describe the liberal arts on your campus, the bottom line is that they are the foundation of a college education upon which all academic specializations (majors) are built; they are what all college graduates should be able to know and do for whatever occupational path they choose to pursue; they are what distinguishes college education from vocational preparation; they define what it means to be a well-educated person.

MAJOR DIVISIONS OF KNOWLEDGE AND SUBJECT AREAS IN THE LIBERAL ARTS CURRICULUM

The divisions of knowledge in today's liberal arts curriculum have expanded to include more subject areas than those included in the original curriculum devised by the ancient Greeks and Romans. These divisions and the courses that make up each division vary somewhat from campus to campus. Campuses also vary in terms of the nature of courses required within each of these divisions of knowledge and the variety of courses from which students can choose to fulfill their liberal arts requirements. On average, about one-third of a college graduate's course credits are required general education courses selected from the liberal arts curriculum (Conley, 2005).

REFLECTION ●—————————————————————

For someone to be successful in any major and career, what do you think that person should:

1. Know; and
2. Be able to do?

Despite campus-to-campus variation in the number and nature of courses required, the liberal arts curriculum on every college campus represents the areas of knowledge and the types of skills that all students should possess, no matter what their particular major may be. The breadth of this curriculum allows you to stand on the shoulders of intellectual giants from a range of fields and capitalize on their collective wisdom.

On most campuses today, the liberal arts curriculum typically consists of general divisions of knowledge and related subject areas similar to those listed in the sections that follow. As you read through these divisions of knowledge, highlight any subjects in which you've never taken a course.

Humanities

Courses in the humanities division of the liberal arts curriculum focus on the human experience and human culture, asking the important "big picture" questions that arise in the life of humans, such as "Why are we here?" "What is the meaning or purpose of our existence?" "How should we live?" "What is the good life?" and "Is there life after death?"

The following are the primary subject areas in the humanities:

- **English Composition.** Writing clearly, critically, and persuasively;
- **Speech.** Speaking eloquently and convincingly;
- **Literature.** Reading critically and appreciating the artistic merit of various literary genres (forms of writing), such as novels, short stories, poems, plays, and essays;
- **Languages.** Listening to, speaking, reading, and writing languages other than the student's native tongue;
- **Philosophy.** Thinking rationally, developing wisdom (the ability to use knowledge prudently), and living an ethically principled life; and
- **Theology.** Understanding how humans conceive of and express their faith in a transcendent (supreme) being.

Fine Arts

Courses in the fine arts division focus largely on the art of human expression, asking such questions as "How do humans express, create, and appreciate what is beautiful?" and "How do we express ourselves aesthetically (through the senses) with imagination, creativity, style, and elegance?"

The primary subject areas of the fine arts are as follows:

- **Visual Arts.** Creating and appreciating human expression through visual representation (drawing, painting, sculpture, photography, and graphic design);
- **Musical Arts.** Appreciating and creating rhythmical arrangements of sounds; and
- **Performing Arts.** Appreciating and expressing creativity through drama and dance.

Mathematics

Courses in this division of the liberal arts are designed to promote skills in numerical calculation, quantitative reasoning, and problem solving.

The primary subject areas comprising mathematics for general education include:

- **Algebra.** Mathematical reasoning involving symbolic representation of numbers in a language of letters that vary in size or quantity;
- **Statistics.** Mathematical methods for summarizing quantitative data, estimating probabilities, representing and understanding numerical information depicted in graphs, charts, and tables, and drawing accurate conclusions from statistical data; and

> "Never mistake knowledge for wisdom. One helps you make a living; the other helps you make a life."
>
> —Sandra Carey, lobbyist to the California State Assembly

> "Dancing is silent poetry."
>
> —Simonides, ancient Greek poet

> "The universe is a grand book which cannot be read until one learns to comprehend the language and become familiar with the characters of which it is composed. It is written in the language of mathematics."
>
> —Galileo Galilei, 17th-century Italian physicist, mathematician, astronomer, and philosopher

© Ekaterina Pokrovskaya, 2013. Under license from Shutterstock, Inc.

- **Calculus.** Higher mathematical methods for calculating the rate at which the quantity of one entity changes in relation to another and calculating the areas enclosed by curves.

Natural Sciences

Courses in this division of the liberal arts curriculum are devoted to systematic observation of the physical world and the explanation of natural phenomena, asking such questions as "What causes physical events that take place in the natural world?" "How can we predict and control these events?" and "How do we promote mutually productive interaction between humans and the natural environment that contributes to the survival and development of both?"

The natural sciences division of the liberal arts curriculum focuses on the observation of the physical world and the explanation of natural phenomena.

The following are the primary subject areas of the natural sciences division:

- **Biology.** Understanding the structure and underlying processes of all living things;
- **Chemistry.** Understanding the composition of natural and synthetic (manmade) substances and how these substances may be changed or developed;
- **Physics.** Understanding the properties of physical matter and the principles of energy, motion, electrical, and magnetic forces;
- **Geology.** Understanding the composition of the earth and the natural processes that have shaped its development; and
- **Astronomy.** Understanding the makeup and motion of celestial bodies that comprise the universe.

Social and Behavioral Sciences

Courses in the division of social and behavioral sciences focus on the observation of human behavior, individually and in groups, asking such questions as "What causes humans to behave the way they do?" and "How can we predict, control, or improve human behavior and human interaction?"

This division of the liberal arts curriculum is composed primarily of the following subject areas:

- **History.** Understanding past events, their causes, and their influence on current events;
- **Political Science.** Understanding how societal authority is organized and how this authority is exerted to govern people, make collective decisions, and maintain social order;

"We cannot defend these [democratic] ideals or protect the vitality of our institutions, including our institutional government, unless we understand their origins and how they evolved over time."

—David Boren, president of the University of Oklahoma and longest-serving chairman of the U.S. Senate Intelligence Committee

- **Psychology.** Understanding the human mind, its conscious and subconscious processes, and the underlying causes of human behavior;
- **Sociology.** Understanding the structure, interaction, and collective behavior of organized social groups, institutions, and systems that comprise human society (e.g., families, schools, and social services);
- **Anthropology.** Understanding the cultural and physical origin, development, and distribution of the human species;
- **Geography.** Understanding how the places (physical locations) where humans live influence their cultural and societal development and how humans have shaped (and been shaped) by their surrounding physical environment; and
- **Economics.** Understanding how the monetary needs of humans are met through allocation of limited resources and how material wealth is produced and distributed.

Physical Education and Wellness

Courses in the physical education and wellness division of the liberal arts curriculum focus on the human body, how to best maintain health, and how to attain peak levels of human performance. They ask such questions as "How does the body function most effectively?" and "What can we do to prevent illness, promote wellness, and improve the physical quality of our lives?"

These primary subject areas fall under this division:

- **Physical Education.** Understanding the role of human exercise for promoting health and performance;
- **Nutrition.** Understanding how the body uses food as nourishment to promote health and generate energy;
- **Sexuality.** Understanding the biological, psychological, and social aspects of sexual relations; and
- **Drug Education.** Understanding how substances that alter the body and mind affect physical health, mental health, and human behavior.

Most of your liberal arts requirements will be fulfilled during your first two years of college. Don't be disappointed if some of these required courses seem similar to courses you recently had in high school, and don't think you'll be bored because these are subjects you've already studied. College courses are not videotape replays of high school courses; you will examine these subjects in greater depth and breadth and at a higher level of thinking (Conley, 2005). Research shows that most of the thinking gains that students make in college take place during their first two years—the years when they're taking most of their liberal arts courses (Pascarella & Terenzini, 2005). Although you will specialize in a particular field of study in college (your major), "real-life" issues and challenges are not neatly divided and conveniently packaged into specialized majors. Important and enduring issues, such as effective leadership, improving race relations, and preventing international warfare, can neither be fully understood nor effectively solved by using the thinking tools of a single academic discipline. Approaching such important, multidimensional issues from the perspective of a single, specialized field of study would be to use a single-minded and oversimplified strategy to tackle complex and multifaceted problems.

REFLECTION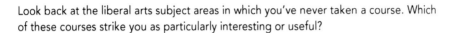

Look back at the liberal arts subject areas in which you've never taken a course. Which of these courses strike you as particularly interesting or useful?

Why?

ACQUIRING TRANSFERABLE SKILLS THAT LAST A LIFETIME

A liberal arts education promotes success in your major, career, and life by equipping you with a set of lifelong learning skills with two powerful qualities:

- **Transferability.** Skills that can be transferred and applied to a range of subjects, careers, and life situations.
- **Durability.** Skills that are enduring and can be continually used throughout life.

> "Intellectual growth should commence at birth and cease only at death."
>
> —Albert Einstein, Nobel Prize–winning physicist

To use an athletic analogy, what the liberal arts do for the mind is similar to what cross-training does for the body. Cross-training engages the body in a wide range of different exercises to promote total physical fitness and a broad set of physical skills (e.g., strength, endurance, flexibility, and agility), which can be applied to improve performance in any sport or athletic endeavor. Similarly, the liberal arts and diversity engage the mind in a wide range of subject areas (e.g., arts, sciences and humanities) and multiple cultural perspectives, which develop a wide range of mental skills that can be used to improve performance in any major or career.

> "You know you've got to exercise your brain just like your muscles."
>
> —Will Rogers, Native American humorist and actor

There's a big difference between learning factual knowledge and learning transferable skills. A transferable skill can be applied to different situations or contexts. The mental skills developed by the liberal arts are transportable across academic subjects you'll encounter in college and work positions you'll assume after college. It could be said that these lifelong learning skills are mental gifts that keep on giving throughout life.

> "If you give a man a fish, you feed him for a day. If you teach a man how to fish, you feed him for life."
>
> —Author unknown

Remember _____

The liberal arts not only provide you with academic skills needed to succeed in your chosen major, they also equip you with skills to succeed in whatever career or careers you decide to pursue. Don't underestimate the importance of these transferable and durable skills. Work hard at developing them, and take seriously the liberal arts courses designed to promote their development. The broad-based knowledge and general, flexible skills developed by the liberal arts will multiply your career options, opening up more career doors for you after college graduation and providing you with greater career mobility throughout your professional life.

The transferable skills developed by the liberal arts are summarized in **Snapshot Summary 2.1**. As you read each of them, rate yourself on each of the skills using the following scale:

4 = very strong, 3 = strong, 2 = needs some improvement,
1 = needs much improvement

Transferable Lifelong Learning Skills Developed by the Liberal Arts

One way the liberal arts "liberate" you is by equipping you with skills that are not tied to any particular subject area or career field, but which can be transferred freely to different learning situations and contexts throughout life. Some key forms of these versatile, durable skills are listed below.

1. **Communication skills.** Accurate comprehension and articulate expression of ideas. Five particular types of communication skills are essential for success in any specialized field of study or work:

   - **Written communication skills.** Writing in a clear, creative, and persuasive manner;
   - **Oral communication skills.** Speaking concisely, confidently, and eloquently;
   - **Reading skills.** Comprehending, interpreting, and evaluating the literal

   meaning and connotations of words written in various styles and subject areas;
   - **Listening skills.** Comprehending spoken language accurately and sensitively; and
   - **Technological communication skills.** Using computer technology to communicate effectively.

2. **Information literacy skills.** Accessing, retrieving, and evaluating information from various sources, including in-print and online (technology-based) systems.

3. **Computation skills.** Accurately calculating, analyzing, summarizing, interpreting, and evaluating quantitative information or statistical data.

4. **Higher-level thinking skills.** Thinking at a more advanced level than simply acquisition and memorization of factual information.

Students often see general education as something to "get out of the way" or "get behind them" so they can get into their major and career (AAC&U, 2007). Don't buy into the belief that general education represents a series of obstacles along the way to a degree. Instead, "get into" general education and take away from it a set of powerful skills that are *portable*—"travel" well across different work situations and life roles—and *stable*—will remain relevant across changing times and stages of life.

REFLECTION ●━━━━━━━━━━━━━━━━━━━━━━━

Reflect on the four skill areas developed by a liberal arts education (communication, information literacy, computation, and higher-level thinking). Which one do you think is most important or most relevant to your future success?

Write a one-paragraph explanation of why you chose this skill.

Remember _____

You may forget the facts you learn in college, but you will remember the ways of thinking, the habits of mind, and the communication skills for the rest of your life.

The skills developed by a liberal arts education are strikingly similar to the types of skills that employers seek in new employees. In numerous national surveys and in-depth interviews, employers and executives in both industry and government consistently report that they seek employees with skills that fall into the following three categories:

Remember _____

When you acquire lifelong learning skills, you're also acquiring lifelong learning skills.

1. **Communication skills.** Listening, speaking, writing, and reading (Business-Higher Education Forum, 1999; National Association of Colleges & Employers, 2007; Peter D. Hart Research Associates, 2006). "There is such a heavy emphasis on effective communication in the workplace that college students who master these skills can set themselves apart from the pack when searching for employment." —Marilyn Mackes, executive director of the National Association of Colleges and Employers (Mackes, 2003, p. 1).

2. **Thinking skills.** Problem solving and critical thinking (Business-Higher Education Forum, 1999; Peter D. Hart Research Associates, 2006; Education Commission of the States, 1995). "We look for people who can think critically and analytically. If you can do those things, we can teach you our business." —Paul Dominski, store recruiter for the Robinson-May Department Stores Company.

Remember _____

The earning potential you acquire after college will depend on the learning potential you develop in college.

3. **Lifelong learning skills.** Learning how to learn and how to continue learning throughout life (Conference Board of Canada, 2000). "Employers are virtually unanimous that the most important knowledge and skills the new employee can bring to the job are problem solving, communication, and 'learning to learn' skills (SECFHE, 2006). The workers of the future need to know how to think and how to continue to learn." —David Kearns, former chief executive officer for the Xerox Corporation.

Student
Perspective

"They asked me during my interview why I was right for the job and I told them because I can read well, write well and I can think. They really liked that because those were the skills they were looking for."

—English major hired by a public relations firm

The remarkable resemblance between the work skills sought by employers and the academic skills developed by a liberal arts education isn't surprising when you think about the typical duties or responsibilities of working professionals. They need good communication skills because they must listen, speak, describe, and explain ideas to co-workers and customers. They are required to read and critically interpret written and statistical reports and write letters, memos, and reports. They also need highly developed thinking skills to analyze problems, construct well-organized plans, generate innovative ideas and so-lutions to problems (creative thinking), and evaluate whether their plans and strategies are effective (critical thinking).

The Liberal Arts Promote Employability

"At State Farm, our [employment] exam does not test applicants on their knowledge of finance or the insurance business, but it does require them to demonstrate critical thinking skills and the ability to calculate and think logically. These skills plus the ability to read for information, to communicate and write effectively need to be demonstrated."

—Edward B. Rust Jr., chairman and chief executive officer of State Farm Insurance Companies (AAC&U, 2007)

The transferable skills developed by the liberal arts have become more and more sought out by employers. In fact, colleges and universities are hearing from em-ployers that these transferable skills are the very abilities their new staff members need to be successful in today's workplace and to effectively take on "real-life" issues. Given the complexity of today's world, this isn't surprising. The 21st cen-tury has increased our interconnectedness with many different countries and cultures. At the same time, the 21st century also has brought with it many new global challenges that were not present even 20 years ago. These changes neces-sitate that college graduates bring with them the knowledge, experience, and abilities to step into the world they will encounter upon graduating. In fact, according to a recent survey of employers (Peter D. Hart Research Associates, 2010, p. 5), new employees are expected to do the following to a much greater degree today than in the past:

- Take on more responsibilities and use a broader set of skills
- Work harder to coordinate with other departments
- Address challenges that are more complex
- Use higher levels of thinking and a wider range of knowledge

Clearly, as the world itself has changed in the 21st century, so has the world of work. Given these changes, it makes sense that employers are seeking new hires with a distinct set of knowledge, values, and skills.

So what are employers looking for in the people they hire? They are seek-ing workers who that can problem-solve and manage projects. They want em-ployees with effective interpersonal skills who can work well with groups. They also want their new hires to be able to adapt to a variety of environments and be skilled communicators. Students develop these qualities while in college through a well-rounded education that balances the curriculum of the liberal arts and their major. In a study conducted by the American Association of State Colleges and Universities (2007, p. 2) employers stated that this curricular bal-ance is ideal since it produces the following highly valued outcomes in students and prepares them for the world of work:

- Integrative learning
  - The ability to apply knowledge and skills to real-world settings
- Knowledge of human cultures and the physical and natural world
  - Concepts and new developments in science and technology
  - Global issues and developments and their implications for the future*
  - The role of the United States in the world
  - Cultural values and traditions in America and other countries*

- Intellectual and practical skills
  - Teamwork skills and the ability to collaborate with others in diverse group settings*
  - The ability to effectively communicate orally and in writing
  - Critical thinking and analytical reasoning skills
  - The ability to locate, organize, and evaluate information from multiple sources
  - The ability to be innovative and think creatively
  - The ability to solve complex problems
  - The ability to work with numbers and understand statistics
- Personal and social responsibility
  - Teamwork skills and the ability to collaborate with others in diverse group settings*
  - Global issues and developments and their implications for the future
  - A sense of integrity and ethics
  - Cultural values and traditions in America and other countries*

Expert's Experience I graduated from college with a BA in political science and sociology. Many of my friends asked me, "What are you going to do with such majors? What kind of job will you get offered?" As it turned out, I received a position in corporate management training after I graduated and spent the next many years working in corporate America. I quickly became aware of the knowledge these liberal arts degrees and my general education bestowed on me. I understood how organizations worked. I could communicate well, orally and written. I understood people and their uniqueness. I could problem solve. I got these degrees in the 20th century and these are the skills still in most demand in the 21st century.

—Aaron Thompson

This study's results further demonstrate the important contributions made by the liberal arts toward your college success and your marketability upon graduation. When you work with your advisor on your academic plan and map out the courses you'll take to complete your degree, think of your liberal arts requirements as courses that will complement the learning you'll do in your major courses. Delve into both! By doing so, you be will be investing in your academic success and future employability.

> "As times goes on, the technical and practical skills vocational majors learn in college become less important to continued success. Such abilities as communication skills, human relations, creativity, and 'big picture thinking' matter more."
>
> —Derek Bok, president emeritus, Harvard University

A Liberal Arts Education Is Preparation for Your Major

For most college students, choosing a major and choosing a career are not decisions made at the same time because their major doesn't turn into their career.

---

*Three items are shown in two learning outcome categories because they apply to both.

It is this belief that leads some students to procrastinate about choosing a major; they think they're making a lifelong decision and are afraid they'll make the "wrong" choice and get stuck doing something they hate for the rest of their life.

The truth is that the trip from your college major to your eventual career(s) is less like climbing a pole and more like climbing up a tree. As illustrated in **Figure 3.3**, you begin with the tree's trunk (the foundation provided by the liberal arts), which leads to separate limbs (choices for college majors), which, in turn, leads to different branches (different career paths or options).

Note that the different sets of branches (careers) grow from the same major limb. So, too, do different sets of careers or "career families" grow from each major. For example, an English major will often lead to careers that involve use of the written language (e.g., editing, journalism, or publishing), while a major in art will often lead to careers that involve use of visual media (e.g., illustration, graphic design, or art therapy).

Don't assume that liberal arts courses you're taking as general education requirements have nothing to do with your specialized field of interest. Liberal arts courses provide a relevant foundation for success in your major. Recall our story at the start of the chapter about Laura, the first-year student with a business major who questioned why she had to take a course in philosophy. Laura needed to take philosophy because she would encounter topics in her business major that related either directly or indirectly to philosophy. In her business courses, she would likely encounter philosophical issues relating to (1) the logical assumptions and underlying values of capitalism, (2) business

FIGURE 3.3

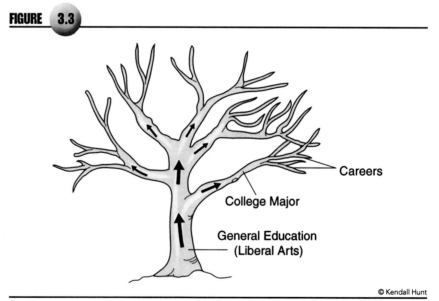

© Kendall Hunt

The Relationship between General Education (Liberal Arts), College Majors, and Careers

ethics (e.g., hiring and firing practices), and (3) business justice (e.g., how profits should be fairly or justly distributed to workers and shareholders). Philosophy would equip her with the fundamental logical thinking and ethical reasoning skills to understand these issues deeply and respond to them humanely.

The same is true for careers other than business. For example, historical and ethical perspectives are needed for all fields because all of them have a history and none of them are value-free.

Keep in mind that the career path of most college graduates does not run like a straight line directly from their major to their career. For instance, most physics majors do not become physicists, most philosophy majors do not become philosophers, and most history majors do not become historians. It is this mistaken belief that may account for the fact that business continues to be the most popular major among college students (Zernike, 2009). Students (and their parents) see that most college graduates are employed in business settings and think that if you want to get a job in business after graduation, you'd better major in business.

> "Virtually all occupational endeavors require a working appreciation of the historical, cultural, ethical, and global environments that surround the application of skilled work."
>
> —Robert Jones, "Liberal Education for the Twenty-First Century: Business Expectations"

REFLECTION ●———————————————

During your college experience, you might hear students say that they need to get their general education (liberal arts) courses out of the way so that they can get into courses that relate to their major and career. Would you agree or disagree with this argument?

Why?

> "The unexamined life is not worth living."
>
> —Socrates, classic Greek philosopher and one of the founding fathers of Western philosophy

The academic skills developed by a liberal arts education are also practical skills that contribute to successful performance in any career.

The Liberal Arts Promote Self-Awareness and Development of the Whole Person

One of the most emphasized goals of a liberal arts education is to "know thyself" (Cross, 1982; Tubbs, 2011). Fully educated people look inward to learn about themselves just as they look outward to learn about the world around them. The ability to turn inward and become aware of ourselves has been referred to as intrapersonal intelligence (Gardner, 1999, 2006). Self-knowledge represents the key first step in any quest toward personal growth and fulfillment.

To become self-aware requires awareness of all elements that comprise the self. As illustrated in **Figure 3.4**, the human self is composed of multiple dimensions that join together to form the whole person.

FIGURE 3.4

© Kendall Hunt

Key Elements of Holistic (Whole-Person) Development

KEY DIMENSIONS OF THE SELF

Each of the following elements of self plays an influential role in promoting human health, success, and happiness:

1. **Intellectual.** Knowledge, multiple perspectives, and different ways of thinking;
2. **Emotional.** Awareness of feelings, self-esteem, emotional intelligence, and mental health;
3. **Social.** Interpersonal relationships;
4. **Ethical.** Values, character, and moral convictions;
5. **Physical.** Bodily health and wellness;
6. **Spiritual.** Beliefs about the meaning or purpose of life and the hereafter;
7. **Vocational.** Economic well-being and career success; and
8. **Personal.** Identity, self-concept, and self-management.

Student
Perspective

"I want to see how all the pieces of me come together to make me, physically and mentally."

—College sophomore

Research strongly suggests that quality of life depends on attention to and development of all elements of the self. It's been found that people who are healthy (physically and mentally) and successful (personally and professionally) are those who attend to and integrate dimensions of the self, enabling them to lead well-rounded and well-balanced lives (Covey, 1990; Goleman, 1995; Heath, 1977).

In Figure 3.4, these diverse dimensions of the self are joined or linked to represent how they are interrelated, working together to promote personal development and well-being (Love & Love, 1995). The dimensions of self are discussed separately in this chapter to keep them clear in your mind. In reality, they do not operate independent of one another; instead, they interconnect and influence each other. (This is why the elements of the self in Figure 3.4 are depicted as links in an interconnected chain.) Thus, the self is a diverse, multidimensional entity that has the capacity to develop along various interdependent dimensions.

One of the primary goals of the liberal arts is to provide a well-rounded education that promotes development and integration of the whole person (Kuh, Shedd, & Whitt, 1987). Research on college students confirms that their college experience affects them in multiple ways and promotes the development of multiple dimensions of self (Bowen, 1997; Feldman & Newcomb, 1994; Pascarella & Terenzini, 1991; 2005).

Since wholeness is essential for wellness, success, and happiness, read carefully the following descriptions and skills associated with each of the eight elements of holistic development. As you read the skills and qualities listed beneath each of the eight elements, place a checkmark in the space next to any skill that is particularly important to you. You may check more than one skill within each area.

SKILLS AND QUALITIES ASSOCIATED WITH EACH ELEMENT OF HOLISTIC (WHOLE-PERSON) DEVELOPMENT

1. **Intellectual development.** Acquiring knowledge and learning how to learn deeply and think at a higher level.
   Goals and skills:
   - ☑ Becoming aware of your intellectual abilities, interests, and learning styles
   - ☑ Maintaining attention and concentration
   - ☑ Improving your ability to retain and apply knowledge
   - ☑ Moving beyond memorization to higher levels of thinking
   - ☑ Acquiring effective research skills for accessing information from various sources and systems
   - ☑ Viewing issues from multiple angles or viewpoints (psychological, social, political, economic, etc.) to attain a balanced, comprehensive perspective
   - ☑ Evaluating ideas critically in terms of their truth and value
   - ☑ Thinking creatively or imaginatively
   - ☑ Responding constructively to differing viewpoints or opposing arguments
   - ☑ Detecting and rejecting persuasion tactics that appeal to emotions rather than reason

2. **Emotional development.** Strengthening skills for understanding, controlling, and expressing emotions.
   Goals and skills:
   - ☑ Dealing with personal emotions in an honest, non-defensive manner
   - ☑ Maintaining a healthy balance between emotional control and emotional expression
   - ☑ Responding with empathy and sensitivity to emotions experienced by others

☑ Dealing effectively with depression
☑ Dealing effectively with anger
☑ Using effective stress-management strategies to control anxiety and tension
☑ Responding effectively to frustrations and setbacks
☑ Overcoming fear of failure and lack of self-confidence
☑ Accepting feedback in a constructive, non-defensive manner
☑ Maintaining optimism and enthusiasm

3. **Social development.** Enhancing the quality and depth of interpersonal relationships.
Goals and skills:
☑ Developing effective conversational skills
☑ Becoming an effective listener
☑ Relating effectively to others in one-to-one, small-group, and large-group situations
☑ Collaborating effectively with others when working in groups or teams
☑ Overcoming shyness
☑ Establishing meaningful and intimate relationships
☑ Resolving interpersonal conflicts assertively, rather than aggressively or passively
☑ Providing feedback to others in a constructive and considerate manner
☑ Relating effectively with others from different cultural backgrounds and lifestyles
☑ Developing leadership skills

4. **Ethical development.** Developing a clear value system for guiding life choices and decisions, building moral character, making ethical judgments, and demonstrating consistency between convictions (beliefs) and commitments (actions).
Goals and skills:
☑ Gaining deeper self-awareness of personal values and ethical assumptions
☑ Making personal choices and life decisions based on a meaningful value system
☑ Developing the capacity to think and act with personal integrity and authenticity
☑ Using technology in an ethical and civil manner
☑ Resisting social pressure to act in ways that are inconsistent with personal values
☑ Treating others in an ethical manner
☑ Knowing how to exercise individual freedom without infringing on the rights of others
☑ Demonstrating concern and commitment for human rights and social justice
☑ Developing the courage to confront those who violate the rights of others
☑ Becoming a responsible citizen

"It's not stress that kills us, it is our reaction to it."
—Hans Selye, Canadian endocrinologist and author of *Stress Without Distress*

"Chi rispetta sara rippetato." ("Respect others and you will be respected.")
—Italian proverb

"The moral challenge is simply to abide by the knowledge we already have."
–Søren Kierkegaard, 19th-century Danish philosopher and theologian

"If you don't stand for something you will fall for anything."
—Malcolm X, African American Muslim minister, public speaker, and human rights activist

5. **Physical development.** Applying knowledge about how the human body functions to prevent disease, preserve wellness, and promote peak performance.

   Goals and skills:
   - ☑ Maintaining awareness of your physical condition and state of health
   - ☑ Applying knowledge about exercise and fitness training to promote physical and mental health
   - ☑ Understanding how sleep patterns affect health and performance
   - ☑ Maintaining a healthy balance of work, recreation, and relaxation
   - ☑ Applying knowledge of nutrition to reduce the risk of illness and promote optimal performance
   - ☑ Becoming knowledgeable about nutritional imbalances and eating disorders
   - ☑ Developing a positive physical self-image
   - ☑ Becoming knowledgeable about the effects of drugs and their impact on physical and mental well-being
   - ☑ Being knowledgeable about human sexuality and sexually transmitted diseases
   - ☑ Understanding how biological differences between the sexes affect male-female relationships and gender orientation

6. **Spiritual development.** Searching for answers to the big questions, such as the meaning or purpose of life and death, and exploring nonmaterial issues that transcend human life and the physical world.

   Goals and skills:
   - ☑ Developing a personal philosophy or worldview about the meaning and purpose of human existence
   - ☑ Appreciating what cannot be completely understood
   - ☑ Appreciating the mysteries associated with the origin of the universe
   - ☑ Searching for the connection between the self and the larger world or cosmos
   - ☑ Searching for the mystical or supernatural—that which transcends the boundaries of the natural world
   - ☑ Being open to examining questions relating to death and life after death
   - ☑ Being open to examining questions about the possible existence of a supreme being or higher power
   - ☑ Being knowledgeable about different approaches to spirituality and their underlying beliefs or assumptions
   - ☑ Understanding the difference and relationship between faith and reason
   - ☑ Becoming aware and tolerant of religious beliefs and practices

7. **Vocational development.** Exploring career options, making career choices wisely, and developing skills needed for lifelong career success.

   Goals and skills:
   - ☑ Understanding the relationship between college majors and careers
   - ☑ Using effective strategies for exploring and identifying potential careers

"A man too busy to take care of his health is like a mechanic too busy to take care of his tools."
—Spanish proverb

Student Perspective

"You may think I'm here, living for the 'now' . . . but I'm not. Half of my life revolves around the invisible and immaterial. At some point, every one of us has asked the Big Questions surrounding our existence: What is the meaning of life? Is my life inherently purposeful and valuable?"
—College student (Dalton, Eberhardt, Bracken, & Echols, 2006)

"Everyone is a house with four rooms: a physical, a mental, an emotional, and a spiritual. Most of us tend to live in one room most of the time but unless we go into every room every day, even if only to keep it aired, we are not complete."
—Native American proverb

☑ Selecting career options that are consistent with your personal values, interests, and talents

☑ Acquiring work experience in career fields that relate to your occupational interests

☑ Developing an effective resume and portfolio

☑ Using effective strategies for identifying personal references and acquiring letters of recommendation

☑ Acquiring effective job-search strategies

☑ Using effective strategies for writing letters of inquiry and applications to potential employers

☑ Developing strategies for performing well in personal interviews

☑ Acquiring effective networking skills for connecting with potential employers

8. **Personal development.** Developing positive self-beliefs, personal attitudes, and personal habits.

Goals and skills:

☑ Developing a strong sense of personal identity and a coherent self-concept (e.g., "Who am I?")

☑ Finding a sense of purpose or direction in life (e.g., "Who will I become?")

☑ Developing self-respect and self-esteem

☑ Increasing self-confidence

☑ Developing self-efficacy, or the belief that events and outcomes in life are influenced or controlled by personal initiative and effort

☑ Setting realistic personal goals and priorities

☑ Developing self-motivation and self-discipline

☑ Developing personal resiliency and perseverance to persist to completion of long-range goals

☑ Acquiring practical skills for managing personal affairs effectively and efficiently

☑ Becoming independent and self-reliant

THE CO-CURRICULUM: USING THE WHOLE CAMPUS TO DEVELOP THE WHOLE PERSON

The power of a liberal arts education is magnified when you take advantage of the total college environment. This includes not only taking advantage of the courses in the college curriculum; it also includes learning experiences that are available to you outside the classroom—referred to as the *co-curriculum.* Co-curricular experiences include all educational discussions you have with your peers and professors outside the classroom, as well as your participation in the various events and programs offered on your campus. As mentioned in Chapter 1, research clearly indicates that out-of-class learning experiences are equally important to your personal development and professional success as the course curriculum (Kuh, 2005; Kuh et al., 1994; 1995; Pascarella & Terenzini, 2005); hence, these experiences are referred to as the *co-curriculum.*

REFLECTION ●━━━━━━━━━━━━━━━━━

Look back and count the number of checkmarks you've placed by each of the eight areas of self-development. Did you find that you placed roughly the same number of checkmarks in all eight areas, or were there large discrepancies across the different areas?

Based on the checkmarks that you placed in each area, would you say that your interests in self-development are balanced across elements of the self, or do they suggest a strong interest in certain dimensions of yourself, with little interest in others?

Do you think you will eventually develop a more balanced set of interests across these different dimensions of self-development? Why?

Learning that takes place in college courses is primarily vicarious—that is, you learn from or through somebody else, by listening to professors in class and by reading outside of class. This type of academic learning is valuable, but it needs to be complemented by experiential learning (i.e., learning directly through firsthand experiences). For example, you don't learn to be a leader solely by listening to lectures and reading books about leadership. To fully develop your leadership skills, you need to have leadership experiences, such as experiences involving "leading a [discussion] group in class, holding office in student government or by being captain of a sports team" (AAC&U, 2002, p. 30). Capitalizing on experiential learning opportunities enables you to take advantage of your whole college to develop yourself as a whole person.

Listed below are some programs and services included in a co-curriculum, accompanied by the primary dimensions of the self that they are designed to develop.

> "To educate liberally, learning experiences must be offered which facilitate maturity of the whole person. These are goals of student development and clearly they are consistent with the mission and goals of liberal education."
>
> —Theodore Berg, "Student Development and Liberal Education"

Dimensions of Holistic (Whole-Person) Development Promoted by Different Co-Curricular Programs and Services

Intellectual Development
- Academic advising
- Learning center services
- College library
- Tutoring services
- Information technology services
- Campus speakers
- Academic workshops
- Concerts, theater productions, and art shows

Social and Emotional Development
- Student activities
- Student clubs and organizations
- Multicultural Center
- International student programs
- Counseling services
- Peer counseling
- Peer mentoring

- Residential life programs
- Commuter programs

Ethical Development

- Judicial Review Board
- Student government
- Integrity committees and task forces

Physical Development

- Student health services
- Wellness programs
- Campus athletic activities and intramural sports

Spiritual Development

- Campus ministry
- Peer ministry
- Religious services

Vocational Development

- Career development services
- Internships programs
- Service learning experiences

- Work-study programs
- Major and career fairs

Personal Development

- Financial aid services
- Campus workshops on self-management (e.g., managing time or money)
- Student development workshops and retreats

Remember _____

A liberal arts education includes both the curriculum and the co-curriculum; it involves strategic use of the total college environment, both inside and outside the classroom.

Note: This list represents just a sample of the total number of programs and services that may be available on your campus. As you can see from the list's length, colleges and universities are organized to promote your development in multiple ways. The power of the liberal arts is magnified when you combine coursework and co-curricular experiences to create a college experience that contributes to your development as a whole person.

BROADENING YOUR PERSPECTIVE OF THE WORLD AROUND YOU

Student *Perspective*

"College was not something I deemed important in order to be really rich later on in life. It was something I considered fundamental to learning about myself and the world around me."

—First-year college student (Watts, 2005)

Learn about things that go beyond yourself—learn about the world around you. A liberal arts education helps you move beyond yourself and expands your perspective to include the wider world around you (Braskamp, 2008). The components of this larger perspective are organized and illustrated in Figure 3.5.

In Figure 3.5, the center circle represents the self. Fanning out to the right of the self is a series of arches that encompasses the *social–spatial perspective*; this perspective includes increasingly larger social groups and more distant places, ranging from the narrowest perspective (the individual) to the widest perspective (the universe). The liberal arts liberate you from the narrow tunnel vision of a self-centered (egocentric) perspective, providing a panoramic perspective of the world that enables you to move outside yourself and see yourself in relation to other people and other places.

To the left of the self in Figure 3.5 are three arches labeled the *chronological perspective*. This perspective includes the three dimensions of time: past

FIGURE   3.5

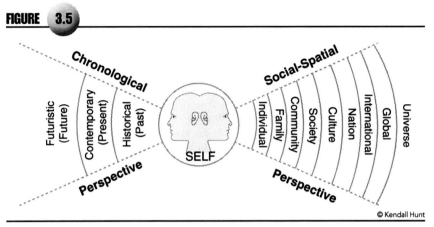

© Kendall Hunt

Multiple Perspectives Developed by the Liberal Arts

(historical), present (contemporary), and future (futuristic). The liberal arts not only widen your perspective, but also lengthen it by stretching your vision beyond the present, enabling you to see yourself in relation to humans who've lived before you and will live after you. The chronological perspective gives you hindsight to see where the world has been, insight into the world's current condition, and foresight to see where the world may be going.

It could be said that the chronological perspective provides you with a mental time machine for flashing back to the past and fast-forwarding to the future, while the social-spatial perspective provides you with a conceptual telescope for viewing people and places that are far away. Together, these two broadening perspectives of the liberal arts enable you to appreciate the experiences of humans living in different places and different times.

The specific elements comprising each of these broadening perspectives are discussed next.

"A quality liberal education leads students to reflect on their place in the world and locate themselves historically and socially."

—Nancy Thomas, "In Search of Wisdom: Liberal Education for a Changing World"

ELEMENTS OF THE SOCIAL-SPATIAL PERSPECTIVE

The Family Perspective

Moving beyond the perspective of yourself as individual, you are part of a larger social unit—a family. The people with whom you were raised have almost certainly influenced the person you are today and how you got to be that way. Moreover, you influence your family. For example, your decision to go to college may make your parents and grandparents proud and may influence the decision of other members of your family to attend college. In addition, if you have children, graduating from college will have a positive influence on their future welfare; as mentioned in the introduction to this book, children of college graduates experience improved intellectual development, better physical health, and greater economic security (Bowen, 1977, 1997; Pascarella & Terenzini, 1991; 2005).

The Community Perspective

Moving beyond the family, you are also a member of a larger social unit—your community. This wider social circle includes friends and neighbors at home, at school, and at work. These are communities where you can begin to take action to improve the world around you. If you want to make the world a better place, this is the place to start—through civic engagement in your local communities.

Civically engaged people demonstrate civic commitment by stepping beyond their narrow self-interests to selflessly volunteer time and energy to help members of their community, particularly those in need. They demonstrate their humanity by being humane—they show genuine compassion for others who are less fortunate than themselves—and by being humanitarian—they work to promote the welfare of other human beings.

The Societal Perspective

Moving beyond your local communities, you are also a member of a larger *society*—a group of people organized under the same social system. Societies include subgroups divided into different regions (e.g., north, south, east, west), different population densities (e.g., urban, suburban, rural), and different socioeconomic classes (e.g., level of income, education, and job status). Within a society, there are typically subgroups that are stratified (layered) into different social classes with unequal levels of economic resources.

In human societies, groups of people are typically stratified into social classes with unequal levels of resources, such as monetary wealth.

The Cultural Perspective

Culture can be broadly defined as a distinctive pattern of beliefs and values that are learned by a group of people who share the same social heritage and traditions. In short, culture is the whole way in which a group of people has learned to live (Peoples & Bailey, 2008); it includes their customary style of speaking (language), fashion, food, art, music, values, and beliefs.

REFLECTION ●———————————————————

What would you say is the factor that is most responsible for poverty in human societies?

———————————————————————————————

Intercultural awareness is one of the outcomes of a liberal arts education (Center of Inquiry, 2011). Being able to step outside of your own culture and see issues from a broader worldview enables you to perceive reality and evaluate truth from the vantage points of different cultural groups. This makes your thinking more comprehensive and less ethnocentric (centered on your own culture).

The National Perspective

Besides being a member of society, you're also a citizen of a nation. The privilege of being a citizen in a free nation brings with it the responsibility of participating in your country's governance through the process of voting. As a democracy, the United States is a nation that has been built on the foundation of equal rights and freedom of opportunity guaranteed by its constitution.

Exercise your right to vote, and when you do vote, be mindful of political leaders who are committed to ensuring equal rights, social justice, and political freedom. When the personal rights and freedom of any of our fellow citizens are threatened, the political stability and survival of our democratic nation is threatened.

The International Perspective

Moving beyond your particular country of citizenship, you are also a member of an international world that includes close to 200 nations (Rosenberg, 2009). Communication and interaction among citizens of different nations is greater today than at any other time in world history, largely because of rapid advances in electronic technology (Dryden & Vos, 1999; Friedman, 2005). The World Wide Web is making today's world a small world after all, and success in this smaller world requires an international perspective. Our lives are increasingly affected by events beyond our national borders; boundaries between nations are breaking down as a result of international travel, international trading, and multinational corporations. By learning from and about different nations, you become more than a citizen of your own country: you become cosmopolitan—a citizen of the world. Moreover, employers of today's college graduates value employees with international knowledge and foreign language skills (Bok, 2006; Fixman, 1990; Office of Research, 1994).

"A liberal [arts] education frees a person from the prison-house of class, race, time, place, background, family, and nation."

—Robert Hutchins, former dean of Yale Law School and president of the University of Chicago

The Global Perspective

Even broader than the international perspective is the global perspective. It extends beyond the relations among citizens of different nations to include all life forms that inhabit planet earth and the relationships between these diverse life forms and the earth's natural resources (minerals, air, and water). Humans share the earth and its natural resources with approximately 10 million animal species (Myers, 1997) and more than 300,000 forms of vegetative life (Knoll, 2003). As inhabitants of this planet and global citizens, we have a responsibility to address environmental issues that require balancing our industrial-technological progress with the need to sustain the earth's natural resources and preserve the life of our planet's cohabitants.

"Treat the Earth well. It was not given to you by your parents. It was loaned to you by your children."

—Kenyan proverb

The Universal Perspective

Beyond the global perspective is the broadest of all perspectives—the universal. The earth is just one planet that shares a solar system with seven other planets

"In astronomy, you must get used to viewing the earth as just one planet in the larger context of the universe."

—Physics professor (Donald, 2002)

and is just one celestial body that shares a galaxy with millions of other celestial bodies, including stars, moons, meteorites, and asteroids (Encrenaz et al., 2004).

Just as we should guard against being ethnocentric (thinking that our culture is the center of humanity), we should guard against being geocentric (thinking that our planet is at the center of the universe). All heavenly bodies do not revolve around the earth; our planet revolves around them. The sun doesn't rise in the east and set in the west; our planet rotates around the sun to produce our earthly experiences of day and night.

> "The sun, with all those planets revolving around it and dependent on it, can still ripen a bunch of grapes as if it had nothing else in the universe to do."
> —Galileo Galilei

ELEMENTS OF THE CHRONOLOGICAL PERSPECTIVE

The Historical Perspective

A historical perspective is critical for understanding the root causes of our current human condition and world situation. Humans are products of both their social and natural history. Don't forget that the earth is estimated to be more than 4.5 billion years old and our human ancestors date back more than 250,000 years (Knoll, 2003). Thus, our current lives represent one very short time frame in a very long chronological reel. Every modern convenience we now enjoy reflects the collective efforts and cumulative knowledge of diverse human groups that have accumulated over thousands of years of history. By studying the past, we can build on our ancestors' achievements and avoid making their mistakes. For instance, by understanding the causes and consequences of the Holocaust, we can reduce the risk that an atrocity of that size and scope will ever happen again.

REFLECTION ●

Look back at the broadening perspectives developed by a liberal arts education. What college course would develop each perspective? If you're unsure or cannot remember whether a course is designed to develop any of these perspectives, look at the course's goals described in your college catalog (in print or online).

The Contemporary Perspective

> "Those who cannot remember the past are damned to repeat it."
> —George Santayana, Spanish-born American philosopher

> "Yesterday is gone. Tomorrow has not yet come. We have only today. Let us begin."
> —Mother Teresa of Calcutta, Albanian Catholic nun and winner of the Nobel Peace Prize

The contemporary perspective focuses on understanding the current world situation and the events that comprise today's news. One major goal of a liberal arts education is to increase your understanding the contemporary human condition so that you may have the wisdom to improve it (Miller, 1988; Harris, 2010). For example, despite historical progress in the nation's acceptance and appreciation of different ethnic and racial groups, the United States today remains a nation that is deeply divided with respect to culture, religion, and social class (Brookings Institution, 2008).

The current technological revolution is generating new information and new knowledge at a faster rate than at any other time in human history (Dryden & Vos, 1999). When there is rapid creation and communication of new information, knowledge quickly becomes obsolete (Naisbitt, 1982). Workers in the today's complex, fast-changing world need to continually update their skills to perform their jobs and advance in their careers (Niles & Harris-Bowlsbey, 2002). This creates a demand for workers who have learned how to learn—a hallmark of the liberal arts.

The Futuristic Perspective

The futuristic perspective allows us to flash forward and envision what our world will be like years from now. This perspective focuses on such questions as "Will we leave the world a better or worse place for humans who will inhabit after our departure, including our children and grandchildren?" and "How can humans living today avoid short-term, shortsighted thinking and adopt a long-range vision that anticipates the consequences of their current actions on future generations of humans?"

To sum up, a comprehensive chronological perspective brings the past, present, and future into focus on a single screen. It enables us to see how the current world is a single segment of a temporal sequence that has been shaped by events that preceded it and how it will shape the events of the future.

Remember

By embracing the perspectives of different times, places, and people, you're embracing the diversity promoted by a liberal arts education. These diverse perspectives liberate or emancipate you from the here and now and empower you to see things long ago and far away.

THE SYNOPTIC PERSPECTIVE: INTEGRATING DIVERSE PERSPECTIVES INTO A UNIFIED WHOLE

A liberal arts education helps you not only appreciate multiple perspectives but also how to integrate them into a meaningful whole (King, Brown, Lindsay, & VanHencke, 2007). Understanding of how the perspectives of time, place, and person interrelate to form a unified whole is referred to as a *synoptic* perspective (Cronon, 1998; Heath, 1977). The word derives from a combination of two roots: *syn*, meaning "together" (as in the word *synthesize*), and *optic*, meaning "to see." Thus, a synoptic perspective literally means to "see things together" or "see the whole." Said in another way, it enables you to see how all the trees come together to form the forest.

REFLECTION ●———————

In light of the information you've read how would you interpret the following statement: "We can't know where we're going until we know where we've been"?

A liberal arts education helps you step beyond yourself to see the wider world and connects you with it. By seeing yourself as an integral part of humankind,

"The only person who is educated is the one who has learned how to learn and change."
—Carl Rogers, humanistic psychologist and Nobel Peace Prize nominee

"In times of change, learners inherit the Earth . . . [they] find themselves beautifully equipped to deal with a world that no longer exists."
—Eric Hoffer, author of *The Ordeal of Change* and recipient of the Presidential Medal of Freedom

"The future is literally in our hands to mold as we like. But we cannot wait until tomorrow. Tomorrow is now."
—Eleanor Roosevelt

"We all inherit the past. We all confront the challenges of the present. We all participate in the making of the future."
—Ernest Boyer and Martin Kaplan, *Educating for Survival*

"A truly great intellect is one which takes a connected view of old and new, past and present, far and near, and which has an insight into the influence of all these on one another, without which there is no whole, and no center."
—John Henry Newman, *The Idea of a University* (1852)

you become integrated with the whole of humanity; you're able to see how you, as an individual, fit into the big picture—the larger scheme of things (Cuseo & Thompson, 2010). When we view ourselves as nested within a web of interconnections with other places, cultures, and times, we become aware of the common humanity we all share. This increased sense of connection with humankind decreases our feelings of personal isolation or alienation (Bellah, Madsen, Sullivan, Swidler, & Tipton, 1985). In his book, *The Perfect Education*, Kenneth Eble (1966) skillfully describes this benefit of a liberal arts education:

> It can provide that overarching life of a people, a community, a world that was going on before the individual came onto the scene and that will continue on after [s]he departs. By such means we come to see the world not alone. Our joys are more intense for being shared. Our sorrows are less destructive for our knowing universal sorrow. Our fears of death fade before the commonness of the occurrence. (pp. 214–215)

Remember _____

A liberal arts education launches you on a quest for two forms of wholeness: (1) an inner wholeness in which elements of your "self" become connected to form a whole person, and (2) an outer wholeness in which you become connected to the whole world. This inner and outer quest will enable you to lead a richer, more fulfilling life that's filled with greater breadth, balance, and wholeness.

EDUCATING YOU FOR LIFE

Research shows that the primary reasons students go to college are to prepare for a career and get a better job (Pryor et al., 2012). While these are important reasons and your career is an important element of your life, a person's vocation or occupation represents just one element of the self. It also represents just one of many roles or responsibilities that you are likely to have in life.

REFLECTION ●━━━━━━━━━━━━━━━━━━━━

In light of the knowledge you've acquired thus far in this chapter, what points or arguments would you make to counter the claim that the liberal arts are impractical?

Remember _____

A liberal arts education not only prepares you for a career but also prepares you for life.

Similar to global issues, personal issues and challenges you face as an individual in your everyday life are multidimensional, requiring perspectives and skills that go well beyond the boundaries of a single academic field or career specialization. Your occupational role represents just one of many roles you will assume in life, which include the roles of family member, friend, co-worker, community member, citizen, and possibly mother or father. A liberal arts education provides you with the breadth of knowledge and the variety of skills needed to successfully accommodate the multiple roles and responsibilities you will encounter throughout life.

Expert's Experience One life role that a liberal arts education helped prepare me for was the role of parent. Courses that I took in psychology and sociology proved to be useful in helping me understand how children develop and how a parent can best support them at different stages of their development. Surprisingly, however, there was one course I had in college that I never expected would ever help me as a parent. That course was statistics, which I took to fulfill a general education requirement in mathematics. It was not a particularly enjoyable course; some of my classmates sarcastically referred to it as "sadistics" because they felt it was a somewhat painful or torturous experience. However, what I learned in that course became valuable to me many years later when my 14-year-old son (Tony) developed a life-threatening disease, leukemia, which is a form of cancer that attacks blood cells. Tony's form of leukemia was a particularly perilous one because it had only a 35 percent average cure rate; in other words, 65 percent of those who develop the disease don't recover and eventually die from it. This statistic was based on patients that received the traditional treatment of chemotherapy, which was the type of treatment that my son began receiving when his cancer was first detected.

Another option for treating Tony's cancer was a bone-marrow transplant, which involved using radiation to destroy all of his own bone marrow (that was making the abnormal blood cells) and replace it with bone marrow donated to him by another person. My wife and I got opinions from doctors at two major cancer centers—one from a center that specialized in chemotherapy, and one from a center that specialized in bone-marrow transplants. The chemotherapy doctors felt strongly that drug treatment would be the better way to treat and cure Tony, and the bone-marrow transplant doctors felt strongly that his chances of survival would be much better if he had a transplant. So, my wife and I had to decide between two opposing recommendations, each made by a respected group of doctors.

To help us reach a decision, I asked both teams of doctors for research studies that had been done on the effectiveness of chemotherapy and bone-marrow transplants for treating my son's particular type of cancer. I read all of these studies and carefully analyzed their statistical findings. I remembered from my statistics course that when an average is calculated for a general group of people (e.g., average cure rate for people with leukemia), it tends to lump together individuals from different subgroups (e.g., males and females or young children and teenagers). Sometimes, when separate statistics are calculated for different subgroups, the results may be different from the average statistic for the whole group. So, when I read the research reports, I looked for any subgroup statistics that might have been calculated. I found two subgroups of patients with my son's particular type of cancer that had a higher rate of cure with chemotherapy than the general (whole-group) average of 35 percent. One subgroup included people with a low number of abnormal cells at the time when the cancer was first diagnosed, and the other subgroup consisted of people whose cancer cells dropped rapidly after their first week of chemotherapy. My son belonged to both of these subgroups, which meant that his chance for cure with chemotherapy was higher than the overall 35 percent average. Furthermore, I found that the statistics showing higher success rate for bone-marrow transplants were based only on patients whose body accepted the donor's bone marrow and did not include those who died because their body rejected the donor's bone marrow. So, the success rates for bone-marrow patients were not actually as high as they appeared to be, because the overall average did not include the subgroup of patients who died because of transplant rejection. Based on these statistics, my wife and I decided to go with chemotherapy and not the transplant operation.

Our son has now been cancer-free for more than five years, so we think we made the right decision. However, I never imagined that a statistics course, which I took many years ago to fulfill a general education requirement, would help me fulfill my role as a parent and help me make a life-or-death decision about my own son.

Joe Cuseo

Planning Your Liberal Arts Education

Since general education is an essential component of your college experience, it should be intentionally planned. This exercise will leave you with a flexible plan that capitalizes on your educational interests while ensuring that your college experience has both breadth and balance.

1. Use your course catalog (bulletin) to identify the general education requirements at your college. The requirements should be organized into general divisions of knowledge similar to those discussed in this chapter (humanities, fine arts, natural sciences, etc.). Within each of these liberal arts divisions, there will be specific courses listed that fulfill the general education requirements for that particular division. (Catalogs can sometimes be difficult to navigate; if you encounter difficulty or doubt about general education requirements, seek clarification from an academic advisor on campus.)

2. You'll probably have some freedom to choose courses from a larger group of courses that fulfill general education requirements within each division. Use your freedom of choice to select courses whose descriptions capture your curiosity or pique your interest. You can take liberal arts courses not only to fulfill general education requirements, but also to test your interest and talent in fields that you may end up choosing as a college major or minor.

3. Highlight the courses in the catalog that you plan to take to fulfill your general education requirements in each division of the liberal arts, and use the form on the following page to pencil in the courses you've chosen. (Use pencil because you will likely make some adjustments to your plan.) Remember that the courses you're taking this term may be fulfilling certain general education requirements, so be sure to list them on your planning form.

General Education Planning Form

Division of the Liberal Arts Curriculum: _____

General education courses you're planning to take to fulfill requirements in this division (record the course number and course title):

_____   _____

_____   _____

_____   _____

Division of the Liberal Arts Curriculum: _____

General education courses you're planning to take to fulfill requirements in this division (record the course number and course title):

_____   _____

_____   _____

_____   _____

Division of the Liberal Arts Curriculum: _____

General education courses you're planning to take to fulfill requirements in this division (record the course number and course title):

_____   _____

_____   _____

_____   _____

Division of the Liberal Arts Curriculum: _____

General education courses you're planning to take to fulfill requirements in this division (record the course number and course title):

_____   _____

_____   _____

_____   _____

Division of the Liberal Arts Curriculum: _____

General education courses you're planning to take to fulfill requirements in this division (record the course number and course title):

_____   _____

_____   _____

_____   _____

4. Look back at the general education courses you've listed and identify the broadening perspectives developed by the liberal arts that each course appears to be developing. (See p. 54 for a description of these perspectives.) Use the form that follows to ensure that your overall perspective is comprehensive and that you have no blind spots in your liberal arts education. For any perspective that's not covered in your plan, find a course in the catalog that will enable you to address the missing perspective.

Broadening Social-Spatial Perspectives

Perspective   Course Developing This Perspective
(See p. 55 for further descriptions of these perspectives.)

Self   _____

Family   _____

Community   _____

Society   _____

Culture   _____

Nation   _____

International   _____

Global   _____

Universe   _____

Broadening Chronological Perspectives

Perspective   Course Developing This Perspective
(See p. 56 for detailed descriptions of these perspectives.)

Historical   _____

Contemporary _____

Futuristic   _____

5. Look back at the general education courses you've listed and identify what element of holistic (whole-person) development each course appears to be developing. (See p. 49 for a description of each of these elements.) Use the form that follows to ensure that your course selection didn't overlook any element of the self. For any element that's not covered in your plan, find a course in the catalog or a co-curricular experience program that will enable you to address the missing area. For co-curricular learning experiences (e.g., leadership and volunteer experiences), consult your student handbook or contact someone in the Office of Student Life.

**Dimensions of Self   Course or Co-Curricular Experience
                            Developing This Dimension of Self**
(See p. 48 for further descriptions of these dimensions.)
(Consult your student handbook for co-curricular experiences.)

Intellectual   _____

Emotional   _____

Social   _____

Ethical   _____

Physical   _____

Spiritual   _____

Vocational   _____

Personal   _____

Remember _____

This general education plan is not set in stone; it may be modified as you gain more experience with the college curriculum and campus life. Its purpose is not to restrict your educational exploration or experimentation, but to give you some educational direction, breadth, and balance.

Dazed and Confused: General Education versus Career Specialization

Joe Tech was really looking forward to college because he thought he would have freedom to select the courses he wanted and the opportunity to get into the major of his choice (computer science). However, he's shocked and disappointed with his first-term schedule of classes because it consists mostly of required general education courses that do not seem to relate in any way to his major. He's frustrated further because some of these courses are about subjects that he already took in high school (English, history, and biology). He's beginning to think he would be better off quitting college and going to a technical school where he could get right into computer science and immediately begin to acquire the knowledge and skills he'll need to prepare him for his intended career.

Reflection and Discussion Questions

1. Can you relate to Joe, or do you know of students who feel the same way Joe does?

2. If Joe decides to leave college for a technical school, how do you see it affecting his future (1) in the short run and (2) in the long run?

3. Do you see any way Joe might strike a balance between pursuing his career interest and obtaining his college degree so that he could work toward achieving both goals at the same time?

PLANNING YOUR CAREER AND EDUCATION

It is always easier to get where you are going if you have a road map or a plan. To start the journey, it is helpful to know about yourself, including your personality, interests, talents, and values. Once you have this picture, you will need to know about the world of work and job trends that will affect your future employment opportunities. Next, you will need to make decisions about which road to follow. Then, you will need to plan your education to reach your destination. Finally, you will need some job-seeking skills such as writing a resume and preparing for a successful interview.

EMPLOYMENT TRENDS

The world is changing quickly, and these changes will affect your future career. To assure your future career success, you will need to become aware of career trends and observe how they change over time so that you can adjust your career plans accordingly. For example, recently a school was established for training bank tellers. The school quickly went out of business and the students demanded their money back because they were not able to get jobs. A careful observer of career trends would have noticed that bank tellers are being replaced by automatic teller machines (ATMs) and would not have started a school for training bank tellers. Students observant of career trends would not have paid money for the training. It is probably a good idea for bank tellers to look ahead and plan a new career direction.

How can you find out about career trends that may affect you in the future? Become a careful observer by reading about current events. Good sources of information include:

- Your local newspaper, especially the business section
- News programs
- Current magazines
- Government statistics and publications
- The Internet

When thinking about future trends, use your critical thinking skills. Sometimes trends change quickly or interact in different ways. For example, since we are using email to a great extent today, it might seem that mail carriers would not be as much in demand in the future. However, since people are buying more goods over the Internet, there has been an increased demand for mail carriers and other delivery services. Develop the habit of looking at what is happening to see if you can identify trends that may affect your future.

Usually trends get started as a way to meet the following needs:[1]

- To save money
- To reduce cost
- To do things faster
- To make things easier to use
- To improve safety and reliability
- To lessen the impact on the environment

The following are some trends to watch that may affect your future career. As you read about each trend, think about how it could affect you.

Baby Boomers, Generation X, and the Millennial Generation

About every 20 years, sociologists begin to describe a new generation with similar characteristics based on shared historical experiences. Each generation has different opportunities and challenges in the workplace.

The Baby Boomers were born following World War II between 1946 and 1964. Four out of every 10 adults today are in this Baby Boom Generation.[2] Because there are so many aging Baby Boomers, the average age of Americans is increasing. Life expectancy is also increasing. By 2015 the projected life expectancy will be 76.4 for men and 81.4 for women.[3] In the new millennium, many more people will live to be 100 years old or more! Think about the implications of an older population. Older people need such things as health care, recreation, travel, and financial planning. Occupations related to these needs are likely to be in demand now and in the future.

Those born between 1965 and 1977 are often referred to as Generation X. They are sometimes called the "baby bust" generation because fewer babies were born during this period than in the previous generations. There is much in the media about this generation having to pay higher taxes and Social Security payments to support the large number of aging Baby Boomers. Some say that this generation will not enjoy the prosperity of the Baby Boomers. Those who left college in the early nineties faced a recession and the worst job market since World War II.[4] Many left college in debt and returned home to live with their parents. Because of a lack of employment opportunities, many in this generation became entrepreneurs, starting new companies at a faster rate than previous generations.

Jane Bryant Quinn notes that in spite of economic challenges, Generation Xers have a lot going for them:[5]

- They have record-high levels of education, which correlate with higher income and lower unemployment.
- There is a demand for more skilled workers, so employers are more willing to train employees. Anthony Carnevale, chairman of the National Commission for Employment Policy, "sees a big demand for 'high-school plus'—a high school diploma plus technical school or junior college."
- Generation Xers are computer literate, and those who use computers on the job earn 10 to 15 percent more than those who don't.
- This group often has a good work ethic valued by employers. However, they value a balanced lifestyle with time for outside interests and family.
- As Baby Boomers retire, more job opportunities are created for this group.
- Unlike the Baby Boomers, this generation was born into a more integrated and more diverse society. They are better able than previous generations to adapt to diversity in society and the workplace.

Many of today's college students are part of the Millennial Generation, born between 1977 and 1995. This generation is sometimes called Generation Y or the Echo Boomers, since they are the children of the Baby Boomers.[6] This new generation of approximately 60 million is three times larger than Generation X and will eventually exceed the number of Baby Boomers. In this decade, they will become the largest teen population in U.S. history. As the Millennials reach college age, they will attend college in increasing numbers. In the next 10 years, college enrollments will increase by approximately 300,000 students per year. Colleges will find it difficult to accommodate rapidly increasing numbers of students, and as a result, the Millennial Generation will face increasingly competitive college admissions criteria.

Millennials are more ethnically diverse than previous generations with 34 percent ethnic minorities. One in four lives with a single parent; three in four have working mothers. Most of them started using computers before they were five years old. Marketing researchers describe this new generation as "technologically adept, info-savvy, a cyber-generation, the clickeratti."[7] They are the connected generation, accustomed to cell phones, chatting on the Internet, and listening to downloaded music.

Young people in the Millennial Generation share a different historical perspective from the Baby Boom Generation. Baby Boomers remember the Vietnam War and the assassinations of President John F. Kennedy and Martin Luther King. For Millennials, school shootings such as Columbine and acts of terrorism such as the Oklahoma City bombing and the 9–11 attack on New York City stand out as important events. The Millennial Generation will see their main problems as dealing with violence, easy access to weapons, and the threat of terrorism.

Neil Howe and William Strauss paint a very positive picture of this new generation in their book *Millennials Rising: The Next Great Generation*:

- Millennials will rebel by tearing down old institutions that do not work and building new and better institutions. The authors predict that this will be the can-do generation filled with technology planners, community shapers, institution builders, and world leaders.
- Surveys show that this generation describes themselves as happy, confident, and positive.
- They are cooperative team players.
- They generally accept authority and respect their parents' values.
- They follow rules. The rates of homicides, violent crime, abortion, and teen pregnancy are decreasing rapidly.
- The use of alcohol, drugs, and tobacco is decreasing.
- Millennials have a fascination with and mastery of new technology.
- Their most important values are individuality and uniqueness.[8]

It is predicted that the world of work for the Millennials will be dramatically different. Previous generations anticipated having a lifetime career. By the year 2020, many jobs will probably be short-term contracts. This arrangement will provide cost savings and efficiency for employers and flexibility for employees to start or stop work to take vacations, train for new jobs, or meet family responsibilities. One in five people will be self-employed. Retirement will be postponed as people look forward to living longer and healthier lives.[9]

Moving from Goods to Services and Technology

Human society has moved through several stages. The first stage, about 20,000 years ago, was the hunting and gathering stage. During this time, society depended on the natural environment for food and other resources. When natural resources were depleted, the community moved to another area. The second stage, some 10,000 years ago, was the agricultural stage. Human beings learned to domesticate animals and cultivate crops. This allowed people to stay in one place and develop more permanent villages. About 200 years ago, industrial societies came into being by harnessing power sources to produce goods on a large scale.

Today in the United States, we are evolving into a service, technology, and information society. Fewer people are working in agriculture and manufacturing. Futurists John Naisbitt et al. note that we are moving toward a service economy based on high technology, rapid communications, biotechnology for use in agriculture and medicine, health care, and sales of merchandise.[10] Service areas with increasing numbers of jobs include health care and social assistance; professional, scientific, and technical services; educational services; administrative and support services; waste management and remediation services; accommodation and food services; government; retail trade; transportation and warehousing, finance and insurance; arts, entertainment, and recreation; wholesale trade; real estate, rental, and leasing; and information and management.

Increased Opportunities in Health Care

If you are interested in science and technology along with helping other people, there are many career opportunities in health care. It is estimated that by 2018, there will be an increase of four million new jobs in health care, which will account for 26 percent of all new jobs.[11] This trend is being driven by an aging population, increased longevity, health care reform, and new developments in the pharmaceutical and medical fields. Because of increased health care costs, many of the jobs done by doctors, nurses, dentists, or physical therapists are now being done by physician's assistants, medical assistants, dental assistants, physical therapy aides, and home health aides. Health care workers will increasingly use technology to do their work. For example, a new occupation is nursing informatics, which combines traditional nursing skills with computer and information science.

Increased Need for Education

In the past, the life pattern for many people was to graduate from school, go to work, and eventually retire. Because of the rapid changes in technology and society today, workers will need additional training and education over a lifetime. Education will take place in a variety of forms: community college courses, training on the job, private training sessions, and learning on your own. Those who do not keep up with the new technology will find that their skills quickly become obsolete. Those who do keep up will find their skills in demand.

As we transition from manufacturing to service and technical careers, education beyond high school will become increasingly important. According to the Bureau of Labor Statistics, occupations that require a postsecondary degree will account for nearly half of all new jobs from 2008 to 2018, with the fastest growth in jobs requiring an associate's degree or higher. In addition, higher education will result in higher earnings and lower unemployment.[12]

FIGURE **3.6**

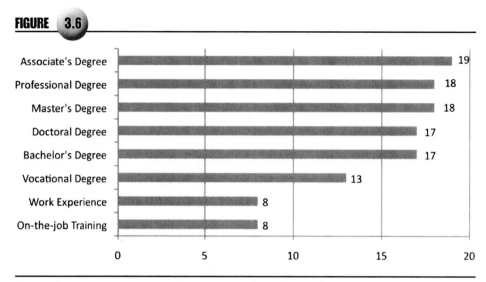

Projected percent increase in employment, 2008 through 2018.[13]

FIGURE **3.7**

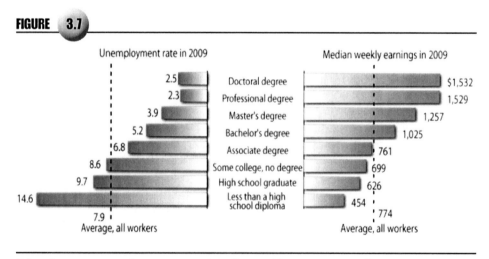

Education pays, unemployment rate and median weekly earnings, 2009.[14]

Young people who do not continue their education are likely to be stuck in lower-paying jobs, while those who continue their education will have higher-paying jobs. Author Joyce Lain Kennedy believes that the middle class is becoming an endangered species.[15] She states that many jobs traditionally held by the middle class have been "dumbed down," making them so simple that anyone can do them. These jobs pay very little and offer no benefits, no employment stability, and little opportunity for advancement. Young people often hold these jobs in their teens and twenties.

At the other end of the job continuum are jobs requiring a college education or training beyond high school. These high-end jobs often require technical or computer skills. These are the jobs that pay better and offer benefits. It seems that we are becoming a nation of haves and have-nots who are separated by their education and technical skills.

Going Green!

Have you purchased organic products or an energy-efficient light bulb, appliance, or car? If so, you are part of a new environmental movement that is gaining impetus in the U.S., the rise of social responsibility and the citizen consumer. Businesses that are seen as green attract consumers who are concerned about using energy efficiently, new sources of energy, and preserving the environment. In addition to profit, businesses are now concerned about the planet and working conditions for people.

As fossil fuels are depleted, the world is facing a major transformation in how energy is generated and used. Sustainability, wind turbines, solar panels, farmer's markets, biofuels, and wind energy are just some of the ways to transition to a post-fossil-fuel world. Jobs in this field will include engineers who design new technology, consultants to audit energy needs, and installers who install and maintain systems. Here are some titles of green jobs: environmental lawyer, environmental technician, sustainability consultant, sustainability project director, green architect, green building project manager, marine biologist, environmental technician, energy efficiency specialist, organic farmer, compliance manager, product engineer, wind energy engineer, and solar engineer.

A Diverse Workforce

The workforce in the United States is becoming increasingly more diverse. Diversity includes many demographic variables such as ethnicity, religion, gender, national origin, disability, sexual orientation, age, education, geographic origin, and skill characteristics. Having an appreciation for diversity is important in maintaining a work environment that is open and allows for individual differences. Increasing diversity provides opportunities for many different kinds of individuals and makes it important to be able to have good working relationships with all kinds of people.

The U.S. Bureau of Labor Statistics has described some trends that will affect the workplace by 2018.[16]

- Whites are expected to make up a decreasing share of the labor force, while Blacks, Asians, and all other groups will increase their share. Persons of Hispanic origin will increase their share of the labor force from 14.3 to 17.6 percent, reflecting a 33.1 percent growth.
- The number of women in the labor force will grow at a slightly faster rate than the number of men. The male labor force is projected to grow by 7.5 percent, as compared with 9.0 percent for the female labor force.
- The number of workers in younger age groups will decline, while workers in the 55 years and older group will increase, reflecting the increase of aging Baby Boomers.
- Total employment is expected to increase by 10 percent from 2008 to 2018. Changes in consumer demand and advances in technology will continue to change the structure of the economy, with decreasing jobs in manufacturing and increasing numbers of jobs in service and technology.

E-Commerce Is Changing the Way We Do Business

E-commerce, the purchasing of goods, services, and information over the Internet, is a new technology that has revolutionized the way business is done in the 21st century. More people are using e-commerce because of convenience, selection, and the ease of shopping for goods at the best price. Online sales are a growing part of the market, increasing 10 to 20 percent a year for the last several years. In 2010, online shopping accounted for 7 percent of all sales, and 42 percent of retail sales were influenced by online marketing.[17] This growth in e-commerce will have implications for education and business. More colleges are offering courses in e-commerce and incorporating e-commerce topics into traditional business offerings. There are more career opportunities in e-commerce and related fields such as computer graphics, web design, online marketing, and package delivery services.

The Microprocessor

The microprocessor is a silicon chip containing transistors that determine the capability of a computer. In the past 20 years, the power of the microprocessor has increased more than one million times. In the next 20 years, the power will increase a million times again.[18] Because of the increased power of the micro-processor, it will be used in new ways and with new devices. Consider the "smart home" of the future:

> As you reach the front door, you are welcomed by a flat screen, rather than a doorbell. You can use this screen to ring the doorbell, talk to the person inside the home or leave a message, which can be accessed by telephone or e-mail.

> If you're the homeowner, walk through the door and the curtains go up, letting light in, and the entire house is soon subtly illuminated. The hi-fi will access its database to play your favorite music, and the air-conditioning will be preset to the temperature you prefer.

> As you move to the kitchen, you take the ingredients for your lunch—say, flour, a piece of fish and a few stalks of broccoli—to a networked table. This will activate a system that will immediately offer you a range of appropriate recipes. Your smart microwave will fix the dish for you, consulting the recipe you prefer, via the Internet.[19]

The microprocessor is increasingly available to all and for less cost. The personal computer would have occupied an entire building 35 years ago. Today we have access to powerful computers and mobile devices that will play an ever greater role in our daily lives.

> It's remarkable how we now take all that power for granted. Using a basic home PC costing less than $1,000, you can balance your household budget, do your taxes, write letters to friends and fax or e-mail them over the Internet, listen to CDs or the radio, watch the news, consult a doctor, play games, book a vacation, view a house, buy a book or a car. The list is endless.[20]

New Advances in Technology and Communication

There has been a recent rapid increase in the development of cell phones and other mobile devices, as well as the use of social media, which will continue to have a major impact on career opportunities. Those who can keep up with the current technology will find increasing career and business opportunities. Graduates will become more marketable if they combine traditional career areas with technology such as social media. For example, students in a marketing degree program will be more in demand if they can use Facebook, LinkedIn, or Twitter to market products.

The Bureau of Labor Statistics reports that two million technology-related jobs will be created by 2018. Jobs in computer systems design and related services are expected to increase by 34 percent by 2018. Jobs that will grow faster than the average include computer-network administrators, data-communications analysts, and Web developers. Some new fields include data-loss prevention, online security, and risk management. Computer science degrees are especially marketable when combined with traditional majors such as finance, accounting, or marketing.[21]

Because we are living in the Information Age, information and technology workers are now the largest group of workers in the United States. Careers in

information technology include the design, development, and support of computer software, hardware, and networks. Some newer jobs in this area include animation for video games, films, and videos as well as setting up websites and Internet security. There are also good opportunities for network programmers who can program a group of computers to work together. Because computer use has increased greatly, it is expected that computer-related jobs will expand by 40 percent or more in the next decade.[22]

In the future, computers will continue to become more powerful, mobile, and connected. It is predicted that by 2018, microprocessors will be replaced by optical computers that function at the speed of light. Technology will be embedded in products used for entertainment as well as for home and business use. It is predicted that in the future, the desktop computer as we know it will cease to exist. Instead of a home computer, we will have computerized homes with sensors that monitor energy use and smart appliances with computer chips. Gestures, touch, and voice communication will rapidly replace computer keyboards. The Nintendo Wii™ and the iPhone are current examples. Computers will move from homes and offices into human bodies. Microchips may be embedded in human bodies to monitor health conditions and to deliver medical care. Some futurists forecast a time when computer chips will be embedded in the brain and connected to the Internet. Of course, computer security will become increasingly important with these new advances.[23]

Radiation and laser technologies will provide new technical careers in the future. It has been said that lasers will be as important to the 21st century as electricity was for the 20th century. New uses for lasers are being found in medicine, energy, industry, computers, communications, entertainment, and outer space. The use of lasers is creating new jobs and causing others to become obsolete. For example, many welders are being replaced by laser technicians, who have significantly higher earnings. New jobs will open for people who purchase, install, and maintain lasers.

Careers in fiber optics and telecommunications are among the top new emerging fields in the 21st century. Fiber optics are thin glass fibers that transmit light. This new technology may soon make copper wire obsolete. One of the most important uses of fiber optics is to speed up delivery of data over the Internet and to improve telecommunications. It is also widely used in medical instruments, including laser surgery.

Another interesting development to watch is artificial intelligence software, which enables computers to recognize patterns, improve from experience, make inferences, and approximate human thought. Scientists at the MIT Artificial Intelligence Lab have developed a robot named Cog. Here is a description of Cog and its capabilities:

> We have given it a multitude of sensors to "feel" and learn what it is like to be touched and spoken to. Cog's ability to make eye contact and reach out to moving objects is also meant to motivate people to interact with it. These features have taught Cog, among other things, to distinguish a human face from inanimate objects (this puts its development at about a 3-month-old's). It can also listen to music and keep rhythm by tapping on a drum (something a 5-year-old can do). One of the most startling moments in Cog's development came when it was learning to touch things. At one point, Cog began to touch and discover its own body. It looked so eerie and human, I was stunned.[24]

Beware of Outsourcing

To reduce costs and improve profits, many jobs in technology, manufacturing, and service are being outsourced to countries such as India, China, and Taiwan, where well-educated, English-speaking workers are being used to do these jobs. For example, programmers in India can produce software at only 10 percent of the cost of these services in the United States. Jobs that are currently being outsourced include accounting, payroll clerks, customer service, data entry, assembly line workers, industrial and production engineers, machine operators, computer-assisted design (CAD) technicians, purchasing managers, textile workers, software developers, and technical support. It is a good idea to consider this trend in choosing your future career and major. Jobs that are most likely to be outsourced are: [25]

- Repetitive jobs, such as accounting,
- Well-defined jobs, such as customer service,
- Small manageable projects, such as software development,
- Jobs in which proximity to the customer is not important, such as technical support.

Jobs that are least likely to be outsourced include:

- Jobs with ambiguity, such as top management jobs,
- Unpredictable jobs, such as troubleshooters,
- Jobs that require understanding of the culture, such as marketing,
- Jobs that require close proximity to the customer, such as auto repair,
- Jobs requiring a high degree of innovation and creativity, such as product design,
- Jobs in entertainment, music, art, and design.

To protect yourself from outsourcing:

- Strive to be the best in the field.
- Be creative and innovative.
- Avoid repetitive jobs that do not require proximity to the customer.
- Choose a career where the demand is so high that it won't matter if some are outsourced.
- Consider a job in the skilled trades; carpenters, plumbers, electricians, hair stylists, construction workers, auto mechanics, and dental hygienists will always be in demand.

New Advances in Biology

Future historians may describe the 21st century as the biology century because of all the developments in this area. If you are interested in biology, it can lead to good careers in the future. One of the most important developments is the Human Genome Project, which has identified the genes in human DNA, the carrier of genetic material. The research done on the human genome has been an impetus for development in some new careers in biotechnology and biomedical technology. Watch the news for future developments that will affect how we all live and work.

Biotechnology will become increasingly important as a way to combat disease, develop new surgical procedures and devices, increase food production, reduce pollution, improve recycling, and provide new tools for law enforcement. Biotechnology includes genomic profiling, biomedical engineering, new pharmaceuticals, genetic engineering, and DNA identification. One of the most promising outcomes of biotechnology will be the production of new pharmaceuticals. About 90 percent of all drugs ever invented have been developed since 1975, and about 6,000 new drugs are waiting for regulatory approval.[26] In the future, biotechnology may be used to find cures for diabetes, arthritis, Alzheimer's disease, and heart disease.

The field of biomedical engineering, which involves developing and testing health care innovations, is expected to grow by 72 percent by 2018.[27] Biomedical technology is the field in which bionic implants are being developed for the human body. Scientists are working on the development of artificial limbs and organs including eyes, ears, hearts, and kidneys. A promising new development in this field is brain and computer interfaces. Scientists recently implanted a computer chip into the brain of a quadriplegic, enabling him to control a computer and television with his mind.[28] Biotechnology also develops new diagnostic test equipment and surgical tools.

Increase in Entrepreneurship

An important trend for the new millennium is the increase in entrepreneurship, which means starting your own business. For the Baby Boom Generation, it was expected that one would have a job for life. Because of rapid changes in society and the world of work, Millennials can expect to have as many as 10 different jobs over a lifetime.[29] A growing number of entrepreneurs operate their small businesses from home, taking advantage of telecommuting and the Internet to communicate with customers. While being an entrepreneur has some risks involved, there are many benefits, such as flexible scheduling, being your own boss, taking charge of your own destiny, and greater potential for future income if your company is successful. You won't have to worry about being outsourced, either.

The Effect of Terrorism and Need for Security

Fear of terrorism has changed attitudes that will affect career trends for years to come. Terrorist attacks have created an atmosphere of uncertainty that has had a negative effect on the economy and has increased unemployment. For example, the airline industry is struggling financially as people hesitate to fly to their vacation destinations. People are choosing to stay in the safety of their homes, offices, cars, and gated communities. Since people are spending more time at home, they spend more money making their homes comfortable. Faith Popcorn, who is famous for predicting future trends, has called this phenomenon "cocooning," which is "our desire to build ourselves strong and cozy nests where we can retreat from the world, enjoying ourselves in safety and comfort."[30] As a result, construction, home remodeling, and sales of entertainment systems are increasing.

Another result of terrorism is the shift toward occupations that provide value to society and in which people can search for personal satisfaction.[31] More people volunteer their time to help others, and are considering careers in education, social work, and medical occupations. When people are forced to relocate because of unemployment, they are considering moving to smaller towns that have a sense of community and a feeling of safety.

As the world population continues to grow, there is continued conflict over resources and ideologies and an increased need for security and safety. Law enforcement, intelligence, forensics, international relations, foreign affairs, and security administration careers will be in demand.

Nontraditional Workers

Unlike traditional workers, nontraditional workers do not have full-time, year-round jobs with health and retirement benefits. Employers are moving toward using nontraditional workers, including multiple job holders, contingent and part-time workers, independent contractors, and temporary workers. Nearly four out of five employers use nontraditional workers to help them become more efficient, prevent layoffs, and access workers with special skills. There are advantages and disadvantages to this arrangement. Nontraditional workers have no benefits and risk unemployment. However, this arrangement can provide workers with a flexible work schedule in which they work during some periods and pursue other interests or gain new skills when not working.

Top Jobs for the Future[32]

Based on current career trends, here are some jobs that should be in high demand for the next 10 years.

Field of Employment	Job Titles
Business	Marketing Manager, Security and Financial Service, Internet Marketing Specialist, Advertising Executive, Buyer, Sales Person, Real Estate Agent, Business Development Manager, Marketing Researcher, Recruiter
Education	Teacher, Teacher's Aide, Adult Education Instructor, Math and Science Teacher
Entertainment	Dancer, Producer, Director, Actor, Content Creator, Musician, Artist, Commercial Artist, Writer, Technical Writer, Newspaper Reporter, News Anchor Person
Health	Emergency Medical Technician, Surgeon, Chiropractor, Dental Hygienist, Registered Nurse, Medical Assistant, Therapist, Respiratory Therapist, Home Health Aide, Primary Care Physician, Medical Lab Technician, Radiology Technician, Physical Therapist, Dental Assistant, Nurse's Aide
Information Technology	Computer Systems Analyst, Computer Engineer, Web Specialist, Network Support Technician, Java Programmer, Information Technology Manager, Web Developer, Database Administrator, Network Engineer
Law/Law Enforcement	Correction Officer, Law Officer, Anti-Terrorist Specialist, Security Guard, Tax/Estate Attorney, Intellectual Property Attorney
Services	Veterinarian, Social Worker, Hair Stylist, Telephone Repair Technician, Aircraft Mechanic, Guidance Counselor, Occupational Therapist, Child Care Assistant, Baker, Landscape Architect, Pest Controller, Chef, Caterer, Food Server
Sports	Athlete, Coach, Umpire, Physical Trainer
Technology	Electrical Engineer, Biological Scientist, Electronic Technician, CAD Operator, Product Designer, Sales Engineer, Applications Engineer, Product Marketing Engineer, Technical Support Manager, Product Development Manager
Trades	Carpenter, Plumber, Electrician
Travel/Transportation	Package Delivery Person, Flight Attendant, Hotel/Restaurant Manager, Taxi Driver, Chauffeur, Driver

QUIZ

Career Trends of the Future

Test what you have learned by selecting the correct answers to the following questions:

1. Most students in college today are in
   a. the Baby Boom Generation.
   b. Generation X.
   c. the Millennial Generation.

2. Use of the Internet will result in
   a. increased e-commerce.
   b. increased use of conventional stores.
   c. decreased mail delivery.

3. The largest group of workers in the United States is in
   a. manufacturing.
   b. information technology.
   c. agriculture.

4. Jobs unlikely to be outsourced include
   a. jobs that require close proximity to the customer.
   b. computer programming jobs.
   c. customer service jobs.

5. Future historians will describe the 21st century as the
   a. art and entertainment century.
   b. biology century.
   c. industrial development century.

How did you do on the quiz? Check your answers: 1. c, 2. a, 3. b, 4. a, 5. b

Work Skills for the 21st Century

Because of rapid changes in technology, college students of today may be preparing for jobs that do not exist right now. After graduation, many college students find employment that is not even related to their college majors. One researcher found that 48 percent of college graduates find employment in fields not related to their college majors.[33] More important than one's college major are the general skills learned in college that prepare students for the future.

To define skills needed in the future workplace, the U.S. Secretary of Labor created the Secretary's Commission on Achieving Necessary Skills (SCANS). Based on interviews with employers and educators, the members of the commission outlined foundation skills and workplace competencies needed to succeed in the workplace in the 21st century.[34] The following skills apply to all occupations in all fields and will help you to become a successful employee, regardless of your major. As you read through these skills, think about your competency in these areas.

Foundation Skills

Basic Skills

- Reading
- Writing
- Basic arithmetic

- Higher-level mathematics
- Listening
- Speaking

Thinking Skills

- Creative thinking
- Decision making
- Problem solving
- Mental visualization
- Knowing how to learn
- Reasoning

Personal Qualities

- Responsibility
- Self-esteem
- Sociability
- Self-management
- Integrity/honesty

Workplace Competencies

Resources

- **Time.** Selects relevant goals, sets priorities, and follows schedules.
- **Money.** Uses budgets, keeps records, and makes adjustments.
- **Materials and facilities.** Acquires, stores, and distributes materials, supplies, parts, equipment, space, or final products.
- **Human resources.** Assesses knowledge and skills, distributes work, evaluates performance, and provides feedback.

Interpersonal

- **Participates as a member of a team.** Works cooperatively with others and contributes to group efforts.
- **Teaches others.** Helps others learn needed skills.
- **Serves clients/customers.** Works and communicates with clients and customers to satisfy their expectations.
- **Exercises leadership.** Communicates, encourages, persuades, and convinces others; responsibly challenges procedures, policies, or authority.
- **Negotiates to arrive at a decision.** Works toward an agreement involving resources or diverging interests.
- **Works with cultural diversity.** Works well with men and women and with people from a variety of ethnic, social, or educational backgrounds.

Information

- **Acquires and evaluates information.** Identifies the need for information, obtains information, and evaluates it.
- **Organizes and maintains information.** Organizes, processes, and maintains written or computerized records.
- **Uses computers to process information.** Employs computers to acquire, organize, analyze, and communicate information.

Systems

- **Understands systems.** Knows how social, organizational, and technological systems work and operates efficiently within them.
- **Monitors and corrects performance.** Distinguishes trends, predicts impacts of actions on systems operations, and takes action to correct performance.
- **Improves and designs systems.** Develops new systems to improve products or services.

Technology

- **Selects technology.** Judges which procedures, tools, or machines, including computers, will produce the desired results.
- **Applies technology to tasks.** Understands the proper procedures for using machines and computers.
- **Maintains and troubleshoots technology.** Prevents, identifies, or solves problems with machines, computers, and other technologies.

Because the workplace is changing, these skills may be more important than the background acquired through a college major. Work to develop these skills and you will be prepared for whatever lies ahead.

HOW TO RESEARCH YOUR CAREER

After you have assessed your personality, interests, values, and talents, the next step is to learn about the world of work. If you can match your interests to the world of work, you can find work that is interesting and you can excel in it. To learn about the world of work, you will need to research possible careers. This includes reading career descriptions and investigating career outlooks, salaries, and educational requirements.

Career Descriptions

The career description tells you about the nature of the work, working conditions, employment, training, qualifications, advancement, job outlook, earnings, and related occupations. The two best sources of job descriptions are the *Occupational Outlook Handbook* and *Occupational Outlook Quarterly*. The *Handbook*, published by the Bureau of Labor Statistics, is like an encyclopedia of careers. You can search alphabetically by career or by career cluster.

The *Occupational Outlook Quarterly* is a periodical with up-to-date articles on new and emerging occupations, training opportunities, salary trends, and new studies from the Bureau of Labor Statistics. You can find these resources in a public or school library, at a college career center.

Career Outlook

It is especially important to know about the career outlook of an occupation you are considering. Career outlook includes salary and availability of employment. How much does the occupation pay? Will the occupation exist in the future, and will there be employment opportunities? Of course, you will want to prepare yourself for careers that pay well and have future employment opportunities.

You can find information about career outlooks in the sources listed above, current periodicals, and materials from the Bureau of Labor Statistics. The following table, for example, lists the fastest-growing occupations, occupations with the highest salaries, and occupations with the largest job growth. Information from the Bureau of Labor Statistics is also available online.

Employment Projections 2008–2018[35]

10 Fastest-Growing Occupations	10 Industries with the Largest Wage and Salary Employment Growth	10 Occupations with the Largest Numerical Job Growth
Biomedical engineers	Management, scientific, technical	Registered nurses
Network systems and data communications analysts	Physicians	Home health aides
Home health aides	Computer systems design and related	Customer service representatives
Personal and home care aides	General merchandise stores	Food preparation workers
Financial examiners	Employment services	Personal and home care aides
Medical scientists	Local government	Retail salespersons
Physician assistants	Home health care services	Office clerks
Skin care specialists	Services for elderly and disabled	Accountants and auditors
Biochemists and biophysicists	Nursing care facilities	Nursing aides, orderlies
Athletic trainers	Full-service restaurants	Postsecondary teachers

Planning Your Education

Once you have assessed your personal characteristics and researched your career options, it is important to plan your education. If you have a plan, you will be able to finish your education more quickly and avoid taking unnecessary classes. You can begin work on your educational plan by following the steps below. After you have done some work on your plan, visit your college counselor or advisor to make sure that your plan is appropriate.

MAKING GOOD DECISIONS

Knowing how to make a good decision about your career and important life events is very important to your future, as this short poem by J. Wooden sums up:

> There is a choice you have to make,
> In everything you do.
> And you must always keep in mind,
> The choice you make, makes you.[36]

Sometimes people end up in a career because they simply seized an opportunity for employment. A good job becomes available and they happen to be in the right place at the right time. Sometimes people end up in a career because it is familiar to them, because it is a job held by a member of the family or a friend in the community. Sometimes people end up in a career because of economic necessity. The job pays well and they need the money. These careers are the result of chance circumstances. Sometimes they turn out well, and sometimes they turn out miserably.

Whether you are male or female, married or single, you will spend a great deal of your life working. By doing some careful thinking and planning about your career, you can improve your chances of success and happiness. Use the following steps to do some careful decision making about your career. Although you are the person who needs to make the decision about a career, you can get help from your college career center or your college counselor or advisor.

Steps in Making a Career Decision

1. **Begin with self-assessment.**
   - What is your personality type?
   - What are your interests?
   - What are your talents, gifts, and strengths?
   - What is your learning style?
   - What are your values?
   - What lifestyle do you prefer?

2. **Explore your options.**
   - What careers match your personal characteristics?

3. **Research your career options.**
   - Read the job description.
   - Investigate the career outlook.
   - What is the salary?
   - What training and education is required?
   - Speak with an advisor, counselor, or person involved in the career that interests you.
   - Choose a career or general career area that matches your personal characteristics.

4. **Plan your education to match your career goal.**
   - Try out courses in your area of interest.
   - Start your general education if you need more time to decide on a major.
   - Try an internship or part-time job in your area of interest.

5. **Make a commitment to take action and follow through with your plan.**

6. **Evaluate.**
   - Do you like the courses you are taking?
   - Are you doing well in the courses?
   - Continue research if necessary.

7. **Refine your plan.**
   - Make your plan more specific to aim for a particular career.
   - Select the college major that is best for you.

8. **Change your plan if it is not working.**
   - Go back to the self-assessment step.

The Decision-Making Process

- **Dependent decisions.** Different kinds of decisions are appropriate in different situations. When you make a dependent decision, you depend on someone else to make the decision for you. The dependent decision was probably the first kind of decision that you ever made. When your parents told you what to do as a child, you were making a dependent decision. As an adult, you make a dependent decision when your doctor tells you what medication to take for an illness or when your stockbroker tells you what stock you should purchase. Dependent decisions are easy to make and require little thought. Making a dependent decision saves time and energy.

The dependent decision, however, has some disadvantages. You may not like the outcome of the decision. The medication that your doctor prescribes may have unpleasant side effects. The stock that you purchased may go down in value. When students ask a counselor to recommend a major or a career, they are making a dependent decision. When the decision does not work, they blame the counselor. Even if the dependent decision does have good results, you may become dependent on others to continue making decisions for you. Dependent decisions do work in certain situations, but they do not give you as much control over your own life.

- **Intuitive decisions.** Intuitive decisions are based on intuition or a gut feeling about what is the best course of action. Intuitive decisions can be made quickly and are useful in dealing with emergencies. If I see a car heading on a collision path toward me, I have to swerve quickly to the right or left. I do not have time to ask someone else what to do or think much about the alternatives. Another example of an intuitive decision is in gambling. If I am trying to decide whether to bet a dollar on red or black, I rely on my gut feeling to make a choice. Intuitive decisions may work out or they may not. You could make a mistake and swerve the wrong way as the car approaches or you could lose your money in gambling.

- **Planful decisions.** For important decisions, it is advantageous to use what is called a planful decision. The planful decision is made after carefully weighing the consequences and the pros and cons of the different alternatives. The planful decision-making strategy is particularly useful for such decisions as:

  - What will be my major?
  - What career should I choose?
  - Whom should I marry?

The steps in a planful decision-making process:

1. **State the problem.** When we become aware of a problem, the first step is to state the problem in the simplest way possible. Just stating the problem will help you to clarify the issues.

2. **Consider your values.** What is important to you? What are your hopes and dreams? By keeping your values in mind, you are more likely to make a decision that will make you happy.

3. **What are your talents?** What special skills do you have? How can you make a decision that utilizes these skills?

4. **Gather information.** What information can you find that would be helpful in solving the problem? Look for ideas. Ask other people. Do some research. Gathering information can give you insight into alternatives or possible solutions to the problem.

5. **Generate alternatives.** Based on the information you have gathered, identify some possible solutions to the problem.

6. **Evaluate the pros and cons of each alternative.** List the alternatives and think about the pros and cons of each one. In thinking about the pros and cons, consider your values and talents as well as your future goals.

7. **Select the best alternative.** Choose the alternative that is the best match for your values and helps you to achieve your goals.

8. **Take action.** You put your decision into practice when you take some action on it. Get started!

THE RESUME AND JOB INTERVIEW

After investing your time in achieving a college education, you will need some additional skills to get a job. Having a good resume and knowing how to successfully interview for a job will help you to obtain your dream job.

Your Resume

A resume is a snapshot of your education and experience. It is generally one page in length. You will need a resume to apply for scholarships or part-time jobs, or find a position after you graduate. Start with a file of information you can use to create your resume. Keep your resume on file in your computer or on your flash drive so that you can revise it as needed. A resume includes the following:

- Contact information: your name, address, telephone number, and email address
- A brief statement of your career objective
- A summary of your education:
  - Names and locations of schools
  - Dates of attendance
  - Diplomas or degrees received
- A summary of your work and/or volunteer experience
- If you have little directly related work experience, a list of courses you have taken that would help the employer understand your skills for employment
- Special skills, honors, awards, or achievements
- References (people who can recommend you for a job or scholarship)

Your resume is important in establishing a good first impression. There is no one best way to write a resume. Whatever form you choose, write clearly and be brief, neat, and honest. If your resume is too lengthy or difficult to read, it may wind up in the trash can. Adjust your resume to match the job for which you are applying. This is easy to do if you have your resume stored on your computer. Update your resume regularly.

Ask for a letter of reference from your current supervisor at work or someone in a position to recommend you, such as a college professor or community member. Ask the person to address the letter "To Whom It May Concern" so that you can use the letter many times. The person recommending you should comment on your work habits, skills, and personal qualities. If you wait until you graduate to obtain letters of reference, potential recommenders may no longer be there or may not remember who you are. Always ask if you can use a person's name as a reference. When you are applying for a job and references are requested, phone the people who have agreed to recommend you and let them know to expect a call.

Print your resume so that it looks professional. Use a good-quality white, tan, or gray paper.

You will probably need to post your resume online to apply for some scholarships and job opportunities. Having your resume on the computer will make this task easier.

The Cover Letter

When you respond to job announcements, you will send a cover letter with your resume attached. Address your letter to a specific person at the company or organization and spell the name correctly. You can call the personnel office to obtain this information. The purpose of the cover letter is to state your interest in the job, highlight your qualifications, and get the employer to read your resume and call you for an interview. The cover letter should be brief and to the point. Include the following items:

- State the job you are interested in and how you heard about the opening.
- Briefly state how your education and experience would be assets to the company.
- Ask for an interview and tell the employer how you can be contacted.
- Attach your resume.
- Your cover letter is the first contact you have with the employer. Make it neat and free from errors.
- Use spell check and grammar check, read it over again, and have someone else check it for you.

The Job Interview

Knowing how to be successful in an interview will help you to get the job that you want. Here are some ideas for being prepared and making a good impression.

- **Learn about the job.** Before the interview, it is important to research both the company and the job. This research will help you in two ways: you will know if the job is really the one you want, and you will have information that will help you to succeed at the interview. If you have taken the time to learn about the company before the interview, you will make a good impression and show that you are really interested in the job. Here are some ways that you can find this information:
  - Your college or public library may have a profile describing the company and the products it produces. This profile may include the size of the company and the company mission or philosophy.

- Do you know someone who works for the company? Do any members of your family, friends, or teachers know someone who works for the company? If so, you can find out valuable information about the company.
- The personnel office often has informational brochures that describe the employer.
- Visit the company website on the Internet.

- **Understand the criteria used in an interview.** The interviewer represents the company and is looking for the best person to fill the job. It is your job to show the interviewer that you will do a good job. Of course you are interested in salary and benefits, but in order to get hired you must first convince the interviewer that you have something to offer the company. Focus on what you can offer the company based on your education and experience and what you have learned about the company. You may be able to obtain information on salary and benefits from the personnel office before the interview.

   Interviewers look for candidates who show the enthusiasm and commitment necessary to do a good job. They are interested in hiring someone who can work as part of a team. Think about your education and experience and be prepared to describe your skills and give examples of how you have been successful on the job. Give a realistic and honest description of your work.

- **Make a good impression.** Here are some suggestions for making a good impression:
   - Dress appropriately for the interview. Look at how the employees of the company dress and then dress a little better. Of course, your attire will vary with the type of job you are seeking. You will dress differently if you are interviewing for a position as manager of a surf shop or an entry-level job in an engineering firm. Wear a conservative dark-colored or neutral suit for most professional positions. Do not wear too much jewelry, and hide excess body piercings (unless you are applying at a piercing shop). Cover any tattoos if they are not appropriate for the workplace.
   - Relax during the interview. You can relax by preparing in advance. Research the company, practice interview questions, and visualize yourself in the interview room feeling confident about the interview.
   - When you enter the interview room, smile, introduce yourself, and shake hands with the interviewer. If your hands are cold and clammy, go to the restroom before the interview and run warm water over your hands or rub them together.
   - Maintain eye contact with the interviewer and sit up straight. Poor posture or leaning back in your chair could be seen as a lack of confidence or interest in the job.

- **Anticipate the interview questions.** Listen carefully to the interview questions. Ask for clarification of any question you do not understand. Answer the questions concisely and honestly. It helps to anticipate the questions that are likely to be asked and think about your answers in advance. Generally, be prepared to talk about yourself, your goals, and your reasons for applying for the job. Following are some questions that are typically asked in interviews and some suggestions for answering them:

1. **What can you tell us about yourself?** Think about the job requirements, and remember that the interviewer is looking for someone who will do a good job for the company. Talk about your education and experience as they relate to the job. You can put in interesting facts about your life and your hobbies, but keep your answers brief. This question is generally an icebreaker that helps the interviewer get a general picture of you and help you relax.

2. **Why do you want this job? Why should I hire you?** Think about the research you did on this company and several ways that you could benefit the company. A good answer might be, "I have always been good at technical skills and engineering. I am interested in putting these technical skills into practice in your company." A not-so-good answer would be, "I'm interested in making a lot of money and need health insurance."

3. **Why are you leaving your present job?** Instead of saying that the boss was horrible and the working conditions were intolerable (even if this was the case), think of some positive reasons for leaving, such as:
   - I am looking for a job that provides challenge and an opportunity for growth.
   - I received my degree and am looking for a job where I can use my education.
   - I had a part-time job to help me through school. I have graduated and am looking for a career.
   - I moved (or the company downsized or went out of business).

   Be careful about discussing problems on your previous job. The interviewers might assume that you were the cause of the problems or that you could not get along with other people.

4. **What are your strengths and weaknesses?** Think about your strengths in relation to the job requirements, and be prepared to talk about them during the interview. When asked about your weaknesses, smile and try to turn them into strengths. For example, if you are an introvert, you might say that you are quiet and like to concentrate on your work, but you make an effort to communicate with others on the job. If you are an extrovert, say that you enjoy talking and working with others, but you are good at time management and get the job done on time. If you are a perfectionist, say that you like to do an excellent job, but you know the importance of meeting deadlines, so you do the best you can in the time available.

5. **Tell us about a difficulty or problem that you solved on the job.** Think about some problem that you successfully solved on the job and describe how you did it. Focus on what you accomplished. If the problem was one that dealt with other people, do not focus on blaming or complaining. Focus on your desire to work things out and work well with everyone.

6. **Tell us about one of your achievements on the job.** Give examples of projects you have done on the job that have turned out well and projects that gave you a sense of pride and accomplishment.

7. **What do you like best about your work? What do you like least?** Think about these questions in advance and use the question about what you like

best to highlight your skills for the job. For the question about what you like the least, be honest but express your willingness to do the job that is required.

8. **Are there any questions that you would like to ask?** Based on your research on the company, think of some specific questions that show your interest in the company. A good question might be, "Tell me about your company's plans for the future." A not-so-good question would be, "How much vacation do I get?"

9. **Write a thank-you note.** After the interview, write a thank-you note and express your interest in the job. It makes a good impression and causes the interviewer to think about you again.

YOUR CAREER MAP

It's estimated that 90 percent of our daily lives is spent doing routine tasks. But habit can be a bad thing, because "if you keep on doing what you've always done, you're going to keep on getting what you've always got."

One of the most important things you can do is to take time to plan your career roadmap this year.

This exercise may take you 20 minutes, or you might devote a few hours to planning where you want to be Next year this time. If you want your life to be different this year, especially your career, take the time to work on your career roadmap.

STEP ONE: TAKE STOCK

The first step is to assess where you are. To figure out where you're going, you must first look at where you've been.

Here are some questions to help you assess where you are:

- What are you most proud of this past year—personally, and professionally?
- What went right this year?
- Did you receive any awards or recognition this year?
- Did you take on any additional responsibility this year? If so, what?
- How did you take initiative in your job this year?
- Have you learned any new skills?
- Did you earn any certifications or licenses?

Record this information in a success journal. This can be a Microsoft Word file on your computer, a note in Evernote, a series of emails you send to yourself (be sure to use email tags so you're able to find the emails again!), or even a physical notebook. And in the coming year, take time to record your accomplishments as you go through the year instead of waiting until the end of the year.

Next, look at opportunities for improvement in your career. How does your salary stack up against your peers? Is your current position in alignment with your priorities and your core values? Where is change needed?

STEP TWO: ARTICULATE YOUR GOAL

Decide what you want. Spell it out: What does it look like; what does it feel like? You have to really want it to invest the time and energy to follow your dream. Describe your ideal job:

- What is your ideal employer? (size, industry, culture, location, structure)

- How much would your dream job pay? (Realistically)

- What are the most important benefits—other than salary—that would prompt you to go to work for a new company?

- Describe your ideal job—the position you would most like to have. What is the job title, responsibilities, who you would report to, who would report to you. Would it involve travel? Do you want to work independently, as part of a team, or both? Do you like short-term projects or long-term projects?

- What do you want your next job to do for you that your last job didn't do? In other words, what will be different about your next job? Is there anything that you do in your current job that you don't want to do in your next job?

Think about the person that you want to be, and imagine the possibilities. Then, identify 2-3 goals you want to tackle. **Use the S.M.A.R.T. goal system to articulate your goals — goals should be "Specific, Measurable, Attainable, Realistic, and Time-Orionted."**

For example, let's imagine you have worked as an accountant for the past three years, but you really want to work in marketing. Your goal might be: "By Jan. 1, 2015, I will be working as a Marketing Assistant in a Fortune 1000 company"

You should also write down why you are interested in making the change. In other words, what is your motivation for taking this path?

Another good question to ask yourself is, "How will I know when I've achieved my goal(s)?"

STEP THREE: MAKE A PLAN

Take time to prepare a game plan for how you will reach your goal. But don't use planning as an excuse to procrastinate. You want to get to Step Four as quickly as possible, because actions create momentum.

Take each of your goals and write down the list of steps under each of them that you will need to take to make the goal happen. The more individual steps you can map out, the easier it will be for you to reach your goals. The steps should be practical tasks that will lead you to achieve the goal.

For example, with my goal of making a career change from accounting to marketing, here are some sample steps:

- Research job postings for entry-level marketing jobs. What are the skills, education, and experience required?

- Join the American Marketing Association and attend one virtual event or in-person boot camp in the next 90-120 days.

- Enroll in semester-long online marketing course focusing on marketing principles.
- Identify a volunteer opportunity to put marketing skills into practice—either in current job or with a community organization.
- Assess transferable skills from accounting that would be useful in marketing role (project management, analysis, financial management, client relations).
- Work with your professional résumé writer, JaneCo's Sensible Solutions, to create a targeted marketing cover letter for your professionally written resume from JaneCo's.
- Join three marketing-related groups on LinkedIn, and follow 5-6 Fortune 1000 companies in the area that have company profiles on LinkedIn.
- Assemble people in network to act as references for marketing interview.
- Connect with 2-3 contacts at Fortune 1000 companies in the area.
- Identify possible employers and submit résumés, or ask JaneCo's to submit them for you.

Give yourself milestones so you can measure your progress. How will you know when you're on the right track? Include specific dates and numbers in your milestones.

STEP FOUR: TAKE ACTION

With the tasks you've outlined in Step Three, this gives you a checklist of items to use to take action. If you are working through the steps and discover you need to add additional items, update your task list. You may also discover additional projects that need to be completed to make the next step—and the overall goal—easier to accomplish.

You may also find that you need to make adjustments to your timeline. For example, if you discover that a six-month program to learn about social media would help you land your new marketing job, you might adjust your goal deadline. This would give you time to put some of the new skills into practice before you put them on your résumé.

As you work your way through your task list, focus on the actions you are taking, realizing that if you are taking the right actions, these should eventually lead to the results you seek. **If you're not getting the results you want, change the plan, not the goal.** Re-examine your tasks and see if there is something you are missing. It can also be helpful to get outside feedback. Enlisting the help of an accountability partner, such as a professional career coach, can provide valuable perspective on your progress. And if there is a specific area where you need help in order to cross the task off your list, make sure you ask for assistance.

For example, a career change can be difficult. Enlisting the help of a professional career coach can help you make informed decisions and help with your personal marketing materials and job search strategies.

STEP FIVE: MEASURE YOUR PROGRESS

When you're on a journey, it can help to periodically assess where you are to make sure you're on the right road. If you miss a step along the way—or take a "wrong turn"—you can find yourself a long way from your intended destination. So plan periodic assessments of your progress along the way. This can be a monthly "check-up" where you review your plan and make any necessary changes, or a quarterly review.

Taking the time to think through—and plan out—**your career roadmap is an important step in helping you create the career you want for yourself.** If you don't, you may find your career stuck or stalled. Or you may wake up five years from now and wonder, "How did I get here?" If you want to achieve more in your professional life, invest the time and effort in completing the Career Roadmap Worksheet.

"If you don't know where you are going,
any road will get you there."

– Author Lewis Carroll

FOCUS ON IT

The more you think about something, the more attention you give to it, the more you focus on it, the more you will experience that something in your life.

Your attention attracts. It brings that which you focus on into existence. If you constantly focus on that which you lack, on that which you dislike, on that which you fear . . . you will get more of it. For that which you focus on expands.

Focus your attention on appreciating what you have, on the things that you can be happy for or grateful for and you will get more of it. What makes you happy? Focus on it.

"The more you focus on what you want, the more you will get of it . . . the more you fill your life with what you want, the less space there's going to exist for that which you do not want." ~Andres Lara

SAMPLE COVER LETTER

Sara Student
222 College Avenue
San Diego, CA 92019
(619) 123-4567

June 20, 2010

Mr. John Smith
Director of Human Resources
Future Technology Company
111 Technology Way
La Jolla, CA 92111

Dear Mr. Smith:

At our college job fair last week, I enjoyed speaking with you about some new engineering jobs available at Future Technology Company. As you suggested, I am sending my resume. I am interested in your opening for an electrical engineer. Is there anything else I need to do to apply for this position?

While at UCSD, I gained experience in laboratory projects, writing scientific reports, and preparing technical presentations. Some engineering projects that I completed relate to work done at your company:

- Constructed a programmable robot with motor and sensors
- Worked with a group of students on the design of a satellite communications system
- Completed lab projects on innovative fiber-optic fabrication techniques
- Proposed a design for a prosthetic device to help the visually impaired

For my senior design project, I used my knowledge of digital signal processing and systems integration to design and construct a voice modulator. This project involved applying theory to hardware and understanding information processing as well as the relation of a computer to its controlled devices.

I am excited about the possibility of continuing work in this field and would enjoy the opportunity to discuss my qualifications in more detail. I am available for an interview at your convenience. I look forward to hearing from you.

Sincerely,

Sara Student

Encl.: Resume

SAMPLE RESUME FOR A RECENT COLLEGE GRADUATE

Sara Student
222 College Avenue; San Diego, CA 92019
(619) 123-4567
saraengineer@aol.com

OBJECTIVE	Electrical Engineer
HIGHLIGHTS	Recent degree in Electrical Engineering
	Specialized coursework in electromagnetism, photonics and lasers, biomedical imaging devices, and experimental techniques
EDUCATION	B.S., Electrical Engineering, University of California, San Diego, CA, 2010
	A.S. with Honors, Cuyamaca College, El Cajon, CA, 2008

KEY RELATED COURSES

- **Circuits and systems:** solving network equations, Laplace transforms, practical robotics development

- **Electromagnetism:** Maxwell's equations, wave guides and transmission, electromagnetic properties of circuits and materials

- **Experimental techniques:** built and programmed a voice processor; studied transducers, computer architecture, and interfacing; applied integrated construction techniques

- **Photonics and lasers:** laser stability and design, holography, optical information processing, pattern recognition, electro-optic modulation, fiber optics

- **Biomedical imaging devices:** microscopy, x-rays, and neural imaging; designed an optical prosthesis

- **Quantum physics:** uncertainty principle, wave equation and spin, particle models, scattering theory and radiation

SKILLS

Computer Skills: PSpice, Matlab, Java, DSP, Assembly Language, Unix, Windows, Microsoft Word, Excel, and PowerPoint

Technical Skills: Microprocessors, circuits, optical components, oscilloscope, function generator, photovoltaics, signal processing, typing, SQUID testing

Personal Skills: Leadership, good people skills, organized, responsible, creative, motivated, hardworking, good writing skills

EMPLOYMENT	Intern, Quantum Design, La Jolla, CA, Summer 2009
	Computer Lab Assistant, UCSD, La Jolla, CA, 2008–2010
	Teacher's Aide, Cuyamaca College, El Cajon, CA, 2005–2007
	Volunteer, Habitat for Humanity, Tijuana, Mexico, 2003–2005
INTERESTS	Optics, computing, programming, physics, electronic music, sampling, marine biology, and scuba diving
ACHIEVEMENTS	Advanced Placement Scholar
	Dean's List, Phi Theta Kappa Honor Society
	Provost's Honors List

Summary and Conclusion

The liberal arts represent the foundation of a college education, upon which all academic majors are built. They promote success in any major and career by supplying students with a set of lifelong learning skills that can be applied in multiple settings and that can be continually used throughout life.

The liberal arts also promote your development as a whole person (intellectual, emotional, social, physical, spiritual, etc.) and broadens your perspective on the world by expanding (1) your social-spatial perspective to include increasingly larger social groups and more distant places, ranging from micro (the individual) to macro (the universe), and (2) your chronological perspective, ranging from the past to the present to the future.

Despite popular beliefs to the contrary, the liberal arts have many practical benefits, including promoting career mobility and career advancement. Most importantly, a liberal arts education prepares you for life roles other than an occupation, including roles such as family member, community member, and citizen. In short, a liberal arts education prepares you for more than a career: it prepares you for life.

Learning More through the World Wide Web

Internet-Based Resources for Further Information on Liberal Arts Education

For additional information related to the ideas discussed in this chapter, we recommend the following Web sites:

Liberal Arts Education:
www.aacu.org/resources/liberaleducation/index.cfm

Liberal Arts Resources:
www.iseek.org/education/liberalarts.html

References

Bahls, Steven. 2011. *Time to Teach Financial Literacy*. Inside Higher Education .com http://www.insidehighered.com/views/2011/06/13/essay_on_responsibility_of_colleges_to_teach_financial_literacy

Caldwell, Miriam. 2013. *What is the Difference Between a Credit Card and a Debit Card*. About.Com. Money in Your 20s. http://moneyfor 20s.about .com/od/managingyouraccounts/f/credit_debit.htm

Mudambi, Aradhana. 2013. *Financial-Aid Vocabulary for the First Generation Student*. Examiner.Com. http://www.examiner.com/article/financial-aid-vocabulary-for-the-first-generation-student

Roberts, Liz. 2008. *What's the Difference Between Good Debt and Bad Debt?* Ezine@rticles.com http://EzineArticles.com/?expert=Liz_Roberts

Bibliography

Carey, K. (2005) *Choosing to improve: Voices from colleges and Universities with better graduation rates.* New York: Education Trust, 2005.

King, J. "Student aid. Who benefits now?" *Educational Record*, 77, no. 1 (1996): 21–27.

Hartle, T. W., and King, J. E. "The end of equal opportunity in higher education?" *College Board Review* 181, (1997): 8–15.

Melvin, M., and Stick, S. "The causes and consequences of the federal student financial aid policy shift from grants to loans. *Journal of College Orientation and Transition* 9, no. 1 (2001): 44–55.

Parsons, M. "The Higher education policy arena: The rise and fall of a community." In *Higher Education in Transition: The Challenges of a New Millennium* edited by J. Losco and B. L. Fife. Westport, CT: Bergin & Garvey, 2000, 83–108.

Pascarella, E. T., and Terenzini, P. T. *How College Affects Students: A Third Decade of Research.* San Francisco: Jossey-Bass, 2005.

Tseng, V. "Family interdependence and academic adjustment in college: Youth from immigrant and U.S. born families." *Child Development* 75, (2004): 966–983.

Notes

1. Michael T. Robinson, "Top Jobs for the Future," from www.careerplanner.com, 2004.
2. Gail Sheehy, *New Passages* (New York: Random House, 1995), 34.
3. U.S. National Center for Health Statistics, National Vital Statistics Reports (NVSR), *Deaths: Final Data for 2006,* Vol. 57, No. 14, April 17, 2009.
4. Jeff Giles, "Generalization X," *Newsweek,* June 6, 1994.
5. Jane Bryant Quinn, "The Luck of the Xers, Comeback Kids: Young People Will Live Better Than They Think," *Newsweek,* 6 June 1994, 66–67.
6. Ellen Neuborne, http://www.businessweek.com, 1999.
7. Claudia Smith Brison, http://www.thestate.com, 14 July 2002.
8. Neil Howe and William Strauss, *Millennials Rising: The Next Great Generation* (New York: Vintage Books, 2000).
9. Neuborne, www.businessweek.com, 1999.
10. John Naisbitt, Patricia Aburdeen, and Walter Kiechel III, "How We Will Work in the Year 2000," *Fortune,* 17 May 1993, 41–52.
11. U.S. Bureau of Labor Statistics, *Occupational Outlook Handbook,* 2010–11 Edition, "Overview of the 2008–18 Projections," accessed from http://data.bls.gov
12. Ibid.
13. Ibid.
14. Ibid.

15. Joyce Lain Kennedy, *Joyce Lain Kennedy's Career Book* (Chicago, IL: VGM Career Horizons, 1993), 32.

16. U.S. Bureau of Labor Statistics, "Overview of the 2008–18 Projections."

17. *The Wall Street Journal*, "E-Commerce Growth Slows, But Still Out-Paces Retail," accessed March 2010, http://blogs.wsj.com

18. Bill Gates, "Microprocessors Upgraded the Way We Live," *USA Today,* 22 June 1999.

19. From "The Microsoft Future According to Bill Gates," accessed from http://www.ameinfo.com/33384.html, 2004.

20. Bill Gates, *Business @ the Speed of Thought: Using a Digital Nervous System* (Warner, 1999). Excerpts available at www.speed-of-thought.com.

21. U.S. Bureau of Labor Statistics, "Overview of the 2008–18 Projections."

22. "Tomorrow's Best Careers," from http://www.future-trends.com, 2004.

23. Dan Tynan, "The Next 25 Years in Tech," www.pcworld.com, January 30, 2008.

24. Anne Foerst, "A New Breed of 'Replicants' Is Redefining What It Means to Be Human," *Forbes ASAP,* 1999.

25. Michael T. Robinson, "Offshoring of America's Top Jobs," from http://www.careerplanner.com, 2004.

26. "Tomorrow's Best Careers," from http://www.future-trends.com, 2004.

27. U.S. Bureau of Labor Statistics, "Overview of the 2008–18 Projections."

28. Roxanne Khamsi, "Paralyzed Man Sends E-Mail by Thought," *News @ Nature.Com*, October 13, 2004.

29. Judith Kautz, "Entrepreneurship Beyond 2000," from www.smallbusinessnotes.com, 2004.

30. Faith Popcorn and Lys Marigold, *Clicking: 16 Trends to Future Fit Your Life, Your Work, and Your Business* (New York: HarperCollins, 1996).

31. James E. Challenger, "Career Pros: Terrorism's Legacy," from www.jobjournal.com, 2003.

32. Michael T. Robinson, "Top Jobs for the Future," CareerPlanner.com, 2008.

33. T. J. Grites, "Being 'Undecided' Could Be the Best Decision They Could Make," *School Counselor* 29 (1981): 41–46.

34. Secretary's Commission on Achieving Necessary Skills (SCANS), *Learning a Living: A Blueprint for High Performance* (Washington, DC: U.S. Department of Labor, 1991).

35. U.S. Bureau of Labor Statistics, "Overview of the 2008–18 Projections."

36. Quoted in Rob Gilbert, ed., *Bits and Pieces,* 7 October 1999.

Resume Worksheet for Your Ideal Career

Name _____   Date _____

Use this worksheet to prepare a resume similar to the sample on the previous page. Assume that you have graduated from college and are applying for your ideal career.

1. What is the specific job title of your ideal job?

2. What are two or three qualifications you possess that would especially qualify you for this job? These qualifications can be listed under Highlights on your resume.

3. List your degree or degrees, major, and dates of completion.

4. List five courses you will take to prepare for your ideal career. For each course, list some key components that would catch the interest of your potential employer. Use a college catalog to complete this section.

5. List the skills you would need in each of these areas.

Computer skills:

Technical or other job-related skills:

Personal skills related to your job objective:

6. List employment that would prepare you for your ideal job. Consider internships or part-time employment.

7. What are your interests?

8. What special achievements or awards do you have?

Interview Worksheet

Name _____   Date _____

Answer the following questions to prepare for the interview for your ideal job. If you do not know what your ideal job is, pretend that you are interviewing for any professional job. You may want to practice these questions with a classmate.

1. What can you tell us about yourself?

2. Why are you leaving your present job?

3. What are your strengths and weaknesses?

4. Tell us about a difficulty or problem that you solved on the job.

5. Tell us about one of your achievements on the job.

6. What do you like best about your work? What do you like least?

7. Are there any questions that you would like to ask?

Rate Your Skills for Success in the Workplace

Name _____   Date _____

Read each statement relating to skills needed for success in the workplace. Use the following scale to rate your competencies:

5 = Excellent   **4** = Very good   **3** = Average   **2** = Needs improvement   **1** = Need to develop

_____ 1. I have good reading skills. I can locate information I need to read and understand and interpret it. I can pick out the main idea and judge the accuracy of the information.

_____ 2. I have good writing skills. I can communicate thoughts, ideas, and information in writing. I know how to edit and revise my writing and use correct spelling, punctuation, and grammar.

_____ 3. I am good at arithmetic. I can perform basic computations using whole numbers and percentages. I can make reasonable estimates without a calculator and can read tables, graphs, and charts.

_____ 4. I am good at mathematics. I can use a variety of mathematical techniques including statistics to predict the occurrence of events.

_____ 5. I am good at speaking. I can organize my ideas and participate in discussions and group presentations. I speak clearly and am a good listener. I ask questions to obtain feedback when needed.

_____ 6. I am a creative thinker. I can come up with new ideas and unusual connections. I can imagine new possibilities and combine ideas in new ways.

_____ 7. I make good decisions. I can specify goals and constraints, generate alternatives, consider risks, and evaluate alternatives.

_____ 8. I am good at solving problems. I can see when a problem exists, identify the reasons for the problem, and devise a plan of action for solving the problem.

_____ 9. I am good at mental visualization. I can see things in my mind's eye. Examples include building a project from a blueprint or imagining the taste of a recipe from reading it.

_____ 10. I know how to learn. I am aware of my learning style and can use learning strategies to obtain new knowledge.

_____ 11. I am good at reasoning. I can use logic to draw conclusions and apply rules and principles to new situations.

_____ 12. I am a responsible person. I work toward accomplishing goals, set high standards, and pay attention to details. I usually accomplish tasks on time.

_____ 13. I have high self-esteem. I believe in my self-worth and maintain a positive view of myself.

_____ **14.** I am sociable, understanding, friendly, adaptable, polite, and relate well to others.

_____ **15.** I am good at self-management. I know my background, skills, and abilities and set realistic goals for myself. I monitor my progress toward completing my goals and complete them.

_____ **16.** I practice integrity and honesty. I recognize when I am faced with a decision that involves ethics and choose ethical behavior.

_____ **17.** I am good at managing my time. I set goals, prioritize, and follow schedules to complete tasks on time.

_____ **18.** I manage money well. I know how to use and prepare a budget and keep records, making adjustments when necessary.

_____ **19.** I can manage material and resources. I can store and distribute materials, supplies, parts, equipment, space, or products.

_____ **20.** I can participate as a member of a team. I can work cooperatively with others and contribute to group efforts.

_____ **21.** I can teach others. I can help others to learn needed knowledge and skills.

_____ **22.** I can exercise leadership. I know how to communicate, encourage, persuade, and motivate individuals.

_____ **23.** I am a good negotiator. I can work toward an agreement and resolve divergent interests.

_____ **24.** I can work with men and women from a variety of ethnic, social, or educational backgrounds.

_____ **25.** I can acquire and evaluate information. I can identify a need for information and find the information I need.

_____ **26.** I can organize and maintain information. I can find written or computerized information.

_____ **27.** I can use computers to process information.

_____ **28.** I have an understanding of social, organizational, and technological systems and can operate effectively in these systems.

_____ **29.** I can improve the design of a system to improve the quality of products and services.

_____ **30.** I can use machines and computers to accomplish the desired task.

_____ **Total**

Score your skills for success in the workplace.

150–121	Excellent
120–91	Very good
90–61	Average
Below 60	Need improvement

From the previous list of workplace skills, make a list of five of your strong points. What do you do well?

From the list of workplace skills, make a list of areas you need to improve.

The Planful Decision Strategy

Name _____   Date _____

Read the following scenario describing a college student in a problem situation. Then, answer the questions that follow to practice the planful decision strategy. You may want to do this as a group activity with other students in the class.

Rhonda is an 18-year-old student who is trying to decide on her major. She was a good student in high school, earning a 3.4 grade point average. Her best subjects were English and American history. She struggled with math and science but still earned good grades in these subjects. While in high school, she enjoyed being on the debate team and organizing the African American Club. This club was active in writing letters to the editor and became involved in supporting a local candidate for city council.

Rhonda is considering majoring in political science and has dreams of eventually going to law school. Rhonda likes being politically involved and advocating for different social causes. The highlight of her life in high school was when she organized students to speak to the city council about installing a traffic light in front of the school after a student was killed trying to cross the street. The light was installed during her senior year.

Rhonda's family has always been supportive, and she values her family life and the close relationships in the family. She comes from a middle-income family that is struggling to pay for her college education. Getting a bachelor's degree in political science and going to law school would take seven years and be very expensive. There is no law school in town, so Rhonda would have to move away from home to attend school.

Rhonda's parents have suggested that she consider becoming a nurse and attending the local nursing college. Rhonda could finish a bachelor's degree in nursing in four years and could begin working part-time as a nurse's aide in a short time. A cousin in the family became a nurse and found a job easily and is now earning a good income. The cousin arranged for Rhonda to volunteer this summer at the hospital where she works. Rhonda enjoys helping people at the hospital. Rhonda is trying to decide on her major. What should she do?

1. State the problem.

2. Describe Rhonda's values, hopes, and dreams.

3. What special interests, talents, or aptitudes does she have?

4. What further information would be helpful to Rhonda in making her decision?

5. What are the alternatives and the pros and cons of each?

Alternative 1	
Pros:	Cons:

Alternative 2	
Pros:	Cons:

Alternative 3 (be creative!)	
Pros:	Cons:

6. Only Rhonda can choose what is best for her. If you were Rhonda, what would you do and why? Use a separate piece of paper, if necessary, to write your answer.

Understanding Student Development through Student Success

4

PURPOSE

Student Development is the way a student grows, progresses, or increases your developmental capabilities. As a first-generation college student, having a clear understanding of your development process allows for better communication with you, your family, and peers. This chapter can be used a compass for you to gauge the direction you should be going.

ACTIVATE YOUR THOUGHTS

What are some of the challenges you foresee as you begin to develop into a young adult?

Do you think as a first-generation college student, your student development experience will differ from students whose parents graduated from college?

UNDERSTANDING STUDENT DEVELOPMENT THROUGH STUDENT SUCCESS

I remember as a child the many visits to the department store. Whether the visit was for clothes or shoes, I always experienced trying different pairs of pants, skirts, blouses, and shoes. The process was often uncomfortable for me because I knew that I had outgrown the clothes and shoes that we purchased before the current visit. I knew that something would be too big, or too tight, or too loose. I knew for a fact that more often than not, I had developed physically in some way, shape, form, or fashion. My mother would often give me prep-talks before the "treasure hunt" of the right jeans, skirt, blouse, and shoes took place. This "talk" never really prepared me from the work it took for me to accept my physical development. I always knew if something was too tight, too big, or too loose, I would not be comfortable. When I outgrew my favorite pair of jeans or shoes, I often denied my outgrowth. I knew the discomfort I felt and even tricked myself into believing that I was comfortable. This analogy can be used when reflecting on the student development growth that you will experience. Your growth in college is intended to be holistic, meaning you should illustrate growth physically, emotionally, mentally, and spiritually.

STUDENT DEVELOPMENT IN COLLEGE

Student and Academic Professionals have researched the importance of student development. However, if you, as a student are not privy to your development, you will find a way to fight the reality of growing and developing into young adults. The habits of high school will try to stick around and plague the idea of growing up. For 12–13 years before college, you have developed study, work, socializing, and communication habits that you have utilized to survive each level of development. When you arrive to college, everything around you will express the need for you to transition from high school to college and eventually develop new habits. The habits developed during your college years will eventually prompt your transition from college into the workforce. Let this chapter be a guide to understanding the skills, tendencies, and habits you need to develop through out your college years. Below are some Student Development Theories for you to explore.

Arthur Chickering seven Vectors of Identity Development*

1. Developing Competence
   a. Intellectual
   b. Physical
   c. Interpersonal
2. Managing Emotions
3. Moving through autonomy toward interdependence
   a. Emotional (no longer need constant reassurance, reduced dependency)
   b. Instrumental (cope with problems without seeking help)
4. Developing mature interpersonal relations
5. Establishing identity
   a. Comfort with body and appearance
   b. Comfort with gender and sexual orientation
   c. Sense of self in relation to social/cultural context (race/ethnicity/culture)
   d. Clarification of self-concept through roles and life-style
   e. Sense of self in response to feedback from others
   f. Self acceptance and self-esteem
   g. Personal stability and integration
6. Developing Purpose-vocational personal interest, family
7. Developing integrity
   a. Humanizing values (relative view of absoluteness of rules)
   b. Personalizing values
   c. Developing congruence between values and behaviors

Vincent Tinto-Individual departure

1. Separation (disassociation with past community membership)
2. Transition (passage from old to new)

Source: *Education and Identity* by A. Chickering, 1969. Jossey-Bass.

3. Incorporation (integration into new community, adopting new norms for behavior)

4. Academic and Social integration–each formal and/or informal (need both, on may be more than the other)

FITNESS FOR FRESHMEN

Time, freedom, and lots of it. You are now responsible for regulating your time and have the freedom to choose how you do it. You decide when you get up, when you go to bed, what you eat and many other aspects of your life previously out of your control. You have more adult responsibilities and decisions to make than any other time in your life.

As for fitness, you are at a cross-road that may determine your fitness level for the rest of your life. The "freshman 15" (a 15-pound weight gain) is a very real problem faced by a great number of first-year college students. You're probably no longer on an organized athletic team with a coach to control your training. You must now motivate yourself to exercise and stay active. Fast food will become a mainstay in your diet.

Keeping Fit

Some strategies to keep fit include eating regular, well-balanced, low-fat meals (don't skip meals.); sleeping at least eight hours a day; and exercising on a regular basis. We are fortunate at Berry to have a registered dietitian as our director of food services. In our school cafeteria you will always have choices of healthful food to eat. Drink lots of water, the fluid of life. It has innumerable ways of helping the body: assisting with digestion, cooling the body, and helping to metabolize fat.

Sleep is important in maintaining fitness. Your body needs time to recover, so take naps in the afternoon if you are not getting enough sleep at night.

We have very diverse intramural offerings; make use of team sports activities and include a variety of individual exercises such as weight lifting and aerobic dance to round out your program. Variety is the spice of life. Variety and a regular exercise partner have been shown to be the major contributors in exercise adherence and success.

Avoid prepackaged diet plans. Such a plan may work, but unless it is a program that you want to continue for a lifetime you are going to quit at some point. The weight will come back because you haven't learned a new, wholesome lifestyle to replace the old one.

Exercise and nutrition combine to make a person fit. Fitness is determined in several categories. Muscular strength, muscular endurance, flexibility, cardiovascular fitness, and body composition (amount of body fat you have compared to lean mass) are all areas which should be addressed in your personal-fitness plan. Take a Survey of Fitness class early in your course of study, and learn how to avoid fitness pitfalls. Exercise increases energy levels and job productivity, which can in turn improve academic performance. It also can decrease stress, depression, and body-fat levels. Exercise can improve the quality of your life and can be tailored to fit anyone's personal preferences. So, don't wait until the "freshman 15" has its grip on you. Make the choice to start now on the road to fitness. If you don't know what to do, go to the gym and ask one of the fitness centers's exercise consultants to help you.

LIVING WITH ROOMMATES

When preparing to attend college for the first time, many students are given advice on how to succeed. Some are told how to be a successful student in the classroom, how to network with professors, and the all-important, how to avoid the "Freshman 15." However, many students tend not to receive advice on how to live successfully on campus, short of making sure they bring and use shower shoes. Living on campus can be an overwhelming experience, and being unprepared can have direct impact on your success as a student.

Think about it, this may be your first time moving outside of your home into a new city, this may be your first time having to share a room or share a room with someone you are not related to you, and this may be your first time having to potentially share a bathroom with 10 or more people. When seeing this short list, one may ask, *why live on campus, when I can stay at home, be comfortable, and commute to college?* Before considering commuting, consider the following:

- Although many factors can influence academic success, one important factor that will determine academic success is living on campus (Astin 1984).

- Students who choose to live on campus tend to have more interactions with their faculty members, take part in extracurricular activities, and become more knowledgeable and take advantage of campus resources (Astin 1984; Chickering and Kuper 1971; Chickering 1974; Pascarella 1984; Pascarella et al. 1994; Welty 1976).

- Students who live on campus tend to have stronger critical thinking skills, show more intellectual growth, are more likely to be more satisfied with their collegiate experience, and most importantly, students who live on campus are more likely to graduate in comparison to those who live off campus (Gellin 2003; Pascarella et al. 1993; Pascarella and Terenzini 1994; Pike 1991; Tinto 1987; Velez 1985).

A research consultant said the following as it pertains to purchasing a car, "As cliché as perhaps it sounds, there's that new-car smell that needs to be experienced firsthand and cannot be experienced over the Internet" (Tuttle 2012). The same concept can be applied to living on campus. Test-driving campus life will make your transition from moving from home to campus an easier transition.

Moving into your residential hall, please find, read, and understand your institution's housing policies and procedures handbook of living on campus. Although you received an actual handbook when you moved onto campus, most institutions have electronic copies of their housing policies and procedures on their residential life websites. The housing policies and procedures handbook will detail the rules and regulations that you have agreed to abide by while living on campus, the course of action that will be taken if you violate any of the policies and procedures, and detail processes that the residential life department oversees (such as room selection, room switching, billing, etc.).

By receiving the handbook or even signing your housing contract, the expectation is that you have read and understood the housing policies and procedures of living on campus. As such, if you unknowingly violate a housing policy, failing to read your handbook will not absolve you from the violation. It is important you read and understand the housing policy and procedures handbook; so you understand how your institution expects you to live responsibly, the consequences for violating housing policies and procedures, and most importantly, your rights as a student living on campus.

Lastly, it is important to understand the roles of the Resident Assistant (RA) and Resident Director, both of whom will live with you in your residence hall.

Resident Assistant

The RA is a student who lives on your floor and will be your mentor, leader, friend, and resource. He or she is tasked with turning your hall into a home. The RA will provide a variety of activities and programs that assist in creating a welcoming and comfortable environment for all the residents on their floor, but also help students grow as scholars and understand the resources available to them. RAs are also responsible for documenting any behavior that violates the housing policies and procedures and reporting it to their supervisor. Due to the nature of the work RAs perform, they typically develop great communication, organization, and leadership skills that make them marketable to employers. Furthermore, RA's are compensated with room and board waivers, and in some instances pay (including room and board). Consider becoming a RA in your sophomore year!

Resident Director

Resident Directors (frequently known as Area Coordinators, Community Directors, Hall Directors, etc.) are professional staff members who supervise RAs. He or she will also live in your building. Among their many duties, Resident Directors oversee the judicial process in their respective residential hall. The judicial process is used when a student violates a housing policy and/or procedure.

Now that you have a basic understanding of the role and function of the RA and Resident Director, you should find and introduce yourselves to these individuals so you can use them as resources while living on campus.

Living on campus means living with other people. In many instances, this may be the first time you have roommate(s), and in most instances this will be the first time you will have to share a room with someone different than you. With this in mind, a commonly asked question is, *how do I pick the right roommate?* The honest answer is there is no formula to ensure you select the "right" roommate. In selecting a roommate, you can nominate someone you would like to live with or have a person(s) randomly assigned to you. In reading this, one may wonder *should I pick my own roommate?* There is no harm in selecting your roommate. When you attended orientation, you meet other students, and in meeting those students, you may find someone who is from your hometown, shares similar interests, etc. If this happens, there is no harm in requesting this individual as your roommate. You may know someone from your high school and want them to be your roommate, *is it wrong to select them as your roommate?* Absolutely not. If you do not select your roommate, your housing office will always assign you a roommate. Whether you select your own roommate or one is randomly assigned to you, having a healthy relationship with your roommate requires the following:

- talk to one another
- respect each other
- seek to find some common interests
- establish rules for the use of shared space/belongings
- have separate groups of friends and interests so when necessary you can take a healthy break from your roommate with your friends
- discuss issues or problems that arise directly, in the room, with your roommate sooner rather than later
- if your roommate brings an issue or concern to you—do not get angry— listen and agree to resolve the problems

While working to have a healthy relationship with your roommate, issues may arise. Knowing this, it is important that within the first week of living on campus, you and your roommate should sit down with each other to discuss and complete a roommate agreement form. Most campuses will encourage you to fill out a roommate agreement form. While it is not mandatory that you complete a roommate agreement, it is strongly recommended that you and your roommate complete one. A roommate agreement form that you and your roommate should complete will detail your likes and dislikes, as well as, expectations of each other while living together. Examples of items that should be discussed in your roommate agreement form are as follows:

- Noise
  - When would a loud situation bother you—while completing homework, sleep, relaxing, etc.?
  - Will your room have quiet hours—if so, when?
  - If noise becomes a problem how will you and your roommate handle this situation?
- Study/homework
  - Do you plan on studying or doing homework in your room? What time do you intend on doing homework/studying? Under what conditions can you do homework (quiet, loud, etc.). If you are unable to study/do homework in your room because of your roommate, how will you handle this situation?
- Cleanliness
  - How often should the room be cleaned? Who will take care of what chore and how often? Personal hygiene—how often do you intend on taking a shower? If cleanliness becomes a problem how will you and your roommate handle this situation?
- Guest
  - What will the guest policy be for your room? How many guests will be allowed at a time? How much notice should be given before guests come

over? Can guests stay overnight? If so, for how long? If a guest becomes a problem—how would your roommate prefer for the other roommate to address this?

- Personal property
  - What items, if any can be shared between roommates?
  - If the sharing of personal property becomes a problem, how will you and your roommate handle this situation?

While this list is not exhaustive, it does give an idea of what should go into a roommate agreement. It is important to have this conversation as early as possible, and put your agreements in writing. In creating your roommate agreement remember:

- Be as specific as possible
- Try to make it as simple as possible, so you and your roommate will be able to remember what has been agreed upon
- Have realistic expectations for one another
- Make time in the beginning of the year to brainstorm ideas in creating a positive living environment with each other
- Have a positive attitude when creating your roommate agreement
- Make sure that you and your roommate create options that will allow for issues to be resolved quickly
- Post your roommate agreement in your room where everyone can see and be reminded of what was agreed upon

Creating a roommate agreement form does not guarantee that you will not have issues with your roommate. However, it does lay the groundwork of how you and your roommate will agree to live, as well as resolve issues when they arise. If issues arise between you and your roommate and you are unable to solve them on your own, you need to contact your RA to intervene in this situation. When your RA is contacted, they will ask if you have completed your roommate agreement. If you have not completed the agreement, they will likely assist you and your roommate in creating one as they help you resolve your situation. After one is created, if issues persist, already exists, but is not being followed, your RA can escalate this situation to the Resident Director faster, and the Resident Director has the ability, if necessary, to make roommate changes. Having completed, your roommate agreement can be the difference in having an issue resolved quickly or having to wait.

Living on campus can be a very overwhelming experience. You are being asked to leave your comfort zone to live and interact in a new environment with new and different people. As overwhelming as this may seem, transitioning to living on campus should not be seen as a challenge but an opportunity for growth. This will be your opportunity to learn about yourself and your ability to be resilient by living in a new environment. This is your opportunity to meet, engage, and establish relationships with people from around the country and the world. Living on campus will give you firsthand experience in how to strategize (test drive living on campus), research and analyze (reading and understanding housing policies and procedures), network (meeting RA and Resident Director), and problem solve (navigating living with a roommate). Gaining these skills will lay the foundation not only for success in the residence hall, but success as a student.

DISABILITY SERVICES

Prior to July 1992, individuals with disabilities were at the mercy of those who cared enough to attempt to provide equal opportunities for all mankind. Those numbers were very small and thus left many individuals with disabilities out in the cold, literally!

At that time, there were very few public institutions of higher learning (universities and colleges) that provided the accessibility of the campus and the academic accommodations in the classroom. One of the premiere institutions that did provide these services prior to the passage of the Americans with Disabilities Act (ADA) is *The University of Illinois at Urbana/Champaign, (UIUC)*. I had the privilege to be the Coordinator and then the Director of the Office of Disability Services at (UIUC). My tenure at UIUC was from May 1989 to September 1996. Several of those years of service were prior to the ADA being passed and enforced. Thus, I have seen so many changes in the lives of students with disabilities as a result of the passage of the ADA.

Thanks to the ADA which was passed and enforced in July 1992, the life for many Americans with disabilities changed! Now they are provided equal opportunity, and this has just been the beginning of the United States changing the accessibility for individuals with disabilities.

What has happened as a result of the ADA in the past 21 years has been astounding. At this time, anywhere an individual with a disability goes there are services to ensure that they have the same opportunities as others too; participate in events/activities; live in the house/opt they like; dine at their favorite restaurants and attend a college/university of their choice. These colleges and universities provide appropriate academic accommodations to "level the playing field" for students to be successful and enjoy life! Individuals with a disability who attend a college or university have provisions (that many do not know exist) to assist with their academic programs in post-secondary education.

Surprisingly, I've had many intelligent people say to me, "you mean students with disabilities can go to college and be successful?"—YES, of course, is always my response. Educate, educate, educate—that is the key to understanding and it has been my professional and personal goal to do just that in my corner of the world.

Having come from a family where my father suffered a medical condition at age 41 that left him with a severe disability never to be employed again, it became my passion to make this world a better place for individuals with a disability. I've found my place in academia helping college students be successful not only in the classroom but also in life. In the past 25 years as a director of disability services at four universities, I've seen the many challenges and obstacles that students with disabilities face on a daily basis. For example, it may be the inability to get to class on time because the student's personal care attendant arrived late to assist with bathing, dressing, feeding breakfast, lunch, or dinner. Or it could be that the electric wheelchair battery runs low and the student is unable to get to class. Students with mobility issues face many environmental obstacles such as snow, ice, and rain, making wheelchairs difficult to go, or must walk slowly with a cane or walker; if blind, depend upon a guide dog on sidewalks impassable.

It is clear the ADA exists to improve the life of an individual with a disability. It gives the students an assurance that; there are many resources available on campus, such as the counseling center, learning center, disability services office, and other offices to assist them in their coursework on campus in general and their overall college experience. The ADA also assures students that the services must be provided to you if they simply follow the appropriate guidelines of the policies and procedures established to protect you (and the institution). Knowing this, let's take it step by step as to what a student with a disability needs to do to be successful at college.

Types of disabilities served include: Learning Disabilities (LD); Attention Deficit Disorder (ADD); Psychological/Psychiatric Disorders; Traumatic Brain Injury; Mobility Disorders; Sensory Disorders; Health Issues and Asperger's Autism Spectrum Disorder; as well as Temporary Disabilities.

It's very important you make an appointment with the Office of Disability Services (ODS) in advance to begin the registration process. This will allow you to be aware of the necessary documentation needed to receive the appropriate academic accommodations for courses. Also the opportunity to meet with ODS staff, get to know them, feel comfortable talking with them and sharing with them your specific needs, whatever they may be.

At the appointment, you will meet with the Disability Specialist and based upon courses you are taking and the approved documentation, a decision is made as to what academic accommodations are needed. Academic accommodations will only be given if there is an appropriate approved documentation to support and justify the accommodations requested from the professors. Once the accommodations are agreed upon by the professor, you and ODS, then the student is assured that the approved academic accommodations will be provided by the professor, unless there is concern of the integrity of the course is being jeopardized. If you aren't sure of using the academic accommodations because you want to try to be successful without them; we still encourage you to register with ODS, get the approved academic accommodations and the letter to give to professors. This way the professor will know and when the student does want to use them everything is in place.

Once the accommodations are established, the student, professor, and disability specialist sign the letter to document the agreed academic accommodations requested, unless there is a concern that the integrity of the course may be jeopardized. If that is the case, there will be discussion and negotiation between you and the professor to ensure that both parties agree with the decision. The ODS will attend the meeting if requested by either you or the professor. In cases where the student or professor is being unreasonable, staff outside ODS, such as a dean or provost, may need to be involved to uphold the integrity of the ADA and/or support the student's academic needs.

Types of academic accommodations requested by students include: extended time on exams, quizzes, and assignments. Time extensions are provided at the discretion of the professor as noted in the accommodation letter presented to the professor by the student. The quiet, distraction-free testing environment may be located in the ODS or another location chosen by the professor, such as a space in close proximity to the classroom where the class is taking the exam. Note takers, scribes, readers, alternate format, and adaptive technology are important accommodations provided. Interpreters, captioning/transcribing service, special housing requests, and adjustable work stations are also available to registered students. At times consultation with the professors may be necessary to ensure these accommodations are provided to the student in a timely manner.

If the student feels uncomfortable presenting the academic accommodation letter to the professor, ODS provides role playing to help them feel more comfortable approaching their professors. Workshops are offered at the beginning of the semester for students registered in ODS. Depending on a professor's availability, one may attend the workshop to role play with the student.

The academic accommodations will be provided as long as the student needs them, the student needs to let ODS know if any change such as additional time on exams, or alternate format for the exam needs to be made. Any new accommodation requested, additional documentation will be necessary, if not currently in the student's file, to justify these requests.

At the beginning of each semester the student must register with ODS to update personal information. Also, any academic accommodations for new courses with possible additions or subtractions of accommodations may be made at that time.

ODS ensures that the student has accessible housing, parking, access to campus activities, and financial assistance with Department of Rehabilitation Services. ODS provides the information to these departments on a need-to-know basis and in a confidential manner never disclosing the student's disability or disorder.

Many students contact ODS with specific requests not realizing that the appropriate documentation is necessary to receive accommodations and is carefully reviewed and approved based upon what the student "needs" not what the student "wants."

Students may need to be encouraged to come to the ODS because they don't want the label of having a disability. Once they come, they may still need to be motivated to use the services/accommodations. Some students are concerned that their professors may look at them differently once they know they are registered in ODS. As professionals in the ODS we need to educate the student about disability to ensure them that all information will be kept confidential by everyone involved with their services. Accommodations are not given unless documentation is current, and without it, the student will need to provide in writing there is a scheduled appointment with a physician, psychologist, or learning specialist for an evaluation. Students may use the outdated documentation for one semester; however, must provide us with the new documentation for the next semester. This policy is enforced without exception.

When professors receive a letter of accommodation from the student with the specific academic accommodations requested, they may question an accommodation if it jeopardizes the integrity of their course. The professor, student, and the disability specialist will meet to absolve the conflict and ensure the student receives a "reasonable" academic accommodation.

ODS is not a student advocacy office, we represent the university to ensure students with disabilities receive appropriate, "reasonable" academic accommodations; yet, also ensure the integrity of the professor's course is not jeopardized. The ADA was passed to "level the playing field" for students, not to give students an academic advantage.

We have come a long way, but we have a long way to go dealing with the stigmas that exist regarding disability. Erving Goffman's classic book, "STIGMA," notes on the management of spoiled identity, is a wonderful resource for defining what stigma is and how it exists in our society in so many facets of life. The way we look at another person who may be different from us has a lot to do with the way we view our world. If we approach life in a positive, accepting manner seeing others having value, we will view disability that way. But if we have a negative, rejecting attitude toward others we will likely view disability that way.

The key to making the world a better place for individuals with disabilities started with a Federal Law, ADA; however, alone it does very little to further the cause. What it takes to make this law successful are dedicated, caring, and passionate people to carry out the charge. Without those who have risen above the stigma of disability, the world for those who have the diagnosis of disability it will not be better for them.

There is an Office of Disability Services at all colleges and universities and it exists to not only ensure that academic accommodations are provided to students, but also, to educate the campus about disability issues. You may be surprised to know that within the world of disability, there are prejudices from one disability to disability. Many disability categories have their own culture and are "funny" about others trying to join their group. Some disability categories question the validity of other disabilities because they are not visible. Judgments and prejudices exist within the disability world and also exist in the big world. Some students with visible disabilities are not convinced; the ADA should include all the disabilities and disorders it represents. Its initial charge was to provide accessibility for those who use wheelchairs to ensure their accessibility for opportunities of those with physical limitations. The law has been lobbied and challenged through the years by the groups who have now been included.

As a professional who has seen all of these additions to the ADA since 1992, it is good to see the world open up to all who need the services set for them by the ADA and to see the successes of students who may not have been successful without the academic accommodations provided for them.

Without the ADA, fewer students with disabilities would be in college and fewer students with college degrees in the work world. To make a difference in the life of an individual with a disability, treat that person just as you would treat any other person; however, with the "reasonable" accommodations needed. If the ADA existed 30 years ago, there are a high number of individuals who didn't attend college at that time because they were labeled lazy, class clown, and "stupid"; however, could have attended college and been successful with academic accommodations used in their courses. There are many adults diagnosed with learning disabilities later in life, now that we are more aware of the symptoms and have medication and academic accommodations to assist them.

It's important to show respect and admiration to an individual with a disability, not patronization and pity, and pass on to others your knowledge about disability issues. Be sure to educate, educate, educate others. Together, we can make the world a better place for an individual with a disability.

SEX, DRUGS, AND ALCOHOL

College student success would not be complete without addressing three things that can turn your future upside down—SEX, DRUGS, and ALCOHOL. With incidents of alcohol poisoning, driving under the influences (DUIs), and date rape, it's important that you are aware of the substance abuse infused culture at college. Substance abuse among young adults aged 18–25 abuse of prescription drugs is second only to abuse of marijuana, according to the 2010 National Survey on Drug Use and Health. Today's college students are abusing prescription drugs, drinking hard liquor, and the number of students using marijuana daily has more than doubled to approximately 4 percent.

Substance abuse is defined as a pattern of drug use leading to significant problems or distress, while substance dependence is defined as continued use of drugs or alcohol, even when significant problems related to use have developed.

Many students believe upon entering college they are abstainers or a low-risk drinker never realizing that your behavior may change as a result of your college experience. College-aged students are abusing a number of prescription medications, over-the-counter drugs, and illegal drugs, including Adderall, alcohol, cold medicine, OxyContin, and medical marijuana.

Today many students are taking "the study drug" as called on campuses across the United States. The name of the drug is called Adderall. It is prescribed for treating attention deficit hyperactivity disorder (ADHD). In fact, one in five college students admits to using Adderall (amphetamine and dextroamphetamine) without an ADHD diagnosis according to the National Institute on Drug Abuse. It's reported that drug heightens the sense of motivation, focus, and concentration which can help when pulling an all-nighter and provide an added boost before an examination. This drug does not make you smarter, it simply helps eliminate distractions and allow students to stay focused.

The risks of Adderall are the following: Depression, low blood pressure, headaches, irritability, dry mouth, rapid mood swings, loss of appetite, and insomnia. When students take Adderall without a medical reason, they can easily become addicted to and dependent on the drug. It's important to note, if you are caught with someone's prescription drugs, you could go to jail and be charged with possession of illegal substance.

In 2006, the Monitoring the Future Study conducted by the University of Michigan found that at least 3 percent of full-time college students in the United States take OxyContin without a prescription in a given year. Students do not understand the detrimental effects this drug has, or how quickly they can be addicted. This drug can damage the brain and impair judgment. The misuse of Oxycontin increases the risk of personal injury and accidents, and can lead to risky sexual behavior, misuse of other drugs, and even death. Prescription drug overdose deaths increased for the eleventh consecutive year and three out of four of the medication overdose deaths were caused by addictive pain killers, including OxyContin.

Over-the-counter drugs, including cold medicines, are becoming the nation's fastest growing drug problem among college students. The OTC drugs are cough and cold medicines containing dextromethorphan (DXM), including Triaminic DM, Coricidin, Tylenol Cold, Robitussin, DM, DayQuil and NyQuill products, and many more.

Students chose cold medications to get high because they don't need a prescription to obtain the medicine. They can also become addicted if taken at least once a week. Addiction increases the likelihood of severe side effects such as death, brain damage, blurry vision, seizures, numbness in toes and fingers, etc.

The drug Ecstasy (methamphetamine and methylenedioxy) has become popular at clubs, concerts, and "rave parties". Many college students across the United States have been transported to the emergency room because of its dangerous side effects. Ecstasy can kill! This is a drug that is illegally made and sold on the streets. It is a stimulant drug that can cause hallucinations. This can last for six hours and increases the heart rate, dry mouth, clenched teeth, blurred vision, chills, confused, and makes you believe someone is trying to hurt or plotting against you. Ecstasy may cause direct damage to brain cells that are involved in thinking and memory. This drug has been slipped into student's drinks since it can be a powder or pill.

Date Rape drugs are also on the rise on and off college campuses. The drugs are Rohypnol, Gamma Hydroxyl Butyrate (GHB) and Ketamine Hydrochloride. The drugs are virtually undetectable, tasteless, odorless, and colorless. All traces of the drugs will leave the body within 72 hours of ingestion and are not found in routine toxicology screen or blood test. Always remember don't accept open drinks from others you do not know. When in bars or clubs always get your drink directly from the bartender and do not take your eyes off the preparation of your drink. Never leave your drink unattended. It's important to note this happens to all individuals regardless of gender, sexual orientation, ethnicity, and social class.

Marijuana is on the rise among college students. Data provides strong evidence that using marijuana continues to pose significant risks to students' health, reputation, and future success. Marijuana use has the potential to impair both physical and mental health. The ingredient THC, (Tetrahydrocannabinol) negatively impacts the lungs, brain, heart, immune system, and reproductive systems of both men and women. Those who use it once a week or more are considerably more likely to experience depression, anxiety, fatigue, and low motivation than the nonusers (Patton et al. 2002).

According to the U.S. Census Bureaus, as of 2012, just over 1 million Americans are medical marijuana patients. Medical marijuana is the same marijuana that is smoked recreationally, and the appeal is largely the same. It can improve mood and relieve pain. It is typically prescribed for patients with cancer, AIDS, ADHD, neurogenic pain, migraines, arthritis, or multiple sclerosis.

The risks of frequent marijuana use may have negative physical and emotional effects, including distorted perception, rapid heartbeat, loss of balance and coordination, difficulty thinking or problem solving, and paranoia, just to name a few. About 9 out of 10 students who use marijuana participate in other high-risk activities such as heavy drinking or cigarette smoking, according to a study by the Harvard School of Public Health. It is also associated with poor academic performance, isolation, and a weakened immune system, which can lead to a number of health problems. In addition to all the possible health issues there's a possibility of arrest and fines and the loss of federal financial aid including access to student loans (Higher Education Amendments, 1998, p.1). For those who do persist, a conviction record may restrict access to law school, medical school, or other professional aspirations and dreams.

Getting "Turnt Up" on the weekend has moved into the weekdays. Alcohol abuse has always been a serious concern on college campuses. Many students drink today at least occasionally during their college career and binge drinking at least once every two weeks (2012 National Institutes of Health). Binge drinking is drinking heavily over a short period of time with the sole intention of becoming intoxicated. This misuse of alcohol could cause alcohol poisoning. It is important for you to understand the concerns of the college regarding alcohol poisoning. Many time students are afraid to call because they are concerned about getting the victim in trouble especially if they are underage. Please understand every year college students die from alcohol poisoning and that outweighs getting into trouble for drinking. The following are symptoms of alcohol poisoning:

- Victims can be conscious or semiconscious
- Slow breathing—8 breaths or less a minute or breathing that stops for more than 8 seconds at a time;
- Cold, clammy, pale, or blush skin;
- Does not respond to being talked to or even shouted at;
- Does not respond to being pinched, prodded, or poked;
- Cannot stand up;
- Rapid pulse rate
- Passing out is NOT sleeping it off!

Alcohol also creates a problem when it is consumed in connection with energy drinks. Mixing alcohol with these drinks in a social setting has become popular on college campuses nationwide and can have harmful and sometimes fatal consequences. Caffeine in energy drinks act as a depressant and slows down the heart. The combination sends mixed signals to the body, which can lead to heart-related problems, speech and walking difficulties, confusion, and exhaustion. The U.S. Food and Drug Administration (FDA) has reported an increase of deaths. Drinkers who consume alcohol with energy drinks are about twice as likely as drinkers who do not report mixing alcohol with energy drinks to report being taken advantage of sexually, to report taking advantage of someone else sexually, and to report riding with a driver who was under the influence of alcohol.

The more a student drinks, the more likely they will experience negative consequences including: unprotected sex, DUI, assault, sexual abuse, and injuries. Excessive drinking can lead to something minor as a hangover or can lead to death. According to NIH, about 25 percent of college students report academic consequences of their drinking, including missing class, falling behind, doing poorly on examinations or papers, and receiving lower grades.

The misuse of alcohol plays a role in the rapidly increasing rate of hazing on college campuses. Hazing occurs in, but extends beyond athletics, Greek-letter organizations and includes behaviors that are abusive, dangerous, and often illegal. In most states, hazing is a state felony. In Illinois, a freshman was found dead at a fraternity house near campus. Officials said the cause of death was hazing related and attributed it to cardiac arrhythmia, with alcohol intoxication as a significant contributor to death. Remember forcing someone to be "Turnt UP" can be Fatal. Be responsible.

CONCLUSION

You have heard people tell you to plan and be prepared and this includes having sex. Sexual health involves more the just intercourse. Studies have shown that college students who drink heavily are more likely to engage in unplanned sexual activity than students who do not drink heavily. Unplanned sexual activity could result in life-altering consequences such as a sexually transmitted infection, sexual assault, or an unwanted pregnancy. Also, drinking or doing drugs prior to intercourse has been consistently related to casual sex as well as a failure to discuss risk-related topics like previous sexual history, contraceptives, and the what if question. You don't have to have sex to fit in. As an independent adult, you'll make your own choices about sex. As with any other decision, you'll want your choices regarding sex, drugs, and alcohol to be informed and thoughtful, not impulsive or pressure-driven by friends or family. Many colleges provide drug, alcohol, and sex information to help students during their life journey on campus. Remember why you came to college and take control of your destiny or someone else will.

GREEK LIFE: BEHIND THE LETTERS

Arguably, fraternities and sororities are the most noticeable symbols of college social life. Dr. Fran Becque, a fraternity history scholar states, "Nationally, fraternity or sorority members are the largest and most visible value-based student organizations" (Becque 2013). As a freshman, from the moment you step on campus, you cannot help but notice the ubiquitous Greek letters in a spectrum of bright colors. A diverse array of college fraternities and sororities exists that should appeal to any demographic, culture, or interest. These range from the centuries-old traditionally White associations, historically Black Greek-lettered organizations (BGLOs), Hispanic/Latino societies, and the newer cultural interest groups that were founded in the past half century. The following chapter presents a history of the American college Greek system; controversies and criticisms of Greek life; the positive attributes and contributions Greeks make to campus life and society; and finally, how to succeed in joining the fraternity or sorority of your choice.

BROTHERLY BONDS: A HISTORY OF AMERICAN FRATERNITIES

Traditional Fraternities

Since before the founding of America, there have been fraternal organizations for men based on religious, occupational, or philosophical grounds. Many of these organizations were centered on an institution of higher learning that had a higher population of men who shared common values (Anderson 2009). American fraternal societies have their origins in the Middle Ages in the brigades of German universities. These fellowships with their high sense of pageantry, elaborate costumes, and symbolic rituals were prevalent in the eighteenth century. The modern American college fraternity has distinctive features from their European predecessors (Wesley 1991; Waszut-Barrett 1996).

On Thursday evening, December 5, 1776, five undergraduates—John Heath, Thomas Smith, Richard Booker, Armistead Smith, and John Jones met for dinner in the Apollo Room of the Raleigh Tavern at William and Mary College in Williamsburg, Virginia. They were members of one of the Latin-named literary societies at William & Mary. On this night, these men decided to form the first Greek-lettered secret society, Phi Beta Kappa, with objectives that included scholarship, inspiration, and fraternity (Parks 2008; Wesley 1991). The development of fraternities was a direct response to students' desire for informal fellowship outside the classroom to balance the rigidity of early American academic primness and formality. The original chapter of Phi Beta Kappa at William and Mary College was deactivated during the American Revolution in 1781, but chapters at Yale and Harvard endured (McKenzie 1986; Waszut-Barrett 1996; Parks and Toberson 2009).

In 1826, public sentiment grew increasingly hostile toward the secret organizations following the disappearance and suspected murder of a local man who threatened to publish Masonic secrets. This began the first anti-Masonic movement in America. Most secret societies were forced to reveal many of their secrets and rituals, including fraternities. As a result, Phi Beta Kappa abandoned its premise as a secret society and emerged as an honor fraternity (Wesley 1991; Waszut-Barrett 1996; McKenzie 2013; Mathiasen 2005).

While popular agitation against fraternities was at its height in America during 1825–1827, three new undergraduate fraternities were organized, Kappa Alpha—the oldest existing general fraternity, Sigma Phi, and Delta Phi. These three fraternities formed what would be referred to as the "Union Triad." Soon after, three other fraternities were founded at Ohio's Miami University: Beta Theta Pi, Delta Theta, and Sigma Chi. These fraternities came to be known as the "Miami Triad" (George Mason University, Office of Student Involvement 2013; James 2000).

The fraternal spirit soon expanded, and new chapters were established at Harvard, Yale, Columbia, Brown, Dartmouth, Amherst, and other colleges. Most traditional fraternities were founded within three major eras: 1840–1850, 1865–1870, and 1900–1920. The first era mostly included fraternities founded in northern liberal arts colleges to counter society's previous puritanical leanings. The second era followed the Civil War with a growth of conservative fraternities in the south dedicated to preserving Southern heritage and reflecting the collective sentiment of the American South during Reconstruction. During the final era, fraternities with more enlightened viewpoints—with less exclusionary considerations written into their charters emerged. However, racial and religious discriminatory policies remained firmly entrenched in most traditional fraternities and sororities until the 1960s. Consequently, the four leading historically Black fraternities were founded during this period (James 2000).

Since the turn of the twentieth century, new fraternities have multiplied in number and influence. In 1883, there were only 26 college fraternities with about 66,000 members. By 1910, this number increased to 32 college fraternities with 1,068 chapters, and by 1912, there were over 40 college fraternities with over a quarter million members. By 1922, there were 66 college fraternities with over 2,000 chapters and more than a 500,000 members nationwide (Wesley 1991).

Most American fraternities are members of the North-American Interfraternity Conference (NIC). NIC was founded in 1909 and currently has 75 member organizations with 5,500 chapters located on over 800 campuses in the United States and Canada with approximately 400,000 undergraduate members and over 4,500,000 alumni members. All of the historically Black fraternities, with the exception of Omega Psi Phi, hold dual memberships in the NIC and National Pan-Hellenic Council (NPHC). In fact, Alpha Phi Alpha, Phi Beta Sigma, and Kappa Alpha Psi actually have the distinction of having the most NIC collegiate charters granted (with the notable exception of Tau Kappa Epsilon)—occupying the second, third, and fourth rankings respectively with almost 1,200 charters between them, Iota Phi Theta Fraternity is in the sixth spot. The NIC stresses fraternal aims such as scholarly pursuit, leadership, service, and fellowship among all of the fraternal organizations (North-American Interfraternity Conference 2014b).

The Historically Black Fraternities

While White students enjoyed the benefits of fraternity life for almost 200 years, this privilege was not initially extended to Black students.

> The collegiate life in which the majority of the black college group lived took its course also from the conditions in which the black college found itself. In the period just prior to and after the Civil War, there was uncertain aid and temporary relief for the education of the black population. Shortly thereafter, definitely organized efforts were launched for the building of colleges and the college training of blacks for service among the more unfortunate members of the black group. This phase of the education was missionary in character and ideals . . . (xi). Consecrated men and women devoted their lives to the work of education for blacks.
>
> The school and college for youth of this early day was a big family. The spirit of brotherhood was in the very air breathed by the student groups of this generation. Clubs, literary societies, personal contact groups were the developments from this condition. College activities found their social outlet in these organizations . . . (xii). Rapidly, the fraternity idea spread into schools whose student body was entirely of the black population.

The coming of one fraternity in these institutions gave rise to the others (xii) (Wesley 1991, xi–xii).

Remarkably, the anti-fraternity sentiment was also shared among the African American intellectual class, most notably faculty and administration at historically Black colleges. Often these early pioneers found more resistance to the fraternal ideal at HBCUs than those students at predominately-White colleges.

National Pan-Hellenic Council (NPHC)

For almost a century, historically Black fraternities and sororities have made profound contributions to collegiate development and provided service and leadership to Black society. The historically Black Greek-letter organizations are all member organizations of the NPHC. From 1930–1997, the NPHC represented the *Original 8* historically Black fraternities and sororities, previously referred to as the *Elite 8*. This consisted of Alpha Phi Alpha Fraternity, Inc., Kappa Alpha Psi Fraternity, Inc., Omega Psi Phi Fraternity, Inc., Phi Beta Sigma Fraternity, Inc., Alpha Kappa Alpha Sorority, Inc., Delta Sigma Theta Sorority, Inc., Zeta Phi Beta Sorority, Inc., and Sigma Gamma Rho Sorority, Inc (National Panhellenic Council, Inc. 2010).

The *Original 8* were founded in the early 1900s as support systems and in response to Black students being formally excluded from traditional fraternities and sororities. They faced extreme racial discrimination, segregation, and sometimes, outright hostility in a post-Reconstruction/Jim Crow-era America. In historical context, many were the children or grandchildren of slaves; they were part of the Progressive Era and the Great Migration—all eight organizations were founded in northern states.

On May 10, 1930, on the campus of Howard University, in Washington DC, the National Pan-Hellenic Council was formed as a permanent organization with the following charter members: Omega Psi Phi and Kappa Alpha Psi Fraternities, and Alpha Kappa Alpha, Delta Sigma Theta and Zeta Phi Beta Sororities. In 1931, Alpha Phi Alpha and Phi Beta Sigma Fraternities joined the Council. Sigma Gamma Rho Sorority joined in 1937 and Iota Phi Theta Fraternity completed the list of member organizations in 1997 (National Panhellenic Council, Inc. 2010; Iota Phi Theta Fraternity, Inc. 2013).

> The stated purpose and mission of the organization in 1930 was "Unanimity of thought and action as far as possible in the conduct of Greek letter collegiate fraternities and sororities, and to consider problems of mutual interest to its member organizations." Early in 1937, the organization was incorporated under the laws of the State of Illinois and became known as "The National Pan-Hellenic Council, Incorporated" (National Panhellenic Council, Inc. 2010, 1–2).

After the *Elite 8*, a number of other BGLOs were founded. Even though during this time, there was greater integration within traditional organizations. The most recognized of these younger Black fraternities is Iota Phi Theta Fraternity. The fraternity was founded by 12 men in the midst of the Civil Rights Movement. While there were already four prominent historically Black fraternities, the Iotas served a unique demographic from the rest of the *Elite 8* fraternities.

Alpha Phi Alpha Fraternity

At first, historically Black fraternities were modeled after their traditionally White counterparts but later they began to incorporate aspects of African and African American culture and heritage that was more historically significant to their population. This was the case with the nation's first Black college fraternity, Alpha Phi Alpha Fraternity. The origin of the fraternity was borne out of survival. During the 1904–1905 school term at Cornell Institute, there were six Black students on campus. Because of intense racial discord, none was retained in the following school year (McKenzie 1986; Wesley 1991; Mason 1999; Alpha Phi Alpha Fraternity, Inc. 2013). Founder Henry Arthur Callis described their situation, "The incoming students in 1905–06 . . . were determined to bind themselves together to ensure that each would survive in the racially hostile environment" (Alpha Phi Alpha Fraternity, Inc. 2013, ¶1). These individuals formed a Social Study Club as a support group (Wesley 1991; Pawley, III 1993).

By October 23, 1906, the club evolved into a Literary Society; Founder, George Biddle Kelley proposed that the society be identified by the Greek letters ΑΦΑ (Alpha Phi Alpha). Founder, Robert Harold Ogle suggested that the organization adopt black and old gold as the official colors. At this time, the club became the "Alpha Phi Alpha Society." There was great divide among the members of the society if they wanted to become an actual fraternity, dissenters believed that African Americans did not have a cultural basis on which to establish a fraternity, especially since there was no precedence (Wesley 1991). However, on a cold Tuesday evening in upstate New York on December 4, 1906, the dispute was put to rest. The motion passed to establish Alpha Phi Alpha as the first fraternity created for Black male college students. Some of the former society members felt strongly enough to depart over this decision. The *Cornell Seven* ". . . who formed Alpha Phi Alpha Fraternity were Henry Arthur Callis A.B. '09, Charles Henry Chapman, Special Agriculture Student '06, Eugene Kinckle Jones, M.A. '08, George Biddle Kelley, Civil Engineering degree '08, Nathaniel Allison Murray B.S. '11, Robert Harold Ogle, Special Agriculture Student, and Vertner Woodson Tandy, Special Architecture Student. They are known as the *Seven Jewels*" (Ross Jr. 2000; Kimbrough 2003) (Cornell University: Division of Rare & Manuscript Collections 2006).

Kappa Alpha Psi Fraternity

On another predominately-White campus in 1910, the only 10 Black students that attended Indiana University—Elder Watson Diggs (affectionately known as *The Dreamer*), Dr. Ezra D. Alexander, Dr. Byron Kenneth Armstrong, Atty. Henry Tourner Asher, Dr. Marcus Peter Blakemore, Paul Waymond Caine, George Wesley Edmonds, Dr. Guy Levis Grant, Edward Giles Irvin, and Sgt. John Milton Lee—formed a temporary association named Alpha Omega until the particulars of developing a full-fledged college fraternity could be realized. Diggs and Armstrong had just transferred from Howard University, where they "were aware of the existence of another historically black Greek-letter organization (Alpha Phi Alpha) and that their contact with this organization motivated them to pursue the idea of a fraternity at Indiana University" (Jennings 2008).

Racial prejudice, hostility, and outright violence towards African Americans were widespread in Indiana. Indiana was emerging as a haven for the new Ku Klux Klan. Indiana was infamous for violence and lynching of Black men. These Black students were thoroughly denied access to all campus recreation facilities, dormitories, and social activities. They faced indignities heaped upon them daily by White administrators, their fellow students, and the community. They remained segregated and isolated from the Indiana University campus (Ross Jr. 2000; Bryson 2003; Jennings 2008).

Similarly, to the founders of Alpha Phi Alpha, racial discrimination inspired them to create their own organization to combat the seclusion they felt being the only Black students on an unfriendly White college campus. They would seldom travel alone as they needed to watch each other's backs; this strengthened their bonds. On January 5, 1911, near the banks of the Jordan River that ran through the campus, they adopted Indiana University school colors, crimson and cream as their fraternity's colors and named it Kappa Alpha Nu (Bryson 2003).

The fraternity hosted house parties that attracted not only IU students but also Black students from around Indiana. Soon camaraderie and friendship replaced their isolation. In time, the house parties evolved into proms that they eventually were able to hold on campus (Bryson 2003; Jennings 2008).

In 1915, the fraternity was renamed as a response to two Kappa founders overhearing some white students refer to a member competing at a track meet as Kappa Alpha *Nig*. They began considering a name change; there was also a secondary desire to have an actual Greek letter in their name. Therefore, on April 15, 1915, members voted and the *Nu* was replaced with the Greek letter Ψ (Psi) which mimicked Indiana University's prominent red interlocking IU logo and Kappa Alpha Psi Fraternity was so designated (McKenzie 1986; Bryson 2003; Jennings 2008).

Omega Psi Phi Fraternity

As previously noted, this period saw unprecedented number of Black students attending historically Black colleges and universities. Howard University saw extraordinary enrollment at this time and the fraternal spirit caught on quickly. Alpha Phi Alpha had already installed their *Beta* chapter at Howard on December 20, 1907 (Wesley 1991; Ross Jr. 2000). Andre McKenzie states, "Omega Psi Phi was founded at Howard University in response to the establishment of an Alpha Phi Alpha chapter on the campus years earlier" (McKenzie 1986).

On Friday evening, November 17, 1911, three Howard University undergraduate students, with the assistance of their faculty adviser, gave birth to the Omega Psi Phi Fraternity. This event occurred in the office of biology Professor Ernest E. Just, the faculty adviser, in the Science Hall (now known as Thirkield Hall). The three liberal arts students were Edgar A. Love, Oscar J. Cooper, and Frank Coleman. From the initials of the Greek phrase meaning, "friendship is essential to the soul," the name Omega Psi Phi was derived. The phrase was selected as the motto. Manhood, scholarship, perseverance, and uplift were adopted as cardinal principles. A decision was made regarding the design for the pin and emblem, and thus ended the first meeting of the Omega Psi Phi Fraternity (OrgSynch 2014).

According to Omega Psi Phi Fraternity,

> On November 23, 1911 in Thirkield Hall, Love became the first Grand Basileus (National President). Cooper and Coleman were selected to be the Grand Keeper of the Records (National Secretary) and Grand Keeper of Seals (National Treasurer), respectively (Omega Psi Phi Fraternity, Inc. 2010, 1).

However, this was only the beginning of a long road to becoming a fully accepted fraternity on Howard's campus, let alone a national fraternity. The Omegas were immediately denied recognition from the administration. The Omega Founders and charter members went on a campaign to win the hearts and minds of the campus by posting cards all around the campus announcing the arrival of the first fraternity founded at Howard University—Omega Psi Phi Fraternity. This did not go over well with the administration, prompting the president of the college, Dr. Wilbur Thirkield, to make a formal speech to the student body denying the very existence of the fraternity (Ross Jr. 2000).

Undeterred, the Omegas decided to make a personal appeal to President Thirkield and that very day, they met with Howard University's head administrator. Despite an immediate admonishment about the posts, Dr. Thirkield received them warmly and listened to their motives and ideas for starting a new fraternity. President Thirkield promised to give them due consideration if they removed the card postings (Ross Jr. 2000).

The administration did not move quickly, waiting until 1912 to make the decision to recognize them as a local fraternity. This flew in the face of Omega Founders who envisioned a national organization from its inception. For over a year, the fraternity went back and forth with the faculty and administration of Howard about its expansion to other campuses. It was not until 1914, that Omega Psi Fraternity finally installed their second chapter at Lincoln University—succeeding in their quest of becoming the first national fraternity founded at Howard University(Ross Jr. 2000; Kimbrough 2003; Ross Jr. 2000; Brown, Parks, and Phillips 2012).

Phi Beta Sigma Fraternity

That same year at Howard University, Phi Beta Sigma Fraternity, Inc. was founded on January 9, 1914 by three young men: A. Langston Taylor, Leonard F. Morse, and Charles I. Brown. However, the groundwork for the fraternity began all the way back in 1910 when A. Langston Taylor was entertained with stories of fraternity life from a friend that attended Howard. By the time Langston enrolled at Howard University during the fall of 1913, he already had the basic structure of the fraternity completed. He enlisted his roommate and another friend to assist in his endeavor (Ross Jr. 2000; McKenzie 2013).

In November 1913, the three founders met at Morse's house and initiated nine more members into their new fraternity. The founders and charter members met on January 9, 1914 at a YMCA in Washington, DC and came up with their motto, *Culture for Service and Service for Humanity*; they elected officers and made plans to submit their application to the university Deans for official recognition. The Deans took three months to approve their request (Ross Jr. 2000; Kimbrough 2003). Phi Beta Sigma describes their Founders' sentiment in establishing the Fraternity:

> The Founders deeply wished to create an organization that viewed itself as "a part of" the general community rather than "apart from" the general community. They believed that each potential member should be judged by his own merits, rather than his family background or affluence…without regard to race, nationality, skin tone or texture of hair. They desired for their fraternity to exist as part of an even greater brotherhood which would be devoted to the "inclusive we" rather than the "exclusive we".

> From its inception, the Founders also conceived Phi Beta Sigma as a mechanism to deliver services to the general community. Rather than gaining skills to be utilized exclusively for themselves and their immediate families, they held a deep conviction that they should return their newly acquired skills to the communities from which they had come. This deep conviction was mirrored in the Fraternity's motto, *Culture For Service and Service For Humanity* (Phi Beta Sigma Fraternity, Inc. 2013, ¶1–3).

Iota Phi Theta Fraternity

On September 19, 1963, during the height of the Civil Rights' Movement, 12 men—Albert Hicks, Lonnie Spruill, Jr., Charles Briscoe, Frank Coakley, John Slade, Barron Willis, Webster Lewis, Charles Brown, Louis Hudnell, Charles Gregory, Elias Dorsey, Jr., and Michael Williams—gathered together on the steps of Morgan State College's Hurt Gymnasium and formed Iota Phi Theta Fraternity. The Iota founders were distinguished from those of the other historically Black fraternities as they were all nontraditional students. They were three to five years older than their fellow students were. Many had served in the military during the Vietnam War, worked full-time while attending classes full-time, and had families with small children. Many were long-time friends. Spruill, Coakley, Dorsey, and Gregory had known one another since grade school, and Spruill and Coakley's friendship extended to when the two were pre-schoolers (Iota Phi Theta Fraternity Inc. 2013a).

> Based upon their ages, heightened responsibilities, and increased level of maturity, this group had a slightly different perspective . . . This perspective [informed] the Fraternity's purpose, "The development and perpetuation of *Scholarship, Leadership, Citizenship, Fidelity, and Brotherhood among Men*" (Iota Phi Theta Fraternity Inc. 2013a, ¶5).

The Iotas first inquired about admission into the NPHC in the 1970s; however, the NPHC did not have criteria in place for new member organizations since the *Elite 8*. After decades of consideration and deliberation, Iota Phi Theta was finally admitted into NPHC in 1996 and the *Elite 8* became the *Divine 9* (Williams-Scurlock 2005; Iota Phi Theta Fraternity, Inc. 2013).

Top 25 Fraternities

In 2012, Newsweek compiled a ranking of the top 25 fraternities of the 75 fraternities that are members of the North-American Interfraternity Conference (NIC).

We first considered the number of active collegiate chapters for each. We also considered the number of alumni who are currently members of the U.S. Senate and the U.S. House of Representatives, as well as the alumni, if any, who became president. Lastly, we considered the amount of money the fraternity's non-profit fund donated to 501(c) (3) organizations according the most recent public filing (funds were normalized using a per-chapter ratio). Funds donated to individual chapters, classified as a 501(c) (7) non-profit social club, were not considered for this aspect of the ranking.

25. Delta Upsilon (ΔΥ)
24. Phi Beta Sigma (ΦΒΣ)
23. Phi Kappa Sigma (ΦΚΣ)
22. Delta Chi (ΔΧ)
21. Beta Theta Pi (ΒΘΠ)
20. Iota Phi Theta (ΙΦΘ)
19. Sigma Alpha Mu (ΣΑΜ)
18. Alpha Tau Omega (ΑΤΩ)
17. Pi Kappa Phi (ΠΚΦ)
16. Tau Kappa Epsilon (ΤΚΕ)
15. Pi Kappa Alpha (ΠΚΑ)
14. Lambda Chi Alpha (ΛΧΑ)
13. Phi Kappa Tau (ΦΚΤ)
12. Kappa Alpha Psi (ΚΑΨ)
11. Delta Tau Delta (DTD)
10. Alpha Phi Alpha (ΑΦΑ)
9. Kappa Alpha Order (KA)
8. Sigma Phi Epsilon (ΣΦΕ)
7. Alpha Gamma Rho (ΑΓΡ)
6. Alpha Epsilon Pi (ΑΕΠ)
5. Sigma Nu (ΣΝ)
4. Theta Chi (ΘΧ)
3. Phi Gamma Delta (FIJI)
2. Sigma Alpha Epsilon (ΣΑΕ)
1. Sigma Chi (ΣΧ) (Newsweek 2012a)

INSIDE THE SISTER CIRCLE: A HISTORY OF AMERICAN SORORITIES

Traditional Sororities

Much like African Americans, women faced intense opposition against attending college. Some administrators and faculty members contended that the female mind was inferior and expressed doubts that women could become proficient in mathematics and the classics. However, Dr. Erastus Otis Haven, after serving as president of University of Michigan and Northwestern University, was selected chancellor at Syracuse University and asserted that women had a place in higher education on par with men. To illustrate this, he confidently enrolled his daughter, Frances Elizabeth, at Syracuse where she became a founder of Gamma Phi Beta Sorority (Haven 1883; Syracuse University n.d.).

The earliest Greek lettered organizations for women were also called fraternities because the term sorority had not yet been conceived. "No such history of sororities existed for women until much later in America's turbulent past, mostly because women did not share the same educational or political opportunities that their male counterparts enjoyed" (Dubroff n.d.). Just prior to the Civil War, secret women literary societies were forming at women colleges as support system for being in a predominately-male environment. Like the fraternities, these literary societies evolved to modern American sororities. The first such secret literary society was Adelphian, which is Greek, for *sister*. Found on May 15, 1851 at Wesleyan Female College in Macon, Georgia by six young women: Eugenia Tucker Fitzgerald, Elizabeth Williams Mitchell, Sophronia Woodruff Dews, Octavia Andrew Rush, Mary Evans Glass, and Ella Pierce Turner, who were between thirteen and eighteen years of age. They founded the organization on the principles of developing the mental, moral, social, and domestic improvement of its members (Anderson 2009). The Adelphian Society changed its name to Alpha Delta Phi in 1905 when it attained a charter as a national organization and changed its name to Alpha Delta Pi in 1913 to avoid confusion with an existing men's fraternity (Dubroff n.d.).

Just a few months later on January 4, 1852, another women's literary society was founded on the same campus. In 1914, three teenage women—Mary Ann DuPont (Lines), Mary Elizabeth Myrick (Daniel), and Martha Bibb Hardaway (Redding) founded a separate society called the Philomathean Society—not to be confused with the Philomathean Literary Society founded at the University of Pennsylvania in 1813 which remains the nation's oldest literary society. In 1904, the name was changed to Phi Mu Fraternity and it became America's second oldest secret organization for women. Formally, the women's organization remains Phi Mu Fraternity, as they chose not change it to *sorority* to preserve their heritage. These first two college women's groups are referred to as the "Macon Magnolias" (Hood 2006; Phi Mu 2010; Velez 2010).

The I.C. Sorosis was founded at Monmouth College in Monmouth, Illinois on April 28, 1867. Later they adopted the Greek letters representing their secret motto as their official name, Pi Beta Phi. It was the first sorority to model itself after the men's fraternities. Three years later on the same campus, Kappa Kappa Gamma was established at Monmouth College on October 13, 1870. These two sororities were known as the "Monmouth Duo" (San Jose State University 2013; Anderson 2009).

There were three women fraternities that were founded at Syracuse University between 1872 and 1904; they comprise the Syracuse Triad. Alpha Phi International Women's Fraternity was the first. "On the afternoon of September 18, 1872, Martha Foote Crow was visiting her friends Clara Sittser Williams and Kate Hogoboom Gilbert in their boarding house at Syracuse University. Martha mused, "Why can't we have a society as well as the men?" (Alpha Phi Fraternity 2010)

The women's fraternity was founded by 10 of the original 20 women first admitted into Syracuse University: Clara Bradley Wheeler Baker Burdette, Hattie Florence Chidester Lukens, Martha Emily Foote Crow, Ida Arabella Gilbert DeLamanter Houghton, Jane Sara Higham, Kate Elizabeth Hogoboom Gilbert, Elizabeth Grace Hubbell Shults, Rena A. Michaels Atchison, Louise Viola Shepard Hancock, and Clara Sittser Williams. In Alpha Phi, the Greek letter *Phi* is pronounced *fee* as the Greeks pronounced it, instead of the more Americanized *fi*. The women used this pronunciation because they felt it sounded more feminine (Alpha Phi Fraternity 2010).

Gamma Phi Beta was founded two years later on November 11, 1874 by Frances Elizabeth Haven, daughter of Syracuse Chancellor Erastus Haven, and three friends Helen M. Dodge, E. Adeline Curtis, and Mary A. Bingham. The word *sorority* was devised for Gamma Phi Beta by their advisor Dr. Frank Smalley, a professor of Latin who felt that *fraternity* was a masculine term; *soror* meant sister in Latin (University of Wisconsin Madison 2013).

Alpha Gamma Delta Women's Fraternity completed the Syracuse Triad on May 30, 1904. Alpha Gamma Delta was founded at the home of Professor Wellesley Perry Coddington by 11 female students: Marguerite Shepard, Estelle Shepard Beswick, Georgia Alberta Dickover, Jennie Titus Smith Morris, Ethel Evelyn Brown Distin, Grace Mosher Harter, Edith MacConnel Hickok, Mary Louise Snider, Georgia Otis Chipman, Emily Helen Butterfield, and Flora Knight Mayer. The organization retained the term *fraternity* rather than a "sorority" because their advisor contended that soror was a Latin word and not consistent with the Greek tradition. Unlike the other members of the Triad, Alpha Gamma Delta Fraternity aspired to become an intercollegiate organization that expanded beyond Syracuse from their onset. To this day, the Syracuse Triad holds some special events together on most campuses where all three organizations are present (Baird and Brown 1920).

In the early days of sorority expansion, there was intense rivalry between the various organizations; they competed for members, distinction, and status. However, the women's groups recognized the benefit of standing together before the men's fraternities. In 1902, seven women's fraternities met in Boston and formed the National Panhellenic Conference (NPC) to encourage unity among the different sororities, to foster positive relations with the host colleges, and to serve as a resource to the different chapters (Anderson. 2009; Dubroff n.d.; San Jose State University 2013).

The Historically Black Sororities

Alpha Kappa Alpha Sorority

As previously stated, women were not given much encouragement to attend college; most men felt that women's greatest contributions were in the home as wives and mothers so there was little need for higher education. Despite the ratification of the fifteenth Amendment, which granted voting rights to citizens regardless of race, color, or previous condition of servitude (gender was not protected), in the post-Reconstruction era, Southern states reverted to the institutional disentranchement of African Americans by rewriting their state constitutions. Twenty million women were also denied the right to vote. If this was the plight of Black men and all women, Black women were subjugated even more. Even at the historically Black, Howard University, there were only a nominal percentage of women enrolled (Ross Jr. 2000) (McKenzie 2013).

Ethel Hedgeman (Lyle) encountered this social and political climate upon returning to Howard for her junior year in fall 1907. Even though she dated—and later married George Lyle, one of the charter members of the Alpha Phi Alpha chapter at Howard—Ethel had envisioned a Black sorority that previous spring after being inspired by accounts of sorority life from her teacher, Ethel Robinson and other Howard faculty. Ethel had already recruited eight other women during the summer: Anna Easter Brown, Beulah Burke, Lillie Burke, Marjorie Hill, Margaret Flagg Holmes, Lavinia Norman, Lucy Slowe, and Marie Woolfolk Taylor. These nine women spent fall 1907 creating the foundation of their sisterhood (Kimbrough 2003; Ross Jr. 2000; McKenzie 2013).

On January 15, 1908, they met in Miner Hall on Howard's campus where they composed the sorority's constitution based on a draft by Lucy Slowe. They conceived their motto, *By Merit and Culture*; selected their colors, salmon pink and apple green; and designed the sorority's insignia, a green enameled ivy leaf with the letters, A K A in each of the leaf's three points. From the first three letters of the three Greek words that formed the Sorority's motto, they christened their sorority *Alpha Kappa Alpha*—the first Greek-lettered sorority for Black college women (Brown, Parks, and Phillips 2012; McKenzie 2013).

All of these nine women were seniors with the exception of Ethel Hedgeman. For their organization to endure, more members were needed. A group of seven sophomore honor students had expressed some interest in the organization and they were invited to join without having to go through initiation. These sophomores: Norma Boyd, Ethel Jones Mowbray, Alice Murray, Sarah Meriweather Nutter, Joanna Berry Shields, Carrie Snowden, and Harriet Terry joined the original eight as the founders for 16 total members. They then sought official recognition from Howard University administration, which granted them status as a local sorority without incident (Ross Jr. 2000) (Brown, Parks, and Phillips 2012).

By the 1911–1912 school term, there were over 20 members but Alpha Kappa Alpha did not exist beyond Howard University. During the spring of 1912, after attending the sorority's annual *Ivy Day*, former chapter Basileus, Nellie Quander was shocked when she discovered that the 22 newly initiated members on campus intended to make profound changes to the sorority. They intended to revise the constitution and extend the organization beyond Howard University.

Since the organization was not incorporated, the members felt they did not have legal authority to form additional chapters. The seven chapter officers proposed changing the sorority colors, its symbols, and had already adopted a new name, *Delta Sigma Theta*. They felt that the letters AKA were not Greek distinctive letters and were merely a feminine derivative of AΦA. These young women had formed a special connection with the founders of the newly organized Omega Psi Phi Fraternity—one of the Delta Founders, Edna Brown Coleman later married an Omega Founder, Frank Coleman (Ross Jr. 2000; Gliddings 2007; McKenzie 2013).

Nellie Quander was stunned; she contacted every alumnae of Alpha Kappa Alpha. With the exception of the campus members, all of the alumnae rebuffed the proposed changes. Nellie gave the 22 members a deadline to cease their efforts to reorganize Alpha Kappa Alpha and to discontinue using the name, Delta Sigma Theta. On January 13, 1913, the entire 22 women of the undergraduate chapter withdrew from Alpha Kappa Alpha to become Delta Sigma Theta Sorority (Gliddings 2007).

Nellie Quander did agree about expanding the sorority to other campuses. She chaired a three-person task force charged with ensuring AKA's continued existence and to oversee its expansion. On January 29, 1913, Alpha Kappa Alpha Sorority was legally incorporated by Nellie Quander; founders Norma Boyd and Ethel Jones Mowbray; and Julia Brooks, Nellie Pratt Russell, and Minnie Smith in Washington, DC. Nellie Quander became Alpha Kappa Alpha's first Supreme Basileus (National President) (Ross Jr. 2000).

Those women who were part of *The Original Group, The Sophomores,* and *The Incorporators* comprise Alpha Kappa Alpha's *20 Pearls.* They are Ethel Hedgeman Lyle, Norma Elizabeth Boyd, Julia Evangeline Brooks, Anna Easter Brown, Beulah Elizabeth Burke, Lillie Burke, Marjorie Hill, Margaret Flagg Holmes, Ethel Jones Mowbray, Alice P. Murray, Lavinia Norman, Sara Meriweather Nutter, Nellie M. Quander, Nellie Pratt Russell, Joanna Berry Shields, Lucy Diggs Slowe, Minnie Beatrice Smith, Carrie Elizabeth Snowden, Marie Woolfolk Taylor, and Harriet Josephine Terry (Brown, Parks, and Phillips 2012).

Alpha Kappa Alpha Sorority's 260,000 members in 958 chapters worldwide have been mission focused on improving the educational, economic, and social development of Black people throughout the Diaspora. They have been at the forefront of the fight for civil rights through marches and sit-ins; promoting global human rights by building schools in post-apartheid South Africa; sponsoring literacy programs for American youth; and raising awareness of health issues that disproportionately affect African Americans such as AIDS, breast cancer, diabetes, heart disease, and sickle cell anemia (Parks 2008; Brown, Parks, and Phillips 2012).

Delta Sigma Theta Sorority

On January 13, 1913, Delta Sigma Theta Sorority was founded by 22 Howard University undergraduate women who had departed Alpha Kappa Alpha: Winona Cargile Alexander, Madree Penn White, Wertie Blackwell Weaver, Vashti Turley Murphy, Ethel Cuff Black, Frederica Chase Dodd, Osceola Macarthy Adams,

Pauline Oberdorfer Minor, Edna Brown Coleman, Edith Mott Young, Marguerite Young Alexander, Naomi Sewell Richardson, Eliza P. Shippen, Zephyr Chisom Carter, Myra Davis Hemmings, Mamie Reddy Rose, Bertha Pitts Campbell, Florence Letcher Toms, Olive Jones, Jessie McGuire Dent, Jimmie Bugg Middleton, and Ethel Carr Watson. Myra Davis Hemmings has the distinction of being President of both Alpha Kappa Alpha and Delta Sigma Theta (Kimbrough 2003; Gliddings 2007; McKenzie 2013).

The Founders wanted to use their collective strength to promote scholarship as well as to provide aid to the needy on a national scope. These women endeavored to be more socially relevant to their community by concentrating their efforts on political activism and public service while distancing themselves from the stereotype of a social sorority. The newly formed Delta Sigma Theta performed their first public service act on March 3, 1913; they participated in the Women's Suffrage March in Washington, DC, in defiance of Howard University administration. They marched side-by-side with the estimated 10,000 women—not behind them (Ross Jr. 2000; Brown, Parks, and Phillips 2012).

During their developmental years, the Deltas became active participants and a force to be reckoned with in the fight for equal rights for African Americans and women. They lobbied for the exoneration of the Scottsboro Boys, the NAACP antilynching campaign, the repeal and dismantling of Jim Crow laws, and most notably, bringing literacy to historically overlooked African Americans in the rural South. Through their National Literacy Project, introduced in 1937, local Delta chapters provided books to Black communities to supplement the inferior schools and libraries. They created some libraries and even operated one of the first bookmobiles, filling buses with books and traveling to rural Black communities in the South (Ross Jr. 2000).

In 1955, Delta Sigma Theta established their Five-Point Programmatic Thrust as a means to realize its objectives of providing public service that benefit the African American community:

1. Economic Development
2. Educational Development
3. Physical and Mental Health
4. Political Awareness and Involvement
5. International Awareness and Involvement (Delta Sigma Theta Sorority, New Orleans Alumnae Chapter 2009).

Since their founding, Delta Sigma Theta Sorority has emerged as the world's largest sorority with over 250,000 members in 900 chapters. During their Centennial Celebration in 2013, more than 40,000 registered Delta sorors attended festivities in Washington, DC. On their hundredth Anniversary on January 13, 2013, President Barack Obama met personally with Delta leadership in the Oval Office and even illuminated the White House in red light in honor of their century of public service. Former Senator and Secretary of State addressed the assembly and summed it up best when she said, "Wherever you see women advancing, you see Deltas!" (Dillard 2013).

Zeta Phi Beta Sorority

While taking a stroll through the Howard University campus in 1919, Phi Beta Sigma member, Charles R.S. Taylor expressed his vision for a sister sorority to Arizona Cleaver and asked if she would be interested in pursuing this endeavor. There were already two sororities at Howard and Arizona had to resolve if there was enough interest to support another. After thoughtful contemplation, Arizona presented her plans to 14 hopefuls at an interest meeting—four of them committed to this undertaking. With the assistance of Charles Taylor and Sigma Founder, A. Langston Taylor, Arizona Cleaver, Pearl Neal, Myrtle Tyler, Viola Tyler, and Fannie Pettie (referred to as the *Five Pearls*) met in the dorm rooms of Miner Hall where they finalized the structure of their new sorority. After receiving approval from the Deans at Howard University, Zeta Phi Beta Sorority was founded on January 16, 1920 (Harrison 1998).

> Zeta Phi Beta was founded on the principles of Scholarship, Service, Sisterly Love, and Finer Womanhood and the precepts that "elitism and socializing had overshadowed the real mission of sororities-to address and correct the problems of society, particularly, those plaguing the African-American community. *(Mission & Vision of Zeta Phi Beta Sorority, Inc.)* (Zeta Phi Beta Sorority, Inc. 2013; McKenzie 2013; Parks 2008)

The *Five Pearls* chose the Greek letters ZΦB, which were derived from ΦBΣ to "seal and signify the relationship between the two organizations" (Harrison 1998, 2). They also constructed the sorority's constitution from Phi Beta Sigma's constitution. They adapted the Sigma's ritual and adopted many of their symbols, therefore making them the only official Brother and Sister organization in the NPHC—constitutionally bound for eternity (Harrison 1998).

Phi Beta Sigma members Charles Taylor and A. Langston Taylor formally introduced Zeta Phi Beta Sorority during a formal held at the Whitelaw Hotel. They were well received by the campus. Alpha Kappa Alpha Sorority and Delta Sigma Theta Sorority hosted a "Welcome to Campus" reception for the Zetas in the assembly room in Miner Hall. In December of that year, Zeta Phi Beta held its first Boule (convention) with Phi Beta Sigma at Howard University (Harrison 1998; McKenzie 2013).

> Since its inception, Zeta has continued its steady climb into the national spotlight with programs designed to demonstrate concern for the human condition both nationally and internationally . . . The sorority takes pride in its continued participation in transforming communities through volunteer services from members and its auxiliaries. Zeta Phi Beta has chartered hundreds of chapters worldwide and has a membership of 100,000+ (Zeta Phi Beta Sorority, Inc. 2013).

Sigma Gamma Rho

The hostile, racist atmosphere in Indiana as described during the early days of Kappa Alpha Psi had actually escalated. In the 1920s, the Ku Klux Klan had a surge of almost 4 million new members and Indiana became their base of operation. Nearly 30% of the white male population in Indiana was initiated klansmen; this earned Indiana the unofficial nickname, *Klandiana*. This was the environment that seven young Black school teachers found themselves emerged in during 1922 (Ross Jr. 2000; Parks 2008).

As the only historically Black sorority that was founded at a predominately-White institution and not Howard University; their mission was simple—help young Black women to succeed so that they could help others through service, leadership development, and education of youth. The *Seven Pearls*: Mary Lou Allison Gardner Little, Dorothy Hanley Whiteside, Vivian White Marbury, Nannie Mae Gahn Johnson, Hattie Mae Annette Dulin Redford, Bessie Mae Downey Rhoades Martin, and Cubena McClure organized Sigma Gamma Rho Sorority on the campus of Butler University in Indianapolis, IN on November 12, 1922 (Kimbrough 2003; Sigma Gamma Rho Sorority, Inc. 2013).

> Sigma Gamma Rho's commitment to service is expressed in its slogan, *Greater Service, Greater Progress*. The sorority has a proud history of offering service wherever chapters exist, including OPERATION BigBookBag, a program designed to address the needs, challenges and issues that face school-aged children who are educationally at-risk in local homeless shelters and extended care hospitals. The objective is for chapters to provide their local homeless shelters and children hospitals with educational materials, equipment and supplies (Sigma Gamma Rho Sorority, Inc. 2013).

During its formative years, Sigma Gamma Rho concentrated on establishing the fundamentals of their sisterhood and building their infrastructure instead of hosting conventions. They held their first Boule in 1925. Since 1922, Sigma Gamma Rho Sorority has expanded to more than 85,000 sisters in over 500 college and alumni chapters in North America, Bahamas, Bermuda, U.S. Virgin Islands, Germany, and Korea (Ross Jr. 2000; Parks 2008; Sigma Gamma Rho Sorority, Inc. 2013).

Sororities are emerging in surprising force at campuses not usually associated with the Greek tradition. Students raised on Facebook and fears about post-college careers view sororities as the ultimate social network and an extension of the community service begun in high school. Nationwide, membership is up, growing a bit more than 15 percent from 2008 to 2011, to 285,543 undergraduates (Moore 2012). Annually, undergraduate sorority members provide more than 1.3 million hours of community service and donate over $5 million for philanthropic endeavors (Anderson. 2009; San Jose State University 2013).

Top 25 Sororities

The NPC has 26 organizations with constituencies and traditions that vary by campus (the NPHC sororities are not part of the NPC). Newsweek analyzed the sororities based on number of chapters, social media popularity, and the amount of donated to philanthropic endeavors as indicated in public filings. Newsweek contacted all 26 sororities to confirm that the information was accurate. The NPC and several sororities declined comment. The following is Newsweek sorority rankings:

25. Theta Phi Alpha
24. Alpha Epsilon Phi
23. Sigma Delta Tau
22. Alpha Sigma Alpha

21. Alpha Sigma Tau
20. Phi Sigma Sigma
19. Sigma Sigma Sigma
18. Alpha Xi Delta
17. Alpha Gamma Delta
16. Sigma Kappa
15. Phi Mu
14. Gamma Phi Beta
13. Alpha Chi Omega
12. Delta Zeta
11. Kappa Alpha Theta
10. Alpha Phi
9. Alpha Omicron Pi
8. Delta Delta Delta
7. Kappa Delta
6. Pi Beta Phi
5. Chi Omega
4. Alpha Delta Pi
3. Kappa Kappa Gamma
2. Delta Gamma
1. Zeta Tau Alpha (Newsweek 2012b)

Latino-Oriented Fraternities and Sororities and Other Cultural Interest Organizations

Latino Greek-Lettered Organizations

The roots of Latino-oriented collegiate secret societies can be traced back even further than historically Black fraternities and sororities, since the late 1800s. Similarly, the first Latino-oriented associations were based on a need for Latino students to have a support system when their social and personal development needs were not being met as a minority on a predominately-White campus (Newsweek 2012b).

Union Hispano Americana was founded at Rensselaer Polytechnic Institute (RPI) in Troy, NY in 1890. It is regarded as the first known collegiate fraternal association for Latin American students. It was an intellectual, cultural secret society for Latin American and Spanish students that were based on principles of Pan-Americanism. This society was one of the four organizations—*Sigma Iota* at Louisiana State University in 1904; *Pi Delta Phi* at the Massachusetts Institute of Technology (MIT) in 1916; and *Phi Lambda Alpha* at UC Berkeley in 1919— that merged to form Phi Iota Alpha Fraternity, Inc. on December 26, 1931, the nation's oldest existing Latino fraternity (Kimbrough 2003; Association of Fraternity/Sorority Advisors, Inc. 2009).

The wars, the Great Depression, and the declining number of Latino college students lead to a drastic drop in membership for Phi Iota Alpha Fraternity until

1973 when it was completely inactive. The mid-1970s through late 1990s saw a resurgence of Latino students returning to college campuses as many predominately-White institutions started using ethnicity and open enrollment policies as part of their admission strategies to increase diversity on their campuses. In addition, political and social activism increased on campus toward the end of the Vietnam War. These factors lead to the emergence of several new Latino-oriented fraternities and sororities being founded on campuses across the United States. Phi Iota Alpha Fraternity returned to RPI in 1984 (Association of Fraternity/Sorority Advisors, Inc. 2009).

Although it is difficult to pinpoint the exact number, Walter Kimbrough has identified over 75 Latino-oriented fraternities and sororities. Only 21 are members of the National Association of Latino Fraternal Organizations, Inc. (NALFO), the primary umbrella associations representing Latino organizations since 1998. The group was incorporated on August 12, 1999 (Association of Fraternity/Sorority Advisors, Inc. 2009).

NAFLO Member Organizations (Association of Fraternity/Sorority Advisors, Inc. 2009)

Organization	Letters	Type	Founding Date	University
Phi Iota Alpha	ΦIA	Fraternity	December 26, 1931	Rensselaer Polytechnic Institute
Lambda Theta Alpha	ΛΘΑ	Sorority	December 1975	Kean College
Lambda Theta Phi	ΛΘΦ	Fraternity	December 1, 1975	Kean College
Lambda Sigma Upsilon	ΛΣΥ	Fraternity	April 5, 1979	Rutgers University
Chi Upsilon Sigma	ΧΥΣ	Sorority	April 29, 1980	Rutgers University
Lambda Upsilon Lambda	ΛΥΛ	Fraternity	February 19, 1982	Cornell University
Alpha Psi Lambda	ΑΨΛ	Coed	February 11, 1985	Ohio State University
Lambda Alpha Upsilon	ΛΑΥ	Fraternity	December 10, 1985	SUNY Buffalo
Lambda Theta Nu	ΛΘΝ	Sorority	March 11, 1986	California State University, Chico
Kappa Delta Chi	ΚΔΧ	Sorority	April 6, 1987	Texas Tech University
Sigma Lambda Upsilon	ΣΛΥ	Sorority	December 1, 1987	SUNY Binghamton
Gamma Zeta Alpha	ΓΖΑ	Fraternity	December 3, 1987	California State University, Chico
Lambda Pi Chi	ΛΠΧ	Sorority	April 16, 1988	Cornell University
Omega Phi Beta	ΩΦΒ	Sorority	March 15, 1989	SUNY Albany
Alpha Pi Sigma	ΑΠΣ	Sorority	March 10, 1990	San Diego State University
Sigma Iota Alpha	ΣΙΑ	Sorority	September 29, 1990	SUNY-Albany, SUNY-Stony Brook, SUNY-New Paltz & RPI
Gamma Phi Omega	ΓΦΩ	Sorority	April 17, 1991	Indiana University
Sigma Lambda Alpha	ΣΛΑ	Sorority	October 5, 1992	Texas Woman's University
Lambda Pi Upsilon	ΛΠΥ	Sorority	November 6, 1992	SUNY-Geneseo
Gamma Alpha Omega	ΓΑΩ	Sorority	January 25, 1993	Arizona State University

Spotlight on Sigma Lambda Beta Fraternity

After months of exploration and research, Baltazar Mendoza-Madrigal, a member of Phi Beta Sigma Fraternity visualized a Latino-oriented fraternity with many of the cardinal principles of Phi Beta Sigma but with a focus on Latin culture. During the spring of 1986, Mendoza-Madrigal took his proposal to the Board of Directors of Phi Beta Sigma Fraternity and was given their blessing to pursue his plan while still maintaining his membership (Parks and Toberson 2009; Sigma Lambda Beta International Fraternity, Inc. 2014).

He returned to the University of Iowa in Iowa City and put in motion his plans for a Latino-based fraternity with a multicultural membership that would promote a positive image of the Latino community (Sigma Lambda Beta International Fraternity, Inc. 2014; Parks and Toberson 2009).

> "The Latino community was divided among several social groups at the time," said Mendoza-Madrigal. The enthusiasm in favor of establishing a social fraternity that could help in unifying the community was so great that word started to spread quickly across the University of Iowa campus. Everyone knew that something great was about to take place (Sigma Lambda Beta International Fraternity, Inc. 2014, ¶3).

On Monday, March 7, 1986, Baltazar held an interest meeting at University of Iowa's Chicano-Indian American Cultural Center (currently the Latino Native American Cultural Center). He related his intentions of establishing a Latino-oriented fraternity that would unite all underrepresented minority students at University of Iowa while promoting cultural understanding and academic excellence. They discussed the need and feasibility of such an organization. The 18 men at this meeting—Mario Buendia, Enrique Carbajal, Thomas Carrasquillo, Manuel Chavarria, Jose Fong, Rudolfo Garza, Luis Jimenez, Luis Marquez, Baltazar Mendoza-Madrigal, Eric Montes, Kuy Ou, Olakunle Oyeyemi, Jaime Ramirez, Olivero Rivera, Eugenio Soria, Juan Valdez, and Ricardo Zamudio—on April 4, 1986, became the Founding Fathers of Sigma Lambda Beta International Fraternity. They represented such diverse continents as North America, South America, Africa, and Asia (Sigma Lambda Beta International Fraternity, Inc. 2014).

Founded on the principles of *Brotherhood, Scholarship, Cultural Awareness, and Community Service*, Sigma Lambda Beta has emerged as the largest Latino-oriented fraternity with over 500 college brothers and 10,000 alumni of all races and ethnicities in 150 college chapters, colonies, and alumni associations in 29 states. As a testament to their inclusionary and diverse aims, they even have chapters located on the campuses of two historically Black universities in Texas, Prairie View A&M University and Huston-Tillotson University (Parks and Toberson 2009) (Sigma Lambda Beta International Fraternity, Inc. 2014).

Spotlight on Sigma Lambda Gamma Sorority

Three years following the historic meeting at University of Iowa's Chicano-Indian American Cultural Center, that gave birth to Sigma Lambda Beta Fraternity. A group of 19 women met at the same location on October 22, 1989 for a similar purpose—the establishment of a Latino-oriented sorority that would provide social and academic support for Latinas and women of all cultures (Parks and Toberson 2009; Sigma Lambda Gamma National Sorority, Inc. 2014).

With support and guidance from their adviser, Esther Materon Arum, and Greek Affairs Coordinator, Mary Peterson, the women met once a week to continue establishing a sisterhood that promoted academic access and excellence and the social development of Latina women. A retreat was held where the women developed their mission, purpose, and started drafting their constitution. Through the course of time only five young women remained Gloria Cuevas, Julieta Maria Miller, Maria Ester Pineda, Danell Marie Riojas, and Guadalupe Temiquel. These five *Founding Mothers* continued to meet and work on their constitution and establish its ideals and became committed to seeing their dream through its completion. The *Founding Mothers* chose five guiding principles: academics, community service, cultural awareness, social interaction, and morals and ethics to unite their members as *Hermanas' por vida* (sisters for life). On April 9, 1990, the University of Iowa Panhellenic Council rewarded their efforts when they officially recognized Sigma Gamma Lambda as a sorority (Sigma Lambda Gamma National Sorority, Inc. 2014).

The *Founding* Mothers immediately began work on the expansion of the sorority to other campuses. Since its founding, Sigma Lambda Gamma has become the largest, Latina-oriented national sorority with sisters from more than 110 nationalities. Boasting more than 3,000 multicultural members in 168 college chapters, colonies, and alumni associations across the nation, Sigma Lambda Gamma is one of the fastest growing fraternal organizations gaining more than 100 chapters in less than 20 years (Kimbrough 2003; Parks and Toberson 2009; Sigma Lambda Gamma National Sorority, Inc. 2014).

Traditions and Customs

Latino-oriented fraternities and sororities have much more in common with NPHC organizations than they do with traditional fraternities and sororities. Like NPHC fraternities and sororities, they do not accept first-semester freshman and require a minimum of 12 earned credit hours and at least a 2.5 GPA. Their two to twelve-week pledge process resembles those that *Elite 8* fraternities and sororities practiced before Membership Intake when they abolished pledging in 1990. Most host informationals, have pledge lines, line numbers, organizational calls, hand signs, and perform strolls and step routines (Association of Fraternity/Sorority Advisors, Inc. 2009). Some other customs and traditions include:

- Artifacts: Artifacts are objects that represent the history and traditions of the organization and can be either nationally recognized or adopted by the individual chapters. Commonly used artifacts include small pins, staffs, machetes, items related to native Latin American culture, and Spaniard and native images.*
- Calls: Calls are used to acknowledge other chapter members in an audible tone (Kimbrough, 2003). Each organization has its own distinct call used by members at various events and venues. Calls are often conducted in a way that prompts another chapter to respond. It can be seen as disrespectful to use the call of an organization to which you do not belong.*

- Colors: Colors are used by organizations to distinguish themselves from each other and can range anywhere from two to five different colors. Sometimes an organization's colors have significant meaning related to its founding or culture. If you are interested in joining that organization, avoid wearing their colors until you are a member.*

- Hand Signs: Hand signs are used as an outward expression of pride in the member's organization. Hand signs can have significant meaning related to the organization's founding and culture. These signs also indicate unity among the membership. It can be seen as disrespectful to use the hand sign of an organization to which you do not belong.*

- Marching: The custom of marching was influenced by their founders, some of whom were military men and/or Masons. As many Latin American countries require all men who reach eight years old to serve in the military, marching is seen as a nod to Latin American countries and their emphasis on the military and discipline. Marching in a line was once part of many NPHC pledge programs as well.*

- Public Ceremonies (Probate/Neophyte Shows, Coming Out, New Member Introduction, etc.): The fraternity or sorority introduces new members to the campus; parents, friends, and other relatives are invited. Usually, the new members' identities are concealed through by masks, hoods, sunglasses, hats, etc. and typically, they perform a step routine and "salute" or "greet" the active members. At the show's conclusion, the new members are unmasked, their identities are revealed, they are formally introduced to the campus, and often their pledge/line names and numbers are revealed. Most times, after the show, established members present gifts bearing the fraternity or sorority letters and/or colors to their pledge son/daughter or little brother/sister. Family and friends also have the opportunity to present gifts.*

- Saluting: A salute involves a line of members performing motions and greetings in tribute to other members. Members tend to write salutes and incorporate modern day songs . . . Saluting "is a means by which members of an organization can praise a particular member within their organization or to honor the organization's past and current accomplishments." In NPHC fraternities and sororities, this is usually referred to as "greeting."*

- Stepping: Stepping, a tradition closely associated with NPHC organizations, is also performed by some NALFO organizations . . . Some elements adopted by Latino-oriented fraternal organizations incorporate customs related to Latino culture, including the addition of salsa and merengue music in the step routines. The adoption of stepping varies among NALFO member organizations.*

- Strolling: Strolling or party walking is a synchronized routine often done in a line formation, which incorporates moves and various expressions to music. Among Latino-oriented fraternal organizations, music associated with strolls is often based on Latino culture, such as salsa, merengue, bachata, reggaeton, etc.*

- Tiki: A tiki or lavalieres are necklaces often made of wood or plastic worn by active members that may have the organization's colors and letters. Lavalieres that are more formal are jewelry consisting of the Greek letters or fraternities and sororities symbols worn on a chain. In traditional fraternities, a lavaliere may be given to a girlfriend as a token of romantic commitment and usually precedes an engagement; this is much like a pinning ceremony.*

- Traditional attire: In recent years the acceptance and approval of specialized attire such as professional dress, uniforms, or other cultural/ceremonial attire has significantly changed due to organizationally driven actions and/or campus policies. Historically, many organizations' new members customarily wore uniforms as a public ritual of their organization. It is important for advisors to direct any questions about this particular practice to specific organizations (Association of Fraternity/Sorority Advisors, Inc. 2009).*

Other Cultural Interest Fraternities and Sororities

The late 1980s through 1990s saw an unprecedented amount of first-generation minority college students, most of whom were on predominately-White campuses. Even though all Greek organizations had abolished all racial, cultural, and religious restrictions, several of these students represented cultures that were outside the primary constituencies of traditionally White fraternities and sororities, historically Black Greek-lettered organizations, and Latino-oriented fraternal organizations. The basic need to belong and seek comfort from the familiar ushered in a new era of cultural-interest and multicultural fraternities and sororities that served those students that were underrepresented in the existing Greek systems. New fraternities and sororities seemed to appear almost monthly from coast to coast. Some were local or regional entities while others had aspirations of being national organizations (Maslow 1943; Parks and Toberson 2009).

A cursory exploration reveals such diverse organizations as an Armenian fraternity, 39 Asian-American fraternities and sororities, 22 Christian-based fraternities and sororities, an Italian-American fraternity, 7 Jewish-oriented fraternities and sororities, 8 fraternities and sororities for LGBQT students, 3 Muslim-based fraternities and sororities, 5 Native American fraternities and sororities, a Persian-oriented fraternity and sorority, 12 South Asian-based fraternities and sororities, and 66 fraternities and sororities that identify themselves as multi-cultural and pride themselves on being inclusive of all cultures, races, religions, and creeds (Parks and Toberson 2009). With such an array of fraternities and sororities, you would be hard-pressed not to find one that suits you, if you desire to participate in Greek life.

REMOVING THE BLINDFOLD: CRITICISMS AND CONTROVERSIES ASSOCIATED WITH GREEK LIFE

Hazing incidents have long tainted the reputation fraternities and sororities. Hazing includes but is not limited to impelled immobility for several hours, forced drinking, humiliation, paddling, hitting, racist activities/racial mockery, sleep deprivation, servitude, and forced excessive calisthenics (AP 1989; Allan and Madden 2008; Applebom December 21, 1994; Jones 2000; Kimbrough 1997; Kimbrough 2003; McKenzie 1986; Shaw et al. 1993). Between 1984 and 2013, there have been 30 hazing deaths that could be directly attributed to fraternity pledge activities. Hazing seems to be less an issue in sororities. Among those 30 deaths, two were from water intoxication (forced consumption of water that results in brain swelling); six were physical—one student died of cardiac arrest from a congenital heart disorder, the medical examiner could not find any bruising or signs of physical violence during the autopsy, and another died of suicide after being beaten; and 22 deaths were caused by alcohol poisoning from binge drinking: including one active member being compelled to drink by pledges; one of the members were charged with minor alcohol and drug misdemeanors, the police emphasized that these individuals had no actual links to the death; two accidental drownings in which alcohol were contributing factors; and one student who died after spending a night at bars with his friends to celebrate his twenty-first birthday. Although there was a lack of culpability in this situation, the college president suspended the entire Greek system (Nuwer 2013). Administrators, researchers, and law enforcement had never ascribed the all too common, birthday binge-drinking deaths to hazing. This association may be undeserved and an incident of scapegoating.

Due to publicity that often surrounds misfortunes; the public often fails to recognize these hazing abuses as isolated incidents perpetrated by a few rogue members. Nor do they distinguish hazing incidents that are unrelated to Greek life and therefore tend to indict the entire Greek system. Substantial anecdotal data corroborates that most hazing incidents involving alcohol abuse are almost exclusive to traditional fraternities while physical hazing occurs more in cultural-interest fraternities. Most sororities are free of this stigma (Williams-Scurlock 2005). Dr. Walter Kimbrough elaborates, "The abuses associated with hazing . . . gave members, as well as the national organizations, a terrible reputation" (Kimbrough 1997, 232).

One of the most publicized hazing incidents concerning a Black fraternity took place in Atlanta during fall 1989. A young sophomore died from cardiac arrest during non-sanctioned, pre-pledging activities held off campus. According to Dr. Joseph Burton, the medical examiner, the death was attributed to an irregular heart rhythm, the result of a congenital heart defect that he had undergone corrective surgery to repair at age 2. Although, the autopsy failed to reveal any bruises or visible injuries (AP 1989), this tragedy prompted the *Elite 8* to abolish pledging altogether during a NPHC Conference in July of 1990. At that time, the *Elite 8* voted to replace pledging with *membership intake*. However, this may have been ill conceived, by not consulting their more than one million members and offering a viable process to replace pledging, they had limited member buy-in. Many members found the membership intake process unsatisfying and argued that the organizations had thrown the baby out with the bathwater and did not actually address the underlying causes behind hazing. Immediately, following the membership intake movement, hazing incidents actually seemed like they increased because many chapters and members continued conducting the prohibited pledging activities, taking them underground where they had less oversight and public scrutiny. All of the NPHC organizations have tinkered with their membership intake process dramatically in the last quarter century (Kimbrough 1997).

Evidence supports that traditional fraternity members are more prone to binge drinking and alcohol related incidents—including accidental drownings, household accidents, vehicular accidents, and assaults. The pledge experience and the fraternity house environment were cited as major contributing factors to hazardous use of alcohol (Allan and Madden 2008; Weshler, Kuh and Davenport 2009). Most fraternity and university leadership have set strict policies and sanctions restricting the use of alcohol at Greek houses and events and most colleges require all Greeks to attend alcohol education and risk management classes about the dangers of binge drinking. It is imperative that students—especially underage students—adhere to existing laws, follow school and fraternity risk management guidelines, and drink responsibly to decrease alcohol related misfortunes.

In several articles, Dr. Molly Stombler (Stombler 1994; Stombler and Padavic 1997) has been extremely critical of gender role doctrines in traditional fraternities. She has accused fraternities with having an oppressive attitude toward women. She alleges that young women are often exploited, subordinated, and sexually objectified by fraternity members. Using inflammatory pejoratives such as "slut", she also contends that many of the women perpetuate this objectification by associating with the fraternity to have access to prospective boyfriends (maybe even husbands) or to engage in promiscuous behavior. Others have also condemned fraternity house lifestyles as a perfect storm for female exploitation. A 2013 article exposed an internal email from a fraternity member in Georgia who gave advice to his chapter brothers on how to use alcohol to take advantage of women at their fraternity house (Kingkade 2013). The Fraternity and university expelled that student and suspended the chapter.

Traditional fraternities have had a checkered history with discriminatory practices. This was the incentive for the founding of the cultural-interest fraternities.

Although discriminatory quotas traditionally guided collegiate admissions, many northern institutions removed or rewrote racial and religious quotas to allow minority students greater access to higher education and the social milieu that accompanied college life. While the incorporation of racial and religious minorities into the extracurricular life of American campuses guaranteed fundamental civil rights, it also challenged accepted patterns of interpersonal relationships. Integrated dining, dancing, and other social relations were perceived as threatening to many whites, who feared even greater intimacy, including intermarriage, might result. In addition, some whites connected anti-discrimination activity with communism and feared the undermining of the democratic process.

From 1945 to 1949, fraternity life became a testing ground for how blacks, whites, Protestants, Catholics, and Jews would relate (to each other) on the postwar campus. . . . A small number of fraternity members, working locally or through their national fraternal organizations, attempted to remove discriminatory clauses in Greek-letter societies. While they were moderately successful, their achievements were limited (James 2000, 303–304).

All NIC fraternities and PHC sororities abolished all racial, religious, and cultural restrictions decades ago.

The Black community has maintained long-held preconceptions about the practices of historically Black Greek-lettered organizations with allegations of elitism, exclusionism, and classism. Charges of being *color-struck*, the unspoken practice of only initiating members who were of light complexion, persisted through most of the twentieth century. A leading motivation for the founding of Phi Beta Sigma Fraternity and Zeta Phi Beta Sorority was to create historically Black organizations that rejected exclusivity and did not discriminate on the darkness of a person's complexion (Graham 2000; Phi Beta Sigma Fraternity, Inc. 2013; Harrison 1998). Fortunately, this practice is a relic of the past, historically Black fraternities and sororities consist of members in all different hues from around the world with a significant population of non-Black members as well.

WHAT CAN GREEK LIFE DO FOR ME? POSITIVE ATTRIBUTES ASSOCIATED WITH BEING GREEK

There have been relatively few positive depictions of Greek life in media and films. Fraternity and sorority members are usually depicted stereotypically in movies and television as drunken, destructive, arrogant, shallow, empty-headed, promiscuous, and unrefined; they seldom show any possible attributes. This and the above criticisms may leave many students questioning why they would be a part of Greek life. There are several benefits to Greek life, both tangible and intangible.

Numerous studies link membership in fraternities and sororities to higher levels of self-confidence, college satisfaction, increased alumni college donations, and community involvement (Jelke and Kuh 2003). In addition, there are indications that over time fraternity members have higher overall ratings in leadership, teamwork, loyalty, helping, duty, equality, collaborative learning, enriching educational experiences, and positive student-faculty interaction. Greeks are more likely to persist in degree attainment and have higher self-reported leadership abilities (Hayek et al. 2002; Asel, Seifert and Pascarella 2009; Pascarella and Terenzini 2005). Dr. Walter Kimbrough reiterates, "Greek organizations are able to assist in the development of students' leadership and social skills, as well as provide a balanced collegiate experience" (Kimbrough and Hutcheson 1998, 4).

> Students who belong to a fraternity (or sorority) . . . are (1) more likely to stay in college than other students; (2) Even after factoring out confounding variables, college graduates who belong to a fraternity (or sorority) . . . tend to become more successfully financially than other college graduates; (3) Colleges receive more gifts, and in greater amounts, from Greek alumni than non-Greek alumni; (4) (Greeks) . . . tend to participate more fully in extracurricular campus activities than do other students; and (5) in later years, (Greek) . . . alumni took part more fully in volunteer organizations, charitable activities and nonprofits than did non-member alumni (Jelke and Kuh 2003, 29).

Many of the positive attributes of Greek life are not usually reported by the media or depicted on screen. However, the following extensive list of noteworthy Greek facts is s a more accurate and fair representation of Greek life:

1. Nationally, 71% of all fraternity and sorority member graduate, while only 50% of nonmembers graduate.

2. The overall fraternity and sorority members' GPA is higher than non-members' GPA.

3. 85% of Fortune 500 Companies are run by Greeks—43 out of the Top 50

4. 76% of the listings in Who's Who in America are fraternity or sorority members.

5. First African American attorney, Violette Anderson was Greek (ZΦB).

6. First Black Rhodes Scholar, Alain Locke was Greek (ΦBΣ).

7. First African American to receive the Nobel Peace Prize, Ralph Bunche was Greek (AΦA).

8. All but five US Presidents since fraternities came into existence have been fraternity members *(Presidents Herbert Hoover, Lyndon B. Johnson, Richard Nixon, Jimmy Carter and Barack Obama are the exceptions).*

9. 70% of the US Presidents' cabinet members since 1900 have been fraternity or sorority members.

10. 75% of Congress is Greek

11. Since 1910, 85% of the Supreme Court Justices have been fraternity or sorority members.

12. The first Black Supreme Court Justice, Thurgood Marshall was Greek (AΦA).

13. The first two women appointed to the US Supreme Court were sorority members.

14. 63% of U.S. Cabinet Members since 1900 are Greek

15. First Black US Senator since Reconstruction, Edward Brook was Greek (AΦA).

16. First female Senator was Greek.

17. First Black female US Senator, Carol Mosely Braun was Greek (ΔΣΘ).

18. First African American Governor since Reconstruction, L. Douglas Wilder was Greek (ΩΨΦ).

19. First elected female head of state in Africa, Ellen Johnson Sirleaf was Greek (AKA).

20. First elected female head of state in the Americas, Eugenia Charles was Greek (ΣΓΡ).

21. First female astronaut was Greek

22. First African American astronaut in space, Guion "Guy" Bluford was Greek (ΩΨΦ).

23. First Black female astronaut in space, Mae Jemison was Greek (AKA).

24. All of the Apollo 11 astronauts were Greek

25. First black woman accepted into membership in the Screen Writer's Guild (SAG), Mary E. Vroman was Greek (ΔΣΘ).

26. First African American to be nominated and first to win an Academy Award, Hattie McDaniel was Greek (ΣΓΡ).

27. Over 85% of the student leaders on 730 campuses are members of Greek-letter organizations.

28. Less than 2% of average college student annual expenses go towards membership expenses.

29. A study by the University of Missouri found that Greeks throughout the U.S. and Canada are more involved on their campuses and rate their overall university experience better.

30. The same study found that fraternity or sorority members are more involved in their communities and give more generously to their alma maters.

31. Fraternity or sorority members form the largest network of volunteers in the U.S. Nationally, fraternity and sorority members volunteer over 10 million hours of community service every year.

32. Fraternity or sorority membership strongly encourages within its community to uphold the ideals that they were founded upon: sisterhood and brotherhood, scholarship, leadership, philanthropy, service, and becoming better citizens of society (Smith 1994; Williams-Scurlock 2005; Asel, Seifert, and Pascarella 2009; Becque 2013; University of Wisconsin Madison 2013; George Mason University, Office of Student Involvement 2013; Cornell University 2014; University of Missouri-Kansas City, Curators of the University of Missouri 2014).

Many studies support that membership in Black Greek-lettered organizations may yield some distinctive attributes. In Black students, membership in Greek-lettered organizations may has an overall more positive influence than with White students. While membership in traditionally White fraternities were believed to be associated with decreased levels of academic achievement and intellectual growth among members, the converse occurred in historically Black organizations (Pascarella and Terenzini 2005). Kimbrough added, "Black Greeks were more motivated to earn grades. . . . On the intellectual values scale, Black Greeks differed significantly with respect to being more independent, more liberal, and more socially conscious than their White counterparts" (Kimbrough and Hutcheson 1998, 37) Other attributes that Black Greeks may contrast with traditional organizations includes strong organizational expectations to exert a positive influence, reflect a positive image, serve as informal and formal role models in their communities, promotion of greater academic achievement through graduate studies, greater intellectual growth, accountability, and supporting the empowerment and edification of Black women (Parks 2008; Brown, Parks, and Phillips 2012; Graham 2000; Stombler and Padavic 1997).

After publishing several inflammatory condemnations of traditional fraternities and sexism, Dr. Molly Stombler resolved that the so-called *little sisters* of historically Black fraternities, sometimes called *sweethearts*, were empowered through the structure of the sweetheart programs. Unlike their counterparts in traditional fraternities, these women made meeting eligible, single men a secondary motive to performing community service, leadership development and experience, and ultimately gaining access to sorority life:

> Because black little sister organizations offered them more room to maneuver than white little sisters—by giving them a say in recruitment and endorsing sisterhood—they created a space for actions on their own behalf. Their emphasis on sisterhood bonds and the desirability of strength in women allowed them to collectively protest injustices with some success(Stombler and Padavic 1997, 37).

Role modeling and mentoring are strong components of Black-Greek lettered organizations (BGLOs). Members are regularly reminded that they are always wearing their letters and not to do anything that would tarnish the impeccable reputation and legacies of their organizations; positive representation is relentlessly reinforced. Members police each other and hold one another accountable for breaches. These qualities attracted most of the members to their organization. This also was the most common reason given from non-Black members who joined BGLOs over traditional fraternities and sororities. Therefore, organizational and peer controls are used to preserve this distinction and this is what primarily influences member selection decisions in BGLOs (Williams-Scurlock 2005; Parks 2008; Parks and Toberson 2009; Graham 2000).

MAKING THE CUT: SUCCESSFULLY JOINING YOUR PREFERRED FRATERNITY OR SORORITY

Finally, you have made up your mind to go Greek! *What should you do now?* First, you should make sure you are a good fit with your selected organization, that your values are complimentary, and that you can live up to the responsibilities and expectations. Do *not* choose a fraternity or sorority just because your mom, dad, or best friend is a member—it might suit their personalities but may clash with yours. Research all of the available organizations and consider what they do on a national scope. Make sure you select the right fraternity or sorority for you because your commitment extends past your campus and your college years.

How should you research the organization? Go to the fraternity or sorority website and learn the basic facts and history of that organization, their national programs and initiatives, partnerships and philanthropies, and get a sense of the "personality" and reputation of that organization. Also, ask questions of members to gain greater knowledge of their organization, most would be pleased to tell you why they joined. Please be honest with yourself. If you are just looking for fun and social outlets then I suggest you join an organization that provides this because you will not be happy in a highly structured organization that primarily focuses on studying, self-development, and public service—and the active members will not be happy with you either.

You have made your decision about the fraternity or sorority you wish to join. *How should you show your interest in joining?* Most schools hold activity fairs within the first weeks of the school year, most fraternities and sororities will participate have someone available to answer questions about the recruitment process—attend the fair and look for the organization that interests you. If you are still undecided about which one is best for you, this is an ideal time to introduce yourself and start getting a feel for the organization. Please remember that these individuals may not be indicative of the chapter—for better or for worse. So, if you do not feel a connection with that person, do not let them deter you from seeking more information. In addition, usually during the first few weeks of school, most fraternities and sororities will host rushes, smokers, socials, informationals or other similarly styled interest meetings. Attend these events, if you are unsure; go to more than one organization. You are not committing to anything; you are merely showing interest or seeking additional information.

Please note, first semester freshman are not eligible to apply for membership in the BGLOs and many of the Latino organizations. Most require you to have a minimum 2.5–2.75 GPA and 12–24 earned credit hours. This is to ensure that you have adjusted to college life; have had time to make an informed decision; developed self-identity; have taken advantage of the time to get to know members and the organization better and vice versa; have demonstrated academic success; and also to give you the time and opportunity to get involved in other aspects of campus life. If you decide to join one of these fraternities or sororities, use this time to develop good study habits, improve time management skills, attend chapter-sponsored activities, get to know members of the organization and decide who would be a good sponsor, get involved with other campus groups, perform community service, and take on some leadership responsibilities. Scholarship and service are the values of these organizations so you must demonstrate that they are important to you as well. Additionally, you should use this time to save money for your initiation fees. Joining fraternities and sororities require a significant, upfront financial commitment of about $500–$1,500.

How should you prepare for the interest meeting, what should you wear, how should you behave? The selection process for fraternities and sororities can be extremely competitive and you want to make the best impression possible so you should take it seriously. There is a historically Black fraternity chapter at a prestigious college in the South; the school has placed a cap of 25 new members per year. As many as 200 young men vie for these 25 spots—with almost half being legacies and a quarter of those being legacies from the same school.

"Sorority recruitment is like no other experience that you will ever have for the rest of your life , , , It's like speed dating meets interviewing meets beauty pageant meets upscale academic summer camp" (Moore 2012). Some parents have gone as far as to enlist the aid of professional consultants and services to give their children an edge during the selection process, costing anywhere from $125 an hour to $8,000 for an intensive three-day workshop.

Most fraternities and sororities expect at least business casual attire to attend interest meetings, if nothing is specified. Women would do well in a conservative but stylish, seasonal dress, or women's suit in muted colors—a "little black dress" with simple accessories is always appropriate. Men can wear khakis/chinos, oxford shirt, blazer (or sweater/vest), and non-athletic casual shoes if the invitation calls for business casual attire. If you do not have a blazer or V-neck sweater or vest, you can wear a tie in a muted color with the oxford shirt—do not roll the sleeves. If the event calls for business attire, men are ALWAYS expected to wear a conservative tie with a white or neutral colored dress shirt, dark suit (or dark dress slacks with a blazer or V-neck sweater), plain dark socks, and polished dress shoes. If possible, avoid wearing the fraternity or sorority's unique colors or those of their rivals. This may seem really trivial or petty but selection in these organizations can be very subjective in nature so why risk offending a member by appearing presumptuous.

Most chapters will hold interviews, treat them as you would a business interview—look the part, speak the part, be prompt, and follow directions. The well-prepared candidate "will have a résumé stressing community service, leadership, academics and teamwork, letters of recommendation from alumni of each chapter, preferably on the campus in question, and reference letters" (Moore 2012). Like many college applications, be prepared to provide a well-written letter of interest stating why you seek membership and a biography.

It is beneficial to prepare possible responses to typical interview questions beforehand. They will definitely ask why you wish to join. Make your responses honest, genuine, and avoid cliché and stock answers. Although, you may feel some anxiety, keep nervous tics in check (saying *uhh*, foot tapping, hair twisting, etc.). Let your personality shine through without being too familiar. Do not be afraid to ask intelligent, nonintrusive questions of the members—inquiries that might clarify something you did not understand during your research. Practice in front of a mirror, or videotape yourself to critique the quality of your responses, the clarity of your delivery, and your physical posture. If possible, have a friend conduct a mock interview with you. By all means, practice, practice, PRACTICE. . . . you want to leave them with the best impression of you possible. Be impressive and confident; make them feel that their organization would be missing out by not selecting you.

Some chapters may hold informal social events like an Open House or tea for prospective candidates. This is an opportunity for them to discern how you behave in a social environment so you are being observed. Good manners, confidence, and interesting conversation will serve you well. Avoid watershed topics like politics and religion—whatever your beliefs, inevitably there will be some that share them and some who will not. Think before you speak and analyze what you say; so you do not accidentally say something that can be perceived as offensive. Finally, do not babble, gush, or lavish them with insincere platitudes; it is not a good look.

CONCLUSION & DISCUSSION

It is my hope that this paper might alleviate some of the negativity associated with Greek life and increase public awareness of their positive attributes. Moreover, that it piques the interest of non-Greeks to seek more information with an open mind and start recognizing these organizations as crucibles for student development rather than frivolous college clubs. In addition, I am optimistic that this will inspire future college students to heed the call of leadership and service that uplifts and encourages others.

OPERATIONAL DEFINITIONS, KEY TERMS, AND ABBREVIATIONS

(Williams-Scurlock 2005; Association of Fraternity/Sorority Advisors, Inc. 2009; National Pan-hellenic Council, Inc. 2010; Brown, Parks, and Phillips 2012; Parks 2008; Kimbrough 2003)

Associate Members: Individuals who are participating in a membership intake process; other terms used include "Caballeros," "Damas," and "Hshinulan" (NAFLO)

Associate Member Educator: Member who oversees the membership intake process (may also be called a Dean).

BGLO or *Black Greek-lettered organizations*: Any of the historically or predominately-Black fraternities or sororities.

Chant: Reciting choruses describing different aspects of the organization; the art of reciting words in unison (NPHC; NAFLO)

Chapters: Organizational divisions within fraternities and sororities, separating different units based on college affiliation or city/area.

College fraternity: Any of the male-only, Greek-lettered, social/service student organizations on college campuses. Initially, "fraternity" also referred to the women societies since "sorority" had not been coined yet.

Crossing the "Burning Sands" or *Crossing Over*: Being initiated as a fully recognized and active member of a Black Greek-lettered organization (NPHC/NAFLO).

Divine Nine: The nine predominately Black fraternities or sororities that has comprised the National Pan-Hellenic Council (NPHC) since 1996: Alpha Phi Alpha Fraternity, Alpha Kappa Alpha Sorority, Kappa Alpha Psi Fraternity, Omega Psi Phi Fraternity, Delta Sigma Theta Sorority, Phi Beta Sigma Fraternity, Zeta Phi Beta Sorority, Sigma Gamma Rho Sorority, and Iota Phi Theta Fraternity.

Elite 8 or *Great 8* or *Original 8*: The original eight historically Black fraternities and sororities that comprised the National Pan-Hellenic Council from 1930–1996 and were established exclusively for African American students prior to integration and the modern civil-rights movement. These BGLOs include Alpha Phi Alpha Fraternity, Alpha Kappa Alpha Sorority, Kappa Alpha Psi Fraternity, Omega Psi Phi Fraternity, Delta Sigma Theta Sorority, Phi Beta Sigma Fraternity, Zeta Phi Beta Sorority, and Sigma Gamma Rho Sorority.

Final Review: Final interview of the membership intake process.

Formal Tea: In-depth meeting about the membership intake process for women who are interested in joining a sorority.

Frat: Brother or shortened term of fraternity.

Graduate or *Alumni Chapters (also referred to as "grad" chapters)*: This is distinctive to BGLO and NAFLO fraternities and sororities; these chapters are formed by and for members beyond their college years. While the majority of alumni members were initiated into their respective fraternity or sorority while in college, members can be initiated directly into graduate chapters after they have obtained a baccalaureate degree.

Greek(s): "Greek" and "Greeks" pertains to members of Greek-lettered organizations—both individually (as in "Greek") and collectively (as in "Greeks").

Hermana(s): Sister(s) (NAFLO)

Hermano(s): Brother(s) (NAFLO)

Iñaca: Individual participating in an IÑACAS Program, (Individuals Networking for the Advancement of Community, Academics, and Service) (NAFLO).

Informal Tea: Meeting at which a potential member of a sorority receives her first introduction to the organization.

Informational: Meeting held by a chapter for prospective members who are seeking general information about the organization.

Intake Process: Process through which an individual becomes a member of the organization; also called a membership recruitment process or leadership development process.

Interest: individual interested in joining an organization.

Membership Intake: In BGLO and some NAFLO fraternities and sororities, the period during which fraternity and sorority aspirants are educated, acclimated, and appraised for membership. If the aspirant is successful, initiation takes place at the conclusion. In BGLOs, this process has officially replaced pledging.

Mid-Review: Midpoint interview during the membership intake process.

National Pan-Hellenic Council or *NPHC:* The umbrella organization comprised of the nine predominately Black Greek-lettered collegiate organizations that provides programming and development. The mission of NPHC is to promote interaction through forums, meetings, and other mediums for the exchange of information and engages in cooperative programming and initiatives through various activities and functions.

Nationals: Popular expression for the national bodies that governs NPHC and NAFLO fraternities and sororities.

Neophyte: Newly initiated member

New Member Educator: See "Associate Member Educator"; also known as a "Dean."

Open House: Program that provides information on a fraternity or sorority.

Pledge Mom/Dad or Sponsor: Mentor with whom new/associate members work with throughout the membership; accompanies new/associate member at all activities, library hours, etc.; similar to a Big Brother/Big Sister for most organizations.

Pinning: Ceremony that begins the membership intake process.

Prophyte: Member that has participated in the membership intake process of their chapter and is no longer the newest member in the chapter.

Prospective: Individual interested in becoming a member; may also be called an Aspirant or Candidate or Interest.

Pledging: The process, by which aspiring fraternities and sororities members were considered, educated, familiarized, appraised, and ultimately initiated. In 1990, the national executive leadership of the *Elite 8* attended a NPHC and unanimously voted to abolish their pledge processes after an initiate died from a preexisting heart condition while pledging Alpha Phi Alpha. The membership intake process replaced pledging. However, many NPHC chapters and individuals continue to engage in unsanctioned, illegal "underground" pledge activities, a direct violation of the official policies of their national organizations.

Sand(s): In BGLO chapters, members may refer to those whom were initiated during the same semester as "sands".

Ship(s): In some BGLOs, specifically in the Midwest, a pledge class may be referred to as a ship (historical origin is most likely derived from the slave ships that brought Africans across the middle passage to America). In addition, the members of a pledge class may refer to each other as ship(s), as a shortened form of shipmate(s) *(see also Line Brothers & Line Sisters).*

Sweethearts or Little Sisters: Members of women's auxiliary groups formally or informally affiliated or associated with college fraternities.

Soror(s): Sister(s).

Traditionally White fraternities and sororities or Predominately White fraternities and sororities: Any of the Greek-lettered collegiate organizations originally founded for White students and currently maintain a predominately-White membership.

Underground: As in pledging "underground"; in BGLOs, an unsanctioned, unauthorized pledge process that often involves illegal hazing activities.

HOMESICKNESS

Making the transition into college can be exciting, overwhelming, and challenging for you. You will experience new friends, sense of freedom, and opportunities to work on/off campus, and become involved in student life. But you will also begin to miss parents, siblings, family pet, and home-cooked meals. Not all students have the same experience at the same time but most encounter HOMESICKNESS.

This is the number one stressor for college students because of the bond established within a relationship between parent/child, etc. that becomes a temporary loss (Ford 2013). Adapting to this loss involves the following:

1. Loneliness—The loss of daily intimacies of having someone or something (pets) special to share significant events with and the sense of being the most important person in someone else's life. Being independent at college than being a child at home is also a difficult transition as is the realization of having to deal with feelings such as anger, guilt, anxiety, helplessness, sadness, and depression.

2. Sense of deprivation—The sense of deprivation following the loss is particularly acute. You may feel deprived financially, socially, physically, and emotionally, in any combination.

3. Freedom and growth—Despite the negative impact of loss, you will find an awareness of freedom and the potential for change. Learning how to effectively cope with adversity is part of your student development process as you look at the potentials of independence and freedom. Along with this sense of freedom comes a sense of choice and greater awareness of "Who am I?" and "What do I enjoy?"

4. Change—You usually have to learn new behaviors that result in personal change. A major lifestyle change, such as starting a new job, moving from the residence hall to apartment living may cause you to feel loss as you are evolving into an adult. Even though these changes can be positive, stress and readjustment are to be expected.

5. New relationships. Forming a new relationship may signify readiness to create a support system for yourself without parental and family guidance.

It's important to note, you are not alone! As many as 70% of your colleagues across colleges and universities will have some concerns that fall under the umbrella term of homesickness. Participating as fully as possible in the activities sponsored by student affairs is essential. There's no better way to meet new people who share your interests and to have some fun. Take time and check your college's website and calendar for student organizations and activities.

Your college years are among the most formative and challenging years of your life. Remember there are people on your campus who can help you through this difficult time called "Homesick." Reach out to your RA (Resident Advisor), Dean of Students or make an appointment at the counseling center. You will be welcomed by all no matter how you feel while at the same time finding your "niche" at your college/university (Ford 2013).

FAMILY ISSUES

Being empowered in your first-generation college student status is important for your college adjustment process. Your self-esteem, locus of control, relationships, and family will catapult your understanding of the tools you will need to be successful.

Higher self-esteem allows for better personal and emotional adjustment into the college environment. Oftentimes as first-generation college students, the weight of success is an extremely heavy load to bear for yourself and your family. Having an understanding of the personal and family expectation, contribute to your esteem while in college. Planning and backup planning is important as a first-generation student because failing a class, receiving your first C in a class, or not landing the job you want can be a serious blow to your self-esteem.

Locus of control speaks to your ability to control your destiny. As a first-generation college student, have the understanding that destiny is not a matter of chance, but a matter of choice. As your environment begins to change, you can attribute success and failure to things you have control over or to force outside of your influence.

Locus of Control*

Are You in Charge of Your Destiny?

Do you feel someone else is pulling your strings?

As the environment around you changes, you can either attribute success and failure to things you have control over, or to forces outside your influence.

Which orientation you choose has a bearing on your long-term success.

This orientation is known as your "locus of control." Its study dates back to the 1960s, with Julian Rotter's investigation into how people's behaviors and attitudes affected the outcomes of their lives.

Locus of control describes the degree to which individuals perceive that outcomes result from their own behaviors, or from forces that are external to themselves. This produces a continuum (see figure 4.1, below) with external control at one end and internal control at the other.

FIGURE 4.1

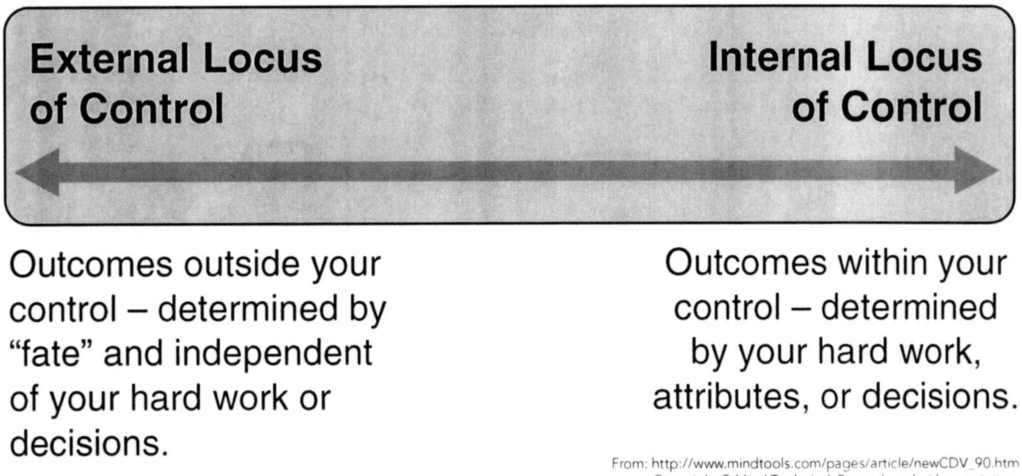
External Locus of Control
Internal Locus of Control
Outcomes outside your control – determined by "fate" and independent of your hard work or decisions.
Outcomes within your control – determined by your hard work, attributes, or decisions.

From: http://www.mindtools.com/pages/article/newCDV_90.htm

Locus of Control Continuum

People who develop an internal locus of control believe that they are responsible for their own success. Those with an external locus of control believe that external forces, like luck, determine their outcomes.

Use the interactive quiz below to determine your current locus of control:

Understanding Your Own Locus of Control

Instructions

For each pair of statements, choose the one that you believe to be the most accurate, not the one you wish was most true. Remember, there are no right or wrong answers. Click the "Calculate My Total" button to add up your score and check your result using the scoring table underneath.

#	Statement	Select the statement you feel is more accurate
1a	Bad luck is what leads to many of the disappointments in life.	○
1b	Disappointments are usually the result of mistakes you make.	○
2a	Political unrest and war normally occur in countries where people don't get involved, or assert their political rights.	○
2b	No matter how much people get involved, war and political unrest will occur.	○

#	Statement	Select the statement you feel is more accurate
3a	You "reap what you sow." In the end, your rewards will be directly related to what you accomplish.	○
3b	Despite your effort and hard work, what you accomplish will probably go unnoticed.	○
4a	Teachers treat students fairly and evaluate their performance as objectively as possible.	○
4b	The grades you earn in school have more to do with factors like how much the teacher likes you, or your mood on the day of a test.	○
5a	To become a leader, you must be in the right place at the right time.	○
5b	Those who are capable of leadership but don't lead have failed to capitalize on the opportunities afforded to them.	○
6a	There are some people in this world that will not like you, no matter what you do.	○
6b	If you have good interpersonal skills and know how to get along with others, then getting people to like you is not difficult at all.	○
7a	If something is meant to happen, it will; there is little you can do to change it.	○
7b	You decide what will happen to you. You don't believe in fate.	○
8a	If you are prepared for an interview, you increase your likelihood of doing well.	○
8b	There is no point in preparing for an interview because the questions they ask are completely random and determined by whim.	○
9a	To be successful in your career takes a lot of hard work and dedication, because effort is what makes the difference.	○
9b	It's who you know, not what you know, that determines how good a job you get.	○
10a	One person can have an impact on government policy and decisions.	○
10b	Normal people can't do much to change the world; the elite and powerful make all the decisions.	○
11a	If you set a reasonable goal, you can achieve it with hard work and commitment.	○
11b	You don't plan ahead or set goals because too much can happen that you can't control.	○

#	Statement	Select the statement you feel is more accurate
12a	Luck doesn't play a large role in getting what you want out of life.	○
12b	Life is like a game of chance. What you get or what happens to you is mostly a matter of fate.	○
13a	Managers and supervisors got those positions by being in the right place and knowing the right people.	○
13b	To be a manager or supervisor you have to demonstrate that you know how to get things done through, and with, people.	○
14a	Accidents or twists of fate are what really determine the course of a person's life.	○
14b	The notion that luck largely determines your life is a fallacy.	○
15a	People have so many ulterior motives; it's impossible to determine who actually likes you and who doesn't.	○
15b	How you treat people is what determines whether they like you.	○
16a	After all is said and done; the positives and negatives of life are basically half and half.	○
16b	When something negative happens, it is usually a result of apathy, lack of knowledge, inability, or a combination of these.	○
17a	Corruption in politics can be eliminated if we all put in enough effort.	○
17b	Once a politician is elected, there is little anyone can do to control him or her.	○
18a	"The assessments I get at work are completely at the whim of my supervisor; I don't understand them at all half the time."	○
18b	"How hard I work and how much pride I take in my job largely determines the results of my performance assessment."	○
19a	You often feel that you have little control over your life, and what happens to you.	○
19b	You don't believe that luck or chance play a large role in determining what happens in your life.	○
20a	If you're lonely, it's because you don't try hard enough to get along with people and be friendly.	○
20b	Despite being friendly and pleasant, if someone doesn't like you, there's not much you can do to change his or her opinion.	○
21a	The things that happen in your life are of your own doing.	○

#	Statement	Select the statement you feel is more accurate
21b	You don't have much control over what happens in life, or in the direction your life is headed.	◯
22a	Why politicians make the decisions they do is anybody's guess!	◯
22b	The people are as much responsible for government decisions as the politicians themselves.	◯
		Total = 0

Score Interpretation

Score	Comment
22–25	Internal Locus of Control (Strong)
26–33	Internal Locus of Control (Moderate)
34–44	External Locus of Control

Note

This assessment has not been validated and is intended for illustrative purposes only. It is patterned after the Locus of Control Scale developed and presented in Rotter, JB (1966), "Generalized expectancies for internal versus external control of reinforcement", Psychological Monographs, 80 (Whole No. 609).

Benefits of an Internal Locus of Control

In general, people with an internal locus of control:

- Engage in activities that will improve their situation.
- Emphasize striving for achievement.
- Work hard to develop their knowledge, skills, and abilities.
- Are inquisitive, and try to figure out why things turned out the way they did.
- Take note of information that they can use to create positive outcomes in the future.
- Have a more participative management style.

Managing the Drawbacks of a Strong Internal Locus of Control

People with an internal locus of control are generally more successful, for very good reasons.

However, there can be times when having an external locus of control can be an advantage, particularly in situations where people need to be considerate and more easygoing. People with a strong internal locus of control tend to be very achievement-oriented, and this can leave people around them feeling "trampled" or "bruised." And with a very strong internal locus of control, there is also a tendency to want to control everything, and this can lead to difficulties in taking direction.

If you have a strong internal locus of control, make sure you pay attention to the feelings of people around you—otherwise you'll seem arrogant, and people may not want to work with you.

Also, make sure that you manage risks properly. Random events do occur for all sorts of reasons. While you can manage many of these with enough determination and hard work, some you can't.

Note

As people grow older they tend towards a more internal locus of control. This comes from the increased ability to influence things going on in their lives and the realization that much of what happens to them is a result of what they do.

Tips for Developing an Internal Locus of Control

Recognize the basic fact that you always have a choice. Making no choice is actually a choice in and of itself, and it's your choice to allow other people or events decide for you.

Set *goals* for yourself and note how, by working towards these and achieving these, you are controlling what happens in your life. As you do this, you'll find that your *self-confidence* quickly builds.

Develop your *decision-making* and *problem-solving* skills so that you can feel more confident, and in control of what happens. With these tools, you'll find that you can understand and navigate through situations that would otherwise damage you.

Pay attention to your *self-talk*. When you hear yourself saying things like, "I have no choice" or "There's nothing I can do," step back and remind yourself that you do, in fact, have some degree of control. It's your choice whether you exercise it or not.

Key Points

You locus of control says a lot about how you view the world and your role in determining the course of your life.

When you believe you have the power to control your own destiny and determine your own direction, you have a strong internal locus of control. In most cases, this is an important attitude to have if you want to be successful.

People with an internal locus of control tend to work harder and persevere longer in order to get what they want. This is not to say that having an external locus of control is always bad: there are some situations where this approach can work well. The key for your own personal development is to understand your natural tendency and then adapting it to the situations you are faced with.

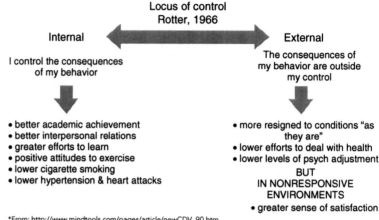

Locus of control
Rotter, 1966

Internal — External

I control the consequences of my behavior

The consequences of my behavior are outside my control

- better academic achievement
- better interpersonal relations
- greater efforts to learn
- positive attitudes to exercise
- lower cigarette smoking
- lower hypertension & heart attacks

- more resigned to conditions "as they are"
- lower efforts to deal with health
- lower levels of psych adjustment

BUT
IN NONRESPONSIVE ENVIRONMENTS

- greater sense of satisfaction

*From: http://www.mindtools.com/pages/article/newCDV_90.htm
Copyright © Mind Tools, Ltd. Reproduced with permission.

Most students come to college expecting a sense of freedom to "grow up." The flight of life started when you got your driver's license, landed your first summer job, and some of you were lucky to have your parents purchase a car for you to take to college. Many parents worry the most about how relationships affect you and how they can affect your family. Yes, parents may have a hard time letting you control your life, not understanding your need to study, but there's the concern about romantic relationships and your past interactions. In college, romantic relationships can support you or can create major conflict and heartbreak, depending on honest communication, and most of all, is the relationship healthy, affirming, or so harmful that it's dysfunctional.

In a national study of 5,000 college students conducted in 2001 by researchers at the University of California, Los Angeles, 29 percent reported they ended a romantic relationship during their first year in college. Breaking up can be emotionally draining. You might find yourself sad, angry, or even depressed. Your family becomes concern by your phone calls, tweets, or Facebook comments. Remember, parents fear you'll harm yourself! Almost everyone has been rejected or "kicked to the curb" at one time or another including your family members. The more irrational you become the more parents suggest removing you from campus to return home to your caretakers—Parents. Remember there are skilled professionals to help you through these experiences at the counseling center, student life professionals, and the list goes on and on. These individuals have assisted many students through similar experiences, and they can be there for you as well.

There are some relationships that are hands off. Never become romantically involved with your professor or someone who works above or for you. If your partner is a person who has power and influence over you, the romance might really represent that person's need for power. Example: You have a relationship with a professor who controls your grade for a class you need to graduate this semester and they give you an unsatisfactory grade. Imagine how you would feel along with your parents when the truth is revealed. When you decide to swim in danger water, the outcomes can be devastating for everyone involved.

Another relationship to be on alert is engaging in online relationships instead of face to face relationships. While there is evidence that online connections might help some students in their college adjustment, there is still evidence of something more disturbingly. It is noted that some students can suffer negative emotional consequences from too much internet use, especially those who use it beyond necessary communication such as dating sites, pornography, etc. It's important to note, your university email address belongs to the school and prohibits usage on numerous sites including illegal downloading of music and movies. Check your computer technology center/website for information.

Family concerns and caregiving lines can become quite blurred. There are so many concerns for families today during this transition. The most common concerns noted today are pregnancy, drug and alcohol usage, domestic violence, suicide, and rape. Parents are caregivers but what happens when you are expected to take care of them due to loss of employment, medical reasons, etc. This is becoming a normal occurrence in the lives of first-generation college students. Many students are sending their work-study money home to help the family stay afloat and going home every weekend to help in the family business. Sound familiar? Here are some suggestions to assist you through this challenging period. First, tell your academic counselor and/or mentor. This helps them to understand the challenges you are facing and how to create a support system for you to succeed in college. There maybe ways to take online classes, register for less credits to help you balance school and work and the possibility of transferring to a community college at home to complete your required general education courses. Second, talk to your parents and family members about the pros and cons of taking a leave from college. If you have student loans and decide to take leave from your educational journey, you will have to start paying them back and any unpaid bills you have at the college, all bills must be paid in full. Transcripts cannot be obtained and employment opportunities can be hindered without transcripts. Important questions to ask yourself are the following: will I be part of the problem than the solution? Can I support myself and the family on minimum wage? What happens if I can't find a job in this economy when I return home ? Am I better off finishing school to be able to take care of the family in the future? These questions are critical to the future of first-generation college students. Think things over and allow the decision to be yours and yours alone. To some it's an honor and a privilege to care for their family as they have cared for them and there are others who regret being stuck in a situation without options. Seek help from your campus's counseling center, career center, and Dean of Students to examine your options in the midst of a difficult family situation.

ACTIVATE YOUR THOUGHTS!

1. Do you think having a romantic relationship with a professor of staff is dangerous?

2. What might be dangerous about online dating?

3. If you met someone online and they showed up at your college residence, what would you do?

4. Examine how you would react if you were dealing with a breakup. Would you tell your parents, friends, siblings, etc.?

5. Your parents lost their jobs and cannot pay the mortgage and might lose the house. Are you obligated to help?

6. A parent dies and leaves you in charge of the family business. You are a junior and received a full scholarship to study abroad next semester. What decision will you make?

Works Cited

Allan, Elizabeth J., and Mary Madden. "Hazing in View: College Students at Risk." Initial Findings of the National Study of Student Hazing, College of Education and Human Development, University of Maine, 2008, 52.

Alpha Phi Alpha Fraternity, Inc. *A Brief History.* 2013. http://www.alpha-phi-alpha.com/Page.php?id=110 (accessed May 17, 2014).

—. *Founding Jewels.* 2013. http://www.alpha-phi-alpha.com/Page.php?id=138 (accessed January 17, 2014).

Alpha Phi Delta Fraternity, Inc. *About APD: The Founding Years.* n.d. http://www.apd.org/?page=FoundingYears (accessed February 17, 2014).

Alpha Phi Fraternity. *Alpha Phi Founded at Syracuse University.* 2010. http://www.alphaphi.org/Mobile/Firsts/22 (accessed January 30 2014, 2014).

Anderson., Ashley. "History of Sororities in America." *Suite.* September 22, 2009. https://suite101.com/a/history-of-sororities-in-america-a150713 (accessed November 30, 2013).

AP. "College Student Dies At Pledging Activity Held by a Fraternity." *The New York Times,* October 1989.

Applebom, Peter. "Lawsuit Shatters Code of Silence Over Hazing at Black Fraternities." *The New York Times,* December 21, 1994.

Asel, Ashley M., Tricia A. Seifert, and Ernest T. Pascarella. "The Effects of Fraternity/Sorority Membership on College Experiences and Outcomes: A Portrait of Complexity." *Oracle: The Research Journal of the Association of Fraternity/Sorority Advisors,* 2009: 1–15.

Association of Fraternity/Sorority Advisors, Inc. *NALFO Resource Guide.* Carmel, IN, 2009.

Astin, Alexander W. "Student involvement: A developmental theory for higher education." *Journal of College Student Personel 25,* no. 4 (1984): 297–308.

Astin, Alexander W. *What Matters in College: Four Critical Years Revisited.* San Francisco: Jossey-Bass, 1993.

Baird, William Raimond, and James Taylor Brown. *Baird's Manual of American College Fraternities.* Menasha, WI: George Banta Company, 1920.

Becque, Fran. *Busting Myths – That Pesky "All But Two Presidents Born Since 1825" Statistic Has Problems.* July 10, 2013. http://www.franbecque.com/2013/07/10/busting-myths-that-all-but-two-presidents-born-since-1825-statistic-just-isnt-true/ (accessed January 11, 2014).

Borsari, Brian E., and Kate B. Carey. "Understanding Fraternity Drinking: Five Recurring Themes in the Literature." *Journal of American College Health,* 1999: 30.

Brown, Tamara L, Gregory S. Parks, and Clarenda M. Phillips. *African American Fraternities and Sororities: The Legacy and the Vision*. Lexington, KY: University of Kentucky Press, 2012.

Bryson, Ralph J. *The Story of Kappa Alpha Psi: A History of the Beginning and Development of A College Greek Letter Organization 1911–1999*. 5th. Philadelphia: Grand Chapter of the Kappa Alpha Psi Fraternity, Inc., 2003.

Chickering, Author W. *Commuting Versus Resident Students*. San Francisco: Jossey-Bass, 1974.

Chickering, Author W., and Kuper, E. "Education outcomes for commuters and residents." *Educational Record 52*, no. 3 (1971): 255–261.

Cornell University: Division of Rare & Manuscript Collections. *Alpha Phi Alpha Fraternity: A Centennial Celebration*. 2006. http://rmc.library.cornell.edu/alpha/introduction/index.html (accessed December 4, 2006).

Cornell University. *Greek Facts*. 2014. http://dos.cornell.edu/greek/about_our_office/facts.cfm (accessed January 22, 2014).

Davis, Tamara L., and Debora L. Liddell. "Getting Inside the House: The Effectiveness of a Rape Prevention Program for College Fraternity Men." *Journal of College Student Devlopment*, 2002: 35.

Delta Sigma Theta Sorority, New Orleans Alumnae Chapter. *Five Point Thrust*. 2009. https://dstnoa.org/Five_Point_Thrust.html (accessed January 15, 2014).

Dillard, Jacqueline. *Hillary Clinton (Part 1)*. YouTube Video. Washington, DC, July 21, 2013.

Dubroff, M. Dee. "History of Sororities: Some Interesting Facts about How Sororities Began." *Catalogs.com Info Library*. n.d. http://www.catalogs.com/info/people/history-of-sororities.html (accessed January 18, 2014).

Ford, Clarice. 2013. "Homesickness." In *How to Survive Your Freshman Year*. 5th Edition. Atlanta, GA: Hundreds of Heads.

Gellin, Alan. "The effect of undergraduate student involvement on critical thinking: A meta-analysis of the literature 1991–2000." *Journal of College Student Development* 44, no. 6 (2003): 746–762.

George Mason University, Office of Student Involvement. *A General History of Greek Life*. Website. Fairfax, VA, 2013.

Gliddings, Paula J. *In Search of Sisterhood: Delta Sigma Theta and the Challenge of the Black Sorority Movement*. New York: William Morrow Paperbacks, 2007.

Graham, Lawrence Otis. *Our Kind of People: Inside America's Black Upper Class*. New York: Harper Collins Publishers, Inc., 2000.

Harrison, Lullelia W. *Torchbearers of a Legacy: A History of Zeta Phi Beta Sorority, Inc. 1920–1997*. Washington, DC: Zeta Phi Beta Sorority, Incorporated, 1998.

Harvard School of Public Health, Boston, MA.

Hauser, Gregory F. "Intimate Associations Under the Law: The Rights of Social Fraternities to Exist and to Be Free from Undue Interference by Host Institutions." *The Journal of College and University Law*, 1997: 59–96.

Haven, Erastus O. *Autobiography of Erastus O. Haven.* Edited by Rev. C.C. Stratton. New York: Phillips & Hunt, 1883.

Hayek, John C., Robert M. Carini, Patrick T. O'Day, and George D. Kuh. "Triumph or Tragedy: Comparing Student Engagement Levels of Members of Greek-Letter Organizations and Other Students." *Journal of College Student Development*, 2002: 643–663.

Higher Education Amendments (1998); pg. 1, Washington, D.C.

Hood, Clifton R. *[Penn] University History - Philomathean Society: A Brief History.* 2006. http://www.archives.upenn.edu/histy/features/studtorg/philo/philo .html (accessed January 21, 2014).

Iota Phi Theta Fraternity Inc. *Historical Overview.* 2013a. http://www .iotaphitheta.org/about/historical-overview (accessed December 8, 2013).

Iota Phi Theta Fraternity, Inc. *Iota Joins the NPHC.* Baltimore, MD, 2013.

James, Anthony W. "The College Fraternity Antidiscrimination Debate, 1945–1949." *The Historian*, 2000: 303–324.

Jelke, Thomas B., and George Kuh. *High Performing Fraternal Groups.* Asheville, NC: College Administration Publications, Inc., 2003.

Jennings, Michael E. "The Pride of All Our Hearts: The Founders of Kappa Alpha Psi Fraternity, Inc." In *Black Greek Letter Organizations in the Twenty-First Century: Our Fight Has Just Begun*, by Gregory Parks. Lexington, KY: University Press of Kentucky, 2008: 115–123.

Jones, Ricky L. "The Historical Significance of Sacrificial Ritual: Understanding Violence in the Modern Black Fraternity Pledge Process." *The Western Journal of Black Studies*, 2000: 112.

Kalof, Linda, and Timothy Cargill. "Fraternity and Sorority Membership and Gender Dominance Attitudes." *Sex Roles*, 1991: 417–424.

Kiesling, Scott F. "Men's Identities and Sociolinguistic Variation: The Case of Fraternity Men." *Journal of Sociolinguistics*, 1998: 69–99.

Kimbrough, Walter L., and Philo A. Hutcheson. "The Impact of Membership in Black Greek-Letter Organizations on Black Students' Involvement in Collegiate Activities and Their Development of Leadership Skills." *The Journal of Negro Education*, 1998: 96–105.

Kimbrough, Walter M. "The Membership Intake Movement of Historically Black Greek-Letter Organizations." *NASPA Journal*, 1997: 229–239.

Kimbrough, Walter M. *Black Greek 101: The Culture, Customs, and Challenges of Black Fraternities and Sororities.* Madison, NJ: Fairleigh Dickinson University Press, 2003.

Kingkade, Tyler. *Georgia Tech Frat Email About 'Luring Your Rapebait' Condemned By Everyone.* November 26, 2013. http://www.huffingtonpost.com/2013/10/08/ georgia-tech-frat-email-rapebait_n_4063101.html (accessed December 28, 2013).

Kuh, George D., and James C. Arnold. "Liquid Bonding: A Cultural Analysis of the Role of Alcohol in Fraternity Pledgeship." *Journal of College Student Development*, 1993: 327–34.

Maslow, Abraham H. "A Theory of Human Motivation." *Psychological Review [Digital Archive/Electronic Version]*, 1943: 370–396.

Mason, Herman "Skip". *The Talented Tenth: The Founders and Presidents of Alpha.* Jackson, MS: Four-G Publishers, Inc., 1999.

Mathiasen, Robert E. "Moral Development in Fraternity Members: A Case Study." *College Student Journal*, 2005: 242–252.

McCabe, Donald L., and William J. Bowers. "The Relationship Between Student Cheating and College Fraternity and Sorority Membership." *NASPA Journal*, 1996: 280–291.

McKenzie, Andre. "In the Beginning: The Early History of the Divine Nine." In *African American Fraternities and Sororities: The Legacy and the Vision*, edited by Tamara L. Brown, Gregory S. Parks, and Clarenda M. Phillips. Lexington, KY: The University Press of Kentucky, 2013, 181–210.

McKenzie, Andre. *Fraters: Black Greek-Letter Fraternities at Four Historically Black Colleges, 1920-1960.* New York: Columbia University, 1986.

Moore, Abigail Sullivan. "Pledge Prep." *The New York Times: Education Life.* July 16, 2012. http://www.nytimes.com/2012/07/22/education/edlife/prepping-students-for-sorority-rush.html?pagewanted=all&_r=1&&pagewanted=print (accessed January 19, 2014).

National Panhellenic Council, Inc. *NPHC, Inc. Mission.* 2010. http://www.nphchq.org/mission.htm (accessed December 2, 2013).

Newsweek. "College Rankings 2012: Top Fraternities." *Newsweek: Education.* August 8, 2012a. http://www.newsweek.com/college-rankings-2012-top-fraternities-64505 (accessed January 19, 2014).

—. "College Rankings 2012: Top Sororities." *Newsweek: Education.* August 8, 2012b. http://www.newsweek.com/college-rankings-2012-top-sororities-64461 (accessed January 19, 2014).

North-American Interfraternity Conference. *About the North-American Interfraternity Conference.* Indianapolis, IN, 2013.

—. *About The North-American Interfraternity Conference.* 2014b. http://www.nicindy.org/about/ (accessed November 10, 2014).

Nuwer, Hank. "Hank Nuwer's List of Deaths by Hazing." *The Hazing Reader.* Bloomington, IN: Indiana University Press, 2013.

Omega Psi Phi Fraternity, Inc. *About Omega.* 2010. http://www.omegapsiphifraternity.org/about_omega.asp (accessed January 17, 2014).

—. *About Omega.* 2010b. http://www.oppf.org/about_omega.asp (accessed January 19, 2014).

OrgSynch. *Omega Psi Phi Fraternity, Inc.: Organizational Overview.* 2014. https://orgsync.com/26517/chapter (accessed January 19, 2014).

Parks, Gregory S. *Black Greek-Letter Organizations in the Twenty-First Century: Our Fight Has Just Begun.* Lexington, KY: University of Kentucky Press, 2008.

Parks, Gregory S., and Craig L. Toberson. *Brothers and Sister: Diversity in College Fraternities and Sororities.* Hackensack, NJ: Fairleigh Dickinson, 2009.

Pascarella, Ernest T. "Reassessing the effects of living on-campus versus commuting to college: A causal modeling approach." *Review of Higher Education* 7, (1984): 247–260.

Pascarella, Ernest T., and Patrick T. Terenzini. *How College Affects Students (Volume 2): A Third Decade of Research.* San Francisco: Jossey-Bass, 2005.

Pascarella, Ernest T., and Patrick T. Terenzini. *How College Affects Students: Findings and Insights.* San Francisco: Jossey-Bass, 1994.

Pascarella, Ernest T., Louise Bohr, Barbara Zusman, and Patricia Inman. "Cognitive impacts of living on campus versus commuting to college." *Journal of College Student Development* 34, no. 3 (1993): 216–220.

Pascarella, Ernest T., Patrick T. Terenzini, and Gregory S. Blimling. "How residence halls impact student learning and personal development." In *Realizing the Educational Potential of College Residence Halls*, by P. Mable and Associates C. Schroeder, 22–52. San Francisco: Jossey-Bass, 1994.

Patton, G., Coffey,C., Carlin, J., Degenhardt, L. Lynskey, M., and Hall, W. 2002. Cannabis use and mental health in young people: cohort study. Center for Adolescent Health, 355: 1195–1198.

Phi Beta Sigma Fraternity, Inc. *A Brief History of Phi Beta Sigma Fraternity, Inc.* 2013. http://www.phibetasigma1914.org/our-history/ (accessed December 8, 2013).

Phi Mu. *Phi Mu: Our Organization At a Glance.* 2010. http://www.phimu.org/aboutus/ourorganizationataglance (accessed January 21, 2014).

Pike, Gary R. "The effects of background, coursework, and involvement on students." *Research in Higher Education*, 1991: 15–30.

Pike, Gary R. "The Influence of Fraternity or Sorority Membership on Students' College Experiences and Cognitive Development." *Research in Higher Education*, 2000: 117–139.

Resident or Community Director, accessed November 20, 2013, http://www.ithaca.edu/reslife/employment/professional_staff/residence_director/rd_job_description/.

"Roommate Agreement Guide," August 2001, November 20, 2013, http://www.american.edu/ocl/sccrs/upload/RoommateAgreement-new-website.pdf.

Ross Jr., Lawrence C. *The Divine Nine: The History of African American Fraternities and Sororities.* New York: Kensington Publishing Corp., 2000.

San Jose State University. *General History of Fraternities and Sororities in the United States: How It All Began.* July 12, 2013. http://www.sjsu.edu/getinvolved/frso/history/usfslhistory/index.html (accessed November 26, 2013).

Sanday, Peggy R. *Fraternity Gang Rape: Sex, Brotherhood, and Privilege on Campus.* New York and London: New York University Press, 2007.

Secret Little Things. *The Elite 8: The Unauthorized Collective History of African American Fraternities and Sororities.* LittleThings Collectible, 2013.

Shaw, David Grogan Bill, Ron Ridenhour, Andrea Fine, and Maria Eftimiades. "Humiliating, Puerile and Dangerous, Fraternity Hazers Keep Claiming New Victims: Their Brother's Keepers?" *People Weekly*, 1993: 65.

Sigma Gamma Rho Sorority, Inc. *About Sigma: History.* 2013. http://www .sgrho1922.org/about-sigma (accessed 30 2014, January).

Sigma Lambda Beta International Fraternity, Inc. *igma Lambda Beta International Fraternity: Our Story.* 2014. http://sigmalambdabeta.com/story/ (accessed January 30, 2014).

Sigma Lambda Gamma National Sorority, Inc. *Sigma Lambda Gamma History.* 2014. http://www.sigmalambdagamma.com/about/history/ (accessed January 20, 2014).

Smith, Jessie C. (Ed.). *Black Firsts: 2,000 Years of Extraordinary Achievement.* Detroit: Visible Ink Press, 1994.

Stombler, Molly, and Irene Padavic. "Sister Acts: Resisting Men's Domination in Black and White Fraternity Little Sister Programs." *Social Problems*, 1997: 257–275.

Stombler, Molly. ""Buddies" or "Slutties": The Collective Sexual Reputation of Fraternity Little Sisters." *Gender & Society*, 1994: 297–323.

Syracuse University. *Erastus O. Haven Papers, Syracuse University Archives.* n.d. http://archives.syr.edu/collections/chancellors/sua_haven_eo.htm#d0e134 (accessed January 30, 2014).

The Beginning of Alpha Phi Alpha Fraternity, Inc.: A Video Lecture by Dr. Thomas D. Pawley, III. DVD. Directed by Vic Taylor. Performed by Thomas D. Pawley, III. 1993.

Tinto, Vincent. *Leaving College: Rethinking the Causes and Cures of Student Attrition.* Chicago: University of Chicago Press, 1987.

Tuttle, Brad. "Would You Buy a Car Without Giving It a Test Drive?" *Time*, August 15, 2012.

United States Department of Health and Human Services; National Institutes of Health (2012), Washington, DC

United States Food and Drug Administration, Washington, D.C.

United States National Survey on Drug and Health: National Institutes of Health (2006); Washington, DC.

University of Michigan; Monitoring the Future Study (2006), Ann Arbor, Michigan.

University of Missouri-Kansas City, Curators of the University of Missouri. *Get Involved! Fraternity & Sorority Affairs: National Statistics.* 2014. http://www .umkc.edu/getinvolved/fsa-national-statistics.asp (accessed January 22, 2014).

University of Wisconsin Madison. *UWGreek: Fraternity Facts.* 2013. http://www .uwgreek.com/frat/home.html (accessed January 22, 2014).

Velez, Phil. *Fraternity Communication: A Blog That Aims To Promote a Positive Image of Fraternities and Sororities. Macon Magnolias.* February 21, 2010. http://fratcomm.blogspot.com/2010/02/macon-magnolias.html (accessed January 21, 2014).

Velez, William. "Finishing college—The effects of college type." *Sociology of Education*, 1985: 191–200.

Waszut-Barrett, Wendy. "Theatre of the Fraternity: Staging the Ritual Space of the Scottish Rite of the Freemasonry, 1896-1929." Burlington, IA: TD & T, 1996: 46–49.

Welty, John D. "Resident and commuter students: Is it only the living situation?" *Journal of College Student Personnel*, 1976: 465–468.

Weshler, Henry, George Kuh, and Andrea E. Davenport. "Fraternities, Sororities and Binge Drinking: Results from a National Study of American Colleges." *NASPA Journal*, 2009: 395–416.

Wesley, Charles H. *The History of Alpha Phi Alpha: A Development in College Life.* Chicago: The Foundation Publishers, 1991.

What is Resident Assistant, accessed November 20, 2013, http://www.residentassistant.com/aboutras.htm.

Williams-Scurlock, Michael C. "Servants of All: Servant Leadership in a Historically Black Fraternity." PhD diss., Regent University, 2005.

Zeta Phi Beta Sorority, Inc. *Our History: About Zeta Phi Beta.* 2013. http://www.zphib1920.org/our-history/ (accessed January 30, 2014).

Discovery: Managing a First-Generation Life Plan*

5

PURPOSE

At the core of each person's life, there exists a set of foundational values the person holds about reality, themselves, and others. As a first-generation college student, discovering who you are and finding your life's purpose is an extremely important transitional process. This chapter will assist you begin to shape your perspective and worldview.

ACTIVATE YOUR THOUGHTS

What do you value the most in your life (or what is most important in your life?)

How do you want to be remembered?

What about your life are you most thankful and grateful for?

Section One deals with the first main component of the Life Calling Model—*Foundational Values.*

At the core of each person's life, there exists a set of foundational values the person holds about reality, themselves, and others. Everybody has these values. It doesn't matter whether people think of themselves as atheists or devout fundamentalists. They have developed a personal creed that attempts to explain the reality of the universe and then from this explanation a valuation of self and others emerges.

A good place to explore for these values during your college experience is in what may be called general education, liberal learning, core requirements, or something similar. One big mistake that many college students make is to dismiss this part of their education as a meaningless waste of time. They have been misled to believe that the courses specifically training them for a selected career are the most important. In reality the opposite is the truth.

A good liberal education empowers students with broad knowledge and transferable skills, and a strong sense of values, ethics, civic engagement and social responsibility. Through challenging encounters with important issues, students come to grips with what they really accept as foundational values.

FIGURE 5.1

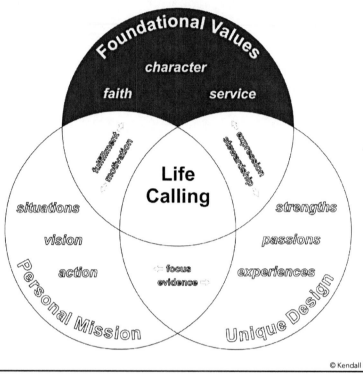

© Kendall Hunt

Life Calling Model Focusing on Faith

As people search to discover their Life Calling, these foundational values play a major role. In many ways this is really where the search for a Life Calling begins because foundational values form the paradigm that creates the "ground rules" for conducting this search.

In this section we will examine each of these foundational values—reality, self, and others—and discover how these values guide the way in which we discover a Life Calling.

The first main component of the Life Calling Model is *Foundational Values*. The first element of this values component focuses on our *faith*.

CONCEPTS

Have you ever looked in the mirror and asked the question, "Why am I here?" If you are like most other people, you have probably answered "Yes, I have asked that question." Nearly everyone wonders at some time in their life where they came from, why they are here, and what happens to them after this life. The most fundamental of the foundational values we hold is the value we hold about reality that comes from the answers we find in response to those basic questions. Everyone has this value; for most of us it is hard to define and remains somewhat mysterious. The dimensions of reality seem infinite. The chronology—past to future—seems infinite. And infinity is something that is hard to measure, let alone comprehend. Furthermore, there is the question of whether or not there is some force behind this reality that causes the reality, yet is separate from the reality. By the very nature of that description, the question is impossible to answer with scientific evidence. So in the end, whether we want to admit it or not, the value we hold about reality comes down to an issue of assumptions—what we presume is true. And these become the *faith* we adopt for our life.

What Is a Principle?

For some people the idea of a *faith* is hard to face because in their minds faith is associated with religion and in many cases more specifically with a particular religion. That concern arises from a too narrow and distorted understanding of faith. We need to broaden the idea of faith more in the direction of a mind-set that emerges from a combination of facts, assumptions, and beliefs. If we look back at the definitions provided at the beginning of this chapter, we could come up with this definition for *faith:* confident belief in the truth, value, or trustworthiness of a person, idea, or thing that does not rely purely on logical proof or material evidence to arrive at such a conclusion.

When we consider reality as being that state beyond logical proof or material evidence, a philosophical *faith* is pretty much the mindset where we all end up—fundamentalists through atheists. This is because there is no material evidence from the initial Creation, Big Bang, or whatever paradigm one uses for origins. Nor is there material evidence from the future. In the short span of what we call the present, we collect as much evidence as we can. We then use this to construct as sound of a logic as we can. But then we all enter into a world beyond evidence and logic, and from what we encounter there, we make our best guess. This is what the nineteenth-century Danish philosopher Søren Kierkegaard called a leap of faith (verb). And around that process we form our faith (noun).

That leaping process is as much an important part in the development of our faith as is the confidence ultimately developed. Sharon Parks (2000), a nationally recognized scholar in faith and leadership, contends that most discussions of faith place too much emphasis on faith as a noun. She advocates the need to include the verb aspects of faith as well in a discussion such as this one related to Life Calling. "Faith is more adequately recognized as the activity of seeking and discovering meaning in the most comprehensive dimensions of our experience."

As we explore the "comprehensive dimensions" related to the Life Calling Model put forth in this book, the process of clarifying the faith for our own life will constantly need to combine our beliefs (noun) and the seeking-discovering (verb) process we engage in to continually clarify and update these beliefs. Whether conscious intent or subconsciously, this faith will become a mind-set that will ultimately shape every other aspect related to the discovery of our Life Calling. Three concepts within our *faith* in particular stand out because they address questions about reality that set the stage for any exploration related to an overriding purpose in life:

1. **Concept of Design.** What do I believe about the nature and pattern of the universe?
2. **Concept of Intent.** What do I believe about the plan behind the universe?
3. **Concept of Personhood.** What do I believe about the intentionality of my personal place in the universe?

Throughout my life, I have encountered a wide variety of answers to these questions. I have also concluded that the Life Calling Model used as the basis for this book can be used by individuals encountering a variety of answers as well. The only persons who will find no help from the Life Calling Model are those who immediately answer all three of those questions with a certainty of "There is none!" For them the search for a Life Calling or overriding purpose is over—they have none according to their conclusion! The fact that this book continues beyond this point rests on the rejection of the "There is none!" conclusion. Instead, the Life Calling Model is based on the assumption that there is a design to the universe and that each person is a part of that design in some way.

Is There a Design to the Universe?

Evidence supports the conclusion that there is a design to the universe. And this evidence comes from a variety of vantage points. In the science classes you may take, you will find them dependent on a design that can be observed, measured, and predicted. You may take a class in comparative religions. If you do, you will quickly realize that the multitude of religions around the world all derive their explanations around what they see as some definable design of the universe. Even in classes where you study economic, political, and social systems, you will discover that they all base their rationalization on some design. Your classes in philosophy will explore the implications of all this.

Let's go back to the study of science. Theoretical physicists focus on trying to understand this design as a framework for the universe. Einstein saw this framework as designed around relativity. Others saw this framework as designed around what they called quantum physics. And now many scientists are looking at something they call String Theory as a unified framework and theory of the universe that postulates fundamental ingredients of nature are not zero-dimensional point particles, but tiny one-dimensional filaments called strings (Green, 2003).

One fascinating look at design comes from a study of Chaos Theory. A quick dictionary definition might lead us to believe that chaos is a condition or place of great disorder or confusion. Chaos Theory, however, suggests that as we observe apparently random data (the "building blocks" of this disorder or confusion) over time, we will discover an underlying order.

For instance, if we roll a standard die with the numbers 1 through 6 on each face, there is no way to predict which number will come up on each successive roll. However, if we plot these rolls on a graph constructed to transfer the six faces of a three-dimensional die to a two-dimensional hexagon, we will find that these totally random rolls produce a very definite pattern—an underlying order or design.

FIGURE 5.2

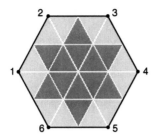

Roll of the Dice

I programmed a computer to help me do this over what would be equivalent of a year—too long a time for me to roll dice. Figure 5-2 shows the results of that computer program that randomly rolls a die and then plots the resulting number from that roll. The program always plots the point halfway between the last number plotted and the new number rolled. That keeps the plots inside the hexagon. The results shown are from a series of 8,640,000 rolls. This is the number of times we would be able to roll a die in a year if we rolled it one time every six seconds. If we were to accept the dictionary definition of chaos, we would expect a random, chaotic plotting pattern, and after just a few rolls, that is what you think you see. But when you are able to amass a large number of rolls, such as year's worth, a definite pattern begins to emerge. There are zones where few to zero plots occur, and there is a zone where a greater density of plots occurs that takes on the shape of a six pointed star (outlined with a solid line for emphasis).

What does this reveal? It reveals that there is some sort of pattern or design underlying the random rolling of dice. It doesn't really reveal to us why there is a design; it just shows us that a design exists.

This same kind of design can be found in many other areas of exploration in theoretical physics. Much of the design comes from the mathematics that underlies all these concepts, and this mathematics may provide the greatest evidence of a design to the universe. To a great extent, mathematics is the very language of design. Does this presence of design prove there is intelligence or God behind the design? It may hint at it, but it does not prove it. It only proves there is a design. An atheist might contend that what we have detected is a self-contained design inherent to the very nature and fabric of the universe free from any outside imposition or influence. An agnostic would agree that there definitely is a design, but would be unsure as to the origins of that design.

To be fair in our discussion, however, we must admit that the majority of the world's population would prefer to attribute this design to God, or at least a god. But even here that approach is widely varied, and that is why we end up with so many religions. The baseline would be what we might call "theistic design"—a definite design with a definite separate designer that has initiated the design and may continue to do so. That designer may be as impersonal as an amorphous power permeating "godness" throughout all aspects of the universe (like the Force described in *Star Wars*) to a very personal, superhuman-like God found in many fundamental religions.

So why go to this extent in answering the question, "Is there a design of the universe?" The reason for this extensive answer is that it shows belief in a design to the universe is widespread, even though the philosophy of the one holding that belief may vary widely. Once we realize this and accept it, this *principle of design* will become the starting point for all subsequent explorations into philosophical questions such as Life Calling.

Earlier we said that we needed to understand that forming the *faith* element of Life Calling contains both a noun and verb component. So what does that mean related to design? Here are two *faith* actions we should take in forming our mind-set:

REFLECTION ●━━━━━━━━━━━━━━━━━━━━━━━━━━━━━

Describe as clearly as you can what you believe right now concerning the design of the universe. Be careful to describe what is truly your belief rather than someone else's.

Continually pursue activities of exploration that will expand your understanding of the design of the universe. Here are some possible classes that can help you:

- Science classes can help you learn how to explore the design of the universe using an objective methodology.
- Philosophy classes can help you learn critical thinking that will enable you to develop conclusion based on cause-to-effect logic.
- Religion classes can help you explore these deeper questions from a more mystical approach. They can also help you explore how others have worked through this subject.

What Do I Believe about the Intentionality of the Universe?

The discovery of a Life Calling begins with the assumption that there is a design to the universe. The intensity and utility of that discovery increases exponentially, however, corresponding to what we assume related to how intentional that design is. In other words, the greater the likelihood of an intention underlying the design, the greater the likelihood there is for a "purpose" to our lives. Here is the reason this is true. Design without intention answers only the question of *how* the universe will occur. Design with intention answers not only *how* it will occur, but also *why* the universe will occur in that manner. Thus, the greater the intention, the greater the *why*, and this greatly increases the likelihood of *purpose*.

The challenge in answering the question of intent, however, is that it requires significantly more speculation than does the question of design by itself. Design is far easier to detect than intention. You may have gone on a field trip to an art museum sometime in your school experience. During the tour your teacher or a guide pointed out various paintings. There was no question that the paintings were there and that you could see them. But then you heard your teacher or guide try to explain what the artists were attempting to convey through their works. That explanation sounded a whole lot more like opinion. In fact, you may have wondered what would happen if you came back with another teacher or guide. Would you hear a different explanation?

The question of whether or not the painting exists is easy to answer. What gave rise to the painting is much more mysterious. The same thing can be said about the relationship between design and intention. Design can be observed and measured; intention cannot. If we go back to our earlier statement that our *faith* emerges from a combination of facts, assumptions, and beliefs, we could differentiate design and intention in this manner:

- *Faith* related to design derives from facts and the assumptions we make about those facts.
- *Faith* related to intention, while incorporating some observable facts, relies much more on assumptions, intuition, and beliefs.

So does belief or faith in an intentional design correlate directly to the existence of God? Once again the answer is "not necessarily," although it is moving more strongly in that direction. The range of philosophies and religions based on intentional design is nearly as broad as our earlier discussion concerning design itself. On one end would be faith in a self-contained intelligence within the universal matter that imprints an intentional design on the evolution of the universe. On the other end would be faith in an anthropomorphic God who systematically plans and implements a specific design as he creates the universe.

Where we fall on this philosophical spectrum depends on several factors. In many cases it has a strong basis in what we have been told by the culture and subculture in which we have grown up. Very few of us start off life with a clean slate. A second factor relates to the conclusions we have drawn from our own observations. This combines both an objective and subjective approach to the interpretations that lead to these conclusions. Finally, our conclusions about intentional design will be impacted by personal encounters with mystical experiences that take place beyond the realm of objective observation and explanation.

So what can we do to enhance the processes forming our *faith* related to intentional design? Here are two faith actions we should take:

REFLECTION ●━━━━━━━━━━━━━━━━━━━━━━━━━━

Describe as clearly as you can what you believe concerning how intentional the design of the universe is. Again, be careful to describe what is truly your belief rather than someone else's.

Explore why you believe what you believe. Engage in activities of exploration that will answer this. Here are some suggested actions that can help you:

- Enroll in a philosophy class that can help you explore this realm. It will help you learn how to develop conclusions based on what you encounter in life.
- Take a religion class that can help you explore these deeper questions from a more mystical approach. As pointed out earlier, they can also help you explore how others have worked through this subject.
- Talk to other people about these issues, especially people you respect. Don't be afraid, however, to include people who disagree with you.
- Pursue spirituality on a mystical as well as rational level.

What Do I Believe about the Intentionality of My Personal Place in the Universe?

The true exploration of an individual Life Calling really takes shape as we answer this third question. Everything prior to this is for the most part general; now it becomes personal. In this whole discussion of design, is there a particular place for me? Was I specifically meant to be here? If so, why was I meant to be here? As those questions are answered, the sense of purpose and calling starts to emerge. The greater my assumption that I am intentionally meant to be here, the greater will be the potential for me to discover a purpose for my life. Richard Leider (1997) calls this the *Power of Purpose*. This assumption that there is an intentional place for me in the universe becomes a spiritual magnet drawing me to something greater than mere existence.

The question of my place in the universe, however, produces a greater challenge than the previous questions about intent. It relies much more on a transcendent level in forming our *faith*. Once my exploration leads me to the assumption that there is a particular intentional place for me in the universe, I enter into the spiritual realm of a cause-and-effect relationship. And there I will encounter the need for an ultimate reality who is the cause of my intentional place in the universe—God. The "who" and "what" of God, however, will be an ongoing exploration as we continue to develop our personal *faith* that will become our guiding mind-set. So here are two faith actions we should take at this level as we continue to form our *mind-set*:

REFLECTION ●──────────────────────

Describe as clearly as you can what you believe concerning how intentional your place is in the design of the universe. Again, be careful to describe what is truly your belief rather than someone else's.

Continually pursue activities of exploration that will increasingly uncover how intentional your place is in the design of the universe. Here are some suggested actions that can help you:

- Take philosophy and religion classes that can help you explore this realm.
- Enroll in classes studying the classics. Here you can learn how some of the greatest minds in history have struggled with uncertainty about their personal place in the universe.
- Continue to talk with other people about these issues. Seek out people who you believe have strong traits of wisdom.
- Pursue mystical spirituality on a very personal level.
- Additionally, continue to explore who and what the ultimate reality is that has specifically intended for you to have a place in the universe. The same actions suggested above will likely help you in this exploration as well.

Faith and Worldviews

The three fundamental questions we have explored exist at some level in the hearts and minds of every person. Is there a design to the universe? If so, is there intention to this design? If there is an intentional design, am I personally a part of it? As our answers to these three questions begin to emerge, they will shape our worldview. James Sire (1997), a noted scholar who has studied worldviews, defines a worldview as a set of preconceived ideas that we hold about the basic makeup of our world (or universe). Our worldview has a very strong impact on our Life Calling because the nature of a Life Calling in our lives is dependent on the basic assumptions of our worldview. Consider the table in Table 5-2. It contrasts the understanding of Life Calling coming from a worldview based on a "naturalist" and a "supernaturalist" assumption. The "naturalist" worldview is formed around the belief that nature contains all there is, and all basic truths are truths of nature. The "supernaturalist" worldview is formed around the belief that there is an order of existence beyond the scientifically visible universe and there is spiritual or mystical truth from this realm that is just as important and reliable as that derived from the visible or natural realm.

Our worldview will begin to have a shaping effect on the way we begin to view ourselves because one will be informed by biblical concepts and the other will be informed by popular culture. Consider the contrasts suggested in Table 5-2. How would you fill in the differing views? We will explore this more in depth in Exercise 3 later in this chapter.

TABLE 5.1

SUPERNATURALIST		NATURALIST
GOD (triangle)		GOD (triangle, circled/crossed out)
Intentional creation	< Origins >	Random chance
Deliberate design	< Blueprint >	Accidental pattern
Unique purpose	< Guidance >	Chaotic possibilities
Permanent place	< Results >	Temporary niche
Response to a Life Calling	< Choices >	Best guess

Supernaturalist vs. Naturalist Understanding of Life Calling

TABLE 5.2

SUPERNATURALIST		NATURALIST
Biblical point of view		Pop-culture point of view
	< Beauty >	
	< Intelligence >	
	< Success >	
	< Fame >	
	< Fun >	
	< Glory >	
	< Dignity >	

© Art Explosion

Supernaturalist vs. Naturalist Understanding of Ourselves

Concepts Summary

Faith: everybody has it . . . it's just a matter of who or what it is in. As we rely on both noun-actions and verb-actions to clarify our faith, we will begin to develop a better sense of reality and our place in it, and our faith will become a clearer mind-set that can also become a stronger guide to our Life Calling.

SCRIPTURAL INSIGHT 1

Faith Is at the Heart of Understanding

Now faith is being sure of what we hope for and certain of what we do not see. This is what the ancients were commended for. By faith we understand that the universe was formed at God's command, so that what is seen was not made out of what was visible.

—Hebrews 11:1-3

INSIGHT

Scripture supplies valuable insight that directly relates to the three important questions of faith related to our origin:

1. What do I believe about the design of the universe?
2. What do I believe about the intentionality of the universe?
3. What do I believe about the intentionality of my place in the universe?

The words at the beginning of Hebrews 11 clearly describe the role of faith when it comes to understanding a Life Calling. There is a great deal of evidence concerning the design of the universe and our place in it, but in the end there will always be an element of things that are not seen that will require a degree of hope and faith.

This passage regarding faith shows three important dimensions. First, faith correlates to what we hope for. That dimension of faith is about the future—we hope something is going to happen. Second, faith correlates to our certainty about what has already happened. That dimension of faith is about the past—we are certain that something happened even though we did not see it. Third, faith is active in what we are trying to understand right now. That dimension of faith is about the present—we engage faith as an active verb to discover meaning in our lives on an ongoing basis.

This 3-dimensional aspect of faith is a very important dynamic in our search for a Life Calling. Faith about the past is foundational in answering the three main questions related to our origins. None of these questions can be answered either "yes" or "no" without relying on faith. Ironic, isn't it? The most devoutly religious person and the dyed-in-the-wool atheist both rely on faith because neither of them can see what happened at the beginning of the universe. The difference between the two is that most religious people openly embrace being persons of faith, while most atheists delude themselves into believing that faith has no place in their thinking.

When Jesus, Peter, James, and John came down from the mountain where Jesus was transfigured, they encountered a crowd in an uproar. A man had brought his son to be healed; the son was possessed by an evil spirit. The other disciples who did not go up the mountain were unable to heal the son, and a great controversy had erupted. Now Jesus was back and the father came to him and pleaded for help in words prefaced with "if you can." Jesus told him if he could believe, all things would be possible. The father answered with one of the most authentic and open responses in the Bible—"I do believe; help me overcome my unbelief!"

Most of us are right there with the father. We want to have faith, and yet our lives are full of doubt as well. We want to believe that we are intentionally here for some greater purpose that God has. Yet when our path is not clear and things go wrong, it so easy for us to give up and start doubting that there is any real meaning, significance, or hope for our lives. The only solution for that dilemma is to hang on to our faith—being sure of what we hope for and certain of what we don't see.

REFLECTION ●

Do you believe there is a divine design to the universe and that you have an intentional place in that design? What is it that you are hoping for in your life right now? What is keeping you from being certain about things you cannot see?

An old saying says that "seeing is believing." These words come from the concept that if you can't show me the evidence or proof, then I will remain skeptical and withhold my belief. On the surface that seems like a good practice that could keep us from being misled and ending up on paths we really did not want to travel. The problem is that if we build our belief about reality on only that which we can see, we will greatly limit our input of information that can help form our faith.

SCRIPTURAL INSIGHT 2

Believing Is Not Necessarily Seeing

We live by faith, not by sight.

—2 Corinthians 5:7

Think about this example. While I am writing this section of the book, I am in a room with an open window. I can hear through that window the sound of water falling into a pond. From where I am writing, however, I cannot see the waterfall. So does it exist or not? You're probably saying, "Of course it exists! Get up and go look out the window." You are probably also wondering if I am crazy. Knowing something exists is not reliant on sight alone. In my example, sound was just a good a source of information.

You might be tempted to counter my example with the notion that "sensory intake is believing." In other words, as long at the senses can take in some measurable input, then you can use that to establish your beliefs; it doesn't have to be just sight. An experience Jesus had during the familiar event we call the Triumphal Entry provides an interesting insight concerning that argument. The story recorded in John 12 describes Jesus coming into Jerusalem riding on a donkey with crowds of people waving palm branches and shouting "Hosanna!" Many people wanted to see Jesus and talk with him; among these were some people of Grecian descent who followed the Jewish faith. A series of conversations went on among these Greeks, Jesus' disciples, and Jesus. At one point Jesus called on God to glorify his name. Immediately a voice called out from heaven, "I have glorified it, and will glorify it again." The interesting thing is that while some people heard the voice, others heard only thunder.

So then, the data we take in through our senses is not necessarily the basis for belief because sometimes it is interpreted differently by different people. As a result of this, it is just as valid to start with faith and let that faith inform our interpretation of data, as it is to gather data and let it inform our faith. That is what Paul meant when he said we live by faith rather than by sight. These words were spoken in the context of a discussion about whether he would rather live in his mortal body in his present situation, or leave this life and live in the life to come in heaven. His conclusion was that he would live by faith in the hope for a better life to come, not by being bound to the hardships that seem so real in the present life.

When we think about the reality of which we are a part and from which we have come, there is evidence within nature itself to provide a rational belief in a divine design to the universe and to our lives. In Romans 1:20 Paul concluded that "since the creation of the world God's invisible qualities—his eternal power and divine nature—have been clearly seen, being understood from what has been made, so that people are without excuse." Our faith, then, is better termed vision-limited rather than totally blind. The data is there if we know how to correctly interpret it.

As devout Christians we may differ in how we interpret the data regarding the manner or length of time in which our creation took place, but our faith can look beyond our sight and be anchored in the belief that there is a design to the universe. This will guide our discovery of a Life Calling.

REFLECTION ⬤

What do you hear in your life right now—the voice of God or thunder? Do you wait to form your faith on what you see, or do you interpret what you see on the basis of your faith? Are you looking for your Life Calling in your faith or in your sight?

As we search for our Life Calling, we can be confident that not only is there a design and Designer behind the universe in which we exist, but that there is also intentionality to that design. The inspirational words of King David reinforce this in another Psalm: "The heavens declare the glory of God; the skies proclaim the work of his hands. Day after day they pour forth speech; night after night they display knowledge. There is no speech or language where their voice is not heard. Their voice goes out into all the earth, their words to the ends of the world" (Psalm 19:1-4). So it is with both faith and reason that we can open the Bible, read and agree with Moses' words in the very first verse: "In the beginning God created the heavens and the earth" (Genesis 1:1).

This is foundational to the concept of a Life Calling because it starts our faith with confidence that our present reality began with a word spoken by God. Without that confidence, everything else that we say about Life Calling will always be doubted. But with that first word of creation, we have hope that God will finish his speech. In other words, he will keep speaking into our creation and our lives. I don't know about you, but that gives me a great sense of assurance.

What is the personal implication for us of God's creative word? Paul gives this illustration in Romans 9. A potter takes a lump of clay and decides to make some pottery. With some of the clay, he decides to make some fancy vases used by high-class people to decorate their houses. But with another lump of the same clay, the potter chooses to form a larger container that can be used to collect trash. When you think about it carefully, both pieces of pottery have a valuable use. Now you might think how much nicer it would be if you were the fancy vase rather than the trash pot, but aren't you glad we have receptacles for trash? Paul's main point in the story, however, is that it is the potter's rightful decision to choose which type of pot the clay will become. And that takes us back to our main verse, "By the word of the Lord were the heavens made." By that same word you and I came into existence. By that word some of us may attain lofty positions in life, and by that word others of us will fill common places of labor. But in the end, it is the same God and the same word that makes each. Therefore, we can accept our Life Calling—wherever it takes us—with faith that God not only spoke it to be, but also commanded it, so that whatever it is, it will stand firm.

REFLECTION ●————————————————————————

Is God speaking your Life Calling into existence or are you bringing it about by your own word? What keeps you from hearing the word of the Lord concerning your life and then trusting it?

————————————————————————————————

The Greek work translated as "Word" in English versions of the Bible is "Logos." This is the root from which our word "logic" has come to us. John, by his choice of the Greek "Logos," saw Jesus as the personification of all knowledge and logic. He then contends that this "Logos" first of all is eternal, second of all is God, and third of all is the Creator of all things. There was no doubt in John's mind as to the intentionality behind the design of the universe.

The question that arises next is, Do I believe that there is an intentional place for me in the universe? In our search for a Life Calling, this is the question that

---

SCRIPTURAL INSIGHT 3

The First Word about Our Life Calling

By the word of the LORD were the heavens made, their starry host by the breath of his mouth. He gathers the waters of the sea into jars; he puts the deep into storehouses. Let all the earth fear the LORD; let all the people of the world revere him. For he spoke, and it came to be; he commanded, and it stood firm.

—Psalm 33:6-9

SCRIPTURAL INSIGHT 4

Something You Can Personally Believe In

In the beginning was the Word, and the Word was with God, and the Word was God. He was with God in the beginning. Through him all things were made; without him nothing was made that has been made.

—John 1:1-3

strikes closest to our hearts. As wondrous and intricate as the universe is, and as clear as its intentional design is manifested, it is all empty and hollow if there is not a personal place for each of us in it.

We can move one step beyond this in our confidence as reflected in Psalm 8:3, 4. "When I consider your heavens, the work of your fingers, the moon and the stars, which you have set in place, what are mere mortals that you are mindful of them, human beings that you care for them?" God, by very nature and definition in the Judeo- Christian tradition, works with intention in designing the universe. And that design includes a personal place and Life Calling for each one of us. Notice those words at the end of the passage. The writer is surprised that God does care for us. That truly is something to believe in!

A favorite parable told by Jesus describes a shepherd who had 100 sheep. At the end of the day, the shepherd brought his sheep together into a tight flock where he could keep them safe during the darkness. However, when the sheep were all together, the shepherd realized that there were only ninety-nine. One sheep had not made it back and was out, lost in the night. The shepherd left the ninety-nine sheep in the safety of the flock and went out in search of the one lost sheep. When he found the sheep he placed it on his shoulders and carried it back to the others.

That parable has multiple applications of meaning, but one that is especially important to our discussion of Life Calling is that the shepherd had great concern for one individual sheep. God created the universe and as part of that creation, he intentionally made each one of us. Our individual lives matter. Can we prove that with hard data from the creation? No. It is something we ultimately have to accept by faith. That is why faith is a foundational value; it may be the most basic of foundational values. Remember, though, no matter which side you're on in these philosophical issues, it takes faith—faith in God or faith that there is no God. Atheists only delude themselves that they are not religious. In reality they just have their own form of religion.

What about your faith? Are you confident that God cares about you and has a plan for you? More importantly, are you living your life according to that faith and confidence?

REFLECTION ●━━━━━━━━━━━━━━━━━━

Have you taken time lately to think about the fact that God is mindful of you and cares about you personally? How does this impact your search for your Life Calling?

While the first and foremost application of this message is specifically to the people of Israel held in captivity by the Babylonians, there is a general principle that can be gleaned from this message regarding God's way of dealing with all of his people down through the ages. God knows the plans he has for each of us, and there are four important elements to each plan.

First, God plans to prosper us. Be careful with the word "prosper," though, because you might think that means to make us financially wealthy. That is not what is meant here. What this means is that God intends for us to be successful

---

SCRIPTURAL INSIGHT 5

God Has a Plan for You

This is what the LORD says: "When seventy years are completed for Babylon, I will come to you and fulfill my good promise to bring you back to this place. For I know the plans I have for you," declares the LORD, "plans to prosper you and not to harm you, plans to give you hope and a future. Then you will call on me and come and pray to me, and I will listen to you. You will seek me and find me when you seek me with all your heart. I will be found by you," declares the LORD, "and will bring you back from captivity. I will gather you from all the nations and places where I have banished you," declares the LORD, "and will bring you back to the place from which I carried you into exile."

—Jeremiah 29:10-14

in carrying out his plans for us. In other words, God does not call any of us to a Life Calling in order to fail. Failure in our lives comes when we stray from his plans and purpose.

Second, God's plans will not harm us. I was born near Waikiki Beach in Hawaii and spent a good share of the rest of my life living along the beaches of California. A few years ago I responded to what I believe was God's plan for me to leave those beaches and come to live and work in the middle of a cornfield in Indiana. When my wife and I went through the first winter, we were tempted to believe that God's plan was bringing us harm. But over the succeeding years we have seen how his plans did not harm us but actually brought us great blessing and fruitfulness.

Third, God's plans give us hope. We all want hope, but what exactly does that mean? It means that we can look forward to what lies ahead of us with desire and confidence. Wouldn't you like to wake up each morning and look ahead to that day with such feelings? By faith you can.

Finally, God's plans guarantee us a future, and a good one at that. That future helps us to keep everything else about our Life Calling in context. No matter what happens along the path we follow, if we are traveling on God's path, the destination will be good. This can be a source of great encouragement with every step we take as we pursue our Life Calling.

REFLECTION ●━━━━━━━━━━━━━━━━━━━

Have you lost hope in your search for a Life Calling? Could that be because you are not searching with all your heart? How can the passage in Jeremiah help you regain that hope?

DISCOVERY

How can the Discovery Guides help you identify, understand, and establish a *faith* that can become a guiding mindset for your life?

T **THEORY**	Study of biblical, philosophical and scientific theories is essential to establish good principles within your mind-set. This study can be pursued in formal classes, but you can also pursue it in your own personal reading. Start creating a list of books that will aid your exploration. Ask others for recommendations.
E **EXAMPLES**	You can learn a great deal about how to explore the deep questions concerning reality by talking with wise people in your life. Find such people and ask them if they would be willing to mentor you for a semester or school year.
A **ASSESSMENT**	Formal assessments do not really play a major role in helping you understand and establish faith in your life.

C COUNSEL	Whether you are attending a secular or faith-based institution, there are likely pastors or spiritual counselors on or near your campus who would be willing to give you guidance in how to explore deep questions related to your life and existence.
H HISTORY	The Concepts section of this chapter already recommended study of the Classics. These great minds in history struggled with the deep questions related to life, and you can learn from their observations. A good place to start would be to read works of St. Augustine, Martin Luther and C.S. Lewis.
E EXPERIENCE	As you develop principles within your faith, you will make assumptions that really are the equivalent of hypotheses as one step in the scientific method. In that methodology, experimentation with a hypothesis is the next step in testing its reliability. Similarly, assumptions of faith and philosophy can be tested in your life experiences, and from these experiences you will modify and solidify them.
R RREFLECTION	In the long run, your *faith* has to be your own. Once you have studied, read, and listened to others, you will need to reflect on what you have learned and heard. Take time for quiet meditation where your own spirit can speak to you. If you don't do this, what you gain will remain theory and likely will not enter into practice in your life.

STORY

It had been a long drive across the desert of Southern California, then crossing the Colorado River into Arizona and on to Williams, where they turned north toward the Grand Canyon. It was late in the evening as Ken Neimon, Diana's father, pulled his large RV into Trailer Village and maneuvered into their reserved campsite.

The six high school graduates were glad to disembark from the motor home, newly christened the *Nautilus*. *Twenty Thousand Leagues Under the Sea* had been one of their favorite books in English class. It seemed appropriate that for a long trip such as theirs (though it would be only two, not twenty, thousand leagues), their "ship" should be named the "Nautilus" after the famed submarine of that tale. The large RV made long trips like the one they had just completed a lot more comfortable than a car . . . but still, it had been a long trip.

Lorena could hardly contain her excitement. Seeing the Grand Canyon had been a dream of hers for a long time. She had read all she could about the park and had secured maps before they had left on their great expedition. Furthermore, she had lectured the rest on the Canyon's wonders for nearly the entire trip across the desert. The others were quite glad to get outside.

"Okay, guys, no sleeping in late tomorrow," Lorena urged. "We'll eat breakfast and then get going. We'll walk to Mather Point. That's traditionally the first view of the canyon because the road from the south entrance leads directly to this overview. We turned into Trailer Village before we went by it, so we'll see it tomorrow."

The others were used to Lorena instructing them, so they just grunted their agreement. They were just as interested in getting to sleep—after a quick snack, of course.

"I'm not done!" Lorena insisted, seeing that she had begun to lose her audience. "We'll ride the shuttle along the West Rim Drive to Hermit's Rest. From there we'll pick up the Hermit Trail and hike a ways down into the canyon. Don't worry. It's no big deal; we're not going to the bottom!"

"Geez, Lor, you're so generous," Ryan responded with a less-than-subtle mocking tone.

The sun was already well above the horizon by the time the travelers woke the next morning. Ground rules had been agreed to concerning the length of time that could be spent getting ready each morning. Adam had been firm on that issue. He had two sisters and more than enough experience! He was concerned that a good part of their day could be wasted if too much time was allowed for getting ready. After all, there were three girls plus a mother on board the *Nautilus*. Everyone cooperated, and after a good breakfast, the adventurers were on their way to Mather Point.

The six stood at the rail looking down into one of the most spectacular sights on earth. Below them lay a very colorful, steep-sided gorge with a dark green river at the bottom.

"Okay, Lor, it's definitely more than a big ditch." Justin was ready to apologize for his disparaging remark made a month earlier. "How do you get something this—as they say—grand?"

Lorena stared down into the canyon as she answered, "Weathering and a whole lot of erosion. That's what Mr. Johnson told us in class."

"Lorena, do you think God created this canyon?" Diana asked.

"Yeah, I do." Lorena looked back up and caught Diana's eyes. "I believe he designed the processes of the universe, and this canyon is a result of those processes."

"The sign here says it took millions of years. My youth pastor said all the earth is less than six thousand years old. Which do you think it is?" Adam asked.

"You know what, Adam? That might not be the most important place to start." Lorena looked over toward him. "There are some who see God as a Force permeating all aspects of the universe—sort of like in *Star Wars*. Many religions, on the other hand, see God as a very personal being who painstakingly created all features of the earth. And as you said, some believe it was in a short amount of time. You know what is remarkable? At either extreme, or all that is in between, it shows faith in a design to the universe exists, even though the philosophy of the people holding that faith may vary widely. When you are looking at this canyon, the rest of the earth, or your life specifically, I think that's the place to begin—faith that there *is* a God and a design behind the reality we're looking at. Don't worry so much about the years."

"Hey, you philosophers, isn't that the shuttle we're supposed to be on?" Abriella pointed back to the top of the stairs, and they all started running.

The ride to Hermit's Rest was filled with more impressive vistas of red, pink, gray, and white rock layers carved into an elaborate network of canyons and chasms. After arriving at their destination, the six began their descent down Hermit Trail. The plan was to hike a couple of miles—enough to get a feel for being in the canyon. The challenge would be that a couple of miles also meant a vertical drop of a thousand feet. The climb back out would test their physical fitness.

They had been hiking for about an hour when Adam called, "Hey, take a look at this!" He pointed to a large sheet of sandstone. Everyone crowded around to see a pattern running down the sandstone that clearly looked like the tracks of a large, lizard-like creature. Footprints bordered what surely was a dragging tail. What was even more remarkable was the fact that the tracks looked like they could have been made yesterday, yet they were solidified in a piece of rock a lot older than that.

After spending some time looking at the fossil tracks and finding some more around the area, the six continued on down the trail a short distance more to an overhang formed in the limestone creating a cave that afforded some relief from the hot, glaring rays of the noonday sun. It also provided a good place to eat the lunch they had brought with them in daypacks.

"You think God cared about that giant lizard or whatever made those tracks?" Ryan asked as he bit off a piece from his sandwich. "Lorena may think that God designed the processes of the universe, but it still makes you wonder if any of the actual parts were intentional—like that lizard, or more important, any of us."

"Yeah, and if that intention includes a plan for what I'm supposed to do with my life," Adam chimed in. "Then maybe I could figure out what to study in college."

"Did it ever occur to you that maybe God's intentional design for you is that you're equipped to explore and figure out your place in that design on your own?" Lorena's question to Adam and the others carried a certain level of intensity.

"I'd rather have it spelled out in one of those rocks on the way back up the trail, like the lizard tracks," Adam answered. "Then I wouldn't have to wonder."

"I'm with you, man," Ryan echoed.

"Yeah, Lorena. Not all of us can figure things out like you can," Diana added.

"Maybe we just don't look in the right places," Lorena responded.

"What do you mean?" Abriella asked.

"I don't know for sure," Lorena answered. "I just think it starts by having faith that we all are part of God's larger design and then using whatever gifts and abilities we have to start exploring what that means. You guys all think that I have it all together because I know where I'm going to college and what I'm going to study. But you know what? There are plenty of times when I'm not sure I'm doing the right thing, so I'm still exploring too. But I have faith that there's something to find."

The looks on the faces of the others indicated that they had just learned a startling new fact about their longtime friend. It would not be the last startling new discovery they would make on their transcontinental adventure.

Works Cited

The following resources may be useful as you explore the development of faith at the start of your exploration of Life Calling.

Alviar, J. J. (1993). Klesis: *The Theology of the Christian Vocation According to Origen*. Dublin, Ireland: Four Courts Press.

Bainton, R. H. (1950, 1977). *Here I Stand: A Life of Martin Luther*. Peabody, Massachusetts: Hendrickson Publishers.

Dykstra, C. R. (1999). *Growing in the Life of Faith: Education and Christian Practices*. Louisville, KY: Geneva Press.

Frankl, F. E. (2006). *Man's Search for Meaning: An Introduction to Logotherapy*. Boston, MA: Beacon Press.

Green, Brian. (2003). *The Elegant Universe*. New York: Vintage Books.

Leider, Richard J. (1997). *The Power of Purpose: Creating Meaning in Your Life and Work*. San Francisco: Berrett-Koehler Publishers.

Lewis, C. S. (2001). *Mere Christianity*, HarperCollins ed. New York, New York: HarperCollins Publishers.

Parks, Sharon. (2000). *Big Questions, Worthy Dreams: Mentoring Young Adults in Their Search for Meaning, Purpose, and Faith*. San Francisco: Jossey-Bass.

Placher, W. C. Ed. (2005). *Callings: Twenty Centuries of Christian Wisdom on Vocation*. Grand Rapids, Michigan: Erdmans Publishing Co.

Saint Augustine, translated by Dods, M. (2009). *The City of God*. Peabody, Massachusetts: Hendrickson Publishers.

Schuurman, D. J. (2004). *Vocation: Discerning Our Callings in Life*. Grand Rapids, Michigan: Erdmans Publishing Co.

Sire, J. W. (1997). *The Universe Next Door: A Basic Worldview Catalog*, 3rd Ed. Downers Grove, Illinois: Intervarsity Press.

Smith, C. S., and Denton, M. L. (2005). *Soul Searching: The Religious and Spiritual Lives of American Teenagers*. New York: Oxford University Press.

Smith, C. S., and Snell, P. (2009). *Soul in Transition: The Religious and Spiritual Lives of Emerging Adults*. New York: Oxford University Press.

Tozer, A. W. (1957). *The Pursuit of God*. Camp Hill, Pennsylvania: Christian Publications.

Wilkens, S., and Sanford, M. (2009). *Hidden Worldviews*. Downers Grove, Illinois: Intervarsity Press.

All of us have values we hold about reality; these form the mindset with which we approach our lives. Sometimes, though we have lived with a mindset for many years, it still is hard for us to define what reality is for us specifically. Use the following exercise to help you understand your concept about reality.

Clarifying Your Faith Using Noun-Actions

In the columns below, statements are made in the left-hand and right-hand columns that for the most part contradict each other. The middle column provides an "I don't know" option. In each case, choose the option that best describes where you are in your thinking at this point in your life, and then explain why you selected that option.

In the beginning God . . .	In the beginning a god . . .	I don't know	In the beginning something . . .	In the beginning nothing . . .
Why I believe this:	Why I believe this:	Why I don't know:	Why I believe this:	Why I believe this:

The universe originally unfolded and continues to unfold from an intentional intelligent design established by God.	The universe originally unfolded and continues to unfold from some sort of intentional design.	I don't know	The universe originally unfolded and continues to unfold from some sort of design, though intention is uncertain.	The universe originally unfolded from an unintentional, chance event and continues to unfold from random events.
Why I believe this:	Why I believe this:	Why I don't know:	Why I believe this:	Why I believe this:

I am an intentional part of God's universal plan.	I am an intentional part of some god's (or gods') universal plan.	I don't know	I am an important part of some universal design.	I am a result of human desire, passion or an accident.
Why I believe this:	Why I believe this:	Why I don't know:	Why I believe this:	Why I believe this:

Summarizing Your Assumptions

1. In one sentence describe your assumption about reality and your place in it based on your answers given in the preceding answers in this exercise. This is the "noun" aspect of your current *faith*.

2. What kind of framework does this place on your search for a Life Calling?

Exercise 2

Strengthening Your Mindset Using Verb-Actions

It is not enough to clearly describe what your *faith* is right now. You need to take actions that continue to clarify and deepen this *faith*. The cycle depicted in Figure 5-3 gives us a good guideline for developing a faith-strengthening exercise program by recommending four main activities that lead from one to another in a continuous cycle.

FIGURE 5.3

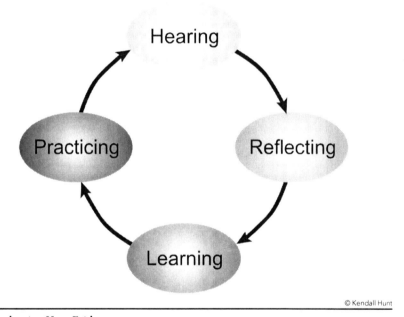

© Kendall Hunt

Strengthening Your Faith

1. Hearing

You might think that we all hear the same way. Actually that is not the case. There are at least three different ways to hear, and each person has a preference.

1. *Ears:* This is what most of us think of when we try to define hearing. It involves actually listening to a message that is audibly delivered to you. Some examples of this might include:
   - Listening to sounds around you
   - Spoken words
   - Sermons
   - Lectures
   - Discussions

- Conversations
- Debates
- Songs

2. *Eyes*: You may not have thought about it in this way, but you not only "see" with your eyes, you also "hear" with your eyes. When you read something or see something happen, it often conveys some level of meaning (a message) to you. Some examples of this might include:
   - Observation of events around you
   - Printed words
   - Pictures
   - Paintings
   - Television
   - Movies
   - Plays
   - Internet
   - Power Point slides

3. *Thoughts*: When you enter the realm of reflective thought, you will often "hear" ideas emerge from these thoughts—messages.
   - Contemplation of ideas presented to you
   - Personal reaction to things you have seen or heard
   - Intentional times of meditation
   - Creative imagination
   - Conscience
   - Inner struggle with issues or problems

> Think back on your life. When you have been successful at hearing a "message," which of the three ways (ears, eyes, thoughts) was usually the most effective one in helping you "hear" the message? Which way was next in effectiveness? Which was third? List them in order below:
>
> 1. First most effective way to hear: _____
> 2. Second most effective way to hear: _____
> 3. Third most effective way to hear: _____

2. Reflecting

Once you hear something, what do you do with it? Probably the worst mistake is to react immediately without even thinking about it. The better choice is to take time and reflect on what you heard. During this reflection you need to ask important questions related to four key areas:

1. *Knowledge* – Does what I've heard match with established information and truth?
   - This does not mean that what you heard might be some discovery never before encountered. But even when that is the case, that discovery still should be examined through the lens of what is already known to be true. For example, a pronouncement that gravity will discontinue as a force in two years should be looked at with a healthy degree of skepticism. Too much current knowledge argues against that prediction.
   - While this Body of Knowledge includes scientific and historical knowledge, it also includes philosophical and religious knowledge.

2. *Wisdom* – Does what I've heard coincide with the understanding of mainstream society throughout ancient and recent history?
   - This does not mean that all new ideas are unacceptable. It basically means the past is a key to interpreting the present and predicting the future. For instance, a sudden contention that murder is now an acceptable premise would be rejected based on the long-standing traditions of most civilized societies to the contrary.
   - Again, the role of religion would come into play.

3. *Reason* – Does what I've heard make sense?
   - Sometimes you don't need to check something out against knowledge or traditions. Sometimes it just plain illogical and doesn't make sense. You don't need to waste your time trying to evaluate the wisdom of someone trying to establish a cult on the new idea that up is down and down is up.
   - The same thing holds true in the world of religion. It is illogical to establish a faith on the claim that evil is good and good is evil.

4. *Experience* – Does what I've heard work?
   - You might consider this the laboratory factor. Try it out. Sometimes things sound reasonable, fit with tradition, and seem to be based on solid theory, but in the end they just plain don't work.
   - Put religious ideas to the same test. Somewhere along the way they need to work if they are truly valid.

Does an idea need to correctly answer all four questions? Not necessarily. For instance, an idea based on solid theory that also makes good sense and works might be worth considering even if it doesn't follow established tradition. However, if it doesn't match any of the four, beware!

Now let's give reflection a trial run. Choose some premise you hold in your faith or have heard. For example, a premise might be that if you go to college, you will have a better job after college. Whatever you choose, write in the appropriate blank below. Continue to evaluate it using the questions given.

PREMISE REFLECTION	
Premise:	
Does the premise match with established information and truth?	☐ Yes ☐ No
Explain your conclusion:	
Does the premise coincide with the understanding of mainstream society throughout ancient and recent history?	☐ Yes ☐ No
Explain your conclusion:	

(Continued)

PREMISE REFLECTION	
Does the premise make sense?	☐ Yes ☐ No
Explain your conclusion:	
Does the premise actually work if it is put into action?	☐ Yes ☐ No
Explain your conclusion:	

3. Learning

As you reflect on a proposed idea or concept and put it through the rigor of your reflection evaluation using the four questions, you will begin to see patterns and information emerge out of this evaluation. Collect these and begin to learn in such a way that you can apply what you learn to other situations that might arise in the future.

To test this out, go back and evaluate the explanations you gave for your answers in the Premise Reflection you just completed. List below three or four concepts you observe that can help you evaluate future ideas proposed to you.

_____

_____

_____

_____

4. Practicing

The final stage in the Faith-Strengthening Cycle involves putting what you have learned into practice. A good way to start is by reviewing some of the premises you currently hold and then running them through the cycle. List below several principles you might evaluate using the cycle. Then find time over the next few weeks to do this.

_____

_____

_____

_____

_____

_____

Exercise 3

What Difference Does Your Worldview Make?

In the Concepts section of this chapter, we proposed that our worldview will begin to have a shaping effect on the way we begin to view ourselves because one will be informed by biblical concepts and the other will be informed by popular culture. Several areas were outlined for consideration as to the contrasting differences a "naturalist" and "supernaturalist" worldview would produce. The table is repeated below. Answer the following questions as a process to develop contrasting views of each area outlined based on that worldview.

1. Describe a "supernaturalist" view of each area based on biblical concepts. Include at least one passage from scripture to support your conclusion.
2. Describe a "naturalist" view of each area based on concepts from popular cultural sources. Include at least one quote or specific example from the popular media to support your conclusion.
3. How can the view you end up adopting impact your understanding of your Life Calling?

TABLE 5.2

SUPERNATURALIST		NATURALIST
Biblical point of view		Pop-culture point of view
	< Beauty >	
	< Intelligence >	
	< Success >	
	< Fame >	
	< Fun >	
	< Glory >	
	< Dignity >	

© Art Explosion

Supernaturalist vs. Naturalist Understanding of Ourselves

Expanding Your Worldview through Liberation Learning

Formation of our Foundational Values and our ultimate worldview does not take place in a vacuum of ignorance. Discovery of our Life Calling includes the need to study and integrate faith, virtue, wisdom and service into a path that leads to intellectual and character development. This is what Paul referred to as transformation by the renewing of your minds in Christ. This then forms the context for pursuing majors and careers in a way designed to prepare you to realize your human potential in Christ. Your transformation also sets the context for living your life to its fullest extent as faithful stewards of the unique gifts God has entrusted to you.

This kind of learning occurs best when we have minds that have experienced "liberation learning." What does this mean? This kind of liberation is not only freeing us from something, it is also freeing us to something. "Liberation learning" liberates students from the captivity of ignorance, closed minds and delusion by revealing to them different ways of looking at the universe. "Liberation learning" liberates students to pursue, engage, and apply truth through a lifelong process of growth that will help them fulfill their full God-given human potential—a Life Calling.

Figure 5-4 depicts eight pillars of study as forming the primary structure of "liberation learning." To accomplish "liberation learning," you need to explore classes within each of these pillars of study to accomplish specified learning outcomes. These learning outcomes may be imbedded in courses related to your major or other majors, or in separate courses developed to provide a learning experience directly related to the specific area of liberation learning. A look at each of the pillars will help you understand this more clearly. You should complete one or more classes in the following subject areas to accomplish specified outcomes that will liberate your learning.

FIGURE 5.4

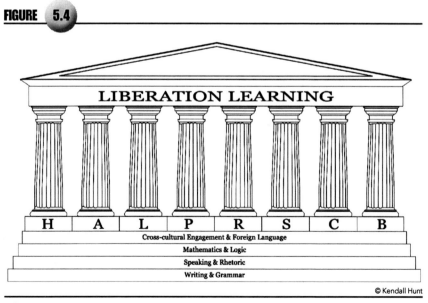

Liberation Learning

© Kendall Hunt

H – History

You should be able to:

- Recognize the prominent world civilizations, periods, events, personalities, and developments.
- Identify the basic techniques of historiography (the methods of studying history).
- Analyze a period of the history of a selected civilization.
- Explain how the historical period analyzed contributed to the development of the selected civilization.
- Apply insights gained from analysis to an understanding of foundational issues related to human existence.
- Demonstrate personal value of the civilizing role of knowing and understanding history in personal and societal direction, purpose, growth and improvement.
- Evaluate history through the lens of your faith and worldview, and evaluate your faith and worldview through the lens of history.
- Integrate a knowledge and understanding of history as a framework for investigating all other areas of liberation learning.

A – Aesthetics

You should be able to:

- Recognize prominent visual and musical artists and their works across a historical framework.
- Summarize classic theories in the philosophy of art and aesthetics.
- Understand the nature of art and aesthetic experience and the ability of this experience to stimulate your imagination, inspire great thoughts, and provoke profound feelings.
- Generate questions of wonder about the nature of the creative process, the work of art, and aesthetic experience.
- Display creative thinking and expression by personally producing visual and musical works of art.
- Differentiate between prominent art forms in both the visual and musical medium.
- Demonstrate personal value of the civilizing role of art and aesthetic experience in personal and societal direction, purpose, growth and improvement.
- Evaluate aesthetics as an expression of God's creativity.
- Integrate a knowledge and understanding of art and the aesthetic experience into the investigation of all other areas of liberation learning.

L – Literature

You should be able to:

- Recognize prominent literary authors and their works across a historical framework.
- Compare and contrast the ideas that have shaped literary works and historical events.
- Understand the nature of literature and its ability to stimulate one's imagination, stir great thoughts, provoke critical thinking, and inspire well-lived lives.
- Write critical analyses that reflect the student's ability to synthesize ideas and themes from selected original texts and secondary sources.
- Explain how the ideas of selected literary works analyzed contributed to the intellectual and social thought of that period as well as to the present.
- Differentiate between prominent literary forms.
- Display critical and creative thinking and expression by personally producing literary pieces.
- Demonstrate personal value of the civilizing role of literature in personal and societal direction, purpose, growth and improvement.

- Evaluate literature through the lens of your faith and worldview, and evaluate your faith and worldview through the lens of literature.
- Integrate a knowledge and understanding of art literature into the investigation of all other areas of liberation learning.

P – Philosophy

You should be able to:
- Recognize and understand at an introductory level a range of prominent philosophers and philosophical problems across a historical framework.
- Analyze selected philosophers and problems with independence of thought and a critical and analytical approach to the theories and concepts, as well as the assumptions on which they are based.
- Explain how the ideas of selected philosophers and philosophies have contributed to the intellectual and social thought of that period as well as to the present.
- Demonstrate skills in careful reading; in comprehension and compression of textual material; in careful analysis; in critical reflection; in rational argument; in sympathetic interpretation and understanding.
- Write and explain your own personal philosophy in a way that demonstrates clear thinking, sound argumentation, the clear and well-organized expression of ideas, impartial pursuit of truth, and a high degree of intellectual autonomy.
- Understand the role of philosophy in shaping intellectual and religious thought.
- Demonstrate personal value of the civilizing role of philosophy in personal and societal direction, purpose, growth and improvement.
- Evaluate philosophy through the lens of your faith and worldview, and evaluate your faith and worldview through the lens of philosophy.
- Integrate a knowledge and understanding of philosophy into the investigation of all other areas of liberation learning.

R – Religion

You should be able to:
- Recognize the major world religions and their basic teachings.
- Summarize the basic themes and beliefs of the religious tradition you personally adopt.
- Analyze the foundational sacred documents of the religious tradition you personally adopt.
- Apply insights gained from the analysis to a reasoned understanding of a worldview.
- Justify how your religious tradition answers the major ontological questions of existence and meaning.
- Outline the relationship between religion-based and moral social responsibility.
- Explain how religion has contributed to the development of civilization.
- Demonstrate personal value of the civilizing role of religion in personal and societal direction, purpose, growth and improvement.
- Integrate a knowledge and understanding of religion into the investigation of all other areas of liberation learning.

S – Science

You should be able to:
- Recognize the major fields of scientific investigation.
- Articulate the steps used in the scientific method for investigating phenomena, acquiring new knowledge, or correcting and integrating previous knowledge.
- Appraise the strengths and weaknesses of scientific inquiry.

- Practice hands-on applications of a selected sub-discipline of science.
- Gather and analyze scientific data through observations.
- Draw conclusions based on observations.
- Hypothesize and design an experiment to test the hypothesis.
- Evaluate sources of information for scientific validity.
- Articulate what is meant by a scientific world-view.
- Value the natural world through the paradigm of stewardship of God's creation.
- Explain how science has contributed to the development of civilization.
- Demonstrate personal value of the civilizing role of science in personal and societal direction, purpose, growth and improvement.
- Integrate a knowledge and understanding of science into the investigation of all other areas of liberation learning.

C – Civitas (citizenship that imparts shared responsibility, a common purpose, and sense of community)

You should be able to:
- Recognize prominent theories and theorists related to civic culture throughout history.
- Understand the basic values of the civic culture in your nation and compare and contrast these with the basic values of other international civic cultures.
- Identify and explain the fundamental roles of government and institutional, political, legal, economic, and educational concepts, policies and processes that work to create a "civilized" society.
- Relate civic theory and concepts to personal responsibility and stewardship.
- Explain how the ideas of selected civic theories have contributed to the intellectual and social thought of that period as well as to the present.
- Value civic culture, including government, through the paradigm of God's ordination.
- Demonstrate personal value of the civilizing role of government, economics and education in personal and societal direction, purpose, growth and improvement.
- Integrate a knowledge and understanding of civics into the investigation of all other areas of liberation learning.

B – Human Behavior

You should be able to:
- Recognize prominent theories and theorists in the fields of sociology, psychology and anthropology.
- Describe the physical and cultural development, biological characteristics, and social customs and beliefs of humankind.
- Understand the nature of culture and social structure.
- Analyze the reciprocal relationship between the individual and society.
- Understand the thought processes and behavior of humans in their interaction with the environment.
- Apply psychological principles to personal, social, and organizational issues.
- Recognize, understand, and respect the complexity of your country's socio-cultural and international diversity.
- Value human dynamics through the paradigm of human beings as temples of God.
- Demonstrate personal value of the civilizing role of the human behavior in personal and societal direction, purpose, growth and improvement.
- Integrate a knowledge and understanding of human behavior into the investigation of all other areas of liberation learning.

Competencies to Support Liberation Learning

You will need basic competencies that will support you in your pursuit of liberation learning, in development within a major area of study, and in life after college. There are four competencies that should be included in any education experience in order for that experience to be complete and successful in liberating the learner. These competencies could be developed through learning experiences that occurred prior to college; are imbedded in the courses related to liberation learning outlined above; are in the courses related to a student's major; or are in separate courses developed to support competency development.

Writing & Grammar

In order to learn, you need to be able to develop correct use of language to communicate effectively. This includes demonstrating skills in expository, analytical, and research methods of writing; and writing with multiple aims including research papers, using the writing process of pre-writing, drafting, revising, and editing.

Speaking & Rhetoric

In order to learn, you need to be able to demonstrate skills in public speaking in a way that instructs and persuades others and stimulates thought. This includes listening, analyzing, organizing, adapting, and delivering ideas effectively.

Mathematics & Logic

In order to learn, you need to be able to develop a correct thought pattern that allows you to logically figure out when some action is taken and what kind of effect it will have. The study of mathematics does this by using numbers. You work with these numbers using a set of commonly accepted rules. The process you learn in doing this becomes a basic language for most types of logic and analysis.

Cross-cultural Engagement & Foreign Language

Finally, if you are going to be a truly global liberated learner, you need to develop an attitude of inclusion characterized by the willingness to interact with persons of different perspectives and cultures without surrendering a commitment to truth. To help develop this attitude, you need to develop fluency in a second, non-native language at a level that enables you to 1) present information, concepts, and ideas about and/or in the target language to an audience of listeners or readers; 2) understand and interpret the target language on a variety of topics; and 3) engage in conversations or correspondence in the target language to provide and obtain information, express feelings and emotions, and exchange opinions.

Getting Started on Your Pursuit of Liberation Learning

1. Identify classes at your college that could help you achieve the learning outcomes for each of the eight pillars of liberation learning. Talk to professors or academic advisors to help you in this task.

   History: _____

   Aesthetics: _____

   Literature: _____

   Philosophy: _____

   Religion: _____

Science: _____

Civitas: _____

Human Behavior: _____

2. Assess what level you believe you are at in each to the Competencies that support liberation learning. If you feel that you need to improve in these areas, identify courses or activities you can engage in to help you.

Writing & Grammar: ☐ Strong   ☐ Adequate   ☐ Weak

Courses/Activities for improvement: _____

Speaking & Rhetoric: ☐ Strong   ☐ Adequate   ☐ Weak

Courses/Activities for improvement: _____

Mathematics & Logic: ☐ Strong   ☐ Adequate   ☐ Weak

Courses/Activities for improvement: _____

Cross-Cultural Engagement & Foreign Language: ☐ Strong   ☐ Adequate   ☐ Weak

Courses/Activities for improvement: _____

WHAT IS DIVERSITY?*

The Spectrum of Diversity

The word "diversity" derives from the Latin root *diversus*, meaning "various." Thus, human diversity refers to the variety of differences that exist among groups of people who comprise humanity (the human species). The relationship between humanity and diversity may be viewed as being similar to the relationship between sunlight and the spectrum of colors. Just as sunlight passing through a prism is dispersed into the variety of colors that comprise the visual spectrum, the human species spanning planet earth is dispersed into the variety of groups that comprise the human spectrum (humanity). The relationship between diversity and humanity is represented visually in **Figure 1.1**.

FIGURE 5.5

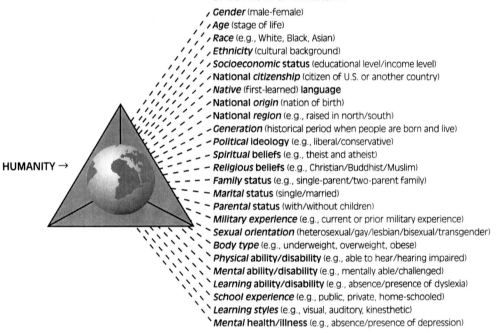

SPECTRUM of DIVERSITY*

HUMANITY →

Gender (male-female)
Age (stage of life)
Race (e.g., White, Black, Asian)
Ethnicity (cultural background)
Socioeconomic status (educational level/income level)
National citizenship (citizen of U.S. or another country)
Native (first-learned) language
National origin (nation of birth)
National region (e.g., raised in north/south)
Generation (historical period when people are born and live)
Political ideology (e.g., liberal/conservative)
Spiritual beliefs (e.g., theist and atheist)
Religious beliefs (e.g., Christian/Buddhist/Muslim)
Family status (e.g., single-parent/two-parent family)
Marital status (single/married)
Parental status (with/without children)
Military experience (e.g., current or prior military experience)
Sexual orientation (heterosexual/gay/lesbian/bisexual/transgender)
Body type (e.g., underweight, overweight, obese)
Physical ability/disability (e.g., able to hear/hearing impaired)
Mental ability/disability (e.g., mentally able/challenged)
Learning ability/disability (e.g., absence/presence of dyslexia)
School experience (e.g., public, private, home-schooled)
Learning styles (e.g., visual, auditory, kinesthetic)
Mental health/illness (e.g., absence/presence of depression)

*This list represents some of the major dimensions of human diversity; it does not represent a complete list of all possible forms of human diversity. Also, disagreement exists about certain dimensions of diversity (e.g., whether certain groups should be considered races or ethnic groups).

© Kendall Hunt

Humanity and Diversity

As can be seen in Figure 5.4, human diversity expresses itself in a multiplicity of ways, including differences in external features, national origins, cultural backgrounds, and sexual orientations. Some of these dimensions of diversity are obvious; others are subtle, and some are invisible.

REFLECTION ●

Look back at the diversity spectrum (Figure 1.1 on p. 2) and review the list of groups that make up the spectrum. Do you notice any groups that are missing from the list that should be added, either because they have distinctive characteristics or because they have been targets of prejudice or discrimination?

Equal rights and social justice are key aspects of diversity; however, they're not the only aspects. In a national survey of American voters the vast majority of respondents agreed that diversity is more than just political correctness (National Survey of Voters, 1998). While diversity may still be viewed narrowly by some people as strictly a "political" issue, in this book we take a broader view of diversity that includes political issues of equal rights and social justice, but also considers diversity to be an essential *educational* issue—an integral element of the college experience that enriches the learning, personal development, and career success of all students.

Keep in Mind
___

Diversity is a human issue that embraces and benefits all people; it's not a code word that stands for "some" people.

___

Since diversity has been interpreted (and misinterpreted) in different ways by different people, we begin by defining some key terms related to diversity that should help clarify its meaning and value.

WHAT IS RACIAL DIVERSITY?

A *racial group (race)* is a group of people who share distinctive physical traits, such as skin color or facial characteristics. The differences in skin color we now see among different human beings are largely due to biological adaptations that evolved over thousands of years among human groups living in different regions of the world. Darker skin tones developed among humans who inhabited and reproduced in hotter geographical regions nearer the equator (e.g., Africans). Their darker skin color helped them adapt and survive by providing their bodies with better protection from the potentially damaging effects of intense sunlight (Bridgeman, 2003). In contrast, lighter skin tones developed over time among humans inhabiting colder climates that were farther from the equator (e.g., Scandinavia). Their lighter skin color enabled their bodies to absorb greater amounts of vitamin-D supplied by sunlight, which was in shorter supply in their region of the world (Jablonski & Chaplin, 2002).

REFLECTION ●

The "Out of Africa" theory is the most widely accepted explanation of the geographic origin of modern humans. Genetic studies and fossil evidence indicate that all Homo sapiens inhabited Africa 150,000–250,000 years ago; over time, some migrated from Africa to other parts of the world (Mendez, et al., 2013; Meredith, 2011; Reid & Hetherington, 2010).

The U.S. Census Bureau (2012) identifies five races:

- **White:** a person having origins in any of the original peoples of Europe, the Middle East, or North Africa.

- **Black or African American:** a person having origins in any of the Black racial groups of Africa.

- **American Indian or Alaska Native:** a person having origins in any of the original peoples of North and South America (including Central America) and who maintains tribal affiliation or community attachment.

- **Asian:** a person having origins in any of the original peoples of the Far East, Southeast Asia, or the Indian subcontinent including, for example, Cambodia, China, India, Japan, Korea, Malaysia, Pakistan, the Philippine Islands, Thailand, and Vietnam.

- **Native Hawaiian or Other Pacific Islander:** a person having origins in any of the original peoples of Hawaii, Guam, Samoa, or other Pacific Islands.

However, as Anderson and Fienberg (2000) caution, racial categories are social-political constructs (concepts) not based on scientific research, but on group classifications constructed by society. No identifiable set of genes distinguishes one race from another, and there continues to be disagreement among scholars about what groups of people constitute a human race or whether distinctive races actually exist (Wheelright, 2005). In other words, you can't do a blood test or some type of internal genetic test to determine a person's race. Humans have simply decided to categorize people into races on the basis of certain external differences in physical appearance, particularly the color of their outer layer of skin. The U.S. Census Bureau could just as easily have divided people into categories based on such physical characteristics as eye color (blue, brown, and green) or hair texture (straight, wavy, curly, and frizzy).

Expert's Experience

My father stood approximately six feet tall and had light brown straight hair. His skin color was that of a Western European with a very slight suntan. My mother was from Alabama and she was dark in skin color with high cheekbones and long curly black hair. In fact, if you did not know that my father was of African American descent, you would not have thought of him as black. All of my life I've thought of myself as African American and all people who know me have thought of me as African American. I have lived half of a century with that as my racial identity. Several years ago, I carefully reviewed records of births and deaths in my family history; I discovered that I had fewer than 50% of African lineage. Biologically, I am no longer black; socially and emotionally, I still am. Clearly, my "race" has been socially constructed, not biologically determined.

Aaron Thompson

The word "race" did not even exist until Americans introduced the term in the 18th and 19th centuries. Prior to that point in history, the term was not used anywhere else in the world. English settlers created the phrase "white race" to distinguish themselves from Native Americans and African Americans whom they deemed to be "uncivilized" and "savages."

At that time, the cotton industry was booming, which create demand for more land and a larger labor force. To meet these needs, white Anglo-Protestant elite devised and disseminated the idea of a privileged "white race" to justify their taking land occupied by Native Americans and using African Americans as slaves to build a larger labor force (Berlin, 2004; Fogel, 1989). This was also seen as a means of providing privileges to incoming British and European immigrants who did not own property. Immigrants who initially defined themselves as German, Irish, or Italian slowly began to refer to themselves as "white" as they began to move up to higher levels of socioeconomic and political status (Feagin & Feagin, 2003). Thus, white privilege was gained at the expense of oppressing groups deemed to be "non-white."

© 2014 Monkey Business Images. Under license from Shutterstock, Inc.

There are many more physical similarities among humans than there are differences in their skin tone.

While humans may display diversity in the color or tone of their outer layer of skin, the reality is that all members of the human species are remarkably similar at an underlying biological level. More than 98% of the genes of humans from all racial groups are exactly the same (Bridgeman, 2003; Molnar, 1991). This large amount of genetic overlap among humans accounts for the many similarities that exist among members of the human species, us, regardless of the differences in color that appear at the outer surface of their skin. All of us have physical features that give us a "human" appearance and clearly distinguish us from other animal species. All humans have internal organs that are similar in structure and function, and whatever the color of our outer layer of skin, when it's cut, we all bleed in the same color.

Expert's Experience

I was sitting in a coffee shop in Chicago O'Hare airport while proofreading my first draft of this chapter. I looked up from my work for a second and saw what appeared to be a white girl about 18 years of age. As I lowered my head to return to work, I did a double-take and looked at her again because something about her seemed different or unusual. When I took a closer look at her the second time, I noticed that although she had white skin, the features of her face and hair appeared to be those of an African American. After a couple of seconds of puzzlement, I figured it out: she was an *albino* African American. That satisfied my curiosity for the moment, but then I began to wonder: Would it still be accurate to say she was "black" even though her skin was not black? Would her hair and facial features be sufficient for her to be considered or classified as black? If yes, then what would be the "race" of someone who had black skin tone, but did not have the typical hair and facial features characteristic of black people? Is skin color the defining feature of being African American or are other features equally important?

I was unable to answer these questions, but found it amusing that all of these thoughts were taking place while I was working on a book dealing with diversity. Later, on the plane ride home, I thought again about that albino African American girl and realized that she was a perfect example of how classifying people into "races" is clearly not based on objective, scientifically determined evidence, but on subjective, socially-constructed categories.

— *Joe Cuseo*

REFLECTION ●

What "race" do you consider yourself to be? Would you say you identify strongly with your race, or are you rarely conscious of it?

What Is Culture?

"Culture" may be defined as a distinctive pattern of beliefs and values learned by a group of people who share the same social heritage and traditions. In short, culture is the whole way in which a group of people has learned to live (Peoples & Bailey, 2008), which includes their style of speaking (language), fashion, food, art and music, as well as their beliefs and values.

Sometimes, the terms "culture" and "society" are used interchangeably as if they have the same meaning; however they refer to different aspects of humanity. *Society* refers to a group of people who are organized under the same social system. For example, all members of American society are organized under the same system of government, justice, and education. On the other hand, culture is what members of a certain group of people actually have in common with respect to their traditions and lifestyle—regardless of how their society or social system may be organized (Nicholas, 1991). Cultural differences can exist within the same society (multicultural society), within a single nation (domestic diversity), or across different nations (international diversity).

Listed below is a snapshot summary of some of the most important dimensions or features of a culture that its members may share, and which may distinguish their culture from others.

Key Components of Culture

Language: How members of the culture communicate through written or spoken words, certain dialect, and nonverbal communication (body language).

Space: How cultural members arrange themselves with respect to the dimension of physical distance (e.g., how closely they position themselves in relation to each other when they communicate).

Time: How the culture conceives of, divides, and uses time (e.g., the speed or pace at which they conduct business).

Aesthetics: How cultural members appreciate and express artistic beauty and creativity (e.g., visual art, culinary art, music, theater, literature, and dance).

Family: The culture's attitudes and habits with respect to parents and children (e.g., customary styles of parenting and caring for aging family members).

Economics: How the culture meets its members' material wants and its habits with respect to acquiring and distributing wealth (e.g., gap between rich and poor).

Gender Roles: The culture's expectations for "appropriate" male and female behavior.

Politics: How decision-making power is distributed in the culture (e.g., power shared equally or held by a minority of its members).

Science and Technology: The culture's capacity and attitude toward the use of science or technology (e.g., the degree to which the culture is technologically "advanced").

Philosophy: The culture's ideas or views on wisdom, goodness, truth, and values (e.g., emphasis on individual competition or collective collaboration).

Spirituality and Religion: Cultural beliefs about a supreme being and an afterlife (e.g., predominant faith-based organizations ad belief systems about the supernatural).

I was once watching a basketball game between the Los Angeles Lakers and Los Angeles Clippers. During the game, a short scuffle broke out between the Lakers' Paul Gasol—who is Spanish, and the Clippers' Chris Paul—who is African American. After the scuffle ended, Gasol tried to show Paul there were no hard feelings by patting him on the head. Instead of interpreting Gasol's head pat as a peace-making gesture, Paul took it as putdown and returned the favor by slapping (rather than patting) Paul in the head!

This whole misunderstanding stemmed from a basic difference in nonverbal communication between the two cultures. Patting someone on the head in European cultures is a friendly gesture; European soccer players often do it to an opposing player to express no ill will after a foul or collision. However, this same nonverbal message meant something else to Chris Paul—who was raised in a very different culture—urban America.

Joe Cuseo

REFLECTION

Fiorello La Guardia, mayor of New York City from 1933–1945 was fluent in English, Italian, and Yiddish. Researchers viewed films of his campaign speeches with the sound turned off and were able to detect which language he was speaking just by observing his nonverbal behavior. For instance, when speaking Italian he used the most body language; when speaking English, he used the least (Adler, Rosenfield, & Protor, 2004).

What Is an Ethnic Group?

An *ethnic group* is simply a group of people that share the same culture. Thus, "culture" refers to *what* an ethnic group has in common and "ethnic group" refers to the *people* who share a common culture. Unlike members of a racial group, whose shared physical characteristics have been *inherited*, members of an ethnic group share similar cultural characteristics that have been *learned* through common social experiences. Members of the same racial group may still be members of different ethnic groups. For instance, white Americans belong to the same racial group, but differ in terms of their ethnic group (e.g., French, German, Irish) and Asian Americans belong to the same racial group, but are members of different ethnic groups (e.g., Japanese, Chinese, Korean).

Members of ethnic minority groups who are white can more easily "blend into" or assimilate into the majority (dominant) culture because their minority status cannot be easily identified by the color of their skin. To further accelerate their assimilation into American culture and acquire the privileges the majority group, a number of white minority immigrants of European ancestry changed their last name to appear to be Americans of English descent. In contrast, the immediately-detectable minority status of African Americans, or darker-skinned Hispanics and Native Americans, didn't allow them the option of presenting themselves as members of an already-assimilated majority group (National Council for the Social Sciences, 1991).

Culture is a distinctive pattern of beliefs and values that develop among a group of people who share the same social heritage and traditions.

Currently, the major cultural (ethnic) groups in the United States include:

- Native Americans (American Indians)
  - Cherokee, Navaho, Hopi, Alaskan natives, Blackfoot, etc.
- European Americans (Whites)
  - Descendents from Western Europe (e.g., United Kingdom, Ireland, Netherlands), Eastern Europe (e.g., Hungary, Romania, Bulgaria), Southern Europe (e.g., Italy, Greece, Portugal), and Northern Europe or Scandinavia (e.g., Denmark, Sweden, Norway)
- African Americans (Blacks)
  - Americans whose cultural roots lie in the continent of Africa (e.g., Ethiopia, Kenya, Nigeria) and the Caribbean Islands (e.g., Bahamas, Cuba, Jamaica)
- Hispanic Americans (Latinos)
  - Americans with cultural roots in Mexico, Puerto Rico, Central America (e.g., El Salvador, Guatemala, Nicaragua), and South America (e.g., Brazil, Columbia, Venezuela)
- Asian Americans
  - Americans who are cultural descendents of East Asia (e.g., Japan, China, Korea), Southeast Asia (e.g., Vietnam, Thailand, Cambodia), and South Asia (e.g., India, Pakistan. Bangladesh)
- Middle Eastern Americans
  - Americans with cultural roots in Iraq, Iran, Israel, etc.

REFLECTION ●▬▬▬▬▬▬▬▬▬▬▬▬▬▬▬▬▬

What ethnic group(s) do you belong to or identify with? What key cultural values do you think are shared by your ethnic group(s)?

European Americans still are the majority ethnic group in the United States; they account for more than 50% of the American population. Native Americans, African Americans, Hispanic Americans, and Asian Americans are considered to be ethnic *minority groups* because each of these groups represents less than 50% of the American population. America's two most populated states, California and Texas, are called "minority-majority" states because more than half of the population in these states is now comprised of people from minority groups; the same is for Hawaii and New Mexico (U.S. Census Bureau, 2008a).

As with racial grouping, classifying humans into different ethnic groups can be very arbitrary and subject to different interpretations. Currently, the U.S. Census Bureau classifies Hispanics as an ethnic group, rather than a race. However, among those who checked "some other race" in the 2000 Census, 97% were Hispanic. This finding suggests that Hispanic Americans consider themselves to be a racial group, probably because that's how they feel they're perceived and treated by non-Hispanics (Cianciotto, 2005). Supporting this perception is use of the term "racial profiling" by American media to describe Arizona's controversial 2010 law that allows police to target people who "look" like illegal aliens from Mexico, Central America and South America. Once again, this illustrates how race and ethnicity are subjective, socially constructed concepts that depend on how society perceives and treats certain social groups, which, in turn, affects how these groups perceive themselves.

In the United States, it's going to be increasingly difficult to categorize groups of people into distinct racial or ethnic groups because it's becoming more common for members of different ethnic and racial groups to form cross-ethnic and interracial families. By 2050, the number of Americans who identify themselves as being of two or more races is projected to more than triple, growing from 5.2 million to 16.2 million (U.S. Census Bureau, 2008a).

Expert's Experience   As a child of a black man and a white woman, someone who was born in the racial melting pot of Hawaii, with a sister who's half Indonesian but who's usually mistaken for Mexican or Puerto Rican, and a brother-in-law and niece of Chinese descent, with some blood relatives who resemble Margaret Thatcher and others who could pass for Bernie Mac, family get-togethers over Christmas take on the appearance of a U.N. General Assembly meeting. I've never had the option of restricting my loyalties on the basis of race, or measuring my worth on the basis of tribe.

Barack Obama

What Is Humanity?

Although humans are members of different cultural groups, all cultures are still cultivated from the same soil—they're all grounded in the common experience of being human. Thus, cultural diversity represents variations on the common theme of *humanity*. Human variety and human similarity coexist and complement each other. To appreciate human diversity is to appreciate both our differences and *similarities* (Public Service Enterprise Group, 2009). Diversity appreciation includes appreciating the unique perspectives of different groups of people as well as the universal aspects of the human experience that are common to all groups—whatever their particular cultural backgrounds happens to be. For example, despite our racial and cultural differences, all of us experience and express the same human emotions with the same facial expressions (see **Figure 5.6**).

Other human characteristics that anthropologists have found to be shared by all groups of people in every corner of the world include storytelling, poetry, adornment of the body, dance, music, decoration with artifacts, families, socialization of children by elders, a sense of right and wrong, supernatural beliefs, and mourning of the dead (Pinker, 2000). Although different ethnic groups may express these shared experiences in different ways, these universal experiences are common to all human cultures.

The relationship between humanity and diversity is well illustrated by the development of language in children. Although groups of people around the world speak distinctively different languages, every newborn baby entering the

FIGURE 5.6

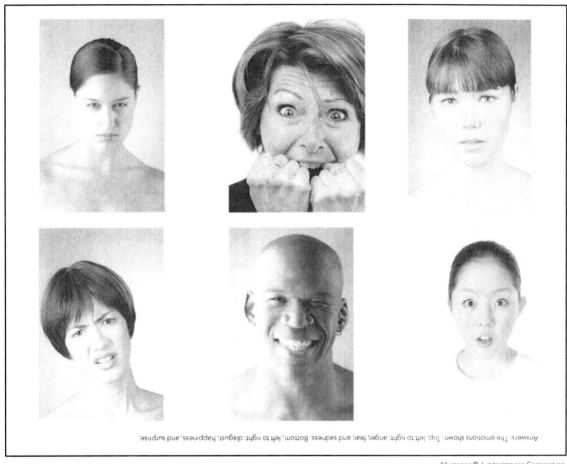

Answers: The emotions shown. Top, left to right: anger, fear, and sadness. Bottom, left to right: disgust, happiness, and surprise.

Humans all over the world display the same facial expressions when experiencing certain emotions. See if you can detect the emotions being expressed in the following faces. (To find the answers, turn your book upside down.)

world babbles in sounds made by all human languages; this gives every new-born human being the potential to speak the sounds of any human language. However, what language(s) that newborns eventually speak will depend on the language sounds they hear spoken by their particular cultural group; the other babbling sounds they used as newborns will eventually drop out of their oral repertoire (Oller, 1981). The same set of sounds that all humans use at birth (the "universal language") reflects our common humanity; the distinctive set of sounds that different groups of humans learn to speak as their "native language" reflects our cultural diversity.

REFLECTION ●

List three human experiences that you think are universal—that are experienced by all humans in all cultures.

1.

2.

3.

Keep in Mind

Although people have different cultural backgrounds, they're still cultivated from the same soil—all forms of ethnic diversity are grounded in the common experience of being human.

You may have heard the question: "We're all human, aren't we?" The answer to this important question is "yes and no." Yes, we are all the same, but not in the same way. A good metaphor for understanding this apparent contradiction is to visualize humanity as a quilt in which we're all united by the common thread of humanity—the universal bond of being human. The different patches comprising the quilt represent diversity—the distinctive or unique cultures that comprise our common humanity. The quilt metaphor acknowledges the identity and beauty of all cultures. It differs from the old American "melting pot" metaphor, which viewed cultural differences as something that should be melted down and eliminated, or the "salad bowl" metaphor that suggested America was a hodgepodge or mishmash of cultures thrown together without any common connection. In contrast, the quilt metaphor suggests that the cultures of different groups should be recognized and valued; yet, these distinctive cultures can be woven together to form a unified whole. This seamless blending of diversity and unity is captured in the Latin expression *E pluribus unum* ("Out of many, one")—the motto of the United States—which you'll find printed on all of its coins. When we appreciate diversity in the context of humanity, we capitalize on the variety and beauty of our differences (diversity) while still preserving the power and strength of our unity (humanity).

© 2014 Alex Melnick. Under license from Shutterstock, Inc.

When I was 12 years old and living in New York City, I returned from school one Friday and my mother asked me if anything interesting happened at school that day. I mentioned to her that the teacher went around the room asking students what we had for dinner the night before. At that moment, my mother began to become a bit concerned and nervously asked me, "What did you tell the teacher?" I said, "I told her and the rest of the class that I had pasta last night because my family always eats pasta on Thursdays and Sundays." My mother exploded and fired back at me, "Why didn't you tell her we had steak or roast beef!" For a moment, I was stunned and couldn't figure out what I'd done wrong or why I should have lied about eating pasta. Then it suddenly dawned on me: My mom was embarrassed about being Italian American. She wanted me to hide our family's ethnic background and make it sound like we were very "American."

As I grew older, I began to understand why my mother felt the way she did. She grew up in America's "melting pot" generation—a time when different American ethnic groups were expected to melt down and melt away their ethnicity. They were not to celebrate diversity; they were to eliminate it.

— *Joe Casco*

What Is Individuality?

It's important to keep in mind that the differences among individual within groups are greater than the average differences between groups. For example, differences in physical attributes (e.g., height and weight) and psychological characteristics (e.g., introvert and extrovert) among individuals within the same racial group are greater than any average difference that may exist between racial groups (Caplan & Caplan, 2009). Thus, the reality is that more variability (individuality) than similarity exists among members of a particular racial or ethnic group.

Keep in Mind

While it's valuable to learn about diverse cultures and common characteristics shared by members of a culture, differences among individuals sharing the same cultural background should neither be ignored nor overlooked. Don't assume that individuals of the same race or ethnicity share the same personal characteristics.

As you proceed through this book, remember the following key distinctions that have been made in this chapter:

- **Humanity.** All humans are members of the *same group* (e.g., the human species).
- **Diversity.** All humans are members of *different groups* (e.g., different gender and ethnic groups).
- **Individuality.** All humans are *unique individuals* who differ from other members of any group to which they may belong.

REFLECTION ●

In what key ways do you think you are:

1. Like all other humans,

2. Like some humans, and

3. Like no other human?

FIGURE 5.7

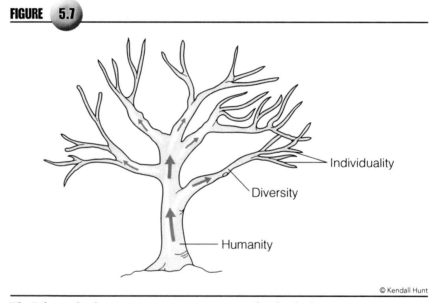

© Kendall Hunt

The Relationship between Humanity, Diversity, and Individuality

Diversity and the College Experience

There are more than 3,000 public and private colleges in the United States. They vary in size (small, mid-sized, large), location (urban, suburban, and rural), and purpose or mission (research universities, comprehensive state universities, liberal arts colleges, and community colleges). This variety makes America's higher education system the most diverse and accessible in the world (Association of American Colleges and Universities, 2002). The diversity and accessibility of educational opportunities provided by American colleges and universities embodies the nation's commitment to the democratic principle of equal opportunity (American Council on Education, 2008).

America's diverse system of higher education is becoming increasingly more diverse with respect to the type of students enrolled. The ethnic and racial diversity of students in America is rapidly rising. In 1960, whites made up almost 95% of the total college population; in 2010, that percentage had decreased to 61.5%. Between 1976 and 2010, the percentage of ethnic minority students in higher education increased from 17% to 40% (National Center for Education Statistics, 2011).

The rise in ethnic and racial diversity on American campuses is particularly noteworthy when viewed in light of the historical treatment of minority groups in the United States. In the early 19th century, education was not a right, but a privilege available only to those who

The ethnic and racial diversity of students in American College is increasing.

could afford to attend private schools. It was experienced largely by Protestants of European descent. Later, white immigrants from other cultural backgrounds began migrating to the U.S. and public education was then made mandatory—with the goal that education would "Americanize" these new immigrants and obliterate their own cultural identities in the process (Luhman, 2007). Members of certain minority groups were left out of the educational process altogether or were forced to be educated in racially segregated settings. Americans of color were taught in separate, segregated schools that were typically inferior in terms of educational facilities. It was not until the groundbreaking Supreme Court ruling in *Brown* vs. *Board of Education* (May 17, 1954) that the face of education was changed for people of color. On that day, the United States Supreme Court ruled that "separate educational facilities are inherently unequal." This decision made it illegal for Kansas and 20 other states to deliver education in segregated classrooms.

FIGURE 5.8

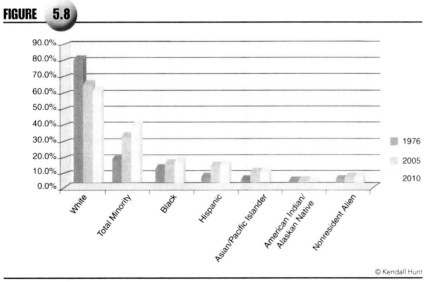

College Enrollment Fall 1976–Fall 2010 Comparison

Source: U.S. Department of Education, National Center for Education Statistics. (2012). Digest of Education Statistics

Expert's Experience

My mother was a direct descendent of slaves and moved with her parents from the deep south at the age of seventeen. My father lived in an all-black coal mining camp, into which my mother and her family moved in 1938. My father remained illiterate because he was not allowed to attend public schools in eastern Kentucky.

In the early 1960s, I was integrated into the white public schools along with my brother and sister. Physical violence and constant verbal harassment caused many other blacks to quit school at an early age and opt for jobs in the coal mines. But my father remained constant in his advice to me: "It doesn't matter if they call you n_____; don't you ever let them beat you by walking out on your education." He'd say to me, "Son, you will have opportunities that I never had. Many people, white and black alike, will tell you that you are no good and that education can never help you. Don't listen to them because soon they will not be able to keep you from getting an education like they did me. Just remember, when you do get that education, you'll never have to go in those coal mines and have them break your back. You can choose what you want to do, and then you can be a free man."

Being poor, black, and Appalachian did not offer me great odds for success, but constant reminders from my parents that I was a good person and that education was the key to my future freedom and happiness enabled me to beat the odds. My parents were not able to provide me with monetary wealth, but they did provide me with the gifts of self-worth, educational motivation, and aspiration for academic achievement.

Aaron Thompson

American colleges have also grown more diverse with respect to gender and age. In 1955, only 25% of college students were female; in 2000, the percentage had jumped to almost 66% (Postsecondary Education Opportunity, 2001). From 1990 to 2009, the proportion of women between the ages of 18 and 29 enrolled in college increased at a rate that was almost triple that of males in the same age range (Kim, 2011). The percentage of college students 24 years of age or older has also grown to 44% of the total student body (Chronicle of Higher Education, 2003), up from 28% in 1970 (U.S. Department of Education, 2002). By 2010, more than one-third of American students enrolled in college were over the age of 25 (Center for Postsecondary and Economic Success, 2011).

Adding further to the diversity on college campuses are *international* students. From 1990 to 2000, the number of international students attending American colleges and universities increased by over 140,000 (Institute of International Education, 2001). By the 2010–2011 academic year, a record-high number of nearly 820,000 international students were enrolled on American campuses (Institute of International Education, 2013).

REFLECTION ●

Persons with disabilities once had little access to colleges and universities, but due primarily to the Rehabilitation Act of 1973 and the Americans with Disabilities (ADA) act of 1990, their access to and participation in higher education has increased dramatically (Schuh, 2000). In 2010, there were over 700,000 students with disabilities enrolled in American colleges and universities (Raue & Lewis, 2011).

Keep in Mind_____

The wealth of diversity on college campuses today represents an unprecedented educational opportunity. You may never again be a member of a community that includes so many people from such a rich variety of backgrounds. Seize this opportunity! You're in the right place at the right time to experience the type of human diversity that will enrich the quality of your educational, personal, and professional development.

REFLECTION ⬤—————————————————————

1. What diverse groups do you see represented on your campus?

2. Are there groups on campus that you didn't expect to see or to see in such large numbers?

3. Are there groups on your campus that you expected to see but don't see or see in smaller numbers than you expected?

Summary

Diversity refers to the wide variety of differences that exist among groups of people who comprise humanity (the human species). Humans can and do differ from one another in multiple ways, including physical features, religious beliefs, mental and physical abilities, national origins, social backgrounds, gender, and sexual orientation. Diversity is concerned with the important political issue of securing equal rights and social justice for all people; however, it's also an important *educational* issue—an integral element of the college experience that enriches learning, personal development, and career preparation.

Racial diversity involves grouping humans into categories that are not scientifically based, but socially determined. There are no specific genes that differentiate one race from another; no "blood test" or genetic marker can be used to detect a person's race. Humans have simply decided to classify themselves into "racial" categories on the basis of certain external differences in physical appearance, particularly the shade of their outer layer of skin.

An ethnic group is a group of people who share a distinctive culture (i.e., a particular set of shared traditions, customs, and behavioral patterns). Unlike a racial group, whose members share physical characteristics that they were born with; an ethnic group's shared characteristics have been *learned* through shared social experiences. Thus, *ethnic diversity* refers to different groups of people with different cultural characteristics. Cultural differences can exist within the same nation (multicultural diversity) and between different nations (international diversity).

Diversity not only involves respecting and valuing human differences; it also involves appreciating our similarities and common experiences. Diverse groups represent variations on the common theme of humanity. Although people have different cultural backgrounds, their group differences emerge from the same soil; they are all grounded in the universal experience of being human. Thus, experiencing diversity not only enhances our appreciation of the unique features of different cultures, it also provides us with a larger perspective on the universal aspects of the human experience that are common to all of us—no matter what our particular cultural background may be.

Embedded within humanity and diversity is *individuality*. Studies show that individual differences *within* the same racial or ethnic group are *greater* than the average differences between groups. The key distinctions among humanity, diversity, and individuality may be summarized as follows:

- **Humanity.** All humans are members of the *same group* (e.g., the human species).
- **Diversity.** All humans are members of *different groups* (e.g., different gender and ethnic groups).
- **Individuality.** All humans are *unique individuals* who differ from other members of any group to which they may belong.

There is greater diversity among college students today than at any other time in the nation's history. This rich diversity represents an unprecedented educational opportunity. By intentionally infusing diversity into your college experience, you can increase the power of your college education and your prospects for future success.

Internet-Based Resources for Additional Information

Race: *RACE—The Power of an Illusion*, at www.pbs.org/race/001_WhatIsRace/001_00-home.htm

Are we so different? A project of the American Anthropological Association, at www.understandingrace.org/home.html

Ethnicity: *Ethnicity Online*, at www.ethnicityonline.net/

Disabilities: *Resources, Programs and Services*, at https://www.disability.gov/

Culture: *Culture Crossing*, at http://www.culturecrossing.net/index.php

Foundational Values

Name _____   Date _____

1.1 Cultural Differences Interview

Find a student, faculty member, or an administrator on campus whose cultural background is differs from yours, and if you could interview that person about his or her culture. Use the following questions in your interview:

a. How is "family" defined in your culture? What are the traditional roles and responsibilities of different family members?

b. What are the traditional gender (male/female) roles associated with your culture? Are they changing?

c. What is the culture's approach to time? (For instance: Is there an emphasis on punctuality? Is doing things fast valued or frowned upon?)

d. What are your culture's staple foods or favorite foods?

e. What cultural traditions or rituals are highly valued and commonly practiced?

f. What special holidays are celebrated by your culture?

Sudden Realization

Name _____   Date _____

You meet someone sitting at a party; after talking with this person for several hours, you realize that you really like this person and you have a lot in common. The attraction is mutual, so you both exchange phone numbers. As you both leave the party, the other person gets into a motorized wheelchair (that you had not noticed previously) and drives away.

What thoughts and feelings do you think would cross your mind immediately after you discovered this person had a physical disability?

Would you still give the person a call? Why?

Source: University of New Hampshire Office of Residential Life (2001)

Gaining Awareness of Your Group Identities

Name _____   Date _____

We are members of multiple groups at the same time, and our membership in these overlapping groups has likely influenced our personal development and identity. In the figure that follows, consider the shaded center circle to be yourself and the six non-shaded circles to be six groups you belong to that you think have influenced your personal development or personal identity.

Fill in the non-shaded circles with the names of groups to which you belong that have had the greatest influence on your personal identity or development. You can use the diversity spectrum that appears on page 2 of this chapter to help you identify different groups. You don't have to come up with six groups and fill all six circles. What's most important is to identify those groups that you feel have had the most influence on your development and identity.

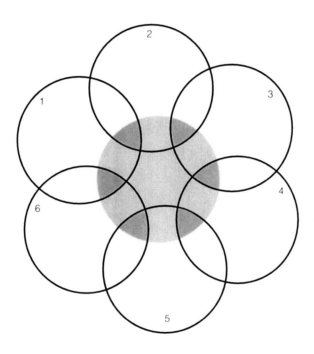

Self-Assessment Questions

a. Of the groups you've identified, which one do you think have had the greatest influence on your personal identity? Why?

b. Have you ever felt limited or disadvantaged by being a member of any particular group(s) you've identified?

c. Have you ever felt that you experienced advantages or privileges because of your membership in any particular group(s) you've identified?

Social Identities

Name _____   Date _____

For each of the identities listed in the far left column:

a. Use the boxes under columns 1 and 2 to rate each identity on a scale from 1–10 (10 = the highest)

b. Use the boxes under columns 3 and 4 to provide a short written response for each identity.

	1	2	3	2
Identity	How important do you consider this piece of your identity?	If someone sees you but does not know you personally, how obvious is this piece of your identity to them?	Is this identity regarded in a positive manner by society at large?	Is this identity regarded in a negative manner by society at large?
Race or ethnicity				
Gender				
Socio-economic class				
Sexual orientation				
Religion				
Generation				
National region (where you were raised)				
Marital status				

Switching Group Identity

Name _____   Date _____

If you were to be born again as a member of a different racial or ethnic group:

a. What group would you choose? Why?

b. With your new group identity, what things would change in your personal life? What things would remain the same in your life despite the fact that your group identity has changed?

c. What group would you not want to be born into? Why?

Source: Adapted from University of New Hampshire Office of Residential Life (2001)

CPSIA information can be obtained at www.ICGtesting.com
Printed in the USA
BVOW 04s0648120815

412896BV00002B/6/P